PILGRIMAGE AND NARRATIVE
IN THE FRENCH RENAISSANCE

To my Family
and in memory
of my Father

PILGRIMAGE AND NARRATIVE IN THE FRENCH RENAISSANCE

'THE UNDISCOVERED COUNTRY'

Wes Williams

CLARENDON PRESS · OXFORD

1998

Oxford University Press, Great Clarendon Street, Oxford OX2 6DP

Oxford New York

Athens Auckland Bangkok Bogotá Buenos Aires Calcutta
Cape Town Chennai Dar es Salaam Delhi Florence Hong Kong Istanbul
Karachi Kuala Lumpur Madrid Melbourne Mexico City Mumbai
Nairobi Paris São Paolo Singapore Taipei Tokyo Toronto Warsaw
and associated companies in
Berlin Ibadan

Oxford is a registered trade mark of Oxford University Press

Published in the United States
by Oxford University Press Inc., New York

British Library Cataloguing in Publication Data
Data available

Library of Congress Cataloging in Publication Data

Williams, Wes.
Pilgrimage and narrative in the French Renaissance :
the undiscovered country / Wes Williams.
Includes bibliographical references and index.
1. Christian pilgrims and pilgrimages—History.
2. Christian pilgrims and pilgrimages in literature.
3. Christian literature—History and criticism.
4. French literature—History and criticism. 5. Discourse analysis, Narrative.
6. Renaissance—France. I. Title
BV5067.W55 1998 263'.04244—dc21 98–27486
ISBN 0–19–815940–4

1 3 5 7 9 10 8 6 4 2

Typeset by Jayvee, Trivandrum, India
Printed in Great Britain
on acid-free paper by
Biddles Ltd,
Guildford and King's Lynn

Preface

AN opportunity, at last, to record my gratitude to those who have helped me in the course of this project. First, the institutions: the British Academy, St John's College, Oxford, New College, Oxford, and the Huntington Library, San Marino all generously supported my research. The first place made such work seem desirable; the second, in providing both the teaching and sabbatical leave—which benefited enormously from the resources and peace of the third—made the sense of it all the clearer. I am grateful to the staff of several libraries for their assistance: the Taylor Institution, the Bodleian Library, the British Library, the Bibliothèque Nationale, the Bibliothèque de l'Arsenal, the Bibliothèque Mazarine, and the Bibliothèque Municipale in Besançon. Both within and without these various institutions, many individual people have read one or other part of the text, supplied advice, references, practical help, or listened to versions of the plot in the making. They know I owe them much, and it is a pleasure to be able to name them here—as pilgrims do companions on the road—Freddie Baveystock, Anna Holland, Neil Kenny, Peter Lanyon, Karen Leeder, Conrad Leyser, Cathy Levy, Christa Mogan, Forbes Morlock, Amy Petersen, Alon Shoval, Sarah Whitehead, Emily Woof. Material in the last chapter and conclusion of this study has already appeared elsewhere—albeit in different form. I am grateful to John O'Brien and Seàn Hand, guest-editors of the journals in question, and to the publishers, for permission to re-integrate it here.

This book is a (much) revised version of a D.Phil thesis; my thanks are now long overdue to Antoine Compagnon and Nigel Smith, its examiners, whose suggestions I have done my best to respond to. I was privileged to enjoy the luxury of joint supervision from Ian

Maclean and Terence Cave, both of whom have continued to listen, cajole, advise, and encourage. I thank them for their patience, for their extraordinary generosity, and their example. It goes without saying that I claim any remaining errors, whether of fact or of interpretation, as my own.

My debt to Terence Cave predates the thesis; that I owe him, and my New College colleague Ann Jefferson, much, both in detail and inspiration, will be abundantly clear in what follows. Less evident to some will be the hand Deana Rankin has had in this book. It is a pleasure to record here some measure of my thanks to all three. For through their own work, and their critical and generous reading of mine, they have, in the past few years, and in their different ways, created the conditions of possibility for meaningful work.

W.W.
Oxford.

Contents

Note on References and Abbreviations

Apart from points where full title, place, and date of publication are germane to the argument, works are referred to in the text, as in the notes, in short title form only. Fuller references are given in the bibliography.

I retain almost all the spelling conventions, punctuation, and diacritical marks of the primary texts—in all their occasionally bewildering inconsistency—whether early printed books, manuscripts, or more recent editions. Exceptions are as follows: abbreviations are resolved and 'u' and 'v' are distinguished in French; some folio numbers have been modernized ('iiij' becoming 'iv', for example).

Introduction

'The undiscovered country, from whose bourn
No traveller returns, puzzles the will,
And makes us rather bear those ills we have
Than fly to others that we know not of.'

Hamlet, III. i. 79–82.

Representing Pilgrimage

Hamlet is talking about death. He imagines an 'undiscovered country' in order both to conjure the loss of his father and to resolve in favour of staying put, not leaving, not yet. The metaphor of the journey is thus, for Hamlet, functional; its function is to be self-sufficient *as metaphor*, enabling him to resist the risks of literalization, and to choose life. Whilst the journey which this study traces is in many ways the antithesis of the unknown—pilgrimage is travel to already discovered country—the movements which pilgrims describe are akin, and often identical, to those enacted by Hamlet's soliloquy.

Many of the writers discussed in this study conceive of pilgrimage as mere metaphor: for them, the idea of leaving is space enough for their purpose, be it devotion or dissent. For others, the metaphor must needs be made literal. They decide to take to the roads, or they are sent by those who have power over them, and so are obliged to make sense of pilgrimage as a journey to a specific place, in real time. Whether they are made to leave, choose to travel, or stay at home, the pilgrims and others whose stories are told in this book find themselves describing the shapes of experience through loss. They understand pilgrimage as a kind of practical philosophy; the project, as Montaigne has it, of 'learning how to die'. In doing so they renegotiate the terms by which they live, their relations to the past, to other cultures, and to places and people they once considered familiar. Setting out to explore, with varying degrees of self-consciousness, the relations of personal narrative to inherited tropes and forms, these travellers and writers find themselves, often to their own surprise, in undiscovered country. In the process, and as if by accident, they bring new life to a long dead metaphor: that of life's pilgrimage.

This book is the history of a few moments in the life of that metaphor, both as institutional practice and paradigm for self-understanding. Rather than a series of propositions about the metaphor, what follows is an account of the force and compulsion of its usage in the Renaissance. It is consequently less an ordnance survey map, than the record of a journey exploring that land which lies between devotional, geographical, and fictional writing, taking as its focus the fortunes of French pilgrimage narrative c.1490–1610. In that the pilgrim's journey is often considered the antithesis of an adventure into the unknown, it represents aspects of Renaissance culture which have received little attention in recent years. For many the Renaissance is a culture primarily concerned with New Worlds, with discovery, invention, and innovation. Traditionally, intellectual and literary history have it that pilgrimage is a medieval phenomenon and the pilgrimage narrative a pre-modern form.[1] What follows is written in part against such a view. My argument is that precisely because of its attachment to the past and its commemoration of places apparently long since fixed in the European imagination, pilgrimage offers a paradigm for reading the world which is under considerable pressure in this time of European expansion abroad and religious conflict at home. And the primary aim of this study is to demonstrate the enduring relevance of pilgrimage to the European Renaissance.

Pilgrimage has, in the past, been variously represented as a medieval phenomenon discarded by the Renaissance, a messy, popular form of belief tidied up by the more literate cultures of

---

[1] The most frequently cited books on pilgrimage stress this point: J. Sumption, *Pilgrimage: An Image of Medieval Religion* (1975), and D. R. Howard, *Writers and Pilgrims: Medieval Pilgrimage Narratives and Their Posterity* (1980). Even the article on pilgrimage in the *Dictionnaire de Spiritualité* simply misses out any reference to sixteenth-century debates (pp. 888–940). An exception in relation to French writing is C. Rouillard, *The Turk in French History, Thought, and Literature* (1941) which is an essential introduction to this field, especially pp. 169–295.

Reformation and Enlightenment, and an overladen, old-fangled mode of travel displaced by the technology and imaginative prowess involved in the invention of the New World. Those who have lent passing attention to the texture of pilgrimage writing—usually as 'background' to the emergent forms of exploration, trade, and missionary literature—have characterized pilgrimage accounts as unresponsive to critical reading. Largely anonymous, and often repetitious, the narratives pilgrims wrote seem to many to have a poor sense of *style*; they ill deserve the attention they once-bafflingly—held. About even the most frequently published pilgrimage account, Atkinson, whose work pioneered serious treatment of Renaissance travel literature in French, is less than sympathetic: 'Giraudet, pour une raison qui nous échappe, a été mieux reçu du public que les autres qui ont décrit leurs pérégrinations à Jérusalem.'[2]

Discussion of travel literature in French followed Atkinson for many years. His most enduring legacy was to perpetuate a rigid distinction between 'real' and 'imaginary' voyages; he also established that there were almost as many Jerusalem pilgrimage accounts published between 1480 and 1610 as accounts of travel to the New World.[3] Whereas the first of these points has received much critical attention, the second, beyond being frequently repeated, has enjoyed next to none. This study attempts to address both. The issue hinges on the function and value of rhetorical readings in relation to the texture of pilgrimage narrative. Thus, for instance, imitative writing proves to Atkinson the poor quality of pilgrim texts, and in this judgement he is not alone, indeed is representative of many: 'On croirait à lire Giraudet, que l'*Evangile* et l'*Ancien Testament* eussent plus de réalité dans son esprit que la Palestine qu'il a visitée.'[4] Rouillard acknowledges that one account seems to him worth reading, but he does so largely in order to stress that 'few of the pilgrimage accounts published in the wake of Regnaut (1573) are of any greater interest, if as much'.[5]

---

[2] G. Atkinson, *Les Nouveaux horizons de la Renaissance française* (1935), p. 24.
[3] 'Il y a, à travers toute l'époque, des voyages au saint sépulchre'; 'Nous avons toujours 35 impressions de Voyages à Jérusalem publiées entre 1480 et 1609, et nous n'en avons que 40 consacrées uniquement au Nouveau Monde', ibid., ix; 11.
[4] Ibid., 38.
[5] Rouillard, p. 229. Of one of the earliest French accounts, that of Huen, Rouillard writes in similar vein: 'its very lack of originality enhances the value of the book as an epitome of Western knowledge on the subject up to that time' (p. 44).

Perhaps in part because of its earlier bad press, pilgrimage has received little attention in recent years, despite the revival of interest in the Renaissance and in travel writing in particular. There exists no synthetic account of the many narratives of the Jerusalem pilgrimage written and published in sixteenth-century Europe; the complex forms of pilgrimage writing which persist and evolve over the period have received serious consideration neither from a rhetorical perspective, nor from that of social history. There is only scattered discussion, largely in late nineteenth-century journals, of the considerably heated early modern debates, in both Latin and the vernacular, concerning the worth of pilgrimage, relics, and physical travel.[6] This critical inattention has led readers, particularly those whose main interest lies in works of literature, to imagine that pilgrimage is of little importance to an understanding of Renaissance culture.[7] The material in this book suggests otherwise. Its argument is that a contextual sense of both the history and the continuing practice of pilgrimage contributes much to an understanding of literary, religious, and social questions central to those cultures we (think we) know as the European, especially French, Renaissance.

Other forms of Renaissance travel writing have, as noted, fared rather better in recent years. The 'return to history' which heralded the advent of New Historicism was in part launched on the ships of discovery and the travel accounts of such writers as Raleigh, Frobisher, and Drake. These travellers' tales were seen to relate usefully to the more canonical concerns of a Spenser or a Shakespeare. American, and more specifically Californian readers led the way in showing how the utopian literary territories staked out by such texts as More's *Utopia* and Shakespeare's *Tempest* are bounded on (almost) all sides by the discourse of colonization. Other recent readers traced in careful detail the ways in which Renaissance handbooks of rhetoric prepared the ground for an understanding of conquest as forensic exploration, teaching both their original addressees and us how to read rhetoric, property, and gender relations as intimately connected.[8]

---

[6] For more on this history, see Chapter 1, below.

[7] All this will soon change: Marie-Christine Gomez-Géraud, who has published a steady stream of illuminating articles on pilgrimage over the past decade is soon to publish her *doctorat d'Etat* on issues related to those I discuss in what follows. Though I have not read the text, it promises to contribute much to our understanding of this body of writing.

[8] The literature here is now vast. The most fruitful texts remain E. O'Gorman, *The Invention of America* (1961); W. Franklin, *Discoverers, Explorers, Settlers* (1979);

Travel writing has been brought to bear on literature, not so much as 'context' or 'background', nor yet as the means of controlling or verifying the sense of a literary text, but by way of elucidating rhetoric at work. Such readings are in large part also anthropological in that they privilege linguistic paradigms for the understanding of culture, use anecdotes as synecdochic indicators of broader truths about a culture, and uncover hidden structures of kinship between apparently unrelated groups of texts. Following in the wake of such re-evaluations of imitation and other rhetorical strategies in Renaissance poetics, we now read the enduring presence of scripture as less a sign of bad style, than very much the point of the narrative.[9] But the work of French pilgrim writers has enjoyed only cursory readings in this context; the few who do read them still seem to find them 'bornés et peu intéressants'; it seems there is '[a]u total, peu de choses à glaner dans cette littérature pieuse'.[10]

In seeking to redress the balance, I shall attempt to represent the rhythm and texture of the pilgrim's experience both as argument at home and as narrative of the road. This means attending closely to those whose texts have survived, those who are named by their companions, and those of whom no record remains. Many of the texts discussed here will be unknown to most readers. This too is a function of recent debate; for although the emphasis on certain figures may have been altered (we now talk, almost, as much about Mandeville and Thevet as we do about Petrarch and Montaigne), the geographical and symbolic co-ordinates of writing about travel remain fundamentally the same from Burckhardt to Greenblatt. The heroic travelling figures of New Historicist, as of Old Positivist, readings are Belon, Léry, or Montaigne, with their

A. Pagden, *The Fall of Natural Man* (1982); P. Parker, *Literary Fat Ladies: Rhetoric, Gender, Property* (1987); S. Greenblatt, *Marvelous Possessions* (1991); A. Kolodny, *The Lay of the Land* (1975); M. B. Campbell, *The Witness and the Other World* (1988); T. Todorov, *La Conquête de l'Amérique* (1982); F. Lestringant's trilogy of studies, *André Thevet* (1991); *L'Atelier du cosmographe* (1991); and *Le Huguenot et le sauvage* (1990); Z. van Martels (ed.), *Travel Fact and Travel Fiction* (1994); and 'Homo viator', *RSH* 245 (janv.–mars 1997).

[9] Lestringant's studies of Thevet's pilgrimage account demonstrate this point persuasively; see in particular his edition of Thevet's *Cosmographie de Levant*, and his 'Un pèlerinage en Terre Sainte récrit par l'évangélisme (1546–1552)', in *André Thevet*, pp. 33–64.

[10] Y. Bernard, *L'Orient du XVIe siècle* (1988), p. 61; N. Broc, *La Géographie de la Renaissance* (1980), p. 138. Broc's complaint echoes that of Atkinson before her: 'le mysticisme n'est pas la meilleure attitude pour regarder le monde matériel et trop de souvenirs bibliques s'interposent entre le pèlerin et les réalités' (ibid.).

accentuated observational detail, or alternatively, Rabelais and Thevet with their extravagant fictions. 'From the Dome of the Rock to the Rim of the World': recent discussions of travel literature still project a grid of reading along axes inherited from the nineteenth-century Orientalists.[11]

By turns indulging and contesting such critical attitudes, the work in this study contributes to the story of the long life of pilgrimage in the European imagination in a manner at once progressive and revisionist. The claim here is not simply that pilgrimage survives into the Renaissance; more is at stake than survival, or the *quantity* of writers still working within the field of pilgrimage writing. For I hope to demonstrate that their texts reveal an insistent concern with the *quality* of the pilgrim experience. The persisting claim of pilgrimage on the imagination is a function of its ability to change, and to demand change in the reader. It is a literary paradigm grounded in repetition, a journey whose very structure is imitation, but one undertaken with a view to metamorphosis. Again and again we find that pilgrims believe, with Paul, and with Hamlet, that for as long as we are still in the body, we are condemned to reiteration; they also believe that we shall all be changed. The central, related claims, whose force pilgrim writers attempt to harness and measure, are that change can be experienced within institutions, that traditional forms best articulate personal experience, and that the possibility for metamorphosis is inscribed in the reiterative details of experience here and now.

Charting the Journey: Structure and Selection

Constructed as a number of dialogues taking place in the course of a journey, this study has two kinds of fellow pilgrims and *co-devisants* in view. This dual destination accounts for its structure and tone: more exploration than proposition. It is written in part on behalf of pilgrim writers now dead, with whom I have been in protracted conversation for the past six years. The form of a series of interrogative dialogues with texts has been adopted in order to give voice to those largely unheard in recent debates about Renaissance culture. But this

---

[11] The title here cited is that of Greenblatt's second chapter, *Marvelous Possessions*, pp. 26–51.

method also has a further aim, that of contributing to the larger realignment of cultural history and literary study which is taking place in contemporary culture. By demonstrating the need for both close scrutiny and the long view, I have attempted both to speak with the dead about the experience which took them across the world and/or into print, and to argue with the living about how we ourselves go about travelling, talking, reading, and writing.

The division of the book into parts seeks to fulfil these aims. Furthermore, as not everyone will want to read the whole book, the different parts foreground different kinds of writing and different thematic concerns. The following, brief account of its structure should enable readers to orient themselves within the book. The first part, 'Coming to Terms: The Subject of Pilgrimage', comprises Chapters 1 to 3. It establishes a history of the terms of Christian pilgrimage from Late Antiquity to Late Renaissance, taking the reception of Augustine and Gregory of Nyssa as test cases. The second part 'Being There: The Experience of Pilgrimage', explores the development of these terms in descriptions of the Holy Land and narratives of the Jerusalem pilgrimage. Chapter 4 presents close readings of a number of texts, all of which seek first to quantify the experience of being in the presence of the sacred, and then to translate this experience home to the reader. Chapters 5 and 6 focus on two pilgrims' accounts, one from each end of the century, and each bearing an explicit relation to a distinct literary form: prose romance and devotional poetry. The pace of these two chapters is slower than that of others; they, like the second chapter, bristle with local detail. This is in part because I am presenting material largely unknown to most readers; I indulge the pilgrims in their own loquacity. But there is also a purpose to the pace of reading here: it is part of the argument of this book that slow, close reading is essential if we are to understand the texture both of the Renaissance debate and of pilgrims' experience.

The third and final part, 'Forms of Return: The Afterlife of Pilgrimage', takes the relation of pilgrimage narrative to literary form as its focus. Here, by way of a close reading of episodes in Rabelais, I examine the reception of the themes and structures of pilgrimage writing by emergent discourses of travel: trade and exploration literature, Protestant anti-pilgrimage polemic, and fictional travel narrative. The richness of textual forms in which pilgrimage figures is indicated by the generic complexity of the writing discussed here: exemplary narratives and translations of both patristic texts and romance adventures (Chapters 1, 5, and 6), guides and letters (Chapters 2 and 3), descriptions (Chapter 4); all of the above (Chapter 7).

Dialogue within the field of pilgrimage takes place on several levels. The first, on which Chapters 1 to 3 concentrate, is that of individual response to historical precedent. As well as detailing the patristic and medieval provenance of pilgrimage discourse, this section demonstrates how it is kept alive in the Renaissance, through translation, argument, and repression. Augustine and Gregory are not the focus merely of my own choosing: the debate about pilgrimage in the Renaissance is a debate about ownership of the Fathers' texts, and in particular these Fathers' texts. It concerns the right to determine the meaning of tradition in the time of *kairos*, the present time of crisis. Each writer discussed is in dialogue with his precursors, and creates in part his own subjectivity by means of this dialogue. Writers within the field of pilgrimage are more aware than most of the effects of such a mode of self-production; they know, and show, that we are most ourselves when imprinting particular inflections on the terms of others; that we experience things most keenly and privately which are inherited, public, banal; and that if an experience, however singular, can be understood and communicated, then it can *ipso facto* be shared. The first two chapters conclude that pilgrimage discourse teaches us—its readers across history—that in attempting to communicate our proper selves, we learn that they are not fully our own, since they already belong in part to others, elsewhere.

The third chapter both confirms that the history of pilgrimage is best characterized as repeated attempts to privilege one sense of the journey over another, and describes the particular shape this history takes in the Renaissance. This, and the subsequent section, together show how Reformers, counter-Reformers, and others unconcerned with polemic reinvent and redescribe the shape of pilgrimage from early to late Renaissance. An initially Erasmian critique of pilgrimage, intent on pointing out the abuses and dangers of the physical journey becomes an argument in favour of a more internalized trajectory, one allied to reading in detail, and harnessing the movement of the imagination. Later, this rhetoric of reading is appropriated by counter-Reformers, who re-establish the worth of the physical journey, while at the same time binding and loosing the imagination with the detail and order of the stations of the cross and the devotional pilgrimage. Chapter 4 confirms how pilgrim writers circumscribe and sanctify the home as the place where the holy can be found. Through reading, the physical enactment of a trajectory within measured space, and the development of rhetorics of sacred description, the Holy Land can be translated into the home. Pilgrimage in this mode is mere metaphor and print is put to practical use, such that readers can measure out Christ's steps to Calvary on their own and—as Adrichomius in particular will show—in their own room.

There is a degree to which the 'dialogue' of pilgrimage, when it becomes confessional in tone, takes on the form of debate, argument, and, eventually, violent battle. The central terms of this dialogue are slippery and they defy definition: curiosity, the body, the literal and the figural, experience, *peregrinatio* itself. Again, as with the selection of texts, I stress that this slipperiness is not merely of my choosing. I have elected to follow the contours of the argument, rather than to lay it out flat: to undertake, and to incite readers similarly to undertake, a journey, rather than to provide a map. This journey produces, as the first two sections of the book suggest, a history in terms of the 'travelling' of rhetorical and physical practices across geographical, generic, and confessional boundaries. This history and its implications, provide the focus of the last three chapters in particular.

Chapters 5 and 6, through discussion of the exemplary narratives of two pilgrims, Cuchermoys and Valimbert, take us away from home, from pilgrimage as metaphor, and back on to the road to Jerusalem. They demonstrate that no pilgrimage occurs in isolation; no pilgrim can, on the road, remain a pure pilgrim, as each becomes in part adventurer, romance hero, trader, and so on. These particular texts are foregrounded because they indicate more clearly than most the extent to which pilgrimage accounts are tied to other literary forms. These literary forms, and the adjacent forms of writing developed by traders, explorers, and missionaries are the focus of the final section of this study. These accounts show, in their different ways, how the narrative of the journey is itself a place where terms central to the experience of pilgrimage—connections between the literal and figural meanings of terms, the pure and impure existence of textual kinds, the integrity of individual bodies, and shared cultures—are the live and complex subject of argument.

'Langages Pellegrins': *Pilgrim Rhetoric*

> Oyez dire metonomie, metaphore, allegorie et autres tels noms
> de la grammaire, semble-t-il pas qu'on signifie quelque forme de
> langage rare et pellegrin? Ce sont titres qui touchent le babil de
> vostre chambriere.[12]

Pilgrimage has been represented in the West as bound up with three categories: exile, the literal journey, and imitation (of Christ and of precursors). These three categories can be productively allied to three modes of articulating experience: exile articulates our relations with the past, the literal journey is enacted in the present and towards a present place, and imitation is a category which has a bearing both on Christian devotional practice and on poetics. It is along these vectors that pilgrims travel, and within this territory that pilgrimage writing is located. These explanatory categories are subdivided here, but they are experienced as simultaneous by the pilgrim. Pilgrim writers are in exile on earth, and more intensely in exile from Christ even as they travel closer to Jerusalem. Exiled from the fullness of the past, they none the less imitate inherited devotional procedures. Exiled from the home community by virtue of leaving for encounters with the Other, they draw closer to the past, and to Christ. Exiled from their sense of themselves by the circuitous procedures of writing, they, or their secretaries, or their friends, piece back together the sense of pilgrimage from a dead companion's manuscript notes, or a nostalgic relative's oral reminiscences.

To separate categories and forms of experience, as this study does for the sake of clarity, is to do a certain kind of violence to the texture of lived history. But it is essential if we are to recognize both the recurring patterns of religious and aesthetic experience, and the very particular weave of the texts composed by individual travellers and writers in the Renaissance. The challenge is to open up these texts to modern readings without collapsing important historical, social, and cultural differences: to make them legible, without rendering them (to use Barthes' term) 'lisible', isolated either from their original contexts, or from further discussion and debate.[13]

The rhetorical argument of this book can thus be summarized as a statement of the need for reading which is at once historical and

---

[12] Montaigne, *Oeuvres*, I, li, p. 294.

[13] The sense of the term 'lisible', and its opposition to 'scriptible', is elaborated in R. Barthes, *S/Z* (1970).

intimate; in ethical terms it argues for acknowledging the strangeness of others, and recognizing their sameness in ourselves. Historically it argues that a number of displacements are operated on the discourse of pilgrimage in the Renaissance such that certain peculiar forms of access to otherness—to the sacred, and to foreign peoples and places—are culturally devalued in the West. Erasmus writes colloquies satirizing aspects of pilgrim experience, but these colloquies, crucially, acknowledge that something is being lost in the process; he also went on a number of pilgrimages himself, writing votary poems to the Virgin without any evident sense of cultural embarrassment. Descartes, by contrast, vows to himself that he will, 'before the end of November', undertake a pilgrimage to Loreto in thanks for having solved a particularly knotty mathematical problem. He notes that he has 'made this promise today, 23 February 1620'; but he never makes it to Loreto, and the vow remains a note, in his private journal.[14]

The worth of such exemplary instances is that they throw sharp light on changes which must also be traced in slow, laborious detail. It is possible that this kind of light distorts the image, and that the experience of the past can best be perceived indirectly, through the dark glass of linguistic detail, filtered through the blinds of rhetoric, or refracted by the lens of fiction. In a sense the entire argument of this book rests on the shifts in usage and significance of one term, grasped in its relation to others: 'pèlerin/pellegrin/peregrin'. Depending on its context, the term can mean strange, foreign, other; and all the while it carries the hidden, and increasingly obscured, charge of pilgrimage.

In tracing the shifting function, aspect, usage, and significance of this term, between noun and adjective, singular and plural, sacred and secular, it becomes clear that problems of reading which pilgrimage poses—poised as it is midway between event and example, between personal record of a journey and reiterative enactment of a prescribed series of rhetorical and devotional moves—inform more canonical forms of devotional and fictional writing. Clear also is the fact that the 'langages pellegrins' of Renaissance pilgrimage have a bearing on recent critical debate concerning both poetics and the ethics of interpretation. For there are important ways in which our own critical languages can usefully be historicized in turn, made strange by the terms of Renaissance writing.

---

[14] We return to Erasmus' *Peregrinatio religionis ergo* frequently in the course of this study. The poem can be found in Erasmus, *Carmina*; Descartes's note is translated in the 'Early Writings' section of his *Philosophical Writings* (1985), I, p. 5.

PART ONE

COMING TO TERMS: THE SUBJECT OF PILGRIMAGE

These all died in faith, not having received the promises, but having seen them afar off, and were persuaded of them, and embraced them, and confessed that they were strangers and pilgrims on the earth. They say such things declare plainly that they seek a country. And truly if they had been mindful of that country from whence they came, they might have had opportunity to have returned. But now they desire a better country.

(Hebrews, 2: 13–16)

Tous princes princesses gens habitans sur la terre en laquelle comme dit sainct paul lapostre ilz nont point de demeure permanente mais ilz sont tous et toutes pelerins pelerines.

(Deguilleville, *Le Pèlerinage de la vie humaine tresutile et puffitable pour cognoistre soymesmes*)

Tous les bons et fideles chrestiens ne sont ils pas en ce monde ici passagers et pellerins? Nostra conversatio in coelis est. Ce dit S. Paul, et ailleurs: Non habemus hic manentem civitatem, sed futuram inquirimus.

(Dublioul, *Le Voyage de Hierusalem*)

CHAPTER ONE

'Linguae peregrinae': *Pilgrim Tongues*

Pilgrimage writing in the Renaissance draws, as the epigraphs to this section suggest, on biblical, patristic, and late medieval tradition. The tradition is not stable, however, nor do all those who speak the language use it in identical ways. Indeed a characteristic of pilgrimage discourse is that its terms are as subject to constant displacement as the pilgrims of our epigraphs: they may find themselves temporarily housed in devotional handbooks, letters, itineraries, dialogues, journals, chronicles, romances, or poems. Pilgrimage writing cannot, therefore, be delimited as a specific genre, nor yet can a straightforward chronological development of its terms be established. There are as many kinds of pilgrims as there are 'princes princesses gens habitans sur la terre'.

Many readers of pilgrimage writing, particularly those who write of medieval texts, none the less argue that generic typologies can indeed usefully be established. Of these the most fruitful categorization is that which divides pilgrim texts into guides, logs, and narrations, with this latter category further subdivided into letters, diaries, and narratives.[1] All of these forms of writing survive into the Renaissance, and a number of texts remain either one or other of the three primary kinds even if they change name: Estienne's *Guides*, for instance, are in effect logs, while Balourdet's *Guide* is in truth a

---

[1] This classification was proposed by Howard, p. 6. Classification by discrete genre remains as impossible as it seems seductive to many: see J. G. Davies, 'Pilgrimage and Crusade Literature' in Sargent-Baur (1992), pp. 1–30; G. Atkinson, *La Littérature géographique de la Renaissance* (1927), p. 30; Bernard, pp. 62–4; C. Zrenner, *Die Berichte der europäischen Jerusalempilger (1475–1500)* (1981), pp. 113–14. This last, concentrating on German texts, is the clearest of the generically motivated studies of pilgrimage writing.

narration, with a polemical defence of pilgrimage attached.[2] But there is more to the changes in kind effected during the Renaissance than changes in name; for pilgrimage writing itself becomes a contested field, a place where the relationships between names, things, and people are put on trial. Categories which are said to have bound medieval pilgrimage writing together cannot hold under the combined pressures of confessional polemic and expansionist trade. Perhaps they never could; the period just before the ones we study so often seem less complex.

Guillaume de Deguilleville's late medieval allegorical dream poem, *Le pelerinage de la vie humaine*, published in both verse and prose treatments throughout the Renaissance, both explains and performs the vernacular recuperative re-enactment of pilgrim traditions most clearly, and most securely. The prose version we cited in epigraph above; the verse text has a margin, which runs throughout in Latin, citing from scripture and the Fathers. From the perspective of later pilgrims' narratives, Deguilleville's does appear to be remarkably free of anxiety about its terms. It begins with Paul: 'dum sumus in hoc corpore peregrinamur a domino, ii Corintiorum quinto capite', and explains his terms as follows:

> Le premier du pelerinaige
> De lhomme durant quest en vie,
> Lautre de lame de la caige
> De son corps desja departie,
> Le tiers declaire et annuncie
> Le pelerinage de crist
> Depuis quil fut ney de marie
> Jusqua lenvoy du sainct esperit.[3]

The poem itself is correspondingly structured as three books, each exemplifying one of three principle ways in which Paul's terms have been extended in the Christian tradition. The first is that of man's journey, within the body, away from God: pilgrimage as exile. The second culminates when the soul is separated from the body, but begins with the first conscious steps towards God: pilgrimage as the

---

[2] See C. Estienne, *La Guide des chemins de France* (1553) and *La Grande Guide des chemins pour aller et venir par tout le royaume de France, Lorraine, partie d'Allemaigne, Savoye, et Italie . . . Augmenté du voyage de S. Jacques, de Rome, de Venise et Hierusalem* (1623); L. Balourdet, *La Guide des chemins pour le voyage de Hierusalem, et autres villes et lieux de la Terre Saincte* (1601).

[3] G. de Deguilleville, *Le Pelerinage de lhomme* (1511), fol. ai[r].

Christian life, centred on conversion. The third is Christ's own life, and its course is repeated by pilgrims who travel to the Holy Land: pilgrimage as literally enacted *imitatio Christi*. Such are, we might think, the ways in which the early Renaissance traveller understood what it was to be a pilgrim.

The dream poem may appear to us to offer a grammar of pilgrimage, but it was not taken up as a model for the narration of pilgrims' experience in the Renaissance. Not one published French pilgrim frames his own account of the journey as such a poem. Rather, early modern pilgrims and their publishers adopt an often bewildering range of positions relative to the place of pilgrimage in their culture. Some argue the holy separation of the pilgrim from other travellers and they publish texts which are simple and unpolished accounts of the Jerusalem journey. Others muddy the waters of clean kind by mixing pilgrimage narratives with a host of adjacent, often non-referential forms of writing. Such texts are in their very nature exercises in generic cross-fertilisation—part travel account, part devotional poem, part romance. In doing so, these writers are to a degree making explicit kinship relations which had long supported the institution of pilgrimage. But they also engender a number of strange and, to many at the time, threatening new forms of traveller and text.

What the apparent confusion of Renaissance writing makes clear is that pilgrimage is—even at its most material—always in part a metaphorical practice; it is consequently open both to allegorical expansion beyond the literal senses of the journey, and to interpretative closure. To talk with Erasmus, for instance, of such figures as Plato, Abraham, and the Queen of Sheba as pilgrims appears initially to widen the terms of reference beyond the institution of Christian pilgrimage.[4] It seems to be part of that marriage of classical, pagan, Hebrew, and Christian myth which characterizes the Renaissance as a cultural movement. As if to prove the point, Erasmus places the terms of *peregrinatio* which are, as he says, 'frequently found in Scripture', in dialogue with others. Paul, the Psalmist, and Socrates are all seen to describe themselves, and by extension all of us, as *peregrini*.[5] And yet to make of all these journeys a form of pilgrimage is

[4] See Erasmus' comments on the adage 'Vita hominis peregrinatio', *Adagiorum*, IV. x. 71 (1541), pp. 1040–1.

[5] Ibid. See also *Enarratio in psalmi xxxviii*, *Opera omnia*, V–3, pp. 237–8.

also to perform a restrictive, recuperative gesture of some force: the founding narratives of other cultures are read as precursors to Christian revelation, making sense only in relation to Christ's incarnation. They are read as being like Us. As Erasmus states it most bluntly in the *Commentary on the 38th Psalm*: 'All men, whether they recognise it or not, are strangers and pilgrims, though not all are pilgrims "with God" '.[6]

This recuperative gesture is, in the Christian tradition, first and most magisterially performed by Paul, in Hebrews 11: 13–16, on which Erasmus, like Deguilleville before him, draws. The centrality of the Pauline epistles to the discourse of pilgrimage is confirmed from early to late Renaissance, on all sides of the pilgrim debate. Erasmus is by no means alone in using Paul to recuperative and polemic effect. Nor, of course, can the tension between the metaphorical and the material properly be understood as a peculiarly modern problem, invented by Erasmus, as certain writers of the counter-Reform claim. Rather, it, like the tension between the claims of the past and the needs of the present, informs discussion of pilgrimage from Augustine to Erasmus and beyond; the history of their separation is the history of pilgrimage.

Where Paul's faithful, in the pre-history of Christian pilgrimage, 'declare plainly . . . that they desire a better country', Jean Dublioul, writing at the start of the seventeenth century, reads this as an argument in favour of plain speech against the 'jargon des errans' of the Reform. For Dublioul, acknowledging the metaphorical sense in which we are all pilgrims in no way makes the journey proper redundant. He has read Erasmus, and understands the argument, but claims that the metaphorical pilgrimage only makes sense with reference to actual travel. It also only makes sense, he suggests, to 'les bons et fideles Chrestiens'. He consequently cites Erasmus' ancient examples only in order to displace them by the more authoritative and 'merveilleux' example of Christ. Having mentioned Plato, Abraham, and Paul as pilgrim precursors, he continues:

Les Anciens ont este curieux d'escrire divers voyages de grands personnages. Que diray-je de ce grand voyageur le Fils de Dieu? lequel comme dit S. Bernard, a fait de merveilleux voyages, du ciel au sacre ventre de la vierge

---

[6] *En. psal.*, *Opera omnia*, v, p. 238. Translation mine. Erasmus sets 'Plato's dream about souls falling down from heaven' alongside Psalm 38: 13 and 2 Cor: 5, 6. The central, repeated terms are 'peregrinus' and 'peregrinare'. I have decided against 'an exile' and 'to sojourn abroad' as renderings, since this empties the adage of its pilgrim charge (and its point).

Marie, de la sans fraction de l'integrite d'icelle, en la creche de Bethleem: de la terre au ciel. Voila un merveilleux pelerinage.[7]

This rhetorical performance, making of Christ himself a pilgrim, and making of pilgrimage an article of faith, is designed to counter Reformers' arguments on two fronts. Pilgrimage is neither an exclusively metaphorical affair (Christ's is a thoroughly bodily *peregrinatio*); nor is it the invention of the corrupt Imperial church. Dublioul had written first in Latin, then, since the message was not getting across, in French, using a different format: 'pour autant que les heretiques de nostre temps y veulent contredire, et empescher les sainctes peregrinations, jargonnans que Dieu est par tout, comme si c'estoit superstition de vouloir adorer et honorer en certain lieu.'[8] The terms of this defence stress that Dublioul's desire for a 'certain lieu' is every bit as rhetorical as it is geographical. Preaching a rhetoric of naive simplicity, Dublioul characterizes the argument that God is everywhere as 'jargon', and in doing so reaffirms the political force of unadorned pilgrim rhetoric. If the pilgrim is called to write, then, Dublioul argues, he must make his text 'comme un abregé, sans autrement pindariser ou farder le langage'.[9]

This is an argument in favour of 'pure' pilgrimage, constructed on a history according to which Reformers' appropriation of Paul's text to their own situation is a distortion of scripture. But this history belies the fact that the Reformers' actions are in truth an imitation of Paul's own performance of the faith. Appropriation of the past to the needs of the present is a possibility inscribed in pilgrim discourse from the outset. Indeed the rhetorical–political underpinning of pilgrimage, to which Erasmus calls attention and counter-Reformers respond, formed the basis of a grammar of pilgrimage evident not only to medieval pilgrims, but also to its founders in Late Antiquity. This metaphorical grammar provides the focus of this chapter, which takes, in turn, Erasmus, Petrarch, and Fabri as exemplars of its three primary formal inflections in Renaissance Latin: dialogue, letter, and narrative. The chapter concludes with a brief return to (Erasmus' edition) of Augustine's *Confessions*, in confirmation of the ways in which the structuring force of Late Antique argument can still be felt

---

[7] J. Dublioul, *Le Voyage de Hierusalem* (1602), p. 4.

[8] Ibid. 6–7. Dublioul's *Hierosolymitanae peregrinationes hodoepicorum* (1599) is more a defence of pilgrimage in general than either a guide or an account of his own journey.

[9] Dublioul, *Voyage*, p. 13.

in Renaissance Latin writing, even in the texts of those Moderns who are said to have brought pilgrimage to an end.

The Politics of Plain Speech: Erasmus' Dialogue

> *Menedemus*—What novelty is this? The resurrection of a body that has been six months in the grave? Unless I am hallucinating this is my neighbour . . . It's the man himself. Welcome, Ogygius.
> *Ogygius*—And well met Menedemus.[10]

Erasmus opens his pilgrimage dialogue with the above resurrection appearance. Ogygius—Mr Gullible—returns to refute accounts of his death and to prove to the likes of Menedemus—Mr Stay-at-Home—the profits of pilgrimage. Those who argue that the Renaissance saw lasting changes effected in the practice and writing of pilgrimage credit Erasmus with an exemplary understanding of the force of change, and more than one critic cites this text in particular as marking a decisive shift in the times.[11] Nor is this an entirely modern story: Greffin Affagart, writing in the 1530s, laments that the ironic standpoint of the *Colloquies* has provoked such a decline in the number and standing of Jerusalem pilgrims that only simple folk accompany him on the journey.[12] Erasmian critiques also reached the 'simple folk': *Von Walfahrt Erasmi Roterdami vermanung wo Christus und sein reich zu suche[n] ist* is one of a number of vernacular pamphlets which bears his name. Erasmus is here made to argue against pilgrimage, both as actual journey and as a way of reading: the true Jerusalem cannot be found at the end of a literal journey, and Christ's face, reflected in the clear springs of scripture, is only ever obscured by the mud of priestly commentary.[13]

It is not difficult to see why Erasmus was, and continues to be, read as an opponent of pilgrimage. The ironic detachment with which the pilgrim Ogygius' return is read by the home-owning bourgeois,

---

[10] Erasmus, *Peregrinatio religionis ergo* (1526), *Opera omnia*, I–3, pp. 470–94. It was not published in French during the Renaissance.

[11] See Sumption, pp. 300–2; F. Bierlaire, *Erasme et ses colloques* (1977), pp. 226–66.

[12] Affagart, *Relation de Terre Sainte* (1533–4), pp. 20–1. For Erasmus' (largely ineffective) self-defence against the censors, see Bierlaire, ibid.

[13] The pamphlet is published, without indication of place, in 1522. For more on Erasmus in the context of German pamphlets, and discussion of the *Divine Mill* illustrations concerning scripture see R. Scribner, *Simple Folk* (1981), pp. 103–6, 224.

Menedemus, would seem to support such a reading. Ogygius returns home with wonders in his bag, and a seemingly endless supply of narratives to underwrite the worth both of his own experience and of inherited forms of understanding. But as the pilgrim unpacks his marvels from his impossibly capacious scrip, they are presented to both Menedemus and the reader for evaluation. While the reader may wonder at Ogygius' goods and admire his faith, for his part, Menedemus systematically subjects the pilgrim's goods to rhetorical unpacking until they are devoid of sacred charge. He reads Ogygius' marvellous possessions as just so many trinkets. But Erasmus is not Menedemus. And a closer reading of the dialogue would show how it blocks identification with Menedemus, and presents a nostalgic indulgence of just those forms of peculiar access to the sacred which the pilgrim—unlike the materialist reader—is able to see represented in signs.[14]

Menedemus' refusal to acknowledge the worth of the pilgrim's most treasured possessions is, nonetheless, frequently repeated in responses to pilgrimage accounts. Ogygius is by no means alone in finding the pilgrim's gifts—both material and metaphorical—dismissed as worse than worthless. As we saw above in the Introduction, most modern readers, ignoring Erasmus' blocking moves, read as Menedemus does. Elsewhere, Erasmus clarifies the nature of his own critique of pilgrims' faith in bones, milk, letters, and other such material extensions of bodily presence. The reading of bones scattered on the ground or encased in gold should, he argues in the *Enchiridion*, be replaced by that of scripture: 'You make much of a piece of his body visible through a glass covering and you do not marvel at the whole mind of Paul shining through his writings?'[15]

The argument against pilgrimage and the cult of relics here is in large part rhetorical. Scripture is a source of *copia*, whereas the bones, and even the letter dictated by an angel, a copy of which Ogygius treasures so dear, are just that: copy. The commodified phials of the Virgin's milk do not so much underwrite the *topos* of scriptural

---

[14] See for instance Menedemus' refusal to acknowledge that either the letter dictated by an angel, or the phial of milk that Ogygius has brought home can really be from the Virgin, *Peregrinatio*, pp. 472–4, 478.

[15] Erasmus, *Enchiridion* (1515 edition), fol. xxviᵛ; it was not translated into French during the Renaissance. The entire fifth section is an eloquent statement of Erasmus' thoughts on the relative values of relics and scripture. For more on this see L. E. Halkin, 'Érasme Pèlerin', in Scrinium Erasmianum II (1969), pp. 245 ff., and 'Le thème du pèlerinage dans les Colloques d'Érasme', in *Actes du Congrès Érasme* (1971), pp. 88–98.

nourishment and digestion as undervalue it. And Erasmus' attention to the rhetorical underpinning of pilgrimage, like the pressure he places on the terms themselves, is not mere play. Even in his most mischievous texts the wit and the games have a questioning purpose. As in the *Colloquies* and the *Enchiridion*, so in the *Adages*, Erasmus interrogates the terms with which we make our meanings, the metaphors by which we live, and die.

The discussion of pilgrimage in the *Adages* appears to widen the terms of pilgrim reference considerably. It takes pilgrimage to encompass both literal journeys within the Christian tradition and a more generally determined philosophical quest, of which the literal journey is the physical sign. This allows Erasmus to draw on, and extend, a traditional understanding of terms, and to recognise as his pilgrim precursors not only Paul, but also Abraham, the Queen of Sheba, and Plato: which is to say everyone, man or woman, who seeks wisdom. All these characters, all these traditions, in dialogue in Erasmus' text, agree: if life is a pilgrimage, this is because we are all pilgrims, simply as a function of our being in the flesh. To be a pilgrim is, in these terms, not so much a Christian, as a human condition.[16]

Identification of the pilgrim with the human condition is however, not the last move in the dance: only a certain (false) kind of pilgrim stays still at this point; the true (Christian) pilgrim keeps on moving. Erasmus explains that 'Christian Philosophy, undertaking, so far as is possible, a pilgrimage away from the body,' offers the hope of release from the condition of estrangement and exile in the body. For the true pilgrim can, by understanding pilgrimage to be a metaphorical move away from attachment to material signs, 'spring forth [*exsilit*] rejoicing, and so return from exile [*ab exsilio*] to his homeland'.[17] The pressure applied to the language of pilgrimage first makes exiles of us all, and then underwrites the means of escape from this condition, for those who can follow the strange music of Erasmus' argument. This music, the dance, and the surface play of signifiers are here underwritten by an extraordinary faith in language. Understanding the metaphors we live by allows us to redescribe the terms of exile as themselves offering a means to redemption.

---

[16] Erasmus, *Enarratio*, p. 238. For Erasmus' care with these words, see M. Screech, *Ecstasy and the Praise of Folly* (1980), pp. 154–7, though I take Erasmus to be more careful to sustain the volatility of the terms in play in his own text than Screech suggests.

[17] Ibid.

It becomes all the more important then to establish the legitimate use of terms of pilgrimage, and to police the motivations of those who use them. Addressing the pilgrim's actual, rather than ideal, motivation in the *Colloquy*, Erasmus has Menedemus assume the worst—'*Menedemus:* For Curiosity, I suppose?'—and Ogygius protest the best—'*Ogygius*: Nay upon the very score of Religion'. This is an echo not of Paul, but of Augustine's argument that 'the law of God, permits the free-flow of curiosity' to be 'stemmed by force' by the laws of religion.[18] Menedemus assumes that his neighbour's pilgrimage had been the exercising of just such free-flowing curiosity, but stems the gullible pilgrim's desire to tell of his journey himself, and does so with rhetorical force. By turns indulgent and cajoling, Menedemus encourages, ironizes, questions, listens to, and upsets his neighbour. The colloquy concludes with Ogygius doubtful of his faith in the laws of religion, and with Menedemus confirmed in his belief in the rightness of home and the folly of curiosity; particularly such curiosity which parades as religion and takes on the form of pilgrimage.

Erasmus perhaps opens the pilgrimage dialogue with the scene of resurrective return for comic effect, but his discussions of pilgrim terms elsewhere suggest good rhetorical and political reasons for such an opening. Not the least of these is to signal the persistence of the traditional understanding of pilgrimage as a specifically one-way journey: a rehearsal for, or doubling of, our journey towards death. Menedemus' taunting reference to the returned pilgrim as a ghost both acknowledges the long life of this tradition and perhaps suggests that its time has come. His supposition that Ogygius travelled 'for Curiosity' echoes one of the enduring critiques of the journey, and further suggests that, by the time Ogygius travels, the pilgrim and the curiously motivated are indistinguishable.

That *curiositas* was subject to repeated translation from Late Antiquity to the Renaissance has been clear for some time.[19] Its imbrication with pilgrimage is discussed by Zacher, who suggests

---

[18] Augustine, *Confessiones*, i, pp. 12–13; see also ii, pp. 82–3. The *Confessions* were not published in French during the Renaissance. For the Latin, I have used O'Donnell's excellent three volume edition (O'D); for translation I have used Pusey (P), for his evident relish in the taste of Augustine's words.

[19] See J. Céard (ed.), *La Curiosité à la Renaissance*, esp. A. Godin 'Erasme: "Pia/Impia curiositas"', pp. 25–36; G. Defaux, *Le Curieux, le glorieux et la sagesse du monde dans la première moitié du XVIe siècle*; N. Kenny, ' "Curiosité" and philosophical poetry in the French Renaissance', *Renaissance Studies*, 5: 3 (1991), pp. 263–76.

that 'from the earliest times it seems to have been understood that *curiositas* could be described most appropriately in metaphors of spatial movement'. It seems that 'the medieval mind' saw in pilgrimage a means to overcome the 'sin of curiosity, which began in Eden'.[20] Curiosity, an expression of the 'libido (sciendi)', forced humankind to travel for the first time, and yet, through the peculiarly regulated form of travel which is pilgrimage, return to a kind of paradise could be effected. To set out on a holy journey and connect the distant place with home through the agency of one's own body was to cure the moral and epistemological wounds endured in the course of the first ever journey. Zacher does not stress this point, but the resolution was achieved by a double movement: physically through the movement of the pilgrim's body, and discursively through the account of his travels. There was no need to choose between the antitheses of 'mundus' and 'patria', or of 'scientia' and 'sapientia'. If the search for knowledge brought the error of oppositional discourse, through further error, now of a different, more literal order, the chance for redemption was asserted. Whereas for Erasmus, such redemption from exile could be effected by means of linguistic redescription, Zacher's medieval pilgrim exemplifies a particular relation of words to experience: the figural can, and can only, be redeemed by literalization.

This understanding of pilgrimage as literally bound up with the word, is, as noted above, not exclusively medieval; nor is the sense in which it articulates our being in language new to the Renaissance. Indeed, the rise of the cult of the saints which accompanied the development of pilgrimage was, its recent historians stress, an activity at once rhetorical and political from the outset. As Ladner points out with reference to Augustine's use of the term *peregrinus* in *The City of God* (itself another gloss on Paul), the terms already carry a political charge in their Late Antique context.[21] The judicial status of the *peregrinus* was that of the free man who was not a Roman citizen; thus the term nicely translated the position of the Christian in, but not of the world. This Augustine recognized as he discussed the pilgrim church in relation to the 'libido dominandi' of humankind, and of Theodosian triumphalism in particular. In adopting this initially legal term as a self-description, early Christians were staging their

---

[20] C. K. Zacher, *Curiosity and Pilgrimage* (1976), pp. 3–13.

[21] See G. B. Ladner, '*Homo Viator*: Medieval Ideas of Alienation and Order', *Speculum*, 42 (1967), pp. 233–59. *Peregrinus* approximates what the US immigration department still terms a 'resident alien'.

own appropriative moves relative to the language of the empire. Augustine's conflation of Paul and Roman law is just one of a number of rhetorico-political gestures which capture the force of the cultural claims of early Christianity, and of the cult of the saints in particular. As Peter Brown has it: 'An element of paradox always surrounded the Christian breaching of the established map of the universe . . . categories which had been held separate in the back of men's minds were brought together and ancient ambiguities resolved.'[22] Along with the terms, gods and places were also appropriated. Classical and pagan figures (*daimon*, *genius*, *potentia*, *praesentia*) were, like Jewish and pagan Holy places, assimilated, through redescription, to that triumphant political synthesis, the rhetoric of the new Christian cult.

From the outset, therefore, pilgrimage was entangled with Empire, with being in, whilst claiming not to be of, the dominant structures of temporal power. In the wake of Brown's studies, recent social and political historians have further explored the genealogy of the practice of pilgrimage as it was developed by the early Church. Origen, it is said, read 'biblical history represented in the contemporary state of Jerusalem'; Eusebius, likewise, developed an exegesis rooted in contemporary political discourse.[23] So too the first (recorded) pilgrim to Palestine, travelling from Bordeaux, 'made his very long journey to the Holy Land against the background of the existing "secular" organization of the empire's communications—and it is this which his *Itinerary* details (in contrast to the emphatically Christian core of the document' devoted to the holy places themselves)'.[24] The roads themselves underwent exemplary conversion: the old imperial *cursus publicus* with its stopping places known as *mansiones* became points along the pilgrim road, and Aelio Capitolina became Jerusalem. The conversion is not purely semantic. And Jerome was to put it most succinctly: 'movetur urbs sedibus suis'—the city has changed address.[25] As with the Empire, so with the City: boundaries were redrawn to accommodate the Christian emphasis on graves as sites of worship, what had been considered defiling became most holy, what

[22] P. Brown, *The Cult of the Saints* (1983), pp. 4, 43.
[23] See E. D. Hunt, *Holy Land Pilgrimage in the Later Roman Empire* (1984), pp. 28–9, 95; R. Markus, *The End of Ancient Christianity* (1990), pp. 139–55; and, from a different perspective, R. Lane Fox, *Pagans and Christians* (1988) on 'canny men' making use of 'uncanny places', pp. 204–5, 253 ff.
[24] Hunt, p. 58.
[25] Jerome, *Ep.* 107.1. See also Brown, *Cult*, pp. 4, 42.

peripheral, the centre of the world.[26] Robert Markus puts the recuperative case most tellingly. He stresses that 'all public and much private life was channelled through a system of sacred spaces in the [pre-Christian] Roman town'. Early Christians consequently had to make the space their own: 'The territory of the empire had to be colonized like a foreign land not long conquered'. The better to colonize, they redescribed the land as empty: 'Like so many white settlers in Africa, they had to impose their own religious topography on a territory which they read as a blank surface.'[27]

Pilgrimage discourse is, then, grounded in politics; as are the terms in which it is discussed by historians of Late Antiquity.[28] Renaissance writers who adapted Paul's terms and the political readings which they generate to their own situation were clearly working in this tradition of appropriation. From Late Antiquity to late Renaissance, for Paul, Jerome, Eusebius, and Augustine, as for Erasmus, Calvin, Dublioul, and Richeome, to use the terms of pilgrimage is to talk about distinctions between forms of language, and between kinds of narrative. Both the figural openness and the political specificity of *peregrinatio* and cognate terms as set down in early Christian writing persistently, repeatedly, invite contemporary redirection. The language of pilgrimage and what we might term 'pilgrim style' is reconfigured in response to the development of new arguments, new imperatives, and new interpretative paradigms.

Nor does this process end with the Renaissance. The linguistic turn of recent years, for instance, when conjoined with anthropology, has given rise to yet another powerful new model for reading pilgrimage. It has provided recent readers whose methods are less historical than structural with something of a dictionary with which to decode the 'linguae peregrinae' which pilgrimage articulates.[29] At once reaffirmed as a literal practice, and reconfigured as a never-ending, constantly renewable project of displacement and liminality,

---

[26] The *topos* of Jerusalem being at the centre of the world, a *topos* at once scriptural, geographical, rhetorical, and political is one to which we shall return in Chapter 4, below. For a broad discussion of symbolic centres see M. Eliade's influential *Patterns in Comparative Religion* (1958), pp. 367–87, and his *The Sacred and the Prophane* (1959), pp. 20–65. For a critique, see J. Z. Smith, *To Take Place* (1987), pp. 1–23. On the Renaissance context, see Greenblatt, *Marvelous Possessions*, pp. 26–51.

[27] Markus, *End of Ancient Christianity*, pp. 141–2.

[28] See A. Cameron, *Christianity and the Rhetoric of Empire* (1991), especially Ch. 4, 'The Power over the Past', pp. 120–54.

[29] V. and E. Turner proposed the long influential model of pilgrimage as 'controlled liminality' in *Image and Pilgrimage in Christian Culture: Anthropological Perspectives*

the drama of pilgrimage is now seen to enact, and so go some way towards resolving, the conflicts which so often arise in the course of linguistic, social, and intersubjective relations.

The stakes of rhetorical readings of social and narrative practices such as pilgrimage are further raised by anthropology's sibling, psychoanalysis.[30] The insistence that the unconscious is structured like a language suggests that concentration on the terms of specific discourses provides access to the concealed motivations for, and investments in, those practices of which they are a part. In this context it suggests the possibility of 'reading' the unconscious of pilgrimage: countering the discursive fatalism of a Foucault, the coupling of anthropology and psychoanalysis grounds a theoretical optimism about how an Erasmian 'rhetoric of presence' (Cave) might animate pilgrimage as both journey and narrative. The social rupture and travelling of distances involved in the journey are recuperated to 'the therapy of distance' (Dupront). Curiosity, the fall, sin, the flesh, distinctions of class, ethnicity, and gender . . . all are staged, and for a time resolved, in the course of the drama which is pilgrimage. Read as a narrative (rather than a drama), pilgrimage is a kind of romance, taking the believer in the regenerative power of rhetoric beyond the exile of illusion, and into the territory of understanding. Passing through the vale of the symbolic, the pilgrim is rewarded for his faith in the literal journey by being offered a glimpse of the real.[31]

Such modern paradigms follow Erasmus in declaring (a sometimes halting) faith in the efficacy of forms of representation, seeing them as reinflecting deeply embedded mental structures and healing their

---

(1978), and 'Pilgrimages as Social Processes', in *Dramas, Fields and Metaphors* (1978). For subsequent anthropological analyses (following those of Eliade and Smith noted above) see J. Chelini and H. Branthomme (ed.), *Les Chemins de Dieu* (1982); and J. Eade and M. Sallnow (ed.), *Contesting the Sacred: The Anthropology of Christian Pilgrimage* (1991).

[30] See F. Huxley, 'Psychoanalysis and Anthropology', in *Freud and the Humanities* (1985); M. Harbsmeier, 'Elementary Structures of Otherness: An Analysis of Sixteenth-Century German Travel Accounts', in *Voyager à la Renaissance* (1987); J. Ries, 'Pèlerinage et pensée mythique', in *Histoire des pèlerinages*; J. Smith, *To Take Place*, pp. 74–95.

[31] See T. C. Cave, '*Enargeia*: Erasmus and the Rhetoric of Presence in the Sixteenth Century' in *French Renaissance Mind* (1976) though this is unconnected to pilgrimage; A. Dupront, *Du Sacré* (1977); Turner's 'liminality' and Dupront's formulation 'une thérapie par l'espace' both underscore Brown's discussion of pilgrimage from *Cult of the Saints* to *The Body and Society* (1989). Among the most forceful critiques of this model is C. Walker-Bynum's 'Women's Stories, Women's Symbols: A Critique of Victor Turner's Theory of Liminality', in *Fragmentation and Redemption* (1991), pp. 27–51. I return to the conjunction of pilgrimage and romance below, Chapter 5.

wounds with the walking, talking cure. Each, in their way, argues that pilgrimage can profit both communities and individuals. For through the drama or the romance of pilgrimage we can rehearse, and so—to refer to the frame of this opening section—come to terms with the every-day partings of existence and with the singular experience of death.

It is the argument of two of pilgrimage's most forceful recent read-ers, Zacher and Howard, that the real sense of the drama of pilgrim-age is already lost by the time Erasmus argues about, and with, its terms. Both critics represent pilgrimage as an essentially medieval phenomenon, and pilgrimage writing proper as a correspondingly pre-modern body of texts. For Zacher it is curiosity which 'over-whelms' pilgrimage and gives birth to the 'literature of discovery' by which it is displaced.[32] Howard sees rather the advent of the home-coming scene in pilgrimage accounts as a mark of the way in which pilgrimage finds itself displaced by 'literature'.[33] Howard's is the more formally (rather than thematically) astute and provocative thesis; his argument is seductive, and it will be seen that I collude with it to some extent. It rests, however, on the existence of a recog-nisable, holy, which is to say separate, body of pilgrimage writing prior to its entanglement with something called literature; it also carries a sense that 'experience' is the preserve not only of moderns, but also, and more importantly, of those who live and work in the territory of literature. Both of these propositions are questionable.

Neither of the above commentators takes pilgrimage narrative as their focus, and neither reads French or late Renaissance texts. Both situate what amounts to a Fall away from pilgrimage and into mod-ernity as one into, rather than out of, grace; their Fall occurs at the onset of the Renaissance, where their story ends. Each adduces an exemplary early Renaissance author to illustrate their theme; for Zacher, this is Petrarch, for Howard, it is Felix Fabri. It will be my argument that the conclusions drawn from these texts misrepresent both the history and the texture of pilgrimage writing in the Renais-sance.[34] I cannot offer full analysis of either Petrarch or Fabri here, still less untie the complex strands of the Augustinian confessional tradition on which both draw. Rather, through brief readings of each

---

[32] See Zacher, pp. 3–25.   [33] See Howard, pp. 1–50.
[34] It should be acknowledged that neither writer calls on either anthropology or psy-choanalysis to 'read' pilgrimage. This in part accounts for the way they construct their his-tory and their understanding of 'modernity'; that I do, of course, accounts in part for the way I construct mine.

text, I shall investigate both the terms which these pilgrims use to describe themselves, and the issues at stake in the critical debate surrounding curiosity, imitation, and confession in which they figure. We begin with Petrarch, climbing a mountain, and then hurrying home to write about the error of what he has done.

A Crisis of Response: Petrarch's Letter

> Mt. Ventoux is an isolated mountain, 6,270 feet in height, commanding a fine view. Today there is an observatory and an hotel on the summit.[35]

Much recent debate about imitation, curiosity, and the travelling self in the Renaissance begins with Petrarch's letter narrating his ascent of Mont Ventoux. Petrarch writes that the climb had begun out of curiosity, developed in response both to the 'frigida incuriositas' of others, and to the desire—'cupiditas'—to emulate a mountain climb he had been reading of in Livy. Some way up the mountain Petrarch meets an old man who tells him he is in error: the journey is worse than a waste of time, as he knows himself, having tried the climb in his youth. Petrarch is deaf to the old man's exemplary tale (perhaps because unlike that of Livy, he cannot 'read' it, still less emulate it, yet), and so he climbs on. At the summit Petrarch sits down, and takes a copy of the *Confessions* out of his pocket with a view to finding a passage from the Father appropriate to the place. He prepares to read this passage out loud to those who have climbed the mountain with him; the stage set, Petrarch opens the *Confessions* and readies himself to perform his part in the drama of dialogue with Augustine:

> Where I fixed my eyes first, it was written: 'And men go to admire the high mountains, the vast floods of the sea, the huge streams of the rivers, the circumference of the ocean, and the revolutions of the stars—and pass themselves by.' I was stunned, I confess.[36]

At this point Petrarch rushes back down the hill, and the letter ends with him alone in a room, writing the letter which tells of the ascent.

---

[35] A. Johnson (ed.), *Franciscae Petrarchae. Epistolae Selectae*, p. 212. I have used Nachod's translation in *The Renaissance Philosophy of Man*, pp. 36–46, occasionally altered. For the Latin see 'Montem Galliae quendam describit', *Opera* (Basel, 1554), pp. 693–6.

[36] Nachod, p. 44. The Latin concludes: 'et reliquunt seipsos. obstupui fateor', *Opera*, p. 695; Petrarch here quotes Augustine, *Conf*, X. 8. 15. (O'D, i, p. 124).

I want in this reading to direct attention to three moments in the letter—that of leaving in response to textual precedent, that of reading at the summit, and that of writing on return—and to suggest that they determine the sense of Petrarch's journey as a pilgrimage. Rather than marking the end of pilgrimage, as Zacher and others argue, the letter stages a crisis of response to the pilgrim tradition, the better to argue its changing and continuing worth. Read as a discussion of the terms of pilgrimage, the letter examines the process by which the travelling man becomes Petrarch by textualising into recognizable narrative form the motions of his body. It is, in other words, and amongst other things, a letter about the creation of a pilgrim voice by means of imitation, and of the pilgrim author by way of exemplary testimony.

The most evident sign of pilgrimage in the letter is the gesture of reading aloud *ad locum*. That he is about to perform this gesture confirms Petrarch's pilgrim identity and underwrites the worth of this particular day's journey. To seal his performance as an orthodox pilgrim Petrarch has only to read the text appropriate to the place, in the place. But he never says his lines; stunned by the sudden realization of the meaning of the particular text he is about to read out loud, he dries. The moment at the summit is one of extraordinary distress. He cannot perform the gesture *as gesture* because he is too struck by the force of the words he reads on the page as it falls open. They produce in him a silence, born of the shock of recognition: of how the journey had started with a moment of imitation; of how further imitation—of the gesture of reading—could now make him an exemplary pilgrim; but of how Augustine suggests that Petrarch's literal imitation of Livy has made a prodigal fool of him. Rather than continue with the pilgrimage and read the text *ad locum* aloud, Petrarch stages a crisis of reading the terms of pilgrimage as they are articulated in the *Confessions*. He closes the book, refuses to read the passage out to his brother, who is waiting, and returns home in silence and a hurry. On returning, rather than explain what has happened to those who are with him, he retires to a room on his own, and begins writing the letter which tells of the event.

This gesture—that of exploring these problems by way of a letter addressed to a man long dead at the time of writing—is telling.[37] For it shows how tradition, for Petrarch, is not so much a stable,

[37] The letter's addressee, Dionigi da Borgo San Sepulchro, had died some time before the letter was composed.

unchanging body of authoritative knowledge, as an enduring, changing conversation, carried out through letters written and read on
mountain tops, between the living and the dead.[38] Certainly Augustine and Petrarch represent reading in different ways: where Augustine
stands amazed before the book of nature and what it reveals about
the human heart, Petrarch stands amazed by Augustine's book and
what it reveals about his own heart. But, for all their differences, both
take reading to be about apposite forms of attention, and about
mutual correction. Petrarch is stunned by how exactly apposite
Augustine's text is to the place and the time of his own rereading, and
reminds himself that Augustine had had a similar experience:

> I could not believe that this [reading these words in this place] could have
> happened to me by chance: I was convinced that whatever I had read there
> was said to me and nobody else. I remembered that Augustine had once sus-
> pected the same himself when reading.[39]

What Augustine represents as a moment of observation regarding the
vagaries of humans in general, Petrarch reads as a corrective injunction, addressed to him in particular. The textual *locus* is an *exem-
plum*, proper to Petrarch's own place atop the mountain. The desire
to find an appropriate text for the event—the rightness of which is
confirmed by Augustine's voice speaking to him through the page—
provides the travelling man with confirmation of his pilgrim identity,
and makes Mont Ventoux into something of a new Jerusalem. Yet
this insistence on the conjoining of travel and reading *ad locum* creates a problem for Petrarch the writer. For having ignored, program-
matically, earlier injunctions to frame his journey as error, he finds
Augustine speaking the same language as the soldiers in Livy—who
warned against the trip—and the old man at the foot of the mountain—who did likewise. All the examples he fails to read about the
worth of literal travel suggest that to give physical expression to the
desire for knowledge must needs lead to error. All these he has
redescribed as not appropriate to him and his position. But there is
no denying that Augustine is speaking to him, just him. He cannot
simply ignore the Father's words in the way that he had the earlier
exemplary warnings, and so stages a crisis of response to the terms of

---

[38] See J. Freccero, 'Autobiography and Narrative', in *Reconstructing Individualism*
(1986), p. 17: 'The modern era may be said to begin with the Petrarchan cult of personal-
ity, when Cicero and Virgil ceased being *auctores* and became pen pals.'
[39] Nachod, p. 45.

pilgrimage. We need to look at the nature of this crisis in some detail, for it bears directly on the kinds of anxiety concerning the reading of tradition and the writing of their own accounts which later Renaissance pilgrims will also encounter. It is a question of coming to terms with the journey as both literal event and metaphorical example, both personal, physical, process, and (inter) textual narrative product. This is the letter, and these are the questions that are said to mark the end of pilgrimage, and the start of the modern era.

This last claim is made by Zacher, who follows the earlier readings of Burckhardt, Cassirer, Kristeller, and Burke in casting Petrarch's ascent as one towards self-fulfilment and individual, heroic self-expression.[40] Petrarch is cast in the role of Renaissance man of parts, new geographer, explorer, and poet. Curiosity here is a mark of the noble new, and Petrarch—writing to a dead medieval father about a textual encounter with a Late Antique father atop a mountain—is himself the founding father of the Moderns who read him in turn. Nor is the tradition of Petrarch as hero of modern experience confined to the writings of Burckhardt and his early humanist followers. Courcelle and Billanovich authorise O'Connell's recent, eloquent reading:

His accomplishment was to assert for the European imagination—and not only for poetry—the value of experience, experience that in its intensity challenges theological or philosophical categories.[41]

A more differentiated, contextualized Petrarch figures in Blumenberg's wide-ranging study of the fortunes of curiosity in relation to the 'secularization' of the European West. The Ascent here represents less a moment of paradigmatic shift than 'one of the great moments that oscillate indecisively between epochs'. For Blumenberg the letter witnesses to an oscillation between 'the Outer' and 'the Inner', between 'the World' and 'the Soul'; in the process modernity is born.[42] For the rhetorically minded reader, the letter, in

---

[40] Zacher, p. 14; J. Burckhardt, *The Civilisation of the Renaissance in Italy* (1944), p. 171; P. Kristeller, 'Augustine and the Early Renaissance', *Review of Religion*, 8 (1944), pp. 57–78; P. Burke, *The Renaissance Sense of the Past* (1969), pp. 21 ff.

[41] M. O'Connell, 'Authority and the Truth of Experience in Petrarch's "Ascent of Mt. Ventoux" ', *PQ* 62 (1983), pp. 507–20; P. Courcelle, 'Petrarque entre Saint Augustin et les Augustins du XVIe siècle', *Studi Petrarchesi* 7 (1954), 45–62 (see also his *Les 'Confessions' de Saint Augustin dans la tradition littéraire: Antécédents et postérité* (1963)); G. Billanovich, 'Petrarca e il Ventoso', *Italia Medievale e Umanistica*, 9 (1966), pp. 369–401.

[42] H. Blumenberg, *The Legitimacy of the Modern Age* (1983), p. 341.

staging the politics and procedures of *imitatio*, negotiates between tradition and the individual talent in order to begin to forge the modern sense of self. Even those, such as Struever and Greene, who read the letter as a failed attempt to form a unified sense of the heroically singular self continue to rally Petrarch to a specific cause: that of the Moderns. That he failed seems to make his revolutionary gesture all the more admirable.[43]

Greene, like the best of recent rhetorical readers, initially takes care to stress the interdependence of the literal and the moral in Petrarch's account: 'it is almost as if the moral character of his errancy had to be articulated in order to be dealt with.'[44] This is to read Petrarch as one of Zacher's medieval pilgrims. But Greene goes on to read the reality out of the letter, and to glimpse proof of Petrarch's proto-modernity in his 'will to purify the mountain of its physical substance, to sublimate it into the summus which is the end of life, just as the existential actuality of the climb is purified to make room for a Christian peregrinatio'.[45] This reading of pilgrimage as sublimated actuality powerfully subtends Greene's understanding of the letter's staging of 'an ego's jealousy toward any distractions from its own absorbing drama'.[46] But it also denies the distractions of the text and in particular it suppresses the force of the term which I am reading less as something the text 'makes room for', than as itself the dramatic focus of Petrarch's understanding of the experience which goes by the name *peregrinatio*.

How we read the letter clearly has implications for our understanding of the Renaissance humanist project and its rhetorical and political legacy. The insistent rereadings to which this (short) open letter has been subjected represent both differing understandings of modernity and Petrarch's own sense of history. Certainly Petrarch's crisis has, in the first instance, to do with how to narrate physical displacement. From here, however, it soon becomes a crisis of a larger order, raising questions about connections between narration and experience, public and personal address, ways of reading and being read. Augustine teaches Petrarch that textual precedent both structures and determines the reading of (what one takes to be one's own)

---

[43] See N. Struever, *The Language of History in the Renaissance* (1970), p. 150; T. Greene, *The Light in Troy* (1982), pp. 104–11; A. Tripet, *Petrarque, ou la connaissance de soi* (1967), pp. 65–73 (good on 'vain curiosity'); R. Durling, 'The Ascent of Mont Ventoux and the Crisis of Allegory', *Italian Quarterly*, 18 (1974), pp. 7–28.
[44] Greene, p. 106.   [45] Ibid.   [46] Ibid.

experience of things. Perhaps, he wonders, experience is only ever a function of imitation, but can my own observation really only ever be read as the discourse of the other speaking through me?

These are large and urgent questions. Petrarch's response to them in the letter turns on his use of the term *peregrinatio*, which first occurs at the point at which he stops quoting others and starts to quote himself:

I said to myself . . . 'The life we call blessed is located on a high peak. "A nar-row way," they say leads up to it. Many hilltops intervene and we must pro-ceed "from virtue to virtue" with exalted steps. On the highest summit is set the end of all, *the goal towards which our pilgrimage is directed*. Everyone wants to arrive there. However, as Naso says: "Wanting is not enough; long and you attain it." '[47]

The degrees of embeddedness of this apparently singular voice are telling: Petrarch is quoting himself, but he is also quoting himself quoting Ovid, and Matthew quoting Christ's sermon on the mount. For some (such as Zacher), the ironic, self-conscious textuality of the letter is a sign of Petrarch's modernity. For others (such as Greene) it reads as reliance on quotation, a 'failure of denotative firmness . . . a failed assimilation'.[48] In our context, Petrarch's modernity is a side-issue: what matters is that those on both sides of the argument ignore Petrarch's own self-description as a pilgrim. Indeed it is striking that in his reading of the letter, Greene elides the italicized phrase in the above quotation: 'the goal towards which our pilgrimage is directed'. His suppression of the term *peregrinatio*, and others' side-stepping of the attendant problematics of pilgrimage, raise a number of important questions. In particular, it causes us to wonder at this desire to characterize Petrarch as, above all, a 'lettered man', this desire *not* to read Petrarch as a pilgrim. For in naming his text a pil-grimage, Petrarch is not so much focusing on his own ego in relation to external things, nor yet staking a claim to a particular new kind of identity, as recognizing the degree to which subjectivity is best under-stood as a function of intersubjective dialogue. As his later readers, Erasmus and Montaigne, in their very different ways, will make plain, even the most personal voice, the most intimate dialogue with the self, is a tissue of quotation.

[47] Nachod, p. 40, my italics. The Latin, punning, reads: 'in summo finis est omnium et vitae terminus, ad quem peregrinatio nostra disponitur', *Opera*, p. 694.
[48] Greene, p. 109.

Petrarch's staging of ways of reading on the mountain certainly points forward to later Renaissance elaborations of lettered self-hood; but it is also a response to Augustine's far earlier narrative of conversion to an awareness of subjectivity, itself structured in time to the rhythms of apposite reading. Petrarch wants his readers to understand Augustine's point that 'the experience of personal conversion is also the conversion of and to the story'.[49] This is not the same as arguing that this scene never actually took place, or that the degrees of textual embeddedness in play here make of all places mere *topoi*. Least of all does it give licence to ignore the specifics of the scene which Petrarch has set—an identifiable mountain, an actual brother, real servants, real stones, and a real spiritual father.[50] For Petrarch takes care to stage allegoresis and imitation as *physical* exercise: in reading, writing, and walking, the body is involved. Robbins concludes her reading with the sense that 'it is not the possibility of seeing real mountains that is at stake, but the possibility of speaking about them'.[51] I am not so sure. It may be that Petrarch's letter is precisely about the difficulty of knowing how to see things about which we cannot speak.

Reading Petrarch's Ascent as a pilgrimage narrative—as the text asks us insistently to do—allows us to recognize the force of inherited imaginings on our own, novel experiences. In such a perspective, the letter represents neither a failure of denotation, nor a failed assimilative allegory. Rather it questions the appropriateness of either mode to exclusive rights over the reading of the way we move and are and have our being. A form of narrative which is not altogether allegoresis, nor yet firm denotation, the letter reads as the account of a journey 'à double sens'. It is at once degree zero register of a particular time, place, and date—26 April 1336, Mont Ventoux, all day—and a rhetorically crafted exemplary travel narrative—'The Ascent of Mont Ventoux', itself a response to others before it, including those of Livy, the old man at the foot of the hill, Augustine, Ovid, and Christ . . .

To read the letter as the account of such a pilgrimage is to return to the three structuring moments with which we began this discussion

---

[49] This point is made by one of Petrarch's most astute recent readers, J. Robbins, in 'Petrarch Reading Augustine: "The Ascent of Mont Ventoux" ', *PQ* 64 (1985), p. 534.

[50] The mountain is one to which literary pilgrimages are now made; Johnson's notes on the state of the summit in 1923, cited above, extend Petrarch and Augustine's conversation.

[51] Robbins, p. 534.

of Petrarch: leaving in response to textual precedent, reading *ad locum*, and writing the experience as part of the journey. We can now understand these moments to be about how available forms of subjectivity are akin to (albeit never quite identical with) available forms of discourse; and how available forms of discourse are entangled with specific times and places. Certainly, as with Augustine, so with Petrarch the stopping points of the *peregrinatio* are scenes of reading occurring at marked times in named places. Unlike Augustine, however, Petrarch never represents himself reading for the first time. This is a substantial point of argument with those who would see Petrarch as hero of bourgeois reading, and consequently the expressive modern self. He represents pilgrimage as a somewhat Barthesian *leçon*: a reading which teaches us not how to consume the world as text, but how to subject our most cherished tenets, including that of experience, or indeed that all the world's a text, to constant critical rereading.[52]

In rereading Petrarch's letter as a pilgrimage account we are shown less the assertion of the value of individually determined experience, than a questioning of ways of reading, and the effects of the forging of something called character. By means of a modulation of the procedures of humanist imitation with those of Christian confession, the travelling man here is being inscribed in a personal mode of narrative which has the effect of generating a character other than the travelling man. A character whose name is legion: moralist, teacher, allegorist, author, Petrarch. Does this mean that the travelling man does not experience the journey? Or does it mean that the travelling man can only talk of experience by becoming a character? Rather than celebrating this process by which authors are made, the letter asks serious questions about the increasing stranglehold which the notions of authorship and experience seem to have on that 'exercise of convictions in quotidian employment' (Struever) which goes by the name of pilgrimage. Can, Petrarch asks, we only come to terms with an experience if we cast ourselves as characters, in a story of an event which purports to represent that experience? Is this surrender of self to story now the cost of the pilgrim cure?[53]

Not entirely. There is no escape from the category of *peregrini*, for we are all exiles from the body and from others in the world; no more

---

[52] See Barthes, *S/Z*, p. 22.

[53] This is certainly how Montaigne will later read pilgrimage; see my '"Rubbing up against others": Montaigne on pilgrimage', in *Voyages and Visions* (forthcoming).

than there is escape from the condition of writing which all this textual talk of conversation elides. But it is still, and always, possible,
Augustine tells Petrarch, to understand pilgrimage to be a means of
bringing dead authors and living readers into a dialogue of mutual
correction. And this dialogue can, in turn, lead to a closer sense of the
physical presence of things which represent the Word, and which the
Word in turn represents. A closer sense, but not a private sense. For
the sense of *peregrinatio* as Petrarch elaborates it has, as the many
voices speaking in his letter make clear, little to do with authenticity
defined as the private ownership of the means of heroic self-
production.

There is, to be sure, something metaphysical about a reading of
pilgrimage which leads from estrangement to a renewed sense of the
world; something metaphysical too in the claims for the eternally resurrective power of language which they make. Certainly they are akin
to the anthropological and psychoanalytic readings of the pilgrim
tradition alluded to above, akin also to the political claims both of
certain kinds of renewed historicism and of a specific moment in the
movement which was Russian Formalism: '[defamiliarization] creates a "vision" of the object instead of serving as a means for knowing it.'[54] This is to read pilgrimage less as a means to satisfying a
desire for knowledge, than as a way of articulating experiences which
take place at the intersections of knowledge and wonder. As Erasmus
suggests—and as I hope to show in the remainder of this study—this
is less a modernist fantasy about the force of representation, than the
compelling and repeated claim underwriting the rhetoric and the
narration of pilgrimage.

'The Lust of Knowing': Fabri's Narrative

I was by no means satisfied with my first pilgrimage, because it
was exceeding short and hurried, and we ran around the holy
places without understanding and feeling what they were.[55]

From Late Antiquity to the Renaissance, Augustine is read and
reread not as endorsing pilgrimage, but as doubting the worth of

---

[54] V. Shklovsky, 'Art as Technique', in *Modern Criticism and Theory* (1988), p. 25. See
also his 'The Resurrection of the Word', in *Russian Formalism* (1973).

[55] Fabri, *The Wanderings of Felix Fabri* (1892), i, p. 48.

leaving home in order to seek God in strange places.[56] Most early modern pilgrimage accounts follow Petrarch's example, and are counter-texts in that they are written with such arguments against travel very much in mind. A particular issue of concern for pilgrim writers is, as Petrarch's haste to rush home makes clear, that of return. As Ogygius discovers, return is a material and a rhetorical matter; arriving home is only the start of the pilgrim's worries. The real difficulty is getting Menedemus to recognize the worth of the things, and the experience, he has brought back with him. The Stay-at-Home displaces the primacy of the scene of leaving, doubts the pilgrim's faith in the power of the represented Word, and calls into question the curative function of travel. In doing so, he demonstrates how homecoming, and its more metaphorical counterpart, rhetorical attentiveness to how an experience may be 'brought home' to the reader, are, from the perspective both of anxious pilgrims and of readers themselves, the central issues of pilgrim narration.

Menedemus' questions exemplify the kind of rhetorical scrutiny which is said to have dealt a death-blow if not to pilgrimage, then to the traditional pilgrimage narrative. I want now to turn to the narrative account of one Jerusalem pilgrim—Felix Fabri, a Dominican from Ulm—who both fears such scrutiny from others, and internalizes it, making of this anxiety a theme within his story. Like Petrarch before him, Fabri stages a kind of dialogue with Augustine; like Petrarch's letter, Fabri's *Evagatorium* uses dialogue to direct attention to the rhetorical problems of return. Like Petrarch, finally, Fabri writes not in order to bring an end to the confessional pilgrim tradition, but to adapt it, and so ensure its dynamic survival. His narrative account of his two Jerusalem pilgrimages, undertaken in 1480 and 1483–4, survives in many forms, having been disseminated in various modes, for various orders of reader at home: manuscript for the brothers in the monastery at Ulm; versified for the use of nuns in meditation; a shortened version printed in 1556 for the families of

---

[56] See B. Kötting, *Peregrinatio Religiosa* (1950); H. Leclercq, 'Mönchtum und peregrinatio im Frühmittelalter', *RQ* 55 (1960), pp. 212–25, and 'Monachisme et pérégrination du IXe au XIIe siècle', *Studia Monastica*, 3 (1961), pp. 33–52; Ladner, '*Homo Viator*'; G. Constable, 'Monachisme et pèlerinage au Moyen Age', *Revue Historique*, 258 (1977), pp. 3–27, and 'Opposition to Pilgrimage in the Middle Ages', *Studia Gratiana*, 19 (1976), pp. 123–46. All of these deal with Late Antique or medieval debates. For their survival in the Renaissance, see P. Maraval, 'Une controverse sur les pèlerinages autour d'un texte patristique (Gregoire de Nysse, Lettre 2)', *Revue d'Histoire et de Philosophie Religieuses*, 66: 2 (1986), pp. 131–46. I return to this below, Chapter 3.

those whom Fabri accompanied; this shortened text reprinted in Feyrabend's *Reyssbuch* in 1584, again by Roth in 1609, and again by Schneider in 1966; the Latin manuscript edited in full in the 1840s; translated, rewritten, and published in two different English versions in the 1950s and 1960s; the section relating to Egypt translated by Masson and published for the IFAO in Cairo; and finally, most recently, told as a series on British television, repeated as I write.[57]

That the story of Fabri's pilgrimages has survived so well is a wonder, given that after his first Jerusalem journey—itself more than most Christians could ever hope to experience—the returned pilgrim could write only about what he could not remember:

The appearance, shape, and arrangements of these and other holy places escaped from my mind, and the Holy Land and Jerusalem with its holy places appeared to me shrouded in a dark mist, as though I had beheld them in a dream.[58]

Initially, Fabri argues that his inability to recall the 'holy places' is due to the speed at which the pilgrimage took place. But it soon becomes clear that the problem relates less to the past journey, than to the present narration: Fabri needs to be able to tell his story in order to reintegrate himself into the home community. To return to the anthropological/analytic model touched on above, the therapy of distance is incomplete if the pilgrim has not come to terms with—in the sense of written about—estrangement. 'We only visited Bethlehem and Bethany once, and that in the dark' is one sort of problem; 'I seemed to myself to know less about all the holy places than I did before I visited them' is quite another.[59]

What Fabri is really suffering from is the inability to give coherent narrative shape to the experience of having been away. That the issue of return is, for the pilgrim, explicitly connected to narrative, is made clear when Fabri is subjected to his brothers' questions back home in Ulm: 'When I was questioned about the holy places I could give no [t]real [*sic*] answers, nor could I write a clear description of my

---

[57] See, for the print story of the German and Latin texts, H. Feilke, *Felix Fabris Evagatorium* (1976), pp. 7–13. K. Hassler's *Evagatorium* is the only edition of the Latin manuscript, and the fullest English translation remains Stewart's *The Book of the Wanderings* (these are the ones to which I refer here). Later English versions were produced by Prescott (*Jerusalem Journey* and *Friar Felix at Large*). Masson's translation, *Le Voyage en Egypte*, has useful bio-bibliographical notes, pp. i–ix.

[58] Fabri, *Wanderings*, i, pp. 48–9.   [59] Ibid.

Wandering.'⁶⁰ Unable to satisfy others' desire for narrative, Fabri finds he can only conjure up images of Jerusalem 'through a mist darkly, as if in a dream'.⁶¹ This is a frankly Pauline admission of inadequate mimetic powers. It could be read as humility, as a healthy, orthodox, Augustinian disregard for the procedures of human representation. But it is, in the context, more immediately an expression of anxiety at Fabri's being unable to give his brothers the 'verum' in answer to their questions, the gift of what Kristeva has termed 'le vréel', and I have ventured as a 'treal'.⁶² This is the true pilgrim present, something which bridges the gap between the real and the true; almost a treat. The terms in which Fabri expects—and is expected—to tell his socialized story are clear even as he expands on his distress:

This left me distressed beyond measure that I had undergone such sufferings, hardships and dangers, and had spent such great sums of money and so much time, without receiving any profit, any consolation, any knowledge.⁶³

'Sine fructu, sine consolatione, sine cognitione': Fabri has returned home without any of those commodities, akin to pearls from the Orient, which he had legitimately hoped to acquire on his journey. Unable to answer the question 'what was it like?', he finds, to his distress, that he has nothing to show for having been away, and so cannot reasonably account for his return. This distress, already 'beyond measure' leads to still greater concern, as he is led to wonder about the actual existence of the events he thought he had experienced. About the need for effective imaginative reconstruction of the past journey in response to the narrative demands of the present, Fabri is startlingly eloquent:

Often when I tried to comfort myself by turning my thoughts to Jerusalem and the holy places, and found that I was only able to conjure up a vague image of them, I have replied to my own questions in anger: 'Please, stop this thinking about those places, for you're only imagining that you were ever there.'⁶⁴

⁶⁰ Fabri, *Wanderings*, p. 49. The Latin reads 'nullum verum dare potui responsum, nec certum conscribere Evagatorium', *Evagatorium*, i, p. 61.
⁶¹ Ibid.
⁶² J. Kristeva, 'Le vréel'. It has been translated as 'The True-Real' in T. Moi (ed.), *The Kristeva Reader* (1986), pp. 214–37. I suggest 'treal' here for its closeness to 'treat'. I have dislodged the term from its specifically Lacanian context; although what Kristeva has to say about disavowal and the irruption of the real into the socialized space of the symbolic is helpful to an understanding of Fabri's text, and the wider issues of pilgrim narration.
⁶³ Fabri, *Wanderings*, p. 49.
⁶⁴ Ibid. (Translation altered slightly.)

The pilgrim here addresses to himself the terms and the questions of those who stayed at home. This internalizing of the desire for the 'verum' leads to an anxiety about the real experience it purports to represent. Such fracturing of consciousness into a drama of self-questioning and self-rebuke is an exemplary confessional manœuvre, as we saw with respect to Petrarch. A question hidden in Petrarch—'Can I truly experience things about which I cannot speak?'—is here clarified and made explicit: 'If I cannot recall this event, did it ever take place?' As Fabri suggests, the rendering explicit of the problem of pilgrim narration does not, however, lead closer to the truth of the event, any more than it necessarily provides the desired treat of coherent narration. What it can do is give voice to the pilgrim's anxiety about the burden he carries on his back: the weight of others' lust of knowing, the desire to be told the tale. The self-confessed inability to conjure up a less than vague image of experience leads to an understanding of the stakes of coherent narration: If I can't tell the story, perhaps it never happened, and if I'm wrong about this, what am I not wrong about?

The drama of self-questioning in Petrarch was a prologue to literal silence, an end to literal travel, and the start of a dialogue with the dead. For Fabri it acts as an impulse to further travel, further narration, in an effort to respond to the desires of the living. Profit, consolation, and knowledge all, he realizes, require a narrative coherence which he is, as yet, unable to provide. As a consequence, he cannot truly come home. By staging a scene in which he doubts the value of the terms of pilgrimage, he gestures towards the chance to live the experience a second time, and to tell the story again: this time for true-real. Fabri conceives the secret and scandalous desire to return to Jerusalem, to test the truth of the experience. The terms of this desire—return, scandal, secret, experience, truth—are explicitly stated in Fabri's text, but they are represented as hidden from his father-confessor. Unlike Augustine or Petrarch, Fabri directly addresses a future reader (rather than a dead Father, or God). This allows him further to play with temporal awareness, not now in relation to his own memory and his sense of private self, but in relation to the reader, who, he stresses, does not always already know what he is going to be told. The narrative act which constitutes the *Evagatorium* is thus not an act of penance, redundant in terms of the knowledge it presents. Rather, it establishes a complicity both between reader and narrator, and between the narrator and his secret self. This Fabri is able to do because—unlike either Augustine or Petrarch—he suggests that there are secret truths, such as the pilgrim's true motivation, which the attentive reader can learn (since the narrator chooses to reveal them), but which will remain hidden from those who police the pilgrim's mind.

Fabri tells his readers that he avoided avowal of his desire for a second pilgrimage during confession, for fear of being recognized as subject to the inventions of the devil and to infection by curiosity. All the while, he planned and prepared his return to Jerusalem, eventually securing a post as secretary and guide to certain nobles intending to make the pilgrimage.[65] They quiz him not about the holy places, but about the requisite preparations for the journey. These are questions he can answer all too easily: he knows from his first trip how to be a guide, but not how to produce a narrative. Employed as a guide and secretary, he is able to travel a second time, and this time produce the longed for narrative. The treat Fabri the pilgrim is then able to afford himself, and others, is that of total revelation, a coincidence of private self and open narration. It is the luxury of hearing him say, again, and again, in the course of over a thousand pages: I am not suffering from a delusion; I was seduced away from home by images more powerful than I could say before; but I really did go away; it really happened; I was there; and it was like this, and this, and this.

Petrarch's letter is read and reread by each new generation. His interrogation of the terms of tradition, imitation, and experience provides a model for critics as they place themselves in the dead Father's position, respond to the crises of history, and establish their own sense of the changing politics of reading. Fabri's *Wanderings* have been similarly resurrected by succeeding generations of readers. Unlike Petrarch's letter, however, his tales are not so much subjected to critical scrutiny, as re-edited, re-told, and re-represented according to the reading habits and new technologies of each new age. If Petrarch suggests that pilgrimage can afford us a clearer sense of the presence of the word and the world, Fabri offers a different kind of pilgrim treat. Both his narrative and the history of its survival bear witness to the way in which pilgrimage accounts satisfy not only the pilgrim's lust for narrative, but also the reader's perennial desire for that peculiar conjunction of secrecy and disclosure which is articulated as anecdotal knowing.

---

[65] Fabri, *Wanderings*, pp. 52–3.

'De Peregrinatione Studiorum Causa': *Augustine's Lesson*

> Who can tell how many times each day our curiosity is tempted
> by the most trivial and insignificant matters? Who can tell how
> often we give way? So often it happens that, when others tell
> foolish tales, at first we bear with them for fear of offending the
> weak, and then little by little we begin to listen willingly.[66]

After his crises of recollection, Fabri eventually accounts for his
absence from his conventual brothers with those narrative tokens
which proved the worth of having been away. Petrarch initially seems
to frustrate the desire for narrative connection with others: he refuses
to read to his brother and makes for home in silence, avoiding open
confession of the continuity of his experience with that of past readers and travellers. But the silence is staged; it is a prelude to writing,
and Petrarch eventually consents to figuring himself as a pilgrim,
thereby conjuring the loss occasioned in the course of travel, of
returning home, and of learning the 'linguae peregrinae' of subjectivity. Like the two exemplary confessional travellers who follow him,
Augustine stages a crisis of reading in relation to experience; his particular focus is the dramatic, unwilling surrender of his body to others' 'lust of knowing'. Whether in the cloisters of Ulm, on Mont
Ventoux, the circus, or the baths at Thagaste, the drama of reading
the self is for Augustine, as for Petrarch, as for Fabri, always played
out at the behest of, in sight of, and in the terms of others. Each pilgrim has, however, a different relation to the demand for disclosure
which others bring to bear on them, and each constitutes his pilgrim
self differently as a consequence. In returning, finally, to Augustine's
Confessions, we shall see how for himself, and for those who follow
in his pilgrim steps, the question of the subject is always, and from
the outset, framed as that of location, exemplarity, and address.

Augustine's most extended discussion of the problematic status of
curiosity and the desire for narrative occurs in *Confessions*, Book X.
It is here that Augustine describes himself as speaking in the presence
not only of God, but also of others, whom he terms fellow-pilgrims;[67]
here also that curiosity is most explicitly defined as driven not by the
urge for salvation, 'sed experiendi noscendique libidine'—'the lust of

---

[66] Augustine, *Conf*, X. 35. 57, p. 215; O'D, p. 141.
[67] Ibid., X. 4. 6, p. 185. The Latin reads: 'confiteor non tantum coram te sed etiam in
auribus civium meorum et mecum peregrinorum' (O'D, p. 121).

making trial and knowing' (Pusey). The terms are forceful, and echo those of an earlier stage in Augustine's narrative, where he had told the story of his friend Alypius' desire to know if, following his conversion, he had been properly 'cured' from the 'infection' of the circus. Alypius is tempted by former friends back into the games and, through a desire to test his own powers of resistance, agrees to enter the arena. As the games approach, Augustine has Alypius take over the narration, giving voice to his own pride:

Though you hale my body to that place, and there set me, can you force me also to turn my mind or my eyes to these shows? I shall then be absent while present; and shall overcome both you and them.[68]

Alypius blocks his eyes and sits in the circus in silence: a pilgrim body in a foreign land, 'he forbade his mind to range abroad'. But he is soon 'overcome by curiosity' as—a liquid force—the sound of the games seeps through his ears and so fills his head as to force open his eyes, and with them the floodgates. What Alypius risks losing here is his newly found, convertite, identity; he risks a second conversion into someone else again. And as the games unfold he becomes increasingly entangled in the sight of what he had gone *not* to see; he becomes someone other than the man who had entered the arena. The passage concludes with a shift back from Alypius' voice to that of Augustine, drawing the moral from his friend's example: 'Nor was he now the man he came, but one of the throng he came to . . . why say more?'[69]

The story of Alypius dramatizes the ways in which curiosity hijacks the body, and with it, the will, wherein, for Augustine, resides our identity. Entanglement in curiosity makes us other to our sacred selves. Nor is Augustine himself free from this danger. He can draw the moral from others' examples, but what of his own experience? In whose voice should events from his own life be told? Turning to consider curiosity in relation to his own, rather than others' desires, Augustine recognizes that he too is bound up with entanglement in the briers of narrative temptation:

In this immense forest, so full of snares and dangers, I have pared away many sins and thrust them from my heart . . . I beseech you, by Christ our

---

[68] Augustine, *Conf*, VI. 8. 13, pp. 95–6; O'D, p. 65.

[69] Ibid., p. 96. The Latin reads: 'non erat iam ille qui venerat sed unus de turba ad quam venerat. quid plura!' (O'D, p. 65).

King and by Jerusalem the chaste, our homeland . . . to ward [the memory of necromancy and astrology] off and keep them still farther from me.[70]

Here the speaking subject is able to speak of itself as subject to correction by the will. Confession, speaking of oneself, naming past deeds the better to set them in the past, can thus be posited as itself a form of husbandry of the heart. The act of narration is not in itself sinful, but rather enables the penitent to identify, to pare away, or stem, the graver curious arts, and so move closer towards the Jerusalem of self-understanding. But necromancy and astrology are not the real obstacles to the pilgrim's progress; the real problem is the 'disease of curiosity' which they exemplify.

In arguing that it is from 'this disease of curiosity that all those strange sights are exhibited in the theatre', Augustine can show that he has learned the lesson of Alypius' example: 'I no longer go to watch a dog chasing a hare at the games in the circus'. But he also, crucially, acknowledges that the circus is not the only theatre. The curiously minded will make a theatre of the world, will make a narration of their own and every experience:

But if I happen to see the same thing in the country as I pass by, the chase easily holds my attention and distracts me from whatever serious things occupy my mind. It might not actually compel me to turn my horse from the path, but such is the inclination of my heart; and unless you make me realize my weakness, and quickly remind me, either to turn my eyes from the sight and raise my thought to you in contemplation, or to despise it utterly and continue on my way, I simply stop and gloat.[71]

The message seems clear: avoid not only the curious arts, the spectacular arts, the narrative arts, but also, since travel is but an enactment of and an occasion for curiosity, stay at home. But the drama of self-questioning does not end there, for now Augustine's curious gaze has learnt, through its attention to detail, to catch itself up in narrative entanglement wherever it falls. Horse-riding is not the problem here. Rather the chase reveals itself as a metaphor for narrative, and the quarry is the self. Confessional self-disclosure, initially posited as a means to control of the will, now proves to be itself a sign of the narrator's fallen state. The narration of 'trivial' example has become his primary desire, and his text sees its own procedures enacted everywhere, even at home: 'What excuse can I make for myself' he asks

---

[70] Ibid. X. 35. 56–7, pp. 214–15; O'D, p. 141.
[71] Ibid.

'when often, as I sit at home, I cannot turn my eyes from the sight of a lizard catching flies or a spider entangling them as they fly into her web?'[72] Even at home, then, curiosity finds itself, and finds itself figured in tropes for narrative.

Augustine offers himself excuses. The first is to argue that these are less tropes, than—at least with regard to lizards and spiders—real animals ('Does it make any difference that these are only small animals?'). The second is to submit to the allegorizing impulse and read them as signs, but as *good* signs, representing the wonder and *varietas* of creation: 'It is true that the sight of them inspires me to praise you for the wonders of your creation and the order in which you have disposed all things.' But the truth is elsewhere, and Augustine forces himself to acknowledge that curiosity cannot properly be recuperated to the order of praise. He knows that he reads his own book figured in nature (and not God's), and he confesses: 'I am not intent upon your praises when I first begin to watch.'[73]

There is, of course, good knowledge and bad knowledge, just as there are good and bad books; but this is not the point. Augustine's real concern is not with distinctions between the circus and lizards—the arts and the sciences. The problem lies elsewhere, as the twinned examples of Alypius and Augustine himself teach: 'concupiscientia', embedded in intent, subverts subsequent redescription of its effects as prayer or praise. Not all travel is pilgrimage, and not all inclinations of the heart, movements of the body, or responses to the desire for narrative, take readers and pilgrims closer to either the world or the Word.

This is Augustine's lesson to his early Renaissance readers; he himself learns it at the conclusion of chapter 3 of the *Confessions*, signalled in Erasmus' edition as 'de peregrinatione studiorum causa'.[74] His father, keen that he should do well in the Empire, had funded Augustine's travels to Carthage, and his studies in rhetoric—the

---

[72] Augustine, *Conf*, X. 35. 56–7, pp. 214–15; O'D, p. 141.

[73] Ibid. See also O'D, iii, pp. 227–8. This example is akin to others in which Augustine's curiosity becomes entangled, listed, with references, in Gibb and Montgomery's edition, p. 318; they include a worm being cut in half, a cock fight, the song of a nightingale, the memory of fishes, the artifice of birds building their nests. H. Marrou, in *Saint Augustin et la fin de la culture antique* (1938), suggests that the connotative message of these animal examples is 'I am a learned man' (pp. 149–50; 278–83). But they also figure the dangers of collecting such examples and applying them to one's own narrative, the danger of becoming a character, or what Petrarch terms 'a man of letters'.

[74] The chapter is pp. 54–5 of volume i of Erasmus' 1529 edition of Augustine's *Opera*.

'linguae peregrinae' of metonomy, allegory, symbolism, and the like—which he there learned. To make these studies and the lessons of their language his own, Augustine needs to convert them into a negative example for his readers; he does so—as he did with his friend Alypius—by distinguishing himself from the bad example of his father. This he does on his return home to Thagaste from Carthage, a homecoming scene which merits brief but close examination.

As Augustine discovers, the self-confessing heart is a lonely hunter; his pilgrim is a stranger even at home. Initially all seems well, and in celebration of the boy's return to the family fold, Augustine is taken to the baths with his father; where he has an erection. It is clear from the text that the young man's first erection is a public event: it occurs in the baths in view of all those present. More than this, the event cannot remain 'insignificant and trivial' since, thanks to the curiosity of his father, it must be spoken of, made meaningful, 'read' as a part of a homecoming narrative. The father clearly reads the movement of his son's body as a sign of the worth of his having been away: a boy left home and a man has returned, as is plain for all in the baths to see.

There is nothing extraordinary about this. Indeed it seems all Roman boys were subject to such public readings of their bodies.[75] But not all boys stage these moments at the point of their return home from travels; nor do all boys read the event itself as heartily publicly as those around them. Augustine, in particular, tells the story of his first erection at this point in his narrative only because it has already been made meaningful by others. In telling it a second time he hopes not so much to regain ownership of the event, as to register the fact of loss, the fact that a certain intimacy has been denied him by virtue of others' curiosity, others' terms. Intimacy is not here synonymous with privacy, rather it connotes a complicity between the speaking subject and his secret self, his listeners, his God.

The terms of the boy's homecoming are not his own, any more than are the movements of his body. What has been taken from Augustine is not ownership of his body (the erection is unwilled, and the boy now knows that the body is not his own); it is rather the right to determine how meaning is ascribed to the event. The question is one of anticipation: does this erection have a specific 'sens', a

[75] See A. Rousselle, *Porneia* (1988), p. 59: 'The appearance of pubic hair and his first ejaculations were a cause for celebration for the whole household, particularly the father' (Quoted, O'D, ii, p. 120).

direction? The Father thinks so, and 'anticipating his descendants', he takes the story off to the Mother, who for her part anticipates 'those crooked ways in which they walk who do turn their back to Thee, and not their face'.[76] Monica's explicit fear here is that with the onset of manhood as defined by his father, Augustine will give himself wholly to the world, and 'turn his back, not his face' to the face not only of other men, but also of God. That is, that in returning home, Augustine will enter the order of the father's language and that in doing so her boy will lose the ability to speak from the heart, either to God, to himself, or to others.

What is at issue in all the above homecoming incidents—those of Ogygius, Petrarch, Fabri, and Augustine—is the language in which we get to talk about what is happening to us, whom we address, and how. These are the confessional pilgrim's abiding concerns; must my story be useful to be worth the telling, and is exemplarity the necessary shape of pilgrim experience? The question is, to repeat, not so much a modern problem, as one central to the discourse of Christian pilgrimage from its outset. It is a question asked, by way of a metaphorical critique of travel, and a literal critique of metaphor, in a revealing passage from *De doctrina christiana*, contemporary in composition with the *Confessions*. Augustine's concern here is explicitly with the legitimate 'use' and 'enjoyment' of figural language in relation to the *peregrinatio* which leads to God. Once again he explores these terms by way of an analogy concerning travel, and in particular, coming home:

Suppose we were travellers or pilgrims [quomodo ergo, si essemus peregrini] who could not live happily except at home, miserable in our travels [peregrinatione], and desiring to end them, to return to our native country. We would need vehicles for land and sea which could be used [utendum] to help us to reach our homeland, which was to be enjoyed [fruendum]. But if the amenities of the journey and the motion of the vehicles itself delighted us, and we were led to enjoy those things which we should use, we should not wish to end our journey quickly, and, entangled in the wrong kind of pleasures, we should be alienated from our country, whose proper pleasures would make us happy.[77]

The passage speaks for itself; it is also an eloquent staging of the difficulties of translating the 'linguae peregrinae' in play here.

[76] Augustine, *Conf*, II. 3. 6, p. 21; O'D, i, p. 17.
[77] Augustine, *De doctrina christiana*, p. 16. For discussion of when different sections of the work were composed, see Green's 'Introduction', ibid., pp. xi–xiv.

Augustine is not talking about pilgrimage as an institutionalized journey; indeed he is not talking about real travel at all. Rather, like Paul whom he follows here, Augustine is discussing the need to be prepared to read the experience of others' and oneself in relation to the masterplot of conversion and redemption. The *De doctrina christiana* is generically more confident of its terms than the *Confessions*: it is less a discussion of subjectivity than an assertion of the terms of the Christian character. If the *Confessions* stage moments of crisis, here there is rather confident redirection of the terms of Pauline Christian tradition. 'So, in this mortal life we are like travellers away from our Lord; if we wish to return to the homeland, where we can be happy, we must use this world, not enjoy it.'[78]

As we have seen in this chapter the pilgrim subject is constituted in response to tradition; the pilgrim speaks in the terms and in the presence of others. In the *Confessions* Augustine speaks both 'before the face of God' and 'in the hearing of his fellow pilgrims'. His narrative negotiates a way between the useful and the pleasurable, and Petrarch, Fabri, and Ogygius who follow him, will do likewise. Erasmus, too, will excitedly adopt the 'uti/frui' distinction to help him think about the worth of learning foreign languages, of the language of pilgrimage, and of the sense of staying at home. Others—whose texts we read in later chapters—will follow him in turn.[79]

All pilgrim narrators recognise that to become entangled in the telling of events from one's own life is to risk being cast as one of the 'errans'. You are pre-empted, told you are too late to determine what may, or may not, matter to you most; in speaking of yourself at all you have risked losing your way. Your speech, your action, and your example, if insufficiently exemplary, risks being of no specific worth. As for Augustine, so too for the early Renaissance travellers discussed in this chapter, to be a pilgrim is to read one's experience for others. As Petrarch learns on the mountain, and as Fabri learns on returning home to his monastery, the pilgrim gains the pleasure of experience by making himself useful, which is to say by surrendering his individual personhood to exemplary character. But secret selves can—cannot but—be forged in the interstices of tradition.

---

[78] Ibid., pp. 16–17. The Latin reads: 'sic in huius mortalitatis vita peregrinantes a domino, si redire in patriam volumus ubi esse possimus, utendum est hoc mundo, non fruendum'. This is a conflation of 1 Cor. 7: 31, 2 Cor. 5: 6, and Rom. 1: 20.

[79] See C. Béné, *Érasme et Saint Augustin* (1969), Annexe N, pp. 447–8 and *passim*.

Such are the terms in which the confessional writer can—and must—negotiate subjectivity. They articulate the peculiar condition of the pilgrim subject, since the entire journey is reiteration, physical enactment of the examples of others. And yet this is not altogether a narration of surrender and loss, for through its alignment with confessional narrative, pilgrimage can also be affirmed as a mode of writing which enables the constitution of a particular kind of narrative subject, one which is not—or not only—the secluded, singular self. For the pilgrim narrator is able to recuperate the dangers of curiosity and digression to a sacred and complex, self-fashioning end; and can do so with both individual pleasure and a sense of connectedness and community. With pilgrimage conceived of as an adventure in subjectivity, few are the travellers, even amongst those who would not class themselves pilgrims, who can fully resist its paradoxical seductions. Few also are those, from Late Antiquity to late Renaissance, who can avoid taking up a position with respect to the ethics of reading, as well as travel, which pilgrimage so powerfully articulates.

CHAPTER TWO

Renaissance Guides to Pilgrimage

chescun desire habunder a son sens . . . La seule art descripre (ainsi que experience le monstre) est de tous embrassee. Parquoy se faict que souvent les
ignorans autant que les instruis se efforcent de escripre: de composer: de
dire.[1]

Not until the early years of the seventeenth century were French-
speaking lay pilgrims to the Holy Land able to buy books telling
them where to go and how to travel. The first two such vernacular
guides to appear in print, both specifically intended for the general
reader, were Loys Balourdet's *La Guide des chemins pour le voyage
de Hierusalem, et autres villes et lieux de la Terre Saincte* (1601) and
Henri de Castela's *La Guide et adresse pour ceux qui veulent faire le
S. voyage de Hierusalem* (1604). Each writer speaks with the experience of the journey behind him; he is one of the survivors come home,
and he writes with the authority both of his priesthood and of his
personal experience. As we shall see in this chapter, however, these
two forms of authority were not always complementary. Indeed one
of the primary purposes of the priests' *Guides* seems to have been to
call into question the value of the experience gained on the pilgrim
journey; certainly they doubt the worth of most pilgrims' narration
of their experience, and bemoan the way in which pilgrimage seems
to offer many a means to 'habunder' about themselves, rather than
the sacred places to which they have travelled, and from which they
have returned.

The appearance of the two *Guides* at this time might initially suggest that the new century saw a new codification of information for

---

[1] Huen, Prologue to *Le grant voyage* (1517), fol. iii[r].

pilgrims hoping to benefit from improved international relations, and the improved technologies of travel. Certainly, the 'grand voyage'—the paradigmatic pilgrimage—was no longer accessible only to the nobility or those who undertook pilgrimages by proxy, on their behalf and at their expense. It is a point stressed by one of the pilgrim authors we saw arguing against Reform above—Dublioul—when he claims in his own call to pilgrimage that, these days, 'ceux qui n'ont grands moyens et voudroyent faire ce pelerinage, pourront facilement faire leur profit et à peu de despens, ou quasi nulz, aller en Hierusalem, et retour jusques à Venise'.[2] By 'quasi nulz despens' he means less than fifty ecus, and in less than four months. Compared with other pilgrims' accounts, these costs seem slightly optimistic, but Dublioul is here concerned less with providing accurate, up-to-date costings, than with proving the worth and general accessibility of pilgrimage. In this he is like his fellow priests, the two *Guide* writers; but the repeated claim of universal access is itself a sign that the institution is under threat. For, in truth, all three priests write not so much in response to developments in the technology of travel, as in reaction to the development of new kinds of traveller, and the threat which is represented by new translations, and new understandings, of the terms of *peregrinatio*.

In offering vernacular advice and encouragement to future pilgrims by way of a prologue, none of these authors was in fact offering anything new. Even the practical advice they give is little more than an addition to material that had long been available to putative pilgrims. Itineraria, logs, and texts offering advice on what to buy, when to travel to Jerusalem, and how much to pay had existed for many years. Most surviving accounts, from that of the Bordeaux pilgrim in the fourth century onwards, included a log of places along the way and the distances between them. Books listing the indulgences to be had on the journey, and a number of inexpensive do-and-don't pamphlets could be bought cheaply from a roadside stall in Venice, or even from the hostel where pilgrims stayed.[3] The hostels also allowed for information to be exchanged between travellers in

---

[2] Dublioul, *Le Voyage*, p. 15.

[3] For examples of (mainly German late fifteenth century) instructions regarding what to take on the journey, see those printed by R. Röhricht and H. Meisner, *Deutsche Pilgerreisen* (1880, 1889), pp. 120, 138, 147, 321. See also A. von Harff, *Pilgrimage* (1967), pp. 69–72. For English accounts, see W. Wey, *Itineraries* (1857), p. 4 ff. and the MS. *Informaçion for Pilgrims*.

person, as did the circulation and copying of manuscript notes on the journey. The printing revolution made such information more widely available; it did not alter radically the organization of the material, nor is it, alone, responsible for the creation of the new form of the *Guide*.

Breydenbach's *Peregrinatio*, to take the most celebrated example, is now considered primarily as an important text in the history of the book. It was also, at the time of its first Latin publication, and within a few years in translation, a compendious and fairly old-fashioned call to pilgrimage both moral and practical. His detailing of the terms of the contract drawn up between pilgrims and the Contarini brothers—ships' captains—in Venice, translated first by Hersin, and then again by Huen as part of his own account, inaugurates the dissemination of such information in print in France. This is important, but the book's function cannot primarily have been to inform prospective pilgrims of the costs of travel. It was itself too costly an object for such a purpose.[4]

Bare itineraries, logs, or the terms of a contract are easily copied, not least because when echoed, pure information carries little or no trace of the personal voice. But even simple details regarding costs can be said to do more than be immediately useful: they also perpetuate a form of pilgrim *style*. Impersonal repetition of another's trajectory is, for many pilgrims, the essence of the experience. A litany of place names, leagues between, and indulgences attached to each place translates their understanding of the sense of the journey. This issue of style, allied to the question of cost but not identical with it, has effects on the pilgrims' published accounts throughout the sixteenth century, many of which are made up of material copied, or only slightly recast, from earlier texts. They are the narratives of pilgrims little concerned to represent themselves as rhetorically skilled authors, or to impress their own sense of place on the reader's imagination.

Anthoine Regnaut, for instance, offers readers of his *Discours du voyage d'outre mer* the most comprehensive practical guide to the Jerusalem journey by way of an eleven-point 'Instruction au voyage', written in such a way as to be easily copied, much as he, or his publisher, has copied a wealth of material from elsewhere.[5] This is

---

[4] B. Breydenbach, *Peregrinatio* (1486), fols. av^{r-v}, Hersin (trans.), *Le saint voyage*, fols. aviii^v–bi^v (1488); Huen, *Le grant voyage*, fols. viii^{r-v}.

[5] A. Regnaut, *Discours du voyage* (1573). We return to this 'Instruction' in detail below. There are also a number of treatises copied out as appendices—on indulgences, the

wilfully useful and reusable writing, and it characterizes a particular kind of pilgrim style. The *Guide* writers' attempts to resurrect this style, just one generation after Regnaut, himself one generation later than Breydenbach, served only to reinforce the sense that it was, almost, already dead.

For the later writers Balourdet, Dublioul, and Castela all fear that being a pilgrim is no longer enough in itself. They want to be both pilgrims and authors, not least because this is how they foresee the survival of pilgrimage. Castela half-apologetically confesses as much when, in elaborate and mixed metaphors, he justifies publishing the *Guide* as a separate pamphlet. In part he does this for reasons of cost—the *Guide* is in a smaller and cheaper format than his own voluminous account of the journey. But there is more than money at stake here, as he writes: 'C'est le dernier mets que je veux te servir. Je le fay suivre mon autre volume à guise de ceux qui attachent les esquifs aux navires afin qu'en plain fortunal ils puissent eschever la cruauté de la mer.'[6] If this is apology, it is also heartfelt argument, in favour of the plain talking of pilgrim travellers, and against their detractors. For the cruel seas Castela refers to, and from which he wishes to protect the pilgrim, are not so much those of the Mediterranean, as those of change. As everyone who travels and writes seems to want to be an author by the early seventeenth century, the pilgrim guides need, amongst other things, to be guides to pilgrim authorship. The *Guide* writers themselves understand that these days the politics and economics of imitation—even imitation of unvoiced information—have become problematic. And all three pilgrim priests are moved to codify the rules of the Jerusalem pilgrimage in the vernacular less by the desire to share up-to-the-minute tips for the journey, than by the need to keep a certain sense of pilgrim style alive.

At first sight, the priests' anxiety seems ill-founded, for imitation clearly both preserves the pilgrim tradition into the late Renaissance, and authorizes the manner in which advice is passed from generation to generation. Even in terms of practical detail little seems to change

travels of Charlemagne, and the like; the journey account proper includes a copy of a log guide of places to stop between Paris and Venice, the 'sauf-conduit' signed by the King, certificates regarding the Order of the Holy Sepulchre, the Jerusalem liturgy, and, most striking of all, a vast number of prints and woodcuts of all sorts and sizes which are scattered throughout the text, often interrupting the narrative mid-phrase without comment. There are also prescriptions in Italian, given to Regnaut by the ship's captain, against seasickness (p. 16), and fleas (p. 24).

[6] Castela, *Guide*, fol. Aiiij[r].

across the long century, since information about where to stay and what to do there is deemed to be still relevant to readers fifty to seventy years after it is first published. But there are none the less clear indicators of change, if not in information, then in tone. For the novelty of the priestly authors lies in their sense of the need to use the *Guide* form to argue the pilgrim's case against the other forms of traveller. This, in time, is understood to be dependent on a sense of themselves, and their readers, as potential authors competing in the market of discourses. Regnaut, with his 'Instruction', had simply assumed the worth of pilgrimage, much as he might have encouraged both the textual and practical imitation of his texts and recipes. None of the pilgrim priests who write guides at the turn of the century can afford to do either. They must argue the cause of pilgrimage, and alongside it, that of their own rights as priestly authors instructed by God to determine the proper scope of the terms of pilgrimage as both practice and narrative. In the process the guide-book finds itself to be a part of polemic. The late Renaissance pilgrim *Guide* writer cannot think of himself as a representative of a large and self-evident community; he is not simply someone writing, but someone writing *against*.

Pilgrims and Authors

Both Balourdet and Castela begin, in the first editions of their texts, by assuming that their enemy is the Reform. In their call to pilgrimage, they recycle Regnaut's 'Instruction' with few changes. He is no longer alive by the time they publish, and no one claims his rights as an author on his behalf; nor should they, for this is pilgrim free trade and what matters is the worth of the practice in general. But Castela also takes material from another pilgrim—Zuallart—and finds that in doing so he has met with an author, who objects to having his words stolen in this way. Zuallart, in the 1608 French version of his *Tresdevot voyage* (originally composed in Italian, and published in Rome, 1587), vents his fury at Castela's having pirated the descriptions of Italy, along with a number of figures, drawings, and plates, from his text. The terms of his anger are revealing. He is unconcerned with the unity of the Church; what matters to him is the integrity of his text and his newly fashioned sense of himself as a writer, with dues. He is, he notes, not against reusing information altogether: Jean de Hault, whom he has never met, has similarly read and profited from his text. But whereas Hault, in his published *Voyage* (1601), acknowledges the debt to Zuallart's account—for which he is in turn grateful—Castela does not.[7]

In the later edition of his own *Voyage* (1612), Castela registers his surprise at the vehemence, and the nature, of Zuallart's attack. The priest had not realized, it seems, that the new kinds of pilgrim which his and others' *Guides* were helping to form would want more than to write texts that were useful to others, would crave acknowledgement, and would want to be known as authors. As the priest learns to his cost, with authorship comes a new sense of the pilgrim subject's relation to others, and a new economy of pilgrim debt.

Castela should, perhaps, not have been surprised. For he had himself outlined the terms of this new economy in his *Guide*. There, value is deemed to be a function of specificity, of difference, and both Castela and Balourdet prescribe attitudes and modes of behaviour which are specific and proper to the pilgrim. Even the opening address to the reader of the first edition of the *Voyage* is an eloquent statement of the pilgrim author's ambiguous position:

Trescher amy, tu m'estimeras en l'entreprise de ce S. voyage d'un coeur presque Herculéen d'avoir prins les armes contre tant de Géants, et tiré en champ de bataille tant de grands personnages confis en toutes sciences. Apres tant de perils que j'ay evité au travail des chemins, je retente une autre fortune.[8]

The 'fortune' Castela fears is—anticipating Zuallart's response, but not explaining why—the reception of his text. It is not the journey, but its retrospective narration which is the most daunting of the Herculean labours he can imagine. The 'Géants' he fears are those of the arena of writing, and he names them by their professions: 'Poëtes, Historiens, Cosmographes, Geometricians, Ingenieurs et Architectes . . . Voilà (Lecteur) de combien d'ennemis je me voys menacé.'[9] Fellow pilgrim authors are not the named enemy. It is as if he expected no competition in his own field.

And indeed his advice to other pilgrims is to avoid the danger of criticism from others altogether: his *Guide* is written not least to

[7] G. Zuallart, *Le Tresdevot voyage* (1608), fol. *4ᵛ. For more on this see M.-C. Gomez-Géraud, 'Contempler Jérusalem', *Littérales*, 3 (1987), pp. 55–67.

[8] Castela, *Le Sainct Voyage*, 'Au Lecteur', *non. pag.*

[9] Ibid. We return to this passage, and this fear, below, Ch. 7.

dissuade pilgrims from writing at all, and to encourage them to adopt a very particular identity: that of the silent witness, free from narrative desire and from all but holy curiosity. He himself stresses that 'ce n'est pas pour repaistre une ame curieuse' that he is writing.[10] The pilgrim must examine his conscience to discover any traces of 'vaine et vicieuse curiosité' and eradicate them altogether, replacing them with 'une vraye et deue intention'. Once in the Holy Land, the pilgrim must seek out 'en premier lieu que les saincts et sacrez vestiges lesquels y ont esté delaissees par l'Antiquité'.[11] If he does not, his journey, and its subsequent narration, will become an incitement only to error:

Dieu n'inspire point d'entreprendre ce S. Pelerinage, pour puis apres se jacter d'avoir veu beaucoup de raretés; ains pour confirmer d'avantage la personne Chrestienne pour [par?] la veue, et l'attouchement des saincts lieux et de la terre saincte sur laquelle il a marché, presché, faict des miracles, souffert mort et passion, et est ressucité.[12]

So Castela warns the pilgrim before he sets out what his motives should be, and implicitly dissuades him from writing about his experience on his return.

Like Castela, Balourdet recognises his task as a *Guide* writer as being that of illustrating the worth of pilgrimage both as a journey and as a form of writing. In arguing the perils of authorship, both priests make explicit the inherited connections between curiosity and narrative digression, elaborated by the writers of the last chapter, and do so in terms specific to the new economy of language operating in their own times. Thus, as well as accounting for the material details and the cost of the journey, they alert the potential pilgrim to the spiritual details and the cost of curiosity; and they do so by way of an elegy for 'simple' pilgrim style. The force of this advice, and the shape of their loss, can be seen in the details of difference between Regnaut's 'Instructions' and the moral and narrative concerns of the *Guides*.

Balourdet urges the pilgrim to travel 'seulement avec intention de contempler, adorer et reverer avec grande effusion de larmes', and 'non point à intention de veoir du monde, ou du Pays, par ambition, ou exaltation de dire, J'ay esté en tel lieu, J'ay veu ceci ou cela, et plusieurs autres choses'. If pilgrims on their return do write, they

---

[10] Castela, *Guide*, fol. Aiiij[r].   [11] Ibid., fol. 20[r].   [12] Ibid., fols. 12[v]–13[r].

must not for example, compose a *Cosmographie* such as Thevet had done after his pilgrimage, still less a Mandevillian compendium of wonders of the kind exemplified most recently by Villamont in his (digressive and often reprinted) *Voyages*.[13] For those who do travel in such a way ('aucuns') do so fruitlessly: 'en ce cas, des maintenant ils ont receu leur loyer et salaire.'[14] These last words, a quotation from the gospels, are near-identical to the advice given by Regnaut; but the differences are telling. Regnaut also speaks of 'effusion de larmes' and of the 'exaltation de dire, j'ay esté voir, et ay veu le pays, pour estre estimé du monde'.[15] But in citing Christ's words against acting in this way, he also explains that this is what he is doing ('nostre Seigneur dit en L'Evangile') and leaves the text in Latin: '*Receperunt mercedem suam*'.[16] Balourdet does neither: in imitating Regnaut, he suppresses reference to scripture, and translates Christ's words as if they were simply (his own) vernacular advice. This is the new pilgrim economy of authorship in practice; for both the words of the earlier pilgrim and those of Christ echo in Balourdet's text, and he might have named both as part of his elegy to the lost style. But it seems he cannot afford to acknowledge his debt to either. Instead, and in order to fortify his own authority, he subsumes their voices to his own, even as he warns his reader against precisely that 'exaltation de dire je' which he perceives to be the primary threat to a pilgrim's integrity.

But as Chaucer's Pardoner had long made clear, even pilgrim priests are not altogether free from the sins against which they preach. And as Augustine before him had shown, knowledge of narrative desire within ourselves both renders us sensitive to its force, and entangles us further in its web. In the event, neither Castela nor Balourdet fully heed their own advice when composing the narratives of their journeys. Balourdet, for instance, despite rarely acknowledging his debt to previous pilgrims does (as shown above), amply demonstrate both his classical learning and his powers of versification; the Egyptians, Cicero, and the Greeks all figure as often as do Saints, and his account includes several of his own poems, which form part of a long digression on the dangers of travel by sea. Castela too displays his erudition from the opening page with that Homeric simile expanding on the Herculean labour which the writing of a

---

[13] Villamont's *Voyages* were originally published in Lyons in 1595; they went through twenty-five re-editions before 1620. For more on his career and 'phenomenal popularity' see Rouillard (p. 230), and Bernard (p. 45).

[14] Balourdet, fols. eii^{r–v}.   [15] Regnaut, p. 1.   [16] Ibid.

pilgrimage account represents. Not for nothing does he, in the quotation cited earlier, attribute the survival of the traces of Christ's presence to 'l'Antiquité'—rather than, for instance, God.

It is clear none the less that both priests write within an economy of exegetical recuperation, which allows such digressions to lead back to meditation on the divine ordering implicit in even the most material aspects of the journey. Clear also is the fact that they argue the continuing relevance of such a mode of writing with some passion. For they are working hard to figure the pilgrim as a certain, special kind of traveller, and one who speaks and writes in a correspondingly particular way. For them, the institution of pilgrimage provides not so much a spiritually sanctioned opportunity for leaving home in search of adventure, nor even the material to tell a powerful tale; rather it is the means to form a character to rival the author, a character whom Castela names 'la personne Chrestienne'.

The *Guide* writers find themselves adopting the role of polemists in response to Castela's 'Géants', and to Balourdet's 'jargonneurs'. The latter are Reformers, and participate in a debate concerning the worth of pilgrimage which centres on editions and translations of Gregory of Nyssa's Letter on pilgrimage. It is this debate, and the terms of those who attack the institution directly, to which we turn in the next chapter. But Castela's professional Giants of the discursive arena present less direct, albeit no less destructive, attacks on pilgrimage; they do so by developing alternative theoretical frameworks for travellers' self-understanding, and these will be our focus here. In particular, we need to look carefully at the theoretical work done by Northern Protestant Humanists who, in the last quarter of the sixteenth century, wrote their own guidebooks, and set about forming their own *method*. For the greatest threat to Castela's 'personne Chrestienne' lay in these writers' construction of a travelling subject dependent on the redeployment of the terms of Christian pilgrimage, but studied in his disregard of its relevence to his cause.

Jerome Turler, with his *De peregrinatione*, was the first and most influential of these new theorists of the road. His guide was translated into English within a year, and provided a model for the Humanist traveller networking his way around northern Europe—or wishing he could do so.[17] Turler's claim is explicitly to correct the

[17] J. Turler, *De peregrinatione, et agro neapolitano, Libri II* (1574). It was translated as *The Traueiler of Jerome Turler* (1575). For the copy given by Spenser to Gabriel Harvey see Baughan's edition. This is the edition to which I refer.

dispersal of advice about how to travel which is 'found here and there in sundrie Bookes and not in any one certeine place'.[18] This phrase, 'one certeine place', is worth pausing to consider. It is used in pilgrimage writing to mean 'a holy place', and specifically to refer to any place marked by the presence of Christ's passage on earth. Dublioul, as we saw, castigates detractors of pilgrimage for 'jargonnans que Dieu est par tout, comme si c'estoit superstition de le vouloir adorer et honorer *en certain lieu*'.[19] But Turler has here made the terms of pilgrimage into the 'jargon' of Humanist learning, and through his translator, he explains what 'one certeine place' now means: 'matter in a readinesse [for 'argument'] in one Booke according to the definitive Methode, as they speak in the schooles.'[20]

The 'Northern Protestant Humanists' whom Turler is here taken to exemplify were not, in fact, a unified movement. The label, much used in recent discussion of these guides, covers a multitude of positions, each arguing a different understanding of how the principles of Aristotelian logic were best applied to the needs of the modern traveller.[21] But certain points do unify them in their relation to the *Guides* which are our focus: not one was translated into French, and none refer—for all their talk of *peregrinatio*—to religious pilgrimage. Nor yet does the one Humanist guide written at this time which does eventually find French translation: Lipsius' *De ratione cum fructu peregrinandi*. Lipsius' guide is written in 1578, as a letter addressed to Philippe de Lannoy in preparation for his Italian journey, but is not published in French until it is translated by Anthoine Brun in 1619. All the travellers imagined by these guides have their sights set on Italy, not Jerusalem, and the tutors are less concerned to cultivate what Augustine termed the fields of the heart, than the flowers of political rhetoric. Lipsius' letter is given the vernacular title: 'Il

---

[18] Turler, fol. Aiiij[v].   [19] Balourdet, pp. 6–7 (emphasis mine).

[20] Turler, fol. Aiiij[v].

[21] T. Zwinger's *Methodus apodemika* (1577), for instance, is opposed, vehemently to H. Pyrckmair's *Commentariolus de arte apodemica* of the same year. For more on these Humanist guides and the development of the form, see J. Stagl, 'Apodemika', *Quellen und Abhandlungen*, 2 (1983); F. D. Liechtenhan, 'Theodor Zwinger, théoricien du voyage', *Littérales*, 7 (1990), pp. 151–64; J. P. Rubiés, 'Instructions for Travellers: Teaching the Eye to See', *History and Anthropology*, 9: 2–3 (1996), pp. 139–90; and (one of the few to relate them to pilgrimage) S. Christensen, 'The Image of Europe in Anglo-German Travel Literature,' in *Voyager à la Renaissance*, pp. 257–80. For an earlier account, see M. T. Hogden, *Early Anthropology in the Sixteenth and Seventeenth Century* (1964), pp. 185–8.

enseigne que l'on doit voyager pour trois sujets.' None of these is pilgrimage.[22]

These guides are of interest here precisely insofar as they establish the extent to which a discourse of travel is emerging which appears to take no account of the pilgrim. The Humanist traveller reformulates the terms of pilgrimage to his own, new ends. When Turler, in his opening chapter to *The Traueiler*, surveys the meanings of the terms *peregrinus* and *peregrinatio* and calls a number of authorities to mind, they are all classical, or legal, or both. Not once does he acknowledge the Biblical and Patristic usage of the terms, nor, when he asks himself '*whether traueyling do a man more good or harme?*'[23] does he refer to the arguments pursued in pilgrim texts, either about the worth of this over that place, or the dangers to the soul of spiritual contagion abroad.

For the thrust of Humanist method was to encourage the traveller in the belief that: '*Many Cuntries tis good to see,* | *Preseruing still our honestie.*'[24] Unlike Castela or Balourdet, Turler is not unduly concerned about either the spiritual or the physical effort involved in preserving honesty. His text does occasionally signal danger in the margin: 'Beware corruption' is the gloss on the couplet quoted above. But he does not directly name the danger, preferring rather to speak of Scylla and Charybdis, and of the 'Syrenes Songes' which the traveller, 'lyke a most expert Pilot', would do well to not to hear.[25] Rather than dwell on the nature of these Siren songs, Turler seeks to train the traveller in the use of his own voice. In this he is like the pilgrim guides, but far less anxious than either about competition from others (Castela), or the pilgrim's own perdition (Balourdet). Rather than counselling silence, he teaches travellers how to produce their own narratives. Ordered perception, he trusts, will lead to a reasoned account, and free from the anxiety about narrative lust or the sin of self-expression, he is able to redefine the nature of the 'fruit' and 'profit' which derive from travel. Independent of sacred rhetoric and dissociated from an exclusively sacred sense of use or pleasure, a new kind of *peregrinatio* gains ground.

This does not mean banishing God from the story of travel, nor

---

[22] A. Brun, *Le choix des Epistres de Lipse traduites de Latin au François*, pp. 17–33. For more on Lipsius in his neo-stoic context and on later travel guides in French, see N. Doiron, *L'Art de voyager* (1995). He reproduces both the Latin and the French text of Lipsius' Letter in appendices.

[23] Turler, pp. 1–6.   [24] Ibid., p. 22.   [25] Ibid., p. 23.

does it mean establishing a purely secular travelling rhetoric, as one of the French writers who travelled according to Turler's method makes clear. Nicolas de Nicolay, writing in 1576, supports his 'louange des pérégrinations' with the argument that God has so ordered the world that every place has its worth, and that the traveller should consequently move everywhere and anywhere:

Par telles pérégrinations et communications, toutes les nations diverses du monde s'apprivoisent et familiarisent les unes aux autres, s'émendent mutuellement les vices barbares, s'enseignent pareillement la vraie religion, les vertus et honnêtetés morales.[26]

This is a powerful claim and did not, for Nicolay, simply mean that the West should be policemen and preachers to the Rest: 'la vraie religion' is not, in his text, that which he has inherited, but something which he discovers by a process of comparative 'communication' with others. The point is stressed by his imitation of the 'vieillard Terentien, qui dit ainsi: "Comme je soie homme, je n'estime rien humain estre de moi étrange".'[27] This amounts to a plea for an understanding of travel as willed hybridity. It is a redefinition of *peregrinatio* as an exercise in secular imitation not of Christ, but of others met in books and on the road. It is travel in the form perhaps most assiduously practised and theorized by that other 'vieillard Terentian': Montaigne.

Proposing himself as a kind of exemplary traveller in the essay 'de la Vanité', Montaigne notes: 'Je peregrine très saoul de nos façons, non pour cercher des Gascons en Sicile (j'en ay assez laissé au logis); je cerche des Grecs, plustost, et des Persans; j'acointe ceux-là, je les considere; c'est là où je me preste et où je m'employe.'[28] The *Journal de Voyage* records the degree to which this process of lending himself to others is, for Montaigne, both dialogic and physical; he talks to local people, of all classes and beliefs, and insists on being served local food. It also stresses the degree to which there should be more gained from travel than a number of gentlemanly skills which can then be rehearsed and repeated at home. Indeed the riding, fencing, and dancing schools at Padua (to which many, many French young men travelled, including a number of pilgrims on their way to the

---

[26] Nicolay, *Dans Empire de Soliman le Magnifique* (1989), p. 46.

[27] Ibid. The quotation is from Terence, *Heautontimoroumenos*, I, I, 25.

[28] Montaigne, *Oeuvres*, III, ix, p. 964; he quotes Terence both on his study walls and in the *Essais*, II, ii, p. 328.

Holy Land), are, Montaigne argues, the worst possible places for the 'jeunes hommes de nostre pays' to learn the estranging essence of travel: 'd'autant que cette société les accoustume aux moeurs et langage de leur nation, et leur oste le moyen d'acquerir des cognoissances estrangieres.'[29]

In their different ways, Turler, Zwinger, and Nicolay are all arguing for what the pilgrim economy fears most, and what Montaigne most desires: 'le commerce des hommes'. The place visited is, in a strict sense, immaterial, for it is the procedure of comparison with home, preparation before leaving, and the construction of the travelling person on the journey, that matters. All these are pilgrim procedures, pilgrim methods. What makes them new are their applicability to any place on earth. Thus Lipsius, for instance, stresses that in order to 'vrayement voyager [id est vere peregrinari]' the young gentleman traveller must, 'avant toute chose propose moi la fin et le fruict que tu vas rechercher'.[30] The tutor then asks: 'quelle est cette région, tant soit-elle heureuse qui reserre tous les plus beaux esprits?' The question is rhetorical, as it would be in a pilgrim context, where its object would not be 'esprit' but 'lieux' and its answer would already be known: 'la Terre Saincte'. Here too the answer is known: 'nowhere', because 'chasque terre a sa petite perle qui l'embellit'.[31]

That these pearls are those of wisdom, sacralized by association with the biblical pearl of great price, and by wider association with the terms of pilgrimage, becomes clear in what follows: 'tend à ceste-là, et entend ceste-là [Hanc adi, hanc audi], et tire de ces poictrines sacrées les fontaines d'une science cachée.'[32] This is Humanism as religion; it also has its sites of pilgrimage, which the traveller must visit in the proper way:

Tu n'y arresteras jamais le pied, tu n'y tourneras pas l'oeil, que tu ne rencontre[s] quelque vestige . . . de l'histoire ancienne . . . l'on te monstrera la demeure [mansio] de Pline, ou celle de Virgile et de Properse, ailleurs les restes de la metairie ou de Varron ou de Ciceron: de combien de joye

---

[29] Montaigne, *Journal de Voyage*, p. 67; see also E. Balmas, *Montaigne e l'Italia* (1994), pp. 3–24; and for his meeting with Zwinger and the similarities of their understanding of the worth of travel, see F. Garavini, 'Montaigne rencontre Theodor Zwinger à Bâle', *Montaigne Studies*, v (1993), pp. 191–205.

[30] Doiron, p. 211. The French translation smooths out the rhythm of Lispius' Latin phrases, which are clearer still in their appropriation of the lexicon—and some of the habits—of the pilgrim; see Doiron, p. 206.

[31] Ibid., p. 213.   [32] Ibid.

interieure sera meslee ceste veuë lors que les ombres des ces grands personnages se representent non seulement à l'esprit, mais presque aux yeux, et
que nous touchons les lieux qu'ils ont tant de fois touchés.[33]

This is, as we shall see in more detail below, pure pilgrim-speak, reap-
plied to the saints of the new learning. Thus, even as the learned fashion themselves as different from those who exhibit 'popular piety',
they perform the ritual actions of pilgrims, and describe their actions
in pilgrims' terms.[34] So Turler, in answer to the question 'what is the
true sense of travel' concludes that travellers leave home:

*either to the ende that they may attayne to such artes and knowledge as they
are desirous to learne or exercise: or else to see, learne, and diligently to
marke suche things in strange Countries, as they shall have neede to use in
the common trade of lyfe, whereby they may profite themselves, their
friendes, and Countreye if neede require.* This definition who so marketh
well, hee shall easely make answere to the question erewhile propounded.[35]

This seems a long way from pilgrimage. And even if, on closer comparison with pilgrim guides, the distance is only illusory, it is none
the less a compelling illusion. One which promises much to the modern traveller in his efforts to picture himself as thoroughly novel, and
his 'carefully marked' accounts as of real contemporary value, unlike
those of the simple and old-fashioned pilgrims.

Though our pilgrim priests might well have known of these texts
(they are, as noted, the training manuals of Castela's Giants and
Balourdet's 'jargonneurs') the pilgrim *Guides* do not seem to be codified in direct competition to them. The priests demonize not the
Latin learned but those—such as Thevet, Villamont, and Belon—
who write in French about pilgrim territory. But there is, with hind-
sight, a certain pathos in their misprision of their enemy: Christian
writers prefer to joust with each other, rather than join forces in an
attempt to regain the ground which is being lost to the new army of
secular travellers. For the 'certain lieu' of pilgrimage was under
threat. Pilgrimage no longer had a hegemony on the definition of the

---

[33] Doiron, pp. 213–14.

[34] Some, even English Protestants such as Thomas Coryate, acknowledged an enduring
desire to combine new and old pilgrimages. See *Coryats Crudities* (1611), in which he
praises, for instance, the ruined houses of Virgil and Cicero alongside the tombs of Saints.

[35] The business of 'marking well' is important. It is, as Baughan points out, adapted
from Machiavelli's *Prince*, and Harvey approvingly 'marks' this definition in the margin
of his own copy, Turler, pp. vi, 5. Turler knew his Machiavelli, and had translated a number of his other writings.

terms of travel either as practice, or as metaphor. Indeed, even amongst those who travelled to the Holy Land, there seemed little consensus on what it meant to be a pilgrim, and to write one's narrative as that of a pilgrim, rather than of a merchant, a soldier, a gentleman traveller, in the retinue of an ambassador, a comosgrapher, a botanist . . .

It was in response to this crisis, at once institutional and rhetorical, at once within pilgrimage writing and beyond it, that priests developed the form of the *Guide*. Their challenge was to define a persuasive, exclusive, and specifically pilgrim subjectivity, and we do them a disservice by simply adding the *Guide* to the list of conduct books in the self-fashioning Renaissance gentleman's library, to be consulted as and when he might wish to play the role of pilgrim for a time. For the thrust of the argument of our *Guide* writers was that a pilgrim is essentially different from other travellers. It is a difference never more telling than when the pilgrim returns home, to narrate, or write, or keep silent, his own story.

The urgency of the logic of difference can be seen to have intensified over the course of the last quarter of the sixteenth century. As the argument raged on, so the number, and kinds of texts increased, for a time; and for a time the survival of the terms of pilgrimage depended on just this argument—as this chapter and the next will show. In order to explore and explain the nature of this polemic concerning pilgrim conduct we need to go in two quite different directions. The first is to detail the kind of information given to pilgrims in the *Guides* about the material costs and the dangers of the literal journey. The second is to explore a quite different kind of handbook, similarly developed for pilgrims in the course of the counter-Reformation: the devotional guide. These texts, exemplified here by the Luis de Granada's influential *Vray chemin et adresse pour acquerir et parvenir à la grace de Dieu*, style themselves as guide-books, but are written for travellers who never leave home, imagining rather their way to Jerusalem. The purpose of reading Granada in this context is to show how, within the devotional guide, even the most material details of trade, exploration, and the like can be moralised, and so made part of the figural pilgrimage. For it is in part thanks to such freeing of pilgrim terms from their literal context that first Turler, and then many others after him can write a treatise entitled *De peregrinatione* and yet be utterly, wilfully, unconcerned with literal pilgrimage. And it is in response to such as Turler that Castela will define the 'personne Chrestienne' as a peculiar kind of half-literal-half-figural pilgrim: walking to, and through Palestine, but as if still on one of Granada's meditative trajectories of reading.

Here too there is pathos. It is the pathos of the surrender by the pastors of the people to the priests of the new learning. For, as I will argue here, the absence of confessional consensus on the worth of pilgrimage leads to a restriction of the terms of legitimate travel, a silencing of many who may otherwise have told of their experience of the road (in relation to those who are known to have travelled, precious few narratives are printed). For polemic brings together those who argue its terms, and excludes those who are unable, or unwilling to do so. Thus, both Catholic and Protestant legislators, Humanists, and clerics find themselves in agreement that silence, or staying at home, is the best option for most pilgrims. Only the properly trained should take to the road, and only the rhetorically adept (preferably learned and priestly) author should presume to tell of his pilgrimage. Meanwhile the 'personne Chrestienne' on pilgrimage, although far from home, finds himself closed to the claims both of the world, and of the others he has travelled in order (not) to hear, talk to, or see.

The Material Details and the Cost of the Journey

> Qui a la garde de ma bourse en voyage, il l'a pure et sans contrerole ... J'oi plus volontiers dire, au bout de deux mois, que j'ai despandu quatre cens escus que d'avoir les oreilles battues tous les soirs de trois, cinq, sept ... O le vilein et sot estude d'estudier son argent, se plaire à le manier, poiser et reconter! C'est par là que l'avarice fait ses aproches.[36]

No *Guides* for pilgrims were published in French before those of Balourdet and Castela. But many pilgrims do offer practical advice in their accounts, either detailing things as they occur to them in the course of the journey, or systematically listing points by way of preface or conclusion. Most systematic of all and the model for those who followed is, as noted above, Anthoine Regnaut. He draws up, by way of introduction to his *Discours du voyage d'outre mer*, an eleven-point guide, which summarized, runs as follows:

---

[36] Montaigne, *Oeuvres*, III, ix, p. 930.

1. Ensure that your motivation is holy, not self-serving.

2. Order your affairs at home, and write your will, so that if God takes you on the journey, your inheritors will not have undue problems.

3. Take two purses: 'l'une sera pleine de vertu de patience, lautre ou il y ait deux cens ducatz d'or de Venise'. You will need one hundred and fifty for the journey and fifty for emergencies.

4. Make sure you are in Venice by the day of the 'Feste Dieu', and arrange to board the pilgrim galley: 'Et avant que s'embarquer en mer faut achepter ses necessitez, et pourvoyances qui s'ensuyvent: Assavoir, une robbe fourrée pour le retour, quant il fera froit. Item des chemises beaucoup pour eviter les poux, et autres immondices, qui croissent en la nave. Item des nappes, serviettes, oreilliers, linceux, une sclavine pour se couvrir, et pour dormir à l'air. Item un matelas en lieu d'un lict, un coffre long pour serrer ses besongnes, deux barilz, l'un pour mettre vin, l'autre eau, fromage lombart, sausisses, langues de beuf, et autres salures.' Once on board and underway, don't leave the boat 'pour chose du monde'.

5. Try to get a place to put your belongings 'au meilleu de la nave pres de l'entrée pour estre plus aëre', especially if you don't travel well. This is where you will sleep.

6. Negotiate the contract with the captain. Pay sixty ducats return for passage and board. If you don't go on the galley, but take a merchant ship, you should pay two ecus a month not including food; five ecus a month gets you a seat at the captain's table, for three you sit at the cook's table. Pay the extra if you possibly can.

7. Buy eggs, chicken, preserves and fruit each time you stop at port. You'll need the extra food for when captain and crew are too busy resisting storms to cook.

8. Dress poorly, so as to avoid having to pay endless tips.

9. Once in the Holy Land carry your bedding with you. Don't, ever, leave the caravan, and don't argue with the locals, 'car il y a grand danger'.

10. Your money should be gold, venetian sequins; for small change carry medins, monsenilz, and marcelz d'argent.

11. Take letters of permission to travel from your bishop, the 'saufconduit' from the king (copied in the text, p. 5); and before leaving Jerusalem, get a certificate from the Pope's commissary to say you have been (also copied).[37]

---

[37] Regnaut, pp. 1–5.

This 'Instruction' is followed by a log of stopping places and distances between Paris and Venice, and copies of the various documents Regnaut collected on his journey.

This, clearly, is a text designed to be used; and it was by many of
those who followed Regnaut on the journey and whose texts have survived. But none—before Castela and Balourdet—follow Regnaut's
systematic arrangement of his material. Most prefer simply to add
specific details to points summarised in the 'Instruction' or to note
changes in the situation since the 1540s when Regnaut travelled.

Carlier de Pinon, for instance, stresses that by 1579 even if you
stipulate in your contract that you will pay the extra to eat at the
captain's table—as Regnaut had suggested—you will need to make
'provision extraordinairement de vin, vinaigre, biscuit, jambons, et
salsizoni ou saulsisses'.[38] A good many shirts and sheets, a mattress,
a large wooden box which doubles as a bed, and a copy of Strabo's
Geographia are all essential for the outward journey; wait until you
get to Constantinople before buying the clothes for the remainder of
the voyage. If you plan to do the Sinai pilgrimage as well, Pinon
advises acquiring an arquebus and a scimitar. Letters of recommen-
dation from the French ambassador asserting your French nationality are ideal; failing that, pretend to be German or Venetian, for the
Turk is said to favour these nations.[39] All the cash you carry should be
sequins, or new Venetian ducats; don't forget to take 'lettres de
faveur': 'au cas que par fortune ou maladie' you fall 'en necessité
d'argent'.[40]

Zuallart, more detailed still, points out that by the time he travels,
late in the sixteenth century, the pilgrim galley no longer exists, but
there are now a number of different ways of getting to Palestine from
France. Boats from Marseilles, being lighter than the Venetian ones,
get you there just as quickly, and are cheaper, but you must cook for
yourself.[41] If you do leave from Venice, take the first boat available,
don't wait until Fête Dieu. Prices have changed, but, though the boat

---

[38] Carlier de Pinon, *Relation du voyage en Orient* (1920), pp. 31–2.

[39] Even those who were not French often obtained such letters; see e.g. the case of
Jacques de Valimbert travelling from Besançon (then an Imperial city) in 1584, Ch. 6,
below.

[40] Carlier de Pinon, p. 32. This account remained in manuscript until this century, and
the words of advice about nationality and money are added in the margin by way of an
afterthought; or perhaps in preparation for publication.

[41] Zuallart, I, p. 51 (all future references to Zuallart are to Book One, unless otherwise
indicated).

now only takes you as far as Cyprus or Tripoly, if you winter in Tripoly, you can, by trading, recoup costs, or even make a profit before taking the Mecca caravan down to Jerusalem in time for Easter weekend. You can go on to Egypt by rejoining the caravan from Jerusalem due south, or (if you don't want to cross the desert), by going to Jaffa and getting a boat to Damiette, and from there across land to Cairo and the pyramids.[42]

Zuallart is of particular interest in that he—like the *Guide* writers with whom he is a contemporary—offers advice not only on practical necessities, but also on issues of conduct. But his understanding of how to be a pilgrim is some way from that of the priestly *Guides*. He is, above all, a canny traveller, keen to adapt to the conditions of the journey, even if it means taking advantage of aspects of the local culture which other pilgrims run in fear of: trade and Islamic pilgrimage. His identity as a pilgrim does not seem dependent on maintaining his difference from others in absolute terms. Like Castela, he advises, for instance, against wearing green, but unlike the *Guide* writers he explains why, and—remarkably—urges pilgrims not to wear the tunic with the red crosses of Jerusalem on them either: such things are offensive to Islamic sensibilities.[43] He accompanies this practical, culturally sensitive advice with his version of who the pilgrim should be: more like Christ, rather than less like others. Is it not remarkable, he asks, 'un grand mystere occult et digne d'admiration', that just as Jesus was born in a stable, and wrapped in poor clothing, so too pilgrims who travel to places where he walked are now obliged to adopt poor clothing, whatever their station in normal life?

The 'bourgeois' gentlemen pilgrim is of course able to pay for extras, and Zuallart urges him to do so. It is, for instance, worth paying the extra six sequins a month to sit at the Captain's table, since the food is so much better than at the Purser's table, where you only pay four. You still need additional stocks as outlined by both Regnaut and Pinon. The biscuit should cost around half an ecu, the Venetian name for 'pain d'espice' is 'Botzelay', and Parmesan cheese is a must. Zuallart's reasons for these added extras—and for adding the foreign words for them in his text—are that you may feel hungry some mornings, you may not know how to explain what you need, you may not

---

[42] Ibid., p. 41. The first book concludes with an exhaustive list of how much each section of the journey cost him, and how much additional extras would cost. Zuallart also details the exchange rates in force at the time (pp. 80–4)

[43] Castela, *Guide*, fol. 52ᵛ; Zuallart, pp. 64–5.

always appreciate the way they prepare their meat, and you are bound to be subject to 'vomissemens ou autres accidens'.[44]

For the pilgrim who is unfortunate enough to be 'degousté ou indisposé' Zuallart has, once again, systematic advice: 'prenez un peu de gingembre, et noix de muscade, confites, de la canelle et cloux de girofle, deux ou trois onces.' There are unspoken social conventions in play here, involving both linguistic and physical decorum. Whereas Regnaut passes on the prescription of ship's captain against sea-sickness in the original (broken) Italian, Zuallart translates the advice into both French and the voice of personal experience:

mon advis est que lon doit se pourveoir de choses adonbees ou confites en vinaigres et qui sont refrigeratives, comme Oranges, Citrons, Limons, Grenades, Raisins de Corinthe, de Pruneaux, et gros raisins de Damas, qu'ils appellent Cibibes, Abricotz seichez qu'il faut mettre tremper en eaue.[45]

Zuallart urges pilgrims to use such curative fruits and medicinal prescriptions only in times of dire need: they should not become habitual, and stop you getting used to life, and food, on board. His aim seems to be to remind his readers—gently—that this journey is also a moral trajectory, that they should not make life too easy for themselves, nor ostentatiously differentiate themselves from their poorer fellow-pilgrims. Most people (by which he means, probably, Regnaut again) advise a 'bon barillet de vin' to console you, which you'll need to keep well hidden and locked away. But even this is not essential: 'bien est-il vray si vous vous contentez de celuy du patron, vous vous en pourrez bien passer.'[46]

It is this concern for practical considerations that leads both Regnaut and Zuallart to a sense that travel is a great leveller, making practical and cultural demands on the pilgrim on board ship as well as on land. Unlike the *Guide* writers neither of these lay pilgrims understand themselves, as pilgrims, to be in some sense essentially different from other travellers. True, Zuallart advises that sailors and the poorer passengers should be avoided as they are likely to pass on their fleas; but when he notes this advice, he is not concerned with

---

[44] Zuallart, p. 60.
[45] Ibid., p. 61. See also Regnaut, 'Recepte pour se gouverner sur mer' (p. 16). The difference between the lay and priestly pilgrims does not stop them copying from, adding to, and correcting the practical advice they offer. Castela copies Zuallart's prescription in turn, adding one of his own against constipation: 'un petit pain de sucre avec un fiolle de cyrop violet, prins avec de l'eau', Castela, *Guide*, fol. 44ʳ.
[46] Zuallart, p. 60.

their morals and makes no connection between dirt and sin. And indeed he suggests that even fleas can be avoided if the reader learns how to wash his clothes—and lose his shame—himself: 'il est bon aussi d'y apporter un peu de savon, et n'estre honteux d'apprendre à blanchir vostre linge.' Castela, when he mentions soap, does not use it to bring different orders of traveller together; and he does not suggest learning how to wash your own clothes.[47]

The primarily social, and socially integrative nature of the lay—as opposed to priestly—pilgrims' understanding of travel is evident throughout their 'Instructions'. It is most clear in moments of apparent similarity. So, like the *Guides*, Zuallart argues against the traveller's primary form of contact with others: trade. But he does so for quite other reasons than those concering the pollution of the pilgrim self. Do not, he urges, fall prey to the temptation of shopping, either for yourself or for your friends. This is not moral advice, it is practical: 'ce qu'aurez acheté, vous donnera de la fascherie et peine à rapporter.'[48]

Resistance to Method

This term—'rapporter'—is crucial. It is a term central to the discourse of Renaissance pilgrimage, as it extends to refer not only to material goods, but also to things of spiritual and experiential value. The question of value connects the pilgrim's 'rapport' of his journey with the 'rapport' between scriptural *topos* and actual place. As a verb, 'rapporter' covers the business of bringing things home, composing an account of one's journey, compiling and editing the texts of others, and drawing out the deeper implications of pilgrim experience.[49] Zuallart's text is striking not least because most of his advice is about the experience of the journey *at the time*. 'Rapporter', in either a retrospective or a prospective sense, causes him only 'fascherie' and 'peine'. For him, pilgrimage is an exercise in improvisation, tied to the present tense, and to movement. Unlike many other pilgrims, who tick off the holy sites and tot up indulgences, and unlike the Humanist travellers obsessed with the 'profit' of travel and the amassing of 'curiositez', he has little time for collecting either

---

[47] Ibid., p. 60. Castela, *Guide*, fol. 41ʳ.   [48] Zuallart, p. 63.
[49] These senses of the term are explored in Ch. 4, below.

material or spiritual goods. The travelling character he creates for himself is a man excited by the practical improvisation of social identity, and by the perpetual circulation both of material goods and of the profits of experience:

J'advertis encore le voyager, qu'il ne doit estre en soing de quelles formes d'oraisons il peut lors user, parce que les esclairs, et tonneres espouventables, les ondes furieuses, assaillantes la nave de toutes parts, quelquefois le recontre et regard hideux des Barbares, luy enseigneront bien la methode, mesme d'estre devot.[50]

Zuallart's main lesson—his reading of experience—is that conditions are subject to change. There can be no traveller's doctrine, no hard and fast rules. For the improvisational pilgrim whose travels his text records is, above all, resistant to method:

Et vous gouvernant . . . en partie selon le temps et les occurrences qui se presenteront, vous vous en trouverez fort bien: car autrement on n'y sçauroit donner aucun conseil absolut à raison que dan [sic] un jour à autre, il y à des evenemens divers, et du changement, comme en toute chose humaine et mondaine il y en a, et plutost en mal qu'autrement.[51]

This is a faith in experience, regulated by the rhetoric of decorum—'the capacity of invention and judgement to order speech and action to meet the demands of the occasion'—rather than by a generally applicable method.[52] Zuallart has Montaigne's understanding of the 'bransloire perenne' of the world, and a concomitant sense of the necessary fluidity of identity.[53] Like Montaigne, he deploys a rhetoric of inadequacy to the task of representing such a changeable world, the better to give voice and body to his experience of travel. As his title suggests and the body of his narrative confirms, even the most cynical pilgrim will be taught practical devotion on the road and at sea.

This is not to say that Zuallart is unaware of the spiritual dangers of pilgrimage, or that he has no sense of the difficulties of maintaining the points of spiritual experience *in situ*. Indeed, like Fabri, he knows that simply being in this place is far from simple:

le diable . . . par ses astuces . . . [fait] sembler que tout ce qu'on veoid n'est rien; mesmes estant aux lieux principaux, comme au mont de Calvaire, au

---

[50] Zuallart, p. 60.   [51] Ibid., p. 80.

[52] This definition of decorum is taken from L. Hutson, *The Usurer's Daughter* (1994), p. 40. See also V. Kahn, *Rhetoric, Prudence, and Scepticism in the Renaissance* (1985), pp. 35, 85; and T. Hampton, *Writing from History* (1990), pp. 134–97.

[53] Montaigne, *Oeuvres*, III, ii, p. 782.

S. Sepulchre et allieurs, ou il nous met tant de difficultez et fantaisies en teste, et par ce moyen rend noz pensees tant egarees, distraictes, et diverties de la vraye devotion que . . . nous n'y sçaurions dire une seule oraison valliable.[54]

Once again, the pilgrim here defines the problem in terms of intention: the mind is hard to control, and can wander and create fictions even when one stands at the 'lieux principaux' of devotion. But, Zuallart insists, this does not mean pilgrimage is a waste of time. The pilgrim should use the real difficulties of the road and the wanderings of the mind to straighten his faith. It is the unexpected details of experience which form a character, and the honest pilgrim can learn more from mistakes than from a method; the journey itself is still the best teacher.

Not everyone agrees: Castela and Balourdet insist in their *Guides*, like Turler and Lipsius in theirs, that travellers must be thoroughly prepared *before* they leave. The priests want their readers to be confirmed pilgrims before the experience of pilgrimage itself begins. They must in effect be vaccinated against the diseases of the soul which infect the very air abroad—or be urged not to leave. It is on the issue of preparation for travel that the competing polemists are most alike; and on this issue that they differ most sharply from Zuallart and his kind. Zuallart has, for instance, much to say about a treacherous interpreter hired in Cyprus, a Greek rogue who led the pilgrims a merry dance which takes a full six pages to narrate. This narrated experience is followed by a terse chapter on how to hire a translator once in the Holy Land: they should cost between seven and twelve ducats for the whole time you need them, and will expect ten maidans a day for food in addition. There are about fifty maidans to a ducat, he adds, by way of financial translation himself.[55] This is precisely the kind of detailed practical advice which is nowhere to be found in *Guides*, be they those of Northern Protestant Humanists, or those of French, Spanish, or Italian counter-Reformers.

What initially appears to be a simple difference in practical emphasis—the priests and tutors expect pilgrims to be escorted everywhere, and therefore in no need of such information—reveals itself to be a question of ideology, bearing on the subjectivity of the traveller, particularly in his relations with others. When Castela addresses the business of coming into contact with the locals, his advice is proscription: don't talk to them; don't listen to what they

---

[54] Zuallart, p. 11.   [55] Ibid., pp. 52–8, 70–1.

are saying, or look at things too closely, neither fortresses, nor things in the bazaar, nor women; don't be seen writing or drawing, or painting pictures either, for if you do, you will be taken for a spy, a 'curieux'. Here the priests and tutors part company; for 'marking well' is essential to Humanist travel, and curiosity can be turned to good account. For Castela, however, curiosity, bound up with narrative desire, is a threat to the pilgrim's identity. It soon finds explicit expression as a problem of male sexual identity in the *Guide*: don't be 'curieux d'aller voir les insolences qu'ils pratiquent la nuit aux bals', or you will be 'induit ou contraint de succumber à la sodomie'. The only sure way to avoid such pollution, he continues, is to maintain absolute difference, achieved through indifference to your surroundings. Thus Castela avoids giving details on how to hire translators, offering advice on how to use decorum to cultivate an adaptable self in the face of the Other, or suggesting how best to order and mark your perception of difference. Instead, he urges preserving what identity one has; and to do so the pilgrim must feign the identity of another. To remain yourself you must pretend to be someone you are not, someone who is radically unable to communicate with others, for communication is pollution. It is a strategy as blunt as it is brutal: 'Parquoy le meilleur luy sera de contrefaire avec eux l'homme aveugle, sourd et muet.'[56]

This is a long way from the 'Instructions' of Regnaut and Zuallart; and it differentiates itself carefully from the Humanist guides' arguments in favour of 'communication' and 'commerce' with Others of all kinds. Where Castela's method is to proscribe all contact, Zuallart's is to narrate encounters gone wrong; where Castela prescribes correct action, Zuallart details the mistakes made by himself, and others he has heard tell of in his travels. Thus precepts are set against exemplary tales as modes of advice. As Montaigne sets 'estude' against 'doctrine' in the construction of his character and that of his text, so too different authors within the field of pilgrimage work out their differing relations to exemplarity, narrative structure, and the construction or preservation of the pilgrim's identity.[57] The central problem is that of the traveller's curiosity, but these differences in their formal approach—precept as against exemplary narrative— point to an important difference in where curiosity is said to reside.

---

[56] Castela, *Guide*, fol. 60ʳ.   [57] Montaigne, *Oeuvres*, II, vi, p. 357.

For Zuallart, curiosity more often than not occurs as a plural noun, and the danger it gives rise to comes from other people. Others are hiding everywhere and the pilgrim should be 'temeraire en ses curiositez'; he should take care not to 's'ecarte[r] indiscretement hors de la compagnie des autres Pelerins ou voyagers, craignant que l'ennemy aux escoutes, ne le surprenne et ensequestre du tout'.[58] But the Other is not hiding within me, nor yet within language itself; the problem here is not that of curiosity polluting the will and threatening identity (as it is in Augustine and his late Renaissance followers, Castela and Granada), so much as being caught out by those who wish to trap you. The pilgrim risks being betrayed by fellow travellers who 'se rendent Turcs et accusent les personnes', but Zuallart does not see silence and self-isolation as an appropriate strategy for avoiding this risk. Rather than counselling counterfeit incomprehension and silence as does Castela, he suggests that 'le meilleur est que le voyager se souvienne de ce que est dit en l'Ecclesiatique *Que la douce parole multiplie les amis et apaise les ennemis, que la langue gracieuse abonde en l'homme de bien*'.[59]

Within this economy of sweet speech, linguistic counterfeiters are Zuallart's greatest enemies.[60] He travels, and above all speaks, not in fear of his own illicit desires, but of being falsely accused by those who distort the conventions of gentle speech, and accuse the pilgrim of being a spy:

encores quilz sceussent fort bien l'intention de l'accusé [himself], de n'estre telle. Ce que j'ay cogneu par experience, tant en Jerusalem, Tripoli, Cipre, que alieurs: car sans y penser (comme je parlois Aleman avec un gentilhomme Tirolois, et une autrefois Espaignol si peu que j'en scavois, avec un prestre Irlandois) j'en trouvay aucuns qui m'arresterent en devise et avec les mesmes langues, me demandans de quel quartier j'estois.[61]

The key term here is 'intention'. Balourdet, Castela, and Granada sense that their own readers may be 'induits ou contraints' into error, which is to say that their curiosity may lead them to experiment with new forms of identity. They may, like the man in Zuallart's story, turn Turk. Zuallart, by contrast, has no such anxiety about his readers. He never considers that they might themselves become spiritual

---

[58] Zuallart, pp. 2–3.   [59] Ibid., p. 3. The margin reads, 'Eccle 6.'
[60] Here again he is kin to Montaigne; see *Oeuvres*, II, v. pp. 346–7, where he writes of his anxiety about counterfeit speech while travelling away from home during the Civil Wars.
[61] Zuallart, p. 3.

casualties of pilgrimage, for he never suspects their intentions. He tells the story of how he himself was tricked, but it is not a story about his own trickery. The function of the tale is not exemplary—'be like me'—except insofar as it imputes similarly pure intentions to the reader in any such encounters they may one day have. Zuallart never suspects himself, and so never imagines that his readers might play the role of the trickster in the story.[62] Never culpabilising his own desire to tell of his experience, he never seeks to block the reader's desire for anecdotal knowing.

Zuallart is no priest, and writes no *Guide*. Rather than staying at home, or urging silence and inattention to others while abroad, his voluminous account advises the pilgrim to master the arts of sweet words and gracious language. Nor, for all its domestication into French of the rhetoric of decorum, is his narration part of the family of the Northern Humanists' *Apodemika*. It is too adamantly an account of lived, recorded experience, gained in time with the rhythms of the road, to be read as a universally applicable model. With its integration of practical advice, scriptural injunction, and narrative luxuriance, Zuallart's *Voyage* brings together the differing forms of travel guide by telling the story of the pilgrim who makes mistakes and learns by experience. And from this experience he crafts an exemplary pilgrim character who will have a long life in later Protestant contexts.[63]

What keeps Zuallart within the Catholic pilgrim fold (and marks him as different from, for instance, either Montaigne or Thevet) is his adherence to scriptural similitude as a means of redeeming curiosity. Thus, even when, in the instance last quoted, he tells how his skill at imitating foreign languages led to his being caught out by more skilful counterfeiters than he, Zuallart provides a scriptural gloss: 'mais craignant que ma parole m'eust manifestee (comme fit celle de S. Pierre qui le fit recognoistre Galileen) je me retiray de leur compagnie au plustost qu'il me fut possible.'[64] The story initially seems to suggest that, like Peter, Zuallart was afraid to be shown up as one of the followers of Jesus. But the parenthetical scriptural gloss also ensures that we recognise the narrator to be, like Peter, a certain kind of

---

[62] Unlike Thevet, whose anxious relation to renegades we return to, in Ch. 7, below.

[63] I am thinking in part of Bunyan's *Pilgrim's Progress*, but more substantially of the narrative form which Northern Protestantism will take some time yet to develop: the *Bildungsroman*.

[64] Zuallart, p. 3.

pilgrim: bluff, subject to making mistakes, an enemy of the rule book, but a true and devout disciple at heart.

The Spiritual Details and the Cost of Curiosity

For Castela and his kind, this vision of Peter as the exemplary pilgrim will not do; nor will the rhetoric of experience suffice as defence against the curse of curiosity. Whilst conceding, somewhat reluctantly, that 'l'experience (comme l'on dict) m'en peut avoir rendu sage', Castela stresses that what it teaches is that most pilgrims will fall fatally prey to curiosity, the lure of strange customs, and strange languages. They will in the process, lose their pilgrim identity.[65] This anxiety about curiosity, like his insistence that good intentions are not enough, derives in part from precisely those narratives of experience that Zuallart and others tell. It also derives from more strictly devotional writers working within the discourse of pilgrimage in the late Renaissance, whose focus is on the pilgrim's legitimate intentions, rather than his improvisational skill on the road. Foremost among these is Luis de Granada, whose name heads a brief pilgrim's guide published in Italian in 1575: the *Istruttione de' Peregrino che vanno alla Madonna di Loreto, et ad altri luoghi Santi*. Granada speaks 'del frutto che si cava dalla Peregrinatione', but stresses that the journey is fruitful only if the heart is well tended. Confession and communion are crucial preparations, and 'la purità dell'intentione con la quale la buona opera si fa' is what determines the degree of its 'utilità'.[66]

Purity, for Granada, is not a natural product of the will; it is cultivated, and must be sustained in its growth by devotional exercise. He affirms that pilgrimage was instituted for those whose minds, like Zuallart's, wander when at prayer: 'quei, che non possono stare per lungo spatio di tempo quieti nell'esercito dell'oratione'.[67] Like Zuallart, Granada stresses that the pilgrim must always be wary of fellow-travellers, for these days 'i lupi si vestono de la pelle di pecorella'.[68] But the pilgrim narrating his experience and the guide writer part

---

[65] Castela, *Guide*, fol. 18ᵛ.

[66] Granada, *Istruttione*, p. 11. As if to stress their interdependence, the guide is published together with a discourse on confession, and another on communion. Both discourses are translated into French, in the 1580s by Jean Chabanet, but the link with pilgrimage is severed, as the guide remains untranslated.

[67] Ibid., p. 10.   [68] Ibid., p. 14.

company on the relation of narration to experience, and on the question of intention. Anticipating Castela and Balourdet, Granada conflates curiosity and the desire to tell one's story. The experience of the journey should be denied to those:

> che si muovono questo peregrinaggio per sola curiosità, cioè per vedere gente nuova, et paesi nuovi, et pascer gli'occhi con la varietà delle cose, che vedono in diverse bande, et per haver molte cose da contar da poi ne' lor paesi.[69]

For the primary temptation of pilgrimage is that of narrative desire, and the real risk of the literal journey is that of doubtful return. It is a problem best understood in terms of the reversal of good intentions into bad effects: 'imperoche è intravenuto à qualche d'uno andar in peregrinaggio per purgare i peccati vecchi et sono tornato à loro paesi carichi d'altri novi.'[70]

There is a curious amount of linguistic play in the serious advice offered here by Granada. Even when prescribing pure speech and plain language, he cannot resist punning to make his point: the 'rich returns' brought home from pilgrimage may be the reverse of what one would expect. The point is doubtless unambiguous, but the fact that it is conveyed by means of a pun is indicative of the shifting, unstable terms in which such advice is dispensed in counter-Reformation devotional writing. Certainly Granada's concentration on the dangers besetting the pilgrim, and the need for rigorous preparatory exercises provide little in the way of publicity for literal pilgrimage. If he was doubtful of the 'profits' to be had from the literal journey, however, he had no doubts about the value, use, and enjoyment of pilgrimage understood as the metaphorical progress of a soul towards God.

The insistence that literal pilgrims should look less to their luggage than to their language serves to publicize other forms of pilgrimage, which Granada develops elsewhere. He marshalls his considerable rhetorical skills to detail the dangers of the literal journey in order to argue the benefits of an alternative, exclusively metaphorical, mode of pilgrimage. This is elaborated in his two influential *Guides*, which both draw on and underline their differences from the practical 'instructions' we have discussed so far: *La Guià dei Peccadores* and the *Le Vray chemin et adresse pour acquerir*

---

[69] Granada, *Istruttione*, p. 13.   [70] Ibid.

et parvenir à la grace de Dieu, et se maintenir en icelle, par le moyen et compagnie de l'Oraison et Contemplation en la Loy et amour de Dieu.[71] In both these texts, as in his guide for Loreto pilgrims, Granada is more fearful even than Castela about the journey itself. He considers purity of intention virtually impossible to maintain on the literal pilgrimage, and consequently proposes the metaphorical journey as the *true* pilgrimage: hence the *Vray* in his title. The daily journey is refigured as one of daily devotion, and the details of movement are moralized throughout.

The commonplace metaphor of the journey and the metaphorical clusters which attach themselves to travel provide the structure for Granada's meditations: time and again we read of the 'voyes au ciel', of how the penitent 's'achemine' towards heaven. The imperatives and collective verbs of motion which structure accounts of the literal journey are redeployed to urge penitents to stay in their rooms, and to follow the author day by day on a journey of reading. Overcoming curiosity and avoiding its entanglement with the self are the aims towards which this journey is directed; reading may be cultivated as pleasurable, but only insofar as it leads to this point. For if it becomes a pleasure in itself, then it is proof of curiosity, and the reading journey will lead not to heaven, but, as surely as any literal journey to 'sites of contagion', directly to the loss of self and sanity figured by hell. The argument here is Granada's; it is also, as we saw above, Augustine's, particularly in its opposition of 'useful' and 'pleasurable' reading.[72] What is a passing metaphor in Augustine—that of readers as 'peregrin'—is for Granada an organizing structure. The intervening invention and elaboration of the institution of Christian pilgrimage makes specific and special sense of Augustine's terms and metaphors.

In the opening *Exhortation* to the *Vray chemin*, the question of style, its enjoyment, and its use, is addressed directly. The 'degoust' of the men of this century, 'plus affectionnez aux viandes d'Egypte, qu'au pain des Anges' is recognised as a serious problem. To counter the 'livres mondains et prophanes' the author has 'deguisé si gentiment cette viande, qu'escrivant avec un doux et plausible stile, il remet en goust les plus desappetissez, et leur donne appetit de taster

---

[71] The *Guià* was not translated into French until after the time of our study; *Le Vray chemin* was translated by Belleforest. I refer to the 1579 edition.

[72] See above, Ch. 1.

de ces choses'.[73] We are some way here from Zuallart's ill-prepared meat on board ship. Taste is a matter of literary style, and meat is metaphor. But this is every bit as much a guide to the devotional pilgrimage as the 'Instruction' is to its literal equivalent; the spicy language is consequently explained—rather than simply spoonfed—to the reader:

Metaphore nous declare l'exercice continuel, et celle perseverance en la contemplation avec laquelle le juste va tousjours espluchant et de tout son coeur espluchant les œuvres merveilleuses de son Dieu.[74]

The terms are perhaps commonplace enough, and they betray the devotional handbook's literary pretensions.[75] But they also lead us to understand what the text expects of its readers, as do Belleforest's own prefatory notes to his translation of Granada's work. Here he explores the uses of a metaphor which we have seen to be central to pilgrimage in a number of ways, that of writing as 'pharmakon'. Those in need of cure, he argues, judge a remedy in terms of its effectiveness: those who know the 'transport d'esprit' which comes of devotional reading 'de toute leur affection', will also know that the repetitive and elaborate strain of 'ceste maniere de stile' produces effects, if it is followed through to the end. This is why he has translated the text in what may appear to be its excessive entirety. Some people, he continues, shifting back to culinary metaphors as he does so, will not be able to stomach such rich writing:

S'il y en a si desgoustez, qui ne puissent demourer si longuement à table, pour la seconde édition nous tascherons à contenter leur appetit, et leur abreger le service.[76]

We are once again some way from the advice given in the travellers' 'instructions' as to what pilgrims should do if they find themselves 'desgoustez ou incommodez'. But we are on the same metaphorical journey; the central difference is in the kind of community of pilgrims the texts imagine. Baroque, self-involved, convoluted: Belleforest's preface to the *Vray chemin* is all of these things. It is also

---

[73] Granada, *Le Vray chemin*, 'Exhortation' (by the Bishop of Cuenca), *non. pag.*
[74] Ibid.
[75] T. C. Cave glosses this passage as owing much to the Horation *utile dulci* topos in his immensely useful discussion of 'The Devotional Treatise as Literature', *Devotional Poetry in France c.1570–1613* (1969), pp. 59–60.
[76] Granada, *Le Vray chemin*, 'Advertissement', *non. pag.*

performative, using the preparation of meat, bread, and the peeling and ingesting of fruit as metaphors for devotional reading in the hope of whetting the reader's appetite for just such reading.[77] By writing in this way, Belleforest, following Granada, implicates his pilgrim readers in the text's own rhetorical self-consciousness, encouraging them to assent to the reinscription of practical information from other territories of guide writing—handbooks to secular poetics and to literal pilgrimage—within the rhetoric of the metaphorical guide. The metaphors can then 'return home' as metaphors for spiritual reading; and the pilgrims themselves need never literally travel.

The physicality of the experience of reading imagined by the *Vray chemin* contrasts sharply with the denial of physical pleasure demanded of the literal pilgrim in the *Guides*. Rather than exposing your body to the dangers of the road, stay at home and enjoy the real pleasures of the text, is Granada's seductively repetitious song. This spiritual siren, luring potential travellers off the pilgrim road, seems to have been heard in France, where the *Vray chemin* grew to be 'one of the most popular devotional handbooks of the later sixteenth century'.[78] It is, however, no uncomplicated celebration of the pleasures of reading. Granada knows that desire is intensified by deferral, and his exercises are more intent on teaching denial than they are on facilitating easy pleasure.

The text is structured as a journey towards Jerusalem, but the devotional pilgrim learns not by progressing merrily along the road, so much as by encountering, and overcoming, obstacles to forward movement. Each of its sections is consequently framed as an 'empeschement à la devotion', and further sub-sub-divisions detail these obstacles as they arise in the course of the journey. As with the *Guides* to literal pilgrimage and to the Humanists' journeys, so here preparation is crucial. The pilgrim's 'intentions' are the focus of the priest's concern, and his heart must be:

---

[77] So, for instance, Bernard likens hearts to a mill which grinds the books we read into flour for bread. This was a favourite image of Reformers; and part of Granada's project is to reclaim close reading from the Reform. See Ch. 1. n. 33 above.

[78] Cave, *Devotional Poetry*, p. 24; see also p. 5: 'there is little doubt that, in France at least, their impact [of Granada's works] was initially far greater than that of Loyola's *Spiritual Exercises*; and this point needs to be emphasised if one is to consider the relationship between devotional method and literature.' It is also important, as Cave demonstrates, to a discussion of how devotional method is made available to a lay readership. Belleforest is central to this process.

ferme comme un mur bien enduit, ou comme un navire bien calfeutré, afin que les ondes aissaillans, il les face escouler, et courir par dessus, sans qu'elles puissent entrer dedans, ny le plonger et abismer.[79]

More is at stake here, of course, than echoes of the advice given to travellers about which kind of ship to board. Rather, it is precisely through attention to, and moralizing of, the material details of travel that the *Vray chemin* achieves its effects. Purity of intention is thus made, as much as a water-tight ship, a real-life travel necessity, in the real-life journey towards salvation. Growing figurally more audacious, and with an introductory 'peut estre que', Granada suggests that:

pour figure de cecy Dieu commanda à Noé qu'il accoustrast et poissast et calfeutrast bien l'arche de toutes parts: car il faut que ainsi soit l'arche de nostre coeur, afin qu'il demeure sec, et sans moüillure au milieu des eaux du deluge tempestueux de ce siecle.[80]

The devotional pilgrim's heart is here imaged by the ark: a figure for movement—a boat—but one which is closed to the claims of the world. If this *is* a journey, it is one made in defiance of the attractions of elsewhere. To illustrate this point further, Granada goes on a textual journey himself, adducing the example of travellers who 'vont espars, cerchans des pailles par la terre d'Egypte . . . et ne cerchent que repaistre les yeux de choses belles, et l'ouye de nouveautez'.[81] It is when such travellers return home that the true state of their intentions is revealed:

Et leur advient tout ainsi qu'à ceux qui vont parler à quelque grand seigneur, ayans l'estomach plein de viandes grossieres, lesquels à demy harengue sont forcez de rejetter la viande une fois avallee: d'autant qu'estans à demy leur priere, et en leur plus grande devotion, ils sont assaillis du desir des auls [sic] et des oignons d'Egypte, je veux dire des pensers et affaires mondains, desquels leurs pensees sont toutes confites.[82]

The text confesses its own excess and acknowledges the need for explication of its increasingly internationalized bodily figures. The 'je veux dire' suggests that the imagery of the 'dépouille d'Egypte' was not altogether familiar to Granada's readers, at least not in so oral and culinary a form. It also highlights the degree to which Granada here, as in his efforts to speak of the 'returns' of pilgrimage

---

[79] Granada, *Le Vray chemin*, fol. 232ʳ.
[80] Ibid.   [81] Ibid.   [82] Ibid.

in the *Istruttione*, has recourse to puns which threaten to distract from his point. Indeed as the passage progresses, so the imagery develops in complexity, culminating in a condemnation of the curious sinner to endless displacement at the mercy of the winds with which his heart will be filled on his return home. Having feasted their eyes on the external beauty of the churches which they visit, the travellers find that they have spilled out their souls like water on the ground, and:

s'en retournent chez eux avec le coeur plein de vent, et vuide de devotion. Et ceux qui cheminent par ceste voye, comme ils sont instables et vagabonds en l'ame, aussi le sont ils au corps, entant qu'à grand'peine peuvent-ils estre en repos en un lieu, ains vaguent d'une part et d'autre, et ne sçachans où aller, ils vont où le vent les pousse pour cercher quelque reception exterieure, à cause qu'ils ont perdu celle de dedans, qui est la vraye et asseuree.[83]

It is for such as these that pilgrimage was instituted, and the rules of pilgrim conduct were elaborated. But the near-chiastic pairing with which Granada speaks of return ('plein de vent/vuide de devotion') casts doubt on the profit to be gained from even the most carefully circumscribed literal journey. For it seems people cannot travel without (enjoying) talking about having done so, and so committing further sins of the mouth. Thus, Granada's advice is clear. At home, as on a journey:

Il faut surtout brider la langue: car (comme dit S. Bernard) c'est un instrument fort propre à faire voguer le coeur et pensee . . . C'est chose notable à voir combien soudain s'evanoüit le goust de devotion quand on ouvre la bouche à trop grand parler, encor que ce soit de choses bonnes.[84]

There follows a paragraph of unbridled movement, in which all the spatial and bodily tropes exploited thus far in the text return with something of a vengeance. The distinctions between the heart and the tongue, figural and devotional sweetness, are submerged in the very flood of words against which the text warns its reader. Images of sweet waters turning sour lead to the conclusion:

Pource la faut serrer et brider [la langue], et si quelque-fois tu es forcé de sortir pour parler et negotier, reviens le plutost que pourras, ainsi que la colombe vers l'Arche, afin que ne perisses au deluge de trop de paroles. Et bien que ceste moderation soit à tous necessaire, elle l'est plus aux femmes qu'aux hommes, et mesmement aux filles, l'ornement desquelles est la honte et le silence pour garder leur chasteté.[85]

---

[83] Ibid., fols. 232ᵛ–233ʳ. [84] Ibid. [85] Ibid., fol. 233ʳ·ᵛ.

The kinds of practical advice pilgrims offer fellow-pilgrims in the course of their writings is, in Granada's *Vray chemin*, literalized, gendered, and made into a restrictive statement in a discourse of power centred on the body. The rhetoric of travel is redirected to construct an internally impregnable space within the body of the immobile believer. The ensuing chapter of the *Vray chemin* details how 'pour brider les sens et le coeur' the penitent must practise 'la solitude exterieure' as the ultimate guard against curiosity; this last named obstacle is the one to which the text has been leading throughout. Anxiety about curiosity, and advice about how to avoid it, get around it, overcome it, sidestep it . . . saturates and structures the entire journey of reading. The only safe recourse is to stay at home; and within the house, to stay closed to the world, and read.

Jerome's letter to Demetrias, imagining the body as a trading city, combines with a reading of the Desert Fathers to offer another powerful image illustrating Granada's point:

> les sens sont comme les portes d'une cité, par où tout entre et sort: . . . pource faut mettre garde aux yeux, et aux oreilles, et à la bouche: car par ces portes entrent et saillent toutes marchandises, et affaires mondains enclos en noz ames. De sorte que l'homme devot faut que soit sourd, aveugle et muet (ainsi que disoient les saincts peres des deserts d'Egypte).[86]

As we saw above, these are precisely the terms of travel which Granada uses in the *Istruttione*, and which the later priest Castela will exploit to instruct his pilgrims: 'contrefaire l'homme aveugle, sourd et muet.'[87] But here in the *Vray chemin* Granada is not talking about pilgrims, rather about penitents at home (primarily women, for all the reference to 'l'homme devot'). Rather than teach people how to travel, he educates his readers in the pleasures to be had from devotional exercise, cultivating in them a sense of the material force of devotional words, images, and metaphors. His *Vray chemin* is structured on a rhetoric of reversal: the 'chemin' turns out not to be a road, so much as a metaphorical 'invitation au voyage' implicating the reader in its own seductions and dangers.[88] And, to stress the point one last time, the chapter ends with a final elaborate verbal/spatial game, another pun. It is one which concludes the text's journey with a telling, self-consuming gloss, purporting to locate not

---

[86] Granada, *Le Vray chemin*, fol. 232ʳ.   [87] Castela, *Guide*, fol. 60ʳ.

[88] I am thinking here of Baudelaire's 'L'invitation au voyage' in *Fleurs du Mal*, pp. 58–9; see also Felman, *Jacques Lacan and the Adventure of Insight*, pp. 26–51.

the presence of the sacred, but rather the archetypal image of narrative temptation, the serpent's tongue. It resides, Granada is sure, in the mouths of young women:

lesquelles sainct Ambroise admonneste, disant: Voy, vierge, par ta voye, afin que ne desvoyes par ta langue: veu que souvent les bonnes paroles sont reputees pour peché en une fille.[89]

This pun, this conclusion to the devotional pilgrimage, demands some attention. The specific dangers which women faced when travelling had earlier been evoked in the *Vray chemin* by way of the scriptural example of Jacob's daughter Dina. Raped at a hidden turning in a road, she lost 'non seulement la devotion, et repos d'esprit, ains encor la chasteté et innocence'.[90] This example is itself worthy of attention, since it is a rare direct reference to sexual violence against women travellers; as we shall see in the next chapter such violence is more imagined and alluded to than narrated in Renaissance pilgrimage writing. And even here it is not contemporary but biblical example.

At this point of the *Vray chemin*, then, the violence is not in the narrated example, but in the words of advice themselves. Pressure is placed on the homophony of 'voy(e)' in order to connect meanings and so make the pun and the fun at the expense of the 'vierge' possible. The 'lesson' is conveyed, and the pun constructed, by the displacement of the phoneme 'voy(e)' along a chain of significance, from 'look' to 'watch where you're going' to 'look out!'. The one sound not accommodated within this echo chamber of advice is the voice of the person ostensibly being addressed. For not only does the pun commend its addressee to linguistic caution even when in her own room, it also effectively silences her by not attending to the very voice—or 'voix'—which it calls repeatedly to mind.

Unlike the *Vray chemin*, none of the *Guides* to literal pilgrimage address women, or ever imply that any advice they have to offer might be of use to women. The pilgrim they envisage is a man. The kinds of connection between reading and action fostered by the *Guides*, and by Zuallart's exemplary character, are, as we have seen, developed in part by way of a response to the Humanist rhetoric of good husbandry, exemplarity, and decorum for a male readership: timely responses to the particular contingencies of the road. The

---

[89] Granada, *Le Vray chemin*, fol. 233ᵛ.   [90] Ibid., fol. 233ʳ.

readerly lessons of the *Vray chemin*, by contrast, are frequently addressed explicitly to young women proscribed from undertaking literal pilgrimages, but wishing to experience both the pleasures and the rigours of the pilgrim experience. It would seem feasible to detect the construction of an ideology of space at work here, one in which a topography of gender represents men as being literal pilgrims on the move, and women as figural pilgrims, safe at home.

But, as Augustine had long since shown and Granada stresses anew, the home is not really safe, and it is, in any case, empty; for the women are not really present in the *Vray chemin*. Rather, woman figures the dangerous pleasures of the text, which the spiritual guide both evokes for his readers (male and female), and tries to keep 'at home', under control. Thus, if it is possible to read Granada's conduct literature as directed towards a female readership, it is also imperative to see that the devotional writer and translator's self-confessed invasion into 'foreign territory' are part of an occasionally desperate attempt to ensure unity 'at home' in the reader's mind. Egyptian meat, the spoils of Spain, and the hearts of women, are all identified as costly, 'foreign' objects of curiosity. This classification of the costs of what we might, connecting Jerome and Rabelais, term 'marchandises peregrines' has little to do with the worth of literal pilgrimage.[91] It has, rather, everything to do with the identification and continuing value of what is understood to be both newly in need of definition, and newly under threat—a place called home.

Pilgrim Method

In all the *Guides* discussed here, the central issue hinges on the instructive power of the writing, and on the use and enjoyment of method. Granada's bold move by way of response to the challenge of writing without either betraying oneself or inducing error in others—a challenge inherited from Augustine—is to suggest that the pleasures of devotion, like those of rhetoric, can be learned. This is bold in so far as it argues that the 'personne Chrestienne' need not define itself in opposition to those who are expert in the 'linguae peregrinae' of rhetoric. Indeed it allows for comparisons to be drawn

---

[91] Following Jerome's letter to Demetrias cited above, and adapting Rabelais' terms for the goods bought on Medamothy (*Quart Livre* 2). For more on this see below, Ch. 7.

between devotional guides and more secular forms of handbook: those of Humanist travellers and those of the poets. This in turn acknowledges that the devotional subject is constructed rather than born, the product of exercise and will, rather than grace alone:

Car tout ainsi que les Rhetoriciens desseignans de former un parfait orateur, ne se contentent de luy enseigner les points principaux esquels consistent les nerfs et forces du bien dire, ains ceux mesme qui sont de peu d'effect, comme la composition et suite des voyelles et consones avec autres menues consid-erations (d'autant que tout cecy ayde à parfaire l'oraison et harangue) ainsi voulans nous former un orateur celeste, priant et orant devant le throne de Dieu, il est raison aussi que nous le marquions et segnalions de tout ce qui est requis en cecy, soit de petite ou de grande consequence, comme ainsi soit que en tels affaires, il n'y a chose qui ne soit fort importante pour l'affaire.[92]

The terms of this self-analysis are perilously close to those of the guides in the other adjacent discourses of travel explored earlier in this chapter. As well as the explicit reference to rhetorical hand-books, the passage also echoes the Humanist guides to educational travel: Turler, remember, urges his reader to 'learne, et diligently to marke suche things . . . as they shall have need' of in the cultivation of the proper travelling self.[93]

To protect the separate, holy, status of the art of prayer, Granada must draw distinctions. Devotional rules are, he stresses, to be learned in order to be forgotten. Others have drawn up 'livrets d'orai-son dressez par art et par reigles' as if prayer were simply a question of speaking according to rules. What they have omitted is the element of grace. No rule is in itself enough, and belief in rules will—he argues with another use of the now tired metaphor—lead you astray:

Et estant la vie spirituelle la chose qui le plus requiert d'estre guidee et con-seillee, l'oraison en estant une partie la plus delicate, et divine, elle ne doibt estre enseignee par art, afin de n'offenser la grace, ains faut seulement don-ner des advis, afin que on ne s'esgare par les chemins.[94]

Granada concedes, here as elsewhere, that the very attention to method on the part of the penitent which his text persistently encour-ages, can prove, if unchecked, to be an 'empeschement à la devotion'. Rhetorical attentiveness should be especially avoided by those sub-ject to the 'curiosité de l'entendement'. For they will find themselves

---

[92] Granada, *Le Vray chemin*, fols. 243ᵛ–244ʳ. [93] Turler, *The Traueiler*, p. 27.
[94] Granada, *Le Vray chemin*, fol. 330ʳ.

being driven to read the wrong books: 'hystoires prophanes, et les livres des Gentils, et antiquitez inutiles, et autres choses semblables.' And even when reading the right books ('Augustin, Paul, Salomon') they will not be able to avoid reading 'avec ceste mesme curiosité, y recerchans le seul artifice et eloquence des paroles, ou quelques poincts, et sentences plus curieuses'. To explain why the *Vray chemin* might seem to some to encourage such modes of rhetorical attention, Granada introduces a further crucial distinction. There are, he argues, those who recuperate rhetorical pleasure to the goal of their own spiritual advancement, and those who read in order to 'enseigner aux autres par ostentation, sans qu'ils facent pour eux prouffit en icelles'.[95]

Once again there are echoes here between the figural and the literal guides. These same terms are taken up by Castela and Balourdet in their *Guides* when they distinguish between good pilgrims (who say little of the experience to others), and bad (who never stop narrating their travels and thus never stop being in error). Method, Granada wants to say, is not enough; but in saying so, he finds it increasingly difficult to proscribe that methodical attention to *writing* which he recognises as the dangerous pleasure of the text. For having adopted the structure of the journey beset by obstacles—a devotional romance—he can never quite extricate himself from a circular argument whereby method is first decried as insufficient, and then impressed on the reader as crucial if she or he is to avoid falling prey to the error of enjoying the romance rather than the goal.

The twists and turns of this discourse had earlier found their way into the prefaces and indeed the body of many pilgrimage narratives. But the point must be clarified: the development of vernacular advice in pilgrims' 'instructions', the elaboration of arts of travel by Latin Humanists, cross-fertilization with spiritual texts such as the *Vray chemin*, all, in their different ways, contribute to the codification and classification of the terms of pilgrim travel exemplified by the *Guides* of Balourdet and Castela. In response to new forms of travel both without and within pilgrimage writing, the pilgrim's reach grew more and more restricted, 'pilgrim' subjectivity more oppositionally defined.

The *Vray chemin* was already available to French readers in a translation by François de Belleforest by the late 1570s; it is thus

---

[95] Granada, *Le Vray chemin*, fol. 265ᵛ.

contemporary in composition with Regnaut's 'Instruction' and the *apodemika* of Turler, Maier, and Lipsius though none of these were translated into French until much later, after the appearance of Castela and Balourdet's vernacular *Guides* to travel. It is important to remember, in other words, that the precise terms of literal pilgrim identity as defined by the vernacular *Guide* writers were not formulated and codified until some time after both the devotional and secular guides were developed. In a sense the accustomed order of rhetorical priority—the literal as *prior* to the figural reading—is reversed by translation history. The vernacular *Guides* to literal pilgrimage are thus not so much the summation of method within travel writing, as the product of twofold resistance: first, against the exclusive appropriation of method by the secular arts of travel, and secondly, against the proliferation of that 'escrivaillerie' within vernacular pilgrimage writing, exemplified here by Zuallart, which the priestly authors considered symptomatic of what Montaigne termed his 'siecle desbordé'.[96]

This needs to be remembered because we must allow for the possibility that the arguments of Granada and others concerning the dangers of literal travel were, in a sense, too persuasive. For the later *Guide* writers sought to counter a decline in the cultural status of pilgrimage which had been brought about in part by Reformist and Humanist critiques, and in part by the stress on interiority in the spiritual writings of the counter-Reform: those of Granada, Loyola, and others. The history of pilgrimage writing over the period is one neither of purely confessional divisions, precise moments of rupture, nor yet of steady development. As the next chapter will demonstrate, focusing on the reception of Gregory of Nyssa's letter on pilgrimage, first in the 1550s and then in 1600–4, its shape is not that of either a straight, or a broken line. Rather than seeking to pinpoint when one paradigm or episteme was displaced by another, we need to acknowledge their competing claims on individuals at the time. The arguments and debates concerning pilgrimage require pilgrims and readers to adopt often incommensurable views at one and the same time. To trace the effects of these larger arguments, we need to look closely, and carefully, at the pressure which the debates bring to bear on the texts of the individual writers and the language in which they speak.[97]

---

[96] Montaigne, *Oeuvres*, III, ix, p. 946.
[97] See below, Ch. 3, for the debate around Gregory of Nyssa.

For this is not, or is not only, a narrative of loss. It is also one of redirection and transplantation. As *Guides* for different orders of reader develop from early to late Renaissance, so the language of pilgrimage lives on by migrating into adjacent discourses of travel, helping, in turn to form those different orders of person. And it is in such texts, which declare their difference from pilgrimage, that concerns long hinted at by pilgrim authors are echoed, and pilgrim anxieties given explicit expression. So for instance Lipsius seems on occasion to be urging his putative traveller to break the rules of pilgrim conduct: 'Regarde, regarde, te dis-je, escoute . . .'[98] His text is peppered with such commands to cast eyes and ears abroad: he urges the young gentleman traveller to write, to take notes, and to speak to almost anyone he encounters. This is travel as accumulation, and the more experience the better. But Lipsius is also concerned about the *quality* of experience, and rather than break with the pilgrim guides follows them in one crucial respect.

Lipsius shares Granada and the *Guide* writers' anxiety about the extent to which *method* and the rhetoric of 'useful pleasure' can guard against the physical force of curiosity. The focal point of this anxiety is curiosity about, and of, women. Unlike the sacred writers, Lipsius speaks of real women; he draws distinctions between kinds of women, and thus confers a degree of humanity on both his traveller (who is himself able to discern good from bad), and on the women themselves. He takes a long time to express his greatest fear, but when he does, he does so clearly: Rome is made up of 'une troupe turbulente', the young man is to '*ne se fier à personne*'.[99]

Others cannot be trusted; least of all other women, and in particular, Roman women, who persist in looking at young men in ways they may not have encountered before. If, Lipsius asks, you make the error of turning to 'ces chaudes, et cautes filles du Soleil, quel homme te pourra garantir?' In such a case all 'profit' derived from the journey would be lost, for 'veritablement tu te perdras, ny je t'en pourray detourner par aucun mien conseil, toutesfois de peur de me taire, et de peur d'amplifier . . .' Lipsius is here caught in the tutor's double bind: to bring the specific temptation to the young man's attention is to bring temptation to mind, to alert his curiosity; but not to do so is to risk his loss. To resolve the problem, he has recourse to an image:

---

[98] Lipsius, *Lettre*, in Doiron, p. 212.   [99] Ibid., p. 216, his italics.

voicy que je te donne une double cuirace, aux yeux, et aux oreilles: ferme, te dis je, les yeux, et les destourne loin de ces regards chatouilleux, car c'est là où est l'entree du méchant mal . . . et comme le desir vient de la veuë, ainsi le vouloyr de l'ouye.[100]

In Pauline mode, Lipsius then follows this advice with the image of an athelete. The hope is that in arousing the boy's desire for the (self-?) image of a strong, disciplined, classical male body, the letter of instruction will displace the sting of his desire for the 'chatouilleux' bodies of the courtesans:

comme donc aux athletes on donnoit des boucliers pour les aureilles, qu'ils appelloyent *amphotides*, afin d'eviter les coups: ainsi pren[ds] ce preservatif contre les armes d'amour, qui n'est entendre rien d'amoureux.[101]

This is a brave attempt on the educator's part to make denial and resistance exciting; he arouses the desire for learning the right (things classical) even as he counsels against learning the wrong. In the original Latin, the term for the athletes' equipment is printed in Greek script, and is the only (exotic, tantalising?) such word in the Letter. It is also the closest anyone in the guide literature we have discussed thus far gets to a specifically sexualized rendering of the workings of curiosity as it is experienced by men when away from home.

A discourse guarding against 'impertinente curiosité' and a corresponding elaboration of pilgrim method had in fact been developing from the earliest French pilgrimage writings onwards. The coupling just noted, for instance, occurs in the account of Huen's pilgrimage to Jerusalem, first published as an extension to a translation of Breydenbach at the end of the previous century. But Huen's argument against curiosity centres not on the destruction of the sexual soul, so much as on the engendering of texts. There are, he writes, too many books these days and curiosity is to blame. Everyone—himself included—wants to be an author: 'et de faict une vielle assotee veult estre escoutee a son hault caquet: et ung sot viellart fera grant debat de parolles vaines.'[102] Huen recognizes that he is no better; he has never drunk from the wells of Minerva. He has, however, been asked to write his story 'comme par maniere de passe temps: a cause que

---

[100] Ibid.
[101] Ibid. The Latin for 'preservatif' here is 'velamentum', a covering of some kind, including, by figural transference, one which allows you to hide what you are doing.
[102] Huen, fol. iii[r].

plusieurs seigneurs et dames sont curieux a demander de la region ou de la terre de promission'.[103]

In this way he explicitly calls on the commonplace linking of *curiositas* and *garrulitas*, implicating also the curiosity of his readers who have prompted him to break his silence and write. If, for the Humanist traveller, looking, speaking, and writing are the point of the journey, Huen suggests that this cannot be so for the pilgrim. His concern about the sins of the mouth defined as *garrulitas* deflects attention away from broader sexual concerns, but the desire to tell one's story is felt with physical force, and is subject to strong repression.

Huen's 'Introduction du sainct voyage' is no guide-book; it pre-dates the drawing of rigid lines between Humanist and pilgrim, and it assumes a generality of pilgrim readers and travellers. But Huen does point towards what will become a central issue of debate in pilgrim discourse: the twinned problem of pilgrims' intentions and readers' attention to rhetoric. He opens his account with a rejection of classical rhetoric: 'Ne la science de Platon ne de Tulle la tresgrande eloquence a dire ta noblesse [that of pilgrimage to Jerusalem] naproche point.' He then goes on, however, to conjoin the Horatian *utile dulci* commonplace with the rhetoric of writerly sacrifice. Since he, the pilgrim, has both taken on himself the rigours of the road and written with pure intentions, the reader at home can travel with the mind free from dangers either of the heart, or the road. Since the pilgrim has overcome temptation and returned home with heart and body intact, his readers can allow themselves to be led 'par les yeux de la pensée' into the presence of Christ crucified, buried, and resurrected. Anyone who listens to this text being read 'ourra le doulx Jhesus preschant tres doulcement comme sil fut present'. The pilgrimage of reading thus becomes paramount, but only because it is predicated on the devotional performance of the literal journey. Articulated through verbs of movement, the reading of the text retro-spectively sanctifies the twists and turns of the literal journey. And both the literal and figurative trajectories culminate in celebration of the host: 'Apres yra par vraye contemplation en la montaigne nom-mee de Syon: et en la cene de Jhesus se trouua; et refectionne de son corps il sera.'[104]

---

[103] Huen, fol. iii[v].   [104] Ibid., fol. v[r].

All of this, Huen is sure, will excite in the reader not the 'impertinente curiosité' of others, but rather a 'saincte curiosité (pour ainsy
parler) pour obvier à vaine evagation'.[105] In this way, the pilgrim
priest first articulates and then redeems curiosity and narrative desire
by predicating pure intentions on the part of the reader. The primal
sin, wandering of the mind, is overcome by the reader's devotional
use of the pilgrim's literal travels. It is possible for Huen—albeit ten-
tatively: the '(pour ainsy parler)' betokens his boldness—to offer this
series of couplings in good faith; he travels, and is first published, in
the last years of the fifteenth century. Later writers will change the coordinates of Huen's world.

The precise contours of change are difficult to trace. Like the
blindfolded men of the fable who each take hold of a different part of
an elephant, we hold fast to believing that the piece of historical
understanding we have grasped gives some sense of the shape of the
age. Certainly, the changes in the status of curiosity within pilgrimage writing are the tail end of a larger beast which is made up of
priestly pilgrim *Guides*, the 'instructions' of earlier pilgrims, the
Humanists' Latin texts, and Granada's *Vray chemin*. What the shifting of terms and metaphors across various and intersecting forms of
Guide makes clear, is that by the time Castela and Balourdet return
home and begin to write, neither the house, nor the body, nor
pilgrimage are quite the same.

---

[105] Ibid., fol. vj^v.

CHAPTER THREE

'Le Jargon des Errans': *Arguments Against Pilgrimage*

Gregory of Nyssa: Deffence (de Voyager)

The edition, translation, and reception of Gregory of Nyssa's second letter on pilgrimage is central to the movement outlined in the last chapter whereby the terms of pilgrimage are redefined by both Reformers and counter-Reformers, especially in France.[1] Gregory's letter was read in ways characteristic of the devotional critiques of pilgrimage we have looked at so far, in that he was thought to cast doubt on the value of the literal journey. In particular, much was made of the way he identified curiosity and the desire for contact with others, particularly women, as the primary temptations which beset the pilgrim. It was in response to this kind of critique that the terms of the *vray pèlerinage* changed. For if it is no longer understood primarily as an encounter with Otherness, then pilgrimage can be made part of the rhetoric of self-examination; it can move from being a journey beyond the bounds of Christendom to a means of policing the borders of home.

Those who, in response to Reformers' critiques, defend the practice of pilgrimage as literal journey adopt one of three positions: they

---

[1] A useful modern edition of Gregory's late fourth-century letter, with facing French translation is P. Maraval, *Lettres* (1990). See also his 'Une controverse'. Maraval's references should be supplemented (and occasionally corrected) by those of M. Altenburger and F. Mann, *Bibliographie zu Gregor von Nyssa* (1988). Because of the nature of the argument in this chapter, date, and place of publication of the Renaissance editions of Gregory will, exceptionally, be indicated in footnotes.

attack Gregory's arguments directly, and thus find themselves in conflict with one of the Church Fathers; they argue that he did not mean
what others—'heretics'—take him to mean; or they claim that the
letter is falsely ascribed to Gregory, and so carries no authority. In
turning first to this text in its original context, and then to its reception in the Renaissance, we need to attend closely to these arguments
as they bear on the motifs and metaphors which have arisen thus far
in this study. We need in particular to listen for the changes in terms
relating to the dangers of travel, and the ways in which they become
gendered. For unlike Augustine, Petrarch, or the Granada of the *Vray
chemin*, Gregory is concerned with literal pilgrimage to Jerusalem.
Like Castela, Balourdet, and Zuallart, he writes from the experience
of the journey; but—and here he is like the Granada of the *Istruttione
de' Peregrini* or Lipsius in his *Lettre* to Philippe de Lannoy—he is
moved to writing not least because he has been convinced by his own
trip of the danger which the journey holds for those who are in search
of the true sense of knowledge or devotion. We begin with a reading
of the letter.

   None of the writers of *Guides* to literal pilgrimage discussed above
have anything specific to say about women pilgrims; none address
their texts to women. Their examples imply that although both men
and women perform local pilgrimages it is only men who travel to
Jerusalem. If this was not entirely true in the Renaissance, it was even
less so in Gregory's time, and his letter is addressed to both men and
women readers, in the knowledge that both men and women travel to
Jerusalem, and in the hope of dissuading both sexes from doing so.
Speaking of the letter in its original context, Peter Brown refers to
Gregory's urgent concern about the mixing of sexes on the journey,
and the 'indiscreta societas', which he and Jerome warn pilgrims
against. Brown calls the concern of the Fathers to mind largely to
decry it as so much patriarchal prurience. He opts rather to stress
that 'therapy of distance' which makes of pilgrims joyously 'liminal'
figures, experiencing in a 'mercifully untaxing form the thrill of
passing an invisible frontier'. Pilgrimage, Brown argues, 'bridges
the greatest cleavage of all in late-antique urban society' by breaking down the segregation of the sexes and making women 'available to the public gaze in a manner rare in a late-antique urban
context'.[2] The experience could, furthermore, be one of liberation

---

[2] Brown, *Cult*, pp. 42–3.

for women: 'All over the Mediterranean area, the controlled liminal-ity of pilgrimage allowed women to experience, for long periods of time, the heartening freedom of the desert.'[3]

These terms owe much to an anthropological understanding of pilgrimage as 'a liminoid phenomenon'; not only a journey *towards* sacred places, but also itself a socially sacralized space. The pilgrim journey is characterized as a kind of Bakhtinian sublime in which the walls of language, class, and gender which normally separate us each from the other are either clambered over or spirited away for a time.[4] The worth of such readings is that they epitomize the kinds of argu-ment for the literal journey which Gregory, and certain of his Renais-sance readers, will reconfigure as proofs of the danger of the practice. For Gregory might well have felt his concern vindicated by the terms of the publicity for pilgrimage which Brown and others present. His own experience of travel to the Holy Land had, he felt, amply demon-strated the dangers of 'mixing' on the pilgrim road. 'Modesty', he argues, 'is preserved in societies that live distinct and separate, so there should be no meeting and mixing up of persons of opposite sex.'[5] The material 'necessities of a journey' have, Gregory insists, spiritual consequences, for they are 'continually apt to reduce this scrupulousness to a very indifferent observance of the rules'. A par-ticular site of pollution are the stopping places on the journey:

The inns and hostelries and cities of the East present many examples of licence and of indifference to vice; how will it be possible for one passing through such smoke to escape without smarting eyes? Where the ear and the eye is defiled, and the heart too, by receiving all those foulnesses through eye and ear, how will it be possible to thread without infection such seats of contagion?[6]

This is a strongly physical account of the conditions of travel to Jerusalem. And if Gregory has the pilgrim's sense of how the phys-ical and the spiritual connect, he also has a strong sense of where the particular danger, as he sees it, lies. He reserves an especial fear for the bodies of women:

It is impossible for a woman to accomplish so long a journey without some-one to *keep her safe*; on account of her natural weakness she has to be lifted

---

[3] Brown, *The Body and Society*, p. 272.

[4] See above, Ch. 1. We return to the idea of pilgrimage as Bakhtinian carnival below, Ch. 7.

[5] *Select Writings and Letters of Gregory of Nyssa*. Select Library of Nicene and Post-Nicene Fathers, 2nd. ser., V (1893), pp. 382–3.

[6] Ibid.

up onto her horse and lifted down again; she has to be supported in difficult situations. Whichever we suppose, that she has an acquaintance to perform this service, or a hired attendant, either way the proceeding cannot escape being reprehensible; whether she commits herself to a stranger, or gives herself to her own servant, she does not *keep the law* of continence.[7]

The woman's body is the focus of the law. Both are represented as fragile, in need of being 'kept'; and if the one object ('her [safe]') is not kept separate from all but those who have legitimate access to it, the other ('the law') cannot be kept either. The therapy for Gregory's pollution anxiety, expressed as it is in such thoroughly bodily terms, cannot be controlled liminality, nor the free movement of his own and womens' bodies subject to the public gaze. He could perhaps have argued, like Granada and Castela, that the pilgrim must travel through the land as though deaf, dumb, and blind.[8] He does not. Like both of the priestly *Guide* writers who follow him, he deals with the problem discursively, but is more radical than either. For he effects a linguistic shift which denies the need for movement, but stresses the need for confession. Geographical space is collapsed into sacred discursive space, which is then internalized and located somewhere deep in the soul.

The first move in this process as Gregory elaborates it is that of negation. He denies that the place proper had any effect at all on him: 'We confessed that the Christ Who was manifested is very God, as much before as after our sojourn at Jerusalem; our faith in Him was not increased afterwards any more than it was diminished.' After negation comes affirmation. He affirms that he has indeed seen the central sites: Bethlehem, the Mount of Olives, 'His grave'. And yet this affirmation of pilgrimage is purely functional. It serves first, to carry the preceding negation over into the specific sites within the Holy Land pilgrimage, and secondly, to reassert the irrelevance of being there for faith: 'Before we saw Bethelehem we knew His being made man by means of the Virgin.'[9] The move away confirms the absence of the need to move away.

This apparently circular, but very powerful, argument is implicit in the paradoxical authority Gregory draws from having experienced

---

[7] Ibid., p. 383, slightly altered; my emphasis.
[8] See above, Ch. 2. Gregory does say that his 'waggon was in fact as good as a church or monastery to us for we were singing Psalms and fasting in the Lord during the whole journey' (ibid.). But he certainly saw, heard, and smelled much, and speaks about all of this.
[9] Ibid.

the place itself. He starts to speak in the voice of the 'witness': 'let our advice be all the more listened to, because we are giving it on matters which came actually before our eyes.' But the witness to the other world in this case tells us only that we should be happy to be at home. The recursive force of his letter is made explicit following the listing of places central to Christ's life. It is expressed in the lexis of profit, and by way of a comparison with home: 'We derived only this much of profit from our travelling thither, namely that we came to know by being able to compare them, that our own places are far holier than those abroad.'[10]

This remarkably direct and subversive understanding of the worth of pilgrimage is argued by none of the *Guide* writers; nor yet as we shall see is it properly acknowledged by those who edit and comment on Gregory's letter in the Renaissance.[11] For his part, Gregory moves on to his starkest—and most consoling—claim:

Change of place does not effect any drawing nearer unto God, but wherever thou mayest be, God will come to thee, if the chambers of thy soul be found of such a sort that He can dwell in thee and walk in thee.[12]

The implication here, as throughout the letter, is that those who need to go to Jerusalem in order to begin confessing their faith are seriously in error. This is Gregory at his most polemical, for his argument renders the literal journey less than an irrelevance. The travelling figure is no longer the pilgrim, but Christ himself, and the places to which he comes are the 'chambers of the soul'. The term Gregory uses here for these 'chambers'—*diversoria*—is identical to that used to refer to the 'inns and hostelries of the East'. He thus operates a displacement of the very sites of anxious contagion from the literal into the figural. This displacement in turn produces its own miniature figural pilgrimage, detailing the most sacred sites, before denying their literal importance to belief:

For if thou keepest thine inner man full of wicked thoughts, even if thou wast on Golgotha, even if thou wast on the Mount of Olives, even if thou stoodest on the memorial rock of the Resurrection, thou wilt be as far away from receiving Christ into thyself, as one who has not even begun to confess him.[13]

[10] Gregory of Nyssa, *Select Writings and Letters*, p. 383.

[11] See, for instance, Richeome, in his *Deffence des pèlerinages* (1604), fol. 19ᵛ. We return to Richeome in detail below.

[12] Gregory, *Select Writings*, p. 383.

[13] Ibid.

The syntax itself stresses that even here, even at the heart of pilgrimage, the pilgrim can be far from Christ. This, as we saw above, is an anxiety expressed by Renaissance pilgrims from Fabri at the end of the fifteenth century to Zuallart at the start of the seventeenth. To articulate the shape of this anxiety for his Late Antique readers, and so attempt to dissuade them from the journey, Gregory gives particular spatial expression to the gulf between the body and the soul, the better to absent the body entirely from pilgrimage. Indeed, at his most emphatic and chiastic, Gregory defines pilgrimage as the gesture of moving away from the body:

Therefore, my beloved friend, counsel the brethren to undertake a pilgrimage away from the body to go to our Lord, rather than to go on pilgrimage away from Cappadocia to go to Palestine.[14]

There is both dialogue and defence in this counsel. Its terms, in particular those of the chiasmus and the displacement into the figural of *peregrinare*, are an echo of II Corinthians 5: 8. Gregory originally writes at a time when the call to *peregrinatio* in Paul's letter was being interpreted as a call to travel, and supporting the new institution of pilgrimage. His resolutely figural reading of Paul thus acts to stake a claim to an understanding of the new practice not as a literal journey, but as the construction of an inner self worthy of Christ's habitation.

This is not, of course, to impose immobility or silence on his readers. But that is one way of extending his interpretation of Paul, and it is, as we shall see (and as might be imagined from discussion in previous chapters), the interpretive road that will be taken by many of Gregory's readers in the late Renaissance. It is a way of reading the terms of pilgrimage which is anticipated in a manuscript addition to Gregory's letter first noted in the fourteenth century, and further copied into the sixteenth. It follows Gregory's advice to 'undertake a pilgrimage away from the body' with a warning, and a resonant exclamation:

spécialement les moniales. Il faut tenir les vierges à l'écart des lieux publics et des vigiles nocturnes. Il le sait, il le sait, ce serpent fertile en inventions et qui a semé son venin à travers de bonnes actions! Il faut que les vierges soient entourées de murs de tous côtés et qu'elles ne quittent leur maison que rarement de toute l'année, lorsque les sorties sont inévitables et indispensables.[15]

---

[14] Ibid. (I have slightly altered the translation to return the pilgrim force to Gregory's punning terms).
[15] The MS. is Cod. Vaticanus gr. 1455 chart., ff. 177–179ᵛ. The addition is given in French by Maraval in his edition of Gregory's *Lettres*, p. 123 n. 1.

Gregory's Letter: Translations and Editions

Gregory's letter was first published, in Greek with anonymous facing Latin translation, as a small octavo booklet by Guillaume Morel in Paris in 1551.[16] This is the first printing of a manuscript which survives in over thirty-five copies, although the source for Morel's Greek text has yet to be found. Morel's reasons for publishing this letter, and for doing so in this format, are similarly lost to us now, as is the reason for bringing the text out again in a number of pamphlet collections, probably in 1558, this time with a different Latin translation.[17] Later generations of readers were assured of Morel's allegiance to the cause of Rome: a 1605 preface to the Letter refers to him as 'Pontificius', publishing the work 'bona fides'.[18] But this is a reading of Morel's motives half a century after the event; and it is part of a polemic arising from the use to which his edition was put soon after its original publication. Whatever Morel's actual intentions, it becomes clear that Gregory's motivations and allegiances in writing the letter are nicely echoed in the discussion concerning those of his first publisher and Latin translator. The repeated, almost obsessive rereadings of this letter further demonstrate how the Late Antique terms of pilgrimage were policed, and their history written and rewritten, from early to late Renaissance.

Morel may not have intended the text to be read as Reformist in tone, and its arguments to become part of (anti-) pilgrim polemic. But it is as such that Gregory is cast, and the letter is next published. Flacius Illyricus twice uses Gregory in support of Reformers' arguments in texts he publishes in 1560. His edition of the fourth of the Magdeburg *Centuries* includes Morel's translation in its entirety; the second version of the *Catalogue of Witnesses to the Truth* offers only a summary of the letter but is all the more clear in its critique.[19]

---

[16] Gregory of Nyssa, *de iis qui adeunt Hierosolyma opusculum* (Paris, Morel, 1551). This was the year Morel was made Greek printer to the king; on his career see P. Renouard, *Répertoire des imprimeurs parisiens* (1965), pp. 314–15.

[17] The difference between the 1551 Latin text and that of 1558, only published as part of larger collections of pamphlets, was noted by Maraval, 'Une controverse', p. 132. The prefatory material of these editions does not provide answers to the questions outlined above.

[18] *De iis qui adeunt Jerosolyma, Juxta editionem Morellianam* (Paris, R. Estienne III, 1606).

[19] Flacius Illyricus [Matthias Francowicz], *Quarta Centuriae Ecclesiasticae historiae* (Basel, 1560), pp. 929–38; *Catalogus testium veritatis* (Basel, 1560). The earlier edition of

Gregory is there made to present eight arguments against pilgrimage. The first five run as follows: scripture is the only conduct manual we need; pilgrimage is nowhere recommended in scripture; it gives rise to numerous crimes and corruptions, particularly regarding women; it is consequently counterproductive to the pursuit of piety; God is no more fully present in Jerusalem than anywhere else where he is worshipped; indeed it appears from the manners and actions of those who live in Jerusalem that Palestine is the devil's own territory. The remaining three arguments, which are more general in nature, are that the truly pious life consists in the sincere pursuit of knowledge of Christ, that God comes close to all those who search for him, and that God's grace and gifts are not confined to any one place.

These are indeed Gregory's arguments, but they are not open to any single reading in the Renaissance. Bellarmine's *Controversies* (1586), for instance, reduces the number of Gregory's points to three: pilgrimage is not one of the beatitudes, it can be dangerous for women, and Christ is omnipresent for believers. These he then counters, in the seventh controversy on the Church Triumphant, with two standard disqualifying clerical gestures. The first is that of reference to Church authority: the decrees of the Council of Trent stress the usefulness of pilgrimage. The second is that of philological authenticity, married to a new anxiety about the good faith of publishers: how do we know that Gregory really was the author of this letter, and even if he were, can we trust the printer to have published the manuscript in front of him without altering it? In this way Bellarmine's strident, much-published tones (1586, 1587, 1588, 1590, 1596, 1599, 1600, 1601 . . .) close the initial rounds of the debate.[20]

Up to this point, the published debate has been conducted in Latin, responding to the Greek and Latin translations of the text. As with the *Guides* discussed above, the debate shifts into the vernacular, becoming there both codified and still more complex, in the first few years of the new century. In the same year as Castela publishes his *Guide*, Robert Estienne III publishes the first French translation of Gregory's letter. This is rapidly followed by a counter-blast:

the *Catalogus* (1556) though it does ally Gregory to the cause, does not mention his letter on pilgrimage (p. 33). For more on this see Maraval, 'Une controverse', p. 133 (though he places Gregory's arguments, incorrectly, in the 1556 *Catalogus*).

[20] Bellarmine, *Controvers*, VII, iii, viii (*Opera*, III, pp. 295–8). For the frequent re-editions of Bellarmine, see C. Sommervogel, *Bibliothèque de la Compagnie de Jésus* (1890–1909), I, pp. 1156–7.

Richeome's *Deffence des pelerinages contre le traducteur d'une lettre pretendue de St Gregoire de Nisse sur les Pelerinages de Hierusalem*.[21] Richeome's *Deffence* in turn generates further Latin argument, as within the year Pierre du Moulin, the peripatetic preacher who was at the time a Pasteur in Paris, brings out yet another edition of the Letter.[22] This amounts to a scholarly, critical edition, offering the Greek text, Morel's translation to counter recent (i.e. Richeome's) claims that it had not been done with reference to the original Greek, and a new translation into Latin. The letter is further published over the next two years, in both Latin translations, and with copious notes and treatises, one on pilgrimage and the other on sacrificial altars, attached. The culmination of the first wave of editions, published in 1607 on Wechel's presses in Hanau, brings together a prefatory letter by Scaliger, Gregory's letter in Greek, based on Morel's edition, du Moulin's Latin translation, and his two treatises. It is, as Maraval points out, 'une sorte d'édition-synthèse . . . le tout suivi d'un *index rerum* fort complet'.[23]

Nor does the battle of books end there. Just as du Moulin's edition and treatise is a direct response to Richeome's attack, so it too finds a response, delivered by the Jesuit Gretser in two texts first published in 1608.[24] They are published again by Sonnius in Paris in the 1615 edition of Gregory's works, along with the 1551 Latin translation of the letter.[25] This facing Greek and Latin edition is reprinted several times, in Köln (1617), and again in Paris (1638).[26] The last early modern facing Greek and Latin edition of the letter is edited by Johann

---

[21] Richeome's *Deffence* was first published by Sonnius, as a separate pamphlet in 1604, and then again, in folio, by Cramoisy in 1628 as part of Richeome's considerable *Oeuvres* (II, pp. 895–907). Page references here are to the 1604 text. Robert Estienne III was the great-grandson of the printer, and was at the time the king's interpreter in Greek and Latin; this argument about the authority of the Father occurs, consistently, close to the centre of temporal power. Hence also the speed of the Jesuit response.

[22] *De euntibus Ierosolyma, Epistola, Latinè versa, et Notis illustrata à Petro Molineo* [s.l.] 1605.

[23] *De euntibus Ierosolyma . . .* (Hanau, 1607). See Maraval, 'Une controverse', pp. 136–7. For more on du Moulin see L. Rimbault, *Pierre du Moulin, 1568–1658* (1966), who gives details of his eventful and much-travelled life, but beyond an allusion (p. 44), does not mention this work or this debate.

[24] Gretser, *Notae in notis Petri Molinei Calvinistae super epistolam Nysseno adscriptam, de euntibus Hierosolymam* (Ingolstadt, Sartorius, 1608); *Examen Tractatus de Peregrinationibus ab eodem Molineo editi* (Ingolstadt, Sartorius, 1608).

[25] *S. Patris Nostri Gregorii Episcopi Nysseni . . . Opera Omnia quae reperiri potuerunt, Graecè et Latinè*, 2 vols. (Paris, Sonnius, 1615). The letter is in vol. ii, pp. 1084–7.

[26] It travelled far and has survived well: there are, for instance, seventeen copies of the 1615 edition in Oxford alone, only two of which are mentioned in Altenburger and Mann.

Heidegger in Trier in 1670, as part of his four-volume discussion and summation of the arguments concerning pilgrimage in the centuries which preceded him.[27]

Gregory's letter was clearly subject to persistent reading, translation, and rereading throughout the Renaissance; and it travelled far.[28] It is of course impossible to know exactly who read (as opposed to bought or sold) these books, but the degree to which the terms of the debate they generate inform the texts of pilgrims and *Guide* writers of all kinds is none the less striking. Following Richeome, the largely Latin and Jesuit divines who engage in the debate about Gregory's letter all seek to restrict the appropriation of his arguments by others, seek to fix the terms of legitimate travel, and to silence their opponents. They do so primarily with reference to philology, arguing that they alone possess a proper understanding of terms, of address, and of translation: Gregory's Greek has been misunderstood by the inept Reformers, it should never have been translated into the vernacular, where it discourages not so much the ascetics to whom it was originally addressed, as the common people who love to go on pilgrimage.

It is the movement of the terms of this argument across linguistic, confessional, and other boundaries which reinforces the sense that the debate around Gregory's letter is not so much about the merits of the journey, as an argument about the politics of interpretation, and the authority of communities of belief. Like Castela, Richeome argues the Catholic pilgrim cause against the Reform. Like his co-religionist, his understanding of what it is to be a pilgrim has less to do with the practical arts of travel, than with the relative merits of what he considers 'errant' (Reformist) and 'propre' (counter-Reformist) narrative method. His *Deffence* is a paradigmatic instance of change in process: it shows how, in the course of the argument around Gregory's letter, the question of whether or not to travel modulates into one of *how* to travel. The true pilgrimage, as the *Guides* of the last chapter suggested, becomes defined as a persuasive performance of the devotional journey; and pilgrimage is, in the process, confirmed to be above all a question of style.

---

[27] Heidegger, *Dissertatio de peregrinationibus religiosis* (Trier, 1670). The letter, with an 'Apologia' is on pp. 414 ff.

[28] For discussion of the travels behind the manuscript tradition and the story of a Cretan refugee from Turkish invasion to whom we owe a particular copy of this text, see P. Canart, 'Recentissimus non deterrimus: Le texte de la lettre II de Grégoire de Nysse dans la copie d'Alvise Lollino (cod Vaticanus gr 1759)', in *Zetesis* (1973), pp. 717–31.

Richeome's Response: Deffence (de Parler)

The only known early modern edition of Gregory's letter in the vernacular, Robert Estienne III's French translation, published in Paris in 1604, is lost. Our discussion of the letter's reception history is thus organized around an absent centre. Gregory might have been pleased by this fact: his central argument about pilgrimage to Jerusalem is, as we saw above, that the journey is worse than a waste of time, since there is, strictly speaking, only absence to be found in the place itself. He summarizes the point most succinctly in another letter, also first published by Estienne. The sacred places, he there argues, are really to be found 'in animo illius qui Deum in se habet'.[29] This is the argument to which Richeome's *Deffence* responds, but he does not need to do so in these terms, for he writes against the French translation of the second Letter in order to silence the vernacular—not the learned Latin—debate.

It might be felt that the subsequent disappearance of the French translation is a witness to Richeome's success. But it is also the case that his polemical method, quoting those sections of the translation he finds offensive, ensure that the text survives. We can read this translation only in fragments, framed by the disqualifying rhetoric of its formidable opponent, but the force of its presence can still be felt in Richeome's counterblast. The *Deffence* was itself translated into Latin, and generated further commentary from his translator Loarte, and, in later years, from Peter Lambeck.[30] The one surviving French contribution to this print war is that of Richeome, and having established the contours of the territory in which he is moving, we can turn to his *Deffence* in detail.

---

[29] *B. Gregorii Nysseni ad Eustathiam, Ambrosiam, et Basilissam epistola* (Paris, R. Estienne, 1606), p. 18. This edition, in Greek, with a Latin translation and notes by Casaubon, also gave rise to crucial arguments concerning the doctrine of Ubiquitism. This reading of Gregory was never elaborated in the French vernacular, and so we cannot pursue it here. See, for more on this, Gregory of Nyssa, *Select Writings*, pp. 542–5.

[30] The Latin translation is in Loarte, *Opusculum de sacris peregrinationibus* (Cologne, Gualter, 1619). See also Loarte's spirited Italian defence, *Trattato delle Sante Peregrinationi* (Venice, 1585). I have not included these later texts in discussion here as they do not bear directly on the French field. Their arguments are essentially those of Richeome, which are those of Bellarmine, but their rhetorical bravado is less evident than either of these. A brief manuscript history, a bibliography of the dispute from Morel to Sonnius, and an argument that 'haeretici eam malè interpretantur' whilst 'Catholici autem rectè contendunt' is found in P. Lambeck's *Commentariorum*, V (Vienna, Cosmerovius, 1672), pp. 81–8.

Richeome engages, clearly, in a considerably entrenched learned debate, and in writing a text such as this in French he changes its terms, as he himself acknowledges. Were it not for the French of others, he says, he would not have written. Now that they have done so, he writes in the assurance that, after reading this book 'ils auront plus d'envie de se retrancher dans les destroicts de leur opiniastrise et se taire, que de faire des saillies de langue ou de plume en vain'.[31] In the last few months, he continues, there have been published in Paris and elsewhere a number of treatises encouraging people to undertake pilgrimages—he could well be referring to the Balourdet and Castela *Guides* though he names no-one. Just as the Devil cannot help but 'sursemer d'yvroye la terre qu'il voit ensemencée de bon grain et d'obscurcir par tenebres d'erreur, le serain de la verité', so certain 'errans' have translated and published a letter, claiming it to have been written by Gregory of Nyssa.[32] They have done so in an attempt to 'empescher le fruict de ces livres-là, et arrester le chemin des bons Pelerins, leur faisant perdre courage de passer outre par la nouvelle d'un faux bruit'.[33] Richeome has taken up his pen in the hope not so much of convincing, as of silencing, and then banishing his devilish opponents. He considers it an 'office de charité' to 'examiner cette traduction' and in doing so to 'descouvrir en passant ce mauvais sursemeur et les tuyaux de son yvroye, et le descriant luy faire quitter et champs et cabane'.[34] The aim, then, is simple: to stop the noise— the 'faux bruit' of the vernacular—and make an exile of the Reformist anti-pilgrim.

It is this disqualifying move, at once rhetorical and political, that constitutes the founding gesture of the *Deffence*. In his studied performance Richeome presents an adept reverse articulation of one of the most persistent arguments against pilgrimage, that most eloquently put by Gregory himself: the pilgrim risks being no better than the vagabond, occupying not only the same literal space, but also 'catching' (as if by way of a disease) the vagabond's social and moral identity. For Gregory, as we saw, the danger of pilgrimage is spiritual, but it is mediated through the body. To defend pilgrimage, Richeome must answer these insistent questions, and he will try to do so late in his *Deffence*. He starts, however, by avoiding the issue, and by reversing the terms of the argument by way of a pun.

---

[31] Richeome, *Deffence*, 'Au Lecteur', fol. aij^r. I refer to the 1604 edition.
[32] Ibid.   [33] Ibid., fol. aij^v.   [34] Ibid.

Pilgrims' literal wandering, Richeome implies, even their wandering into such places as those Gregory feared most, is nothing compared to the error of Reformist readers. The argument (always implied, never quite explicitly stated) pivots on the double meaning of the word which allows for an identity of Reformers and masterless men to be posited: 'errer'. It is, Richeome says, those who refuse to see the worth of leaving home to seek God who are in error, and the treatise opens with the marginal note: 'Façon de faire des errans.' In thus defining the Reformers as 'errans' Richeome evacuates the danger of literal error from pilgrimage; he also suggests that his own text can be read as belonging to the *useful* genre of the *Guide* to literal pilgrimage. The success of this defence lies in what is never quite addressed. In order for this critical procedure to be effective Richeome must, as I have suggested, ignore both the message of Gregory's letter and the warnings of the other *Guides* to which he himself refers. This he does in the hope that his pilgrim readers will imitate him in his simple (but studied) ignorance. The learned debate which they may have heard of which casts them as in error is, he urges, irrelevant: 'Les bons Pelerins tandis poursuivront en paix leur chemin, se servant de ce petit traicté ou comme de guide, ou comme de mont-joye.'[35]

Thus far Richeome is all teeth and smiles, flattery and reassurance. When he turns to face his opponent, however, his sword is already drawn and his teeth bared: the 'enfan des tenebres' who translated Gregory's letter declines to declare himself 'à teste levée'. He is afraid, it seems, to be struck in the face and thus have his argument disfigured.[36] Or does he hide his own face, his own name, because he knows that the letter is not properly Gregory's at all?

Ceste traduction, dict-il, *est faicte sur l'original Grec imprimé à Paris par Guill. Morel.* Ceste preface, dis-je, est tracée sur les mensonges des Centuriateurs de Magdebourg Lutheriens, et non sur l'original Grec de Gregoire de Nysse, que ce traducteur n'a possible veu qu'au Latin de ces bons interprètes, aussi fideles en l'histoire Ecclesiatique, qu'en la religion.[37]

If this is dialogue ('dict-il . . . dis-je'), it is staged only to disqualify the

---

[35]   Richeome, *Deffence*, 'Au Lecteur', fol. aij[v].

[36]   The image-cluster of the text and name as face, along with that of concealment and disfigurement saturates the piece. For the specific instance of being 'frappé au visage en se monstrant' see fol. 2[v].

[37]   Ibid. In common with Renaissance typographical convention, the opponent's voice is italicized in Richeome's text.

terms in which the other speaks, the better to ensure their silence. There is, in this drive to impose silence, a hidden gendering at work in Richeome. It draws on the advice of the spiritual guides, but is concealed either in terms of 'fidelity' as in the above quotation, or in those of 'modesty' coupled with a desire to be praised: 's'il vouloit estre à bon esceint modeste et en estre loüé, il se devoit taire du tout.'[38] The tactic here is of course not so much to argue that the translator was in fact a woman, as to—gently and quietly—feminize the opponent, so as to render 'her' speech, and those of 'her' kind effeminate, untrustworthy, and inauthoritative.

The underlying force of this line of attack grows in pressure as Richeome's *Deffence* retraces the translation and publishing history of the letter. He summarizes half a century of argument in one long sentence, and by way of a catalogue of misogynist and homophobic tropes:

Et ce Grec fut jadis supposé comme je diray tantost par gens de mesme esprit qu'eux et de mesme foy, et mis au vent pour faire peur aux idiots l'an 1551 quand l'heresie de Luther avoit jà sa teste formée et les cornes levé contre le ciel pour reformer le monde en le defigerant, et mettant le degast à toutes les bonnes moeurs, et quand la fumée du PVIS de l'abysme, dont parle S. Jean, estoit jà espanduë par la Chrestienté, et les SAUTERELLES engendrées de cette fumée-là voltigeoient à grands esquadrons par l'Europe pour piquer de leurs queües à guise de scorpions infernaux à la mort eternelle les hommes charnels, hommes de ventre comme sauterelles et ennemis de longs voyages et plus de longues peines: et partant mensonge en cet original et mensonge en Grec, et mauvais commencement de preface fondé sur deux mauvais pilotis.[39]

Richeome is enjoying himself here. The polemic has a lexicon derived in part from the apocalyptic scriptures and in larger part from Bellarmine, but it has a rhythm and underlying direction all of its own. He cannot, yet, quite embrace the argument concerning the inauthenticity of the letter with conviction and so adduces reasons why Gregory meant something other than what Reformers took him to mean. But when he returns to the question of authenticity, he does so with all the more vigour. Did, he asks, the translator really have no 'autre machine pour combatre les Pelerinages que la banderolle d'une epistre esgareé, portant à faux l'inscription et le nom de sainct Gregoire?'[40] This letter is no more by Gregory of Nyssa than

---

[38] Ibid.   [39] Ibid., fols. 2ᵛ–3ⁱ.   [40] Ibid., fols. 4ⁱ–5ⁱ.

heretics, in 1551 or 1604, are part of the Catholic, Apostolic, and Roman Church. Gregory was a saint, who talks of celebrating mass at the altars of Cappadocia, and must therefore have been a Catholic, therefore not a Huguenot, and therefore could not have written a letter condemning pilgrimage. In this way Richeome warms to his theme. But thus far he has been fencing, and the real thrust comes when he turns the knife into the *style* of his adversary, attacking him not for his inadequate use of a foreign language, but for his improper understanding of the terms of rhetoric, and of French.

Quoting once again, Richeome shows how his opponent divides pilgrims into 'ignorants, timides et obstinez'; but this is false 'division' and only demonstrates what, in a resonant phrase, he terms the 'jargon des errans':

qui lors qu'ils redoutent l'auctorité des Docteurs Catholiques et n'y peuvent responre, recourent aux lettres closes et disent que ceux-là sçavent bien la verité, mais qu'ils ne la veulent pas dire; c'est deviner regardant la Lune, c'est aller trop avant à la conscience d'autruy et calomnier sans conscience.[41]

In using the 'jargon des errans' the translator proves himself to be 'aussi peu conscientieux en son assertion que pauvre Logicien en sa division, en laquelle, comme je viens de monstrer, il distribue un TOUT, en des membres qui ne sont point'.[42] There follows one of Richeome's customary combinations of reversal and identification: it is the heretics who are 'tous timides et ignorants' and this unnamed translator 'en est le patron et les represente en soy tous'.[43]

Accusing the other of using jargon is a means to reinforce orthodox language; declaring the rhetorical incompetence of his kind allows you to parade your own rhetorical prowess. Having widened the scope of his attack, established its broad outlines, and laid a number of metaphorical mines ('errans', 'jargon', 'hommes de ventre'), Richeome can focus on a closer demolition of the translator's sentence style. Heretics write badly and this one proves it by concluding the preface with the accusation that those who favour pilgrimage *'ne veulent entrer au Royaume celeste, et en defendent l'entrée aux autres'*.[44] What matters to Richeome here is not whether this is true or false, but that it is a badly constructed argument. The margin

---

[41] Richeome, *Deffence*, fols. 7ʳ⁻ᵛ.   [42] Ibid., fol. 7ᵛ.
[43] Ibid., fol. 8ʳ.   [44] Ibid., fol. 9ᵛ.

signals 'vaines nuances', and the text proper offers an alternative lesson in sentence construction, imaged by way of the performance of a masculine, muscular art:

C'est une periode finale d'une plume evantée et un javelot jetté par un bras sans art et sans nerfs: car au lieu de donner à sa bute et boucler son discours par sa conclusion, il s'oublie de sa fin et tire en l'air. Il falloit conclurre en particulier contre ceux qui font ou approuvent les Pelerinages de bouche et les condamnent en leur conscience: car de ceux-cy il parloit en particulier, et non de prendre un si grand large pour conclusion: C'estoit donner au blanc encor que la bale fut de plume.[45]

It is a feature of effeminate heretical 'jargon', then, to make a habit of quibbling over the 'sens' of words, to dispute 'sur la pointe d'une exception', to create 'vaines nuances', and leave a host of ambiguities open. They should take more care not to do so, Richeome warns, lest the orthodox turn the jargon—or the javelin—against them. This he duly does, leading to a graphic, bodily, and gendered conclusion to this stage of the argument, in which reversal is followed, again, by identification. The accusation of 'superstition' levelled against pilgrims rebounds back onto their critics, and the present translator is identified as being kin to the heretics of 1551.[46] Together, this faithless and monstrous brood have brought forth unwanted offspring: 'ce Grec mentionné chez Guill. Morel par les Centuriateurs et emprunté par ce traducteur, est un avorton.'[47] The translator's claim to have consulted the original Greek text published by Morel in 1551 is thus refigured as the last in a series of illicit couplings—revealed most tellingly in the writer's inability to put sentences together properly. The 'hommes de ventre' cannot, it seems, but produce an unwanted, foreign, thing; and one unworthy of having seen the light of publication.

Richeome's sexually aggressive rhetoric echoes the gendered and sexually fearful tone of Gregory's arguments against pilgrimage, exemplified in his anxiety about 'mixing' on the journey. Gregory counsels against travel in order to keep the body pure, but Richeome uses Gregory's rhetoric to reverse effect, urging all those (men) able to do so, to take to the roads, so as to clear them of those who travel in illegitimate ways. This combinatory rhetoric of reversal, identification, and disqualification structures the entire *Deffence*. Richeome does directly quote passages from the translation, and at one stage

---

[45] Ibid., fols. 9ᵛ 10ʳ.   [46] Ibid., fol. 11ᵗ.   [47] Ibid., fol. 12ᶠ.

transcribes the Greek; he seems in doing so to be taking on the voice of his opponent.[48] But this is less dialogue than ventriloquism. He mimics the 'faux bruit' of the translator in such a way as to render his voice comic, and so disqualify his arguments as logically absurd; all of which allows Richeome to identify his own voice as the sweetest and best.[49]

The same procedure applies to the translator's central argument about the letter's real addressees. Gregory warns that ascetics, monks, and nuns should not travel, and the Reformer takes this to refer, in this age of the priesthood of all believers, to everyone.[50] Richeome quotes this reading, but does so only in order to highlight the error in logical consistency it exemplifies: 'tirant une conclusion generale d'un faict particulier. Cette façon d'argumenter n'est pas bonne.' It is, he continues, as absurd as arguing as follows:

Le VIN n'est pas bon aux Febricitans, LA MARCHANDISE n'est pas seante aux gens nobles; LES ARMES ne conviennent poinct aux Ecclesiastiques, DONC personne ne doibt boire vin, ny estre marchant, ny gendarme; seroit-ce bien devider la fusée?[51]

Here again, rather than determine the validity of such an argument in its own terms—those of historical and social change—Richeome questions its validity in terms of logical competence, which he considers not subject to history. What for others is dialogue, for Richeome becomes 'deffence': the voice of the adversary, in its offending translation, is printed, captured, and incorporated into Richeome's own text, so as to be disfigured, italicized, and rhetorically erased by the force of his own.

The further, and final, effect of this method is to recuperate Gregory's concerns to counter-Reformation argument. Thus, for instance, Gregory's episcopal anxiety regarding the security of the holy household in the absence of the pilgrim father is, for Richeome, less a matter for bishops and elders than for the individual house-

[48] Richeome, 'Au Lecteur', margin, fol. 14ʳ.

[49] This is a tactic Richeome had learned from Erasmus' *Ciceronianus;* he had rehearsed it the year before in his *Plainte apologétique* against Arnauld. See M. Fumaroli, *L'Age de l'éloquence* (1980), pp. 101–6, 240–2 (though he is silent on the *Deffence*).

[50] This was recognized as a wilful reading of the Greek by Casaubon, in his (1607) notes to du Moulin's (1605) edition. Gretser later admires Casaubon's scholarly integrity, but, like Lambeck after him, regrets Casaubon's being without the camp: 'viro docto, sed quod dolendum, in castris Calvinianis militanti' (see Gregory of Nyssa, *Select Writings*, p. 542). Richeome has no room for admiration or regret regarding his opponents in the war.

[51] Richeome, *Deffence*, fol. 13ʳ⁻ᵛ.

holder. What in Gregory (and his Reformist readers) is of concern to everyone and should be the subject of public debate (hence the translation), is for Richeome a matter of private discernment. It is between a man and his conscience, and, perhaps, his 'directeur de conscience'. The public debate about the worth of pilgrimage is thus displaced by a technology of divisive discernment; divisive in two crucially interdependent respects: externally, since it enables readers to distinguish between true and false guardians of the pilgrim tradition, and internally, since it allows them to question their own motivation.

This encapsulates the change in pilgrim terms effected from early to late Renaissance; what is initially a question of substance—'is pilgrimage a good or a bad thing?'—is suspended, and replaced by one of character and performance: 'what is my motivation?' This is a series of moves akin to those which mark the stages in the development of the *Guides* outlined above. Advice becomes codified as 'method', and once pilgrimage becomes grasped as a question of style, there are those who have it and those who do not. An argument about the worth of pilgrimage is displaced first into an argument about ways of travelling, and then, as if by accident, into ways of arguing. In the process, the identification of the 'true' pilgrim with Castela's 'personne Chrestienne' is confirmed in ways we now recognize as orthodox. Rehearsing the terms of the devotional handbooks and the *Guides*, Richeome outlaws curiosity (almost always, in this text, 'vaine'), and outlines the 'intention' of the 'bon Pelerin'. He (for it is always he) leaves home:

avec une pure intention . . . pour honorer Dieu avec plus grande affection, pour faire penitence et apprendre l'humilité et la patience et retourner en sa maison plus sage et plus riche de vertu, et non pour vaine curiosité, pour voir les païs et les villes, pour prendre ses passetemps.[52]

Richeome does not always ignore the arguments against him, nor does he only echo the terms of others. The manner in which the above sentence continues acknowledges that local pilgrimage in particular can become a carnivalesque suspension of social norms. But it does so only in order to assert the need to punish such abuses: '[non pour prendre ses passetemps/] moins encor pour semer noises et exercer des inimitiez; comme souvent il est advenu ez Pelerinages qui se font ez lieu voisins par gens de mesme contree, qui sont faictes dignes de punition exemplaire.'[53]

[52] Ibid., fol. 18ᵛ.   [53] Ibid., fol. 19ᵛ.

'Noises' again; though of course in French the term does not primarily have to do with sound, it does, across languages, echo the 'faux bruit' of what opponents say pilgrimage can be all about. Even in the French this is a teasing reference to just that side of the practice of pilgrimage which Gregory most fears, and which, in Richeome's own terms, 'est advenu souvent'. But where it does happen, he argues for 'punition exemplaire'. He also suggests a number of further, apparently material, points which should maintain the purity of the literal practice. The first is to accept that certain people should not travel:

ceux qui ne les peuvent accomplir sans prejudice de leur famille ou de leur charge, ou encor sans risque de leur vie et santé; Et partant ceux qui ont femme et enfans qu'ils doivent regir et gouverner, ou encor nourrir de leur travail, ou qui sans femme exercent quelque charge publicque, qui administrent la justice, qui preschent en l'Eglise, enseignent aux escoles d'importance ou font choses semblables, ou finalement sont maladifs et de petite vie.[54]

This applies to all pilgrimages. It is even more true for the Jerusalem journey, which should not be seen as essential for such people—despite Jerome's having stated ('avec une clause hardie et preignante') that pilgrimage is 'une partie de la foy':

Car la providence divine a si bien pourveu de moyens de devotion à ses enfans en cecy, qu'elle n'a laissé aucun païs, aucune ville ou village, ny presque aucun endroit de la Chrestienté, où elle n'ait faict reluire quelque particulier rayon de ses graces, y faisant des lieux celebres et propres pour servir d'exercice de religion et pieté aux bons Pelerins.[55]

This is characteristic of Richeome's method. He first adopts the literal terms of Gregory's anxiety about the social dangers of pilgrimage, identifying himself with the Father; he then adapts, or reverses these concerns, by making them figural; his final move is to disqualify those who insist on reading the fears literally. Privileging a figural over a literal reading of the Greek has the effect of emptying Gregory's 'inns and hostelries of the East' of actual foreign bodies, and so making them safe for French pilgrims to visit. It further generates a host of sites all over Europe for those who cannot undertake the Jerusalem pilgrimage. And, finally, it produces a technology of discernment which, in distinguishing between 'true' and 'false' pilgrims, displaces the fundamental opposition between those who are for, and those who are against the practice altogether.

[54] Richeome, *Deffence*, fol. 17ʳ⁻ᵛ.   [55] Ibid., fol. 18ʳ⁻ᵛ.

There follow several pages of examples of the antiquity of pilgrimage, from Gregory's own time through to the present day. Grounding his conclusion on the authority of the Church, Richeome ends with a disingenuously gentle statement of faith in the literal journey: 'Il n'est pas voirement necessaire d'aller chercher la piété en païs estrange quand on la peut treuver chez soy, mais on la treuve quelquefois plus heureusement ailleurs que chez soy.'[56] This seems an odd summation to a defence of pilgrimage, but it is consonant with the rhetorical design of the *Deffence*. For Richeome argues that the true pilgrims' investment in figural language is what enables them either to travel or to remain at home. Over-literal readings (such as those of the 'errans') lead to attachment to the details of the journey, and so to sin. The true reader of the pilgrim tradition knows that the real *can* be found at home, but can also occasionally be found more happily— 'quelquefois plus heureusement'—in the course of a journey elsewhere. The journey is neither inherently dangerous nor inherently sacred: it is all a matter of style.

In this way Gregory's reminders of the dangers of the road, like those of spiritual error which underlie pilgrimage and about which Castela and Granada both obsess in their *Guides*, are forgotten. They are displaced by the cultivation of two connected kinds of pleasure: that which comes of being on the winning side in a polemic, and that of knowing oneself to be one of the happy few who read the world properly. At once appropriating and silencing the voices both of outright opponents and of priestly doubters of literal pilgrimage, Richeome is thus able to generate a host of sanitized sacred sites, all 'particuliers et propres', for his projected community of readers, the 'bons Pelerins'. And it is all done, as if by accident, in the course of an argument about translation.

Go to Jerusalem if you feel happy about it, if you do not, there are lots of other places you can go which are just as good: such is the gentle summation of Richeome's otherwise violent argument. Resting on Church tradition it is also supported with reference to scripture, itself not 'commandement, mais advertissement, et douce semonce', and by a note in the margin: 'Dieu est plus admirable en certains lieux.'[57] Towards its conclusion, then, the *Deffence* softens, and Richeome's strident voice modulates into personable, reasonable

---

[56] Ibid., fol. 32ʳ⁻ᵛ.
[57] Ibid., fol. 33ʳ The reference is to Deut. 16, which legislates where Passover should be

tones. Defensive ventriloquism gives way to a more dialogic form of quotation and reference, as texts other than the offending translation are brought into play. The Psalmist, Paul, Jerome, Ambrose, Augustine, Eusebius, Bede, Church Councils, the Queen of Sheba, Plato, Aristotle. . . . Authorities are cited, and analogies are drawn between pilgrims and other travellers: all to the good of the pilgrim, and offending none but enemies of the Church.

So, for instance, the Queen of Sheba was moved to acquire 'la sapience de Salomon', Plato and Aristotle travelled for 'quelque gain de sciences humaines', and merchants travel for 'les presens perissables'.[58] We have seen that pilgrims from Erasmus to Castela commonly called on such figures to authorize their journeys, with a greater or lesser degree of anxiety about extending the terms of pilgrimage to merchants or pagan philosophers. By this stage in his *Deffence* Richeome is no longer anxious about anything. He has won his own battle, and so suggests, quietly, that it seems unreasonable to prevent true pilgrims from travelling if all these other characters are able to do so, moved as they are by what he terms—for once changing the adjective, and with some cheek—'honeste curiosité'. This he follows by bringing the 'variété' *topos* to bear on the pilgrims' travels, by drawing an analogy with networks of friendship and trade. These are lines of argument Castela found painful to draw; Richeome does not:

Et comme nous voyons qu'il [Dieu] faict produire plusieurs choses naturelles en des lieux qu'il ne donne pas aux autres pour lier l'amitié des hommes par le commerce des choses qu'il se communiquent entre eux, ainsi donne t'il de ses graces en un lieu qu'il ne donne point aux autres, c'est sa bonté, et sagesse . . . si Dieu les faicts tels pour sa gloire et pour le proffict de ses enfans font-ils mal de se mettre en chemin pour y aller admirer la gloire de leur pere et tirer profit de ses biens?

Voyla ce qu'en bref on peut dire de ce subject pour la foy Catholique contre la mescreance des errans.[59]

This is a powerfully persuasive final gesture. Richeome concludes the defence with the lexis of profit, and with a metaphor of paternal inheritance, performatively recuperating as he does so both the general argument, and the central terms of his opponents' criticism. 'Curiosité, proffict, gain, commerce, communication, gloire', all are

celebrated. Though it does indeed read as a defence of pilgrimage, it is hard to see how it supports the voluntarist approach Richeome here adopts.

[58] Richeome, *Deffence*, fol. 33ʳ.   [59] Ibid., fols. 33ʳ⁻ᵛ.

made part of (his) sacred design. To underline the degree to which the terms belong, as if by rights and nature, to the Church, and have been usurped by the illegitimate and unnatural Reformers, Richeome has one last gesture of attack to perform. It is, again, one of reversal, followed by identification. 'Le traducteur', he begins, 's'est esgaré voulant couper le chemin aux passans'. The reason 'les errans haïssent les pelerinages' is that they themselves are too concerned with literal 'commerce' which he defines in two connected ways.[60] The first is to argue that it is Reformers who calculate things in terms of financial rather than spiritual cost, claiming as they do that economic 'fraiz' and the physical 'frain, regle et travail' of pilgrimage are ruinous. Their attachment to an over-literal understanding of the real is what prevents them from undertaking the real, and spiritual, journey; thus the reversal. There follows the identification and attendant disqualification by way of the second sense of 'commerce': gendered, eroticized, and a representation of the Reformers' effeminate bodies: 'ilz veulent aller au Ciel par un chemin de velours parsemé de lis et de roses, et ont en haine tout ce qui contrarie à leur sensualité.'[61]

Richeome clearly derives more than just the gendering and physical emphasis of his argument from Gregory. Certainly, the insistent shifts between affirmation and negation which structure Gregory's Late Antique attack on pilgrimage are rehearsed and replayed to work as a defence of the practice in the very different context of counter-Reformation. Richeome is able to adopt Gregory's method because he ignores its meaning; in particular, he leaves unaddressed the central critique of the Letter: that the literal journey is all too often an excuse for pleasure, and that even those whose hearts are closed to the world cannot help but find themselves subject to the temptations of the road. In identifying Reformers' bodies as sites of sensual excess, Richeome distracts attention from the minds and bodies of pilgrims themselves. In this way he avoids discussion of the danger that the pilgrim might, on the journey, lose his specific identity to that of the *voyeur*, or the sexual tourist.

But there is a rhetorical price to be paid for arguing in this way. Richeome does not re-enact Gregory's sublimation of the body to figure; perhaps because he cannot. For his is a sacred rhetoric dependent on reference to the physical body, and his understanding of pilgrimage is consequently, and resolutely, physical. To sanction the

---

[60] Ibid., fol. 34ʳ.   [61] Ibid., fols. 34ᵛ–35ʳ.

body on the road, he must argue for journey as a potentially healthy activity, for those who know how to travel. This in turn depends on the construction of a proper pilgrim traveller, much as it does for the *Guide* writers. Richeome's essential contribution to this argument is to capture the terms of the Reformers' critique, and the Reformers' reading of Gregory in particular, in order to reinvent them as central to his defence of literal pilgrimage.

He knows that he cannot enjoy, let alone match the rhetorical play of difference between literal and figural place, between actual and metaphorical journeys that Gregory's Letter sets in motion. Gregory has no institutional allegiance to a literal understanding of pilgrimage; he writes at a time when pilgrimage is first being developed, and he argues that the rise of this new practice should be resisted. Nor does he have the Jesuit's sense of how the body can be engaged in the performance of devotion. Richeome is, however, committed, along with his Church, to the idea of pilgrimage as embodied in actual men and women's journeys beyond the bournes of their parishes and that this demands a physical reading of terms. So, with some considerable, and disingenuous, skill, he acknowledges the rigours of travel, the better to then reconfigure them as invigorating for the *vray* pilgrim, who rejects the lassitude and sensual overindulgence of his detractors. It then becomes possible to argue, in good conscience, that the literal pilgrimage is a heroic spiritual act; it becomes possible to leave home on a pilgrimage 'pour faire penitence et apprendre l'humilité et la patience'. And, crucially, the chance to 'retourner en sa maison plus sage et plus riche de vertu' is reasserted even, or especially, after a literal pilgrimage, with all its material and devotional dangers.[62] Indeed, being able to do so identifies the 'bon Pelerin' with Castela's 'personne Chrestienne', one of the 'heureux', the blessed few.

Other readers of Gregory, from his own time to the late Renaissance, are less convinced. They will dispute the rightness of reading of pilgrim culture that Richeome presents, arguing in terms more focused than either Richeome or the pilgrim *Guides*. To these dissident readings we turn in conclusion to this chapter. Our focus—like theirs—will be the attempt to configure a different understanding of the worth of the journey, and of reading, from that of the polemists. What emerges from this attempt is the creation not so much of a

---

[62] Richeome, *Deffence*, fol. 18ᵛ.

person as a *place*, at once metaphorical, and physical; and from within this place, voices silenced by polemic begin to be heard.

Within Walls: The Pilgrim's Place

Dans la cellule ou Richeome nous fait méditer, pas une place
qui ne soit ou fresque ou vitrail.[63]

The early Renaissance convent was a very different place to the churches found in Late Antique Cappadocia to which Gregory originally refers, and for which he longs while in riotous and sin-soaked Jerusalem.[64] The seminary in which Richeome served, the churches in which he preached the defence of pilgrimage, and the rooms in private houses in which he was read, were different again. It is these places, and their relation to the kinds of changes in pilgrim discourse we have traced here, that the manuscript and publishing history of Gregory's letter encourages us to investigate. Seemingly insignificant details, such as additions to texts and arguments about translating the precise reach of this or that term within a Late Antique letter, reveal much about both the construction of the pilgrim person and of the pilgrim's place in the Renaissance. They also give some sense of the role of pilgrimage within the larger changes in the understanding of place and of persons brought about in early modern France.

Not least of the differences between the kinds of place listed above was likely to be found on their walls. The study walls of Richeome's readers, particularly within church institutions, were, very possibly, hung with paintings or tapestries, perhaps displaying the kinds of sacred image which Richeome wrote of so extraordinarily eloquently elsewhere.[65] And the churches in which readers worshipped may well have had stations of the cross tracing their way around the space. For by the time Richeome argues that literal pilgrimage is not essential to faith, but in truth a question of style, the counter-Reform has developed a number of compensatory rituals for those who could not,

---

[63] H. Bremond, *Histoire littéraire*, i. *L'Humanisme dévot* (1916), p. 37.

[64] See the seventeenth letter for Gregory's evocation of the town, *Select Writings*, pp. 542–5.

[65] See Richeome, *Tableaux Sacrez* (Paris, Sonnius, 1601) and *La Peinture spirituelle* (Lyon, Pierre Rigaud, 1611). As Fumaroli points out, the latter is in effect a guided tour, describing 'les peintures ornant le Séminaire des Jésuites de Rome, à Sant' Andrea del Quirinale', *L'Age de l'éloquence*, p. 262. See also Cave, *Devotional Poetry*, pp. 278–80.

or should not, travel to Jerusalem. Some of these Richeome refers to, in evoking the countryside bristling with local pilgrimage sites.

Others, such as the stations of the cross and the meditative pilgrimage, he leaves unaddressed: they will be the focus of our next chapter. There we shall see how the rhetorics of figural travel developed in the course of the Renaissance took Gregory's image of Christ's indwelling and figural movement within the penitent, and gave it intense physical force. For writers in this mode, acknowledgement of the place of the body need not merely be implied, it is explicitly recognized as central to pilgrimage, and even the sexual desires of the reader can be aroused and directed to a sacred end by meditation properly directed. Belleforest's translation of Guevara's *Livre du Mont de Calvaire* (1578) is one of several devotional guides which take the model of the 'descriptions de la Terre Sainte' to a graphic, bodily limit. The reader at home, concentrating on the details of the crucifixion, performs a substitutive ascent of Calvary, and in the process his or her body is engaged in intensely physical worship. Much devotional poetry of the period similarly displays and dissects exemplary bodies—those of Christ, of Saints, or of the reader—in lush and occasionally gory detail. Prayerful reading is made physical, useful, and also, on occasion, self-consciously pleasurable.[66]

As a guide to the way in which devotional writing developed to involve the body in imagined trajectories, we could usefully take Baxandall's discussion of the relations between painting and experience in the Italian Renaissance.[67] He writes persuasively of how orators and painters effect a 'marriage between the painting and the beholder's previous visualizing activity on the same matter'; the 'marriage' legitimizes visual pleasure, bringing together as it does so both the represented and the physical body. The way this is achieved becomes clear in the following passage from a *Garden of Prayer* composed, Baxandall tells us, for young girls:

The better to impress the story of the Passion on your mind and to memorise each action of it more easily, it is helpful and necessary to fix the places and people in your mind: a city for example which will be the city of Jerusalem— taking for this purpose a city that is well known to you. In this city find the principal places in which all the episodes of the Passion would have taken place . . . And then too you must shape in your mind some people, people

---

[66] See *Le Vray chemin* discussion above, with reference to fol. 40ʳ⁻ᵛ; and see Guevara, *Livre du Mont de Calvaire*, pp. 23–9. See also Cave, *Devotional Poetry*, pp. 32–8, 51–7.

[67] M. Baxandall, *Painting and Experience in Fifteenth Century Italy* (1972), p. 46.

well known to you, to represent for you the people involved in the Passion . . . every one of whom you will fashion in your mind. When you have done all this, putting all your imagination into it, then go into your chamber. Alone and solitary, excluding every external thought from your mind, start thinking of the beginning of the Passion, starting with how Jesus entered Jerusalem on the ass. Moving slowly from episode to episode, meditate on each one, dwelling on each single stage and step of the story. And if at any point you feel a sensation of piety, stop: do not pass on as long as that sweet and devout sentiment lasts.[68]

The 'marriage' is that of Christ's imagined body with that of the female reader; the pleasure legitimized by this marriage is at once visual, spiritual, and erotic. It also, in its emphasis on solitude, secures the protection of the virgins that Gregory's annotator had in mind. It seeks to occupy both their minds and their bodies, while they themselves are being kept within walls. This is also true of another imagined trajectory, suggested for other early Renaissance people unable to go on pilgrimage proper. Writing soon after the *Garden* was published, Johann Geiler, the popular preacher in Strasbourg, declares in his *Christliche Bilgerschaften zum ewigen Vatterland* that a prisoner incarcerated in a dungeon, and so unable to go to Rome for the 1500 Jubilee, need not be excluded from the benefits of the indulgences which were to be had that year. He calculated, from pilgrims' accounts, that it would take three weeks to walk to Rome, a week to visit all the churches, and three weeks to return: the prisoner should walk around his cell for six weeks, and sit still and pray for one. The pacings of a prisoner are transfigured through a rhetoric of reading: his restricted movements 'describe' the literal displacement of pilgrimage, and his literally arrested body is read as a figure for penitence.[69] The prisoner himself may or may not be able to read, we are not told. It is not his reading which is at issue, rather his body has, like those of the young girls to whom the *Garden* is addressed, been appropriated.

Like the young girls in the *Garden*, and yet also unlike them. For the man's body must literally move in order for the surrogate pilgrimage to be effective. The women's bodies, by contrast, are not addressed, and they move in the mind. What is the status of this difference? Does it express a fact akin to the fact that few women

---

[68] *Garden of Prayer* (Venice, 1494), quoted, Baxandall, ibid.
[69] J. Geiler, *Christliche Bilgerschaften zum ewigen Vatterland* (Strasbourg, 1512), fol. 206ᵛ.

travelled to Jerusalem; does it correspond to a historically located difference in gendered understandings of the pilgrim's place? Even in surrogate pilgrimages and even within prisons, men do actually move whereas women are moved—motion is for men, emotion for women? If so, then these images of immurement are complementary rather than identical; one is the negative of the other.

And yet, in defiance of the warnings of the figural *Guides* and the re-edited Fathers, and despite the alternative technologies of imaginary travel available to them, early modern men and women persisted in setting out from home on pilgrimage. They persisted in 'reading' pilgrimage literally with their bodies. Not all, of course, were Richeome's blissfully ignorant 'bons pelerins', unaware of the arguments and dangers they faced, pursuing their ways 'en paix'. Many were subject to bodily anxiety: they feared being eaten by wolves after losing their possessions to thieves, or being eaten by giants when they hid behind lettuce leaves; they risked being forced into slavery, skewered like a kebab and covered in bacon while slowly roasted over charcoal fire, or more prosaically, burned, or cut to pieces, and sold as relics to Franciscans for having dared to peer into Solomon's temple.[70] Others were assailed by questions, both before setting out and on the road itself. They worried about how to keep the laws of pilgrim conduct. They asked, with Erasmus, himself echoing Gregory: 'What use is physically going to Jerusalem, when you carry Sodom, Egypt and Babylon deep within you?'[71] Or they asked themselves what Turler's margin notes tells us is 'a common question': '*Whether traueyling do a man more good or harm?*'[72]

Gregory is one of the few to ask this question for a woman traveller as well as for 'a man'. Following his example, we need to ask this 'common question' again, and to question the way it is gendered in relation to what I have termed the pilgrim's *place*. Gregory's greatest concern is expressed in reference to women's bodies. One of his letters—the seventeenth—addressed to three Godly women thinking of undertaking a pilgrimage urges them to think hard about the dangers involved; another—the second—is read in the Renaissance as authorizing the immurement of virgins, ostensibly to save them from

[70] For more on these instances, culled from Balourdet, Castela, Thevet, and Rabelais, see below, Ch. 7.

[71] Erasmus, *Enchiridion*, fol. xxxi[v]. The Latin reads 'An magnum est quod corpore Hierosolymam adis, cum intra temeteipsum sit Sodoma, sit Aegiptus, sit Babylon.'

[72] Turler, *The Traueiler*, p. 4. See above, Ch. 2.

themselves.[73] Richeome, in commenting the second, feminizes his opponent, but he clearly does not have women in mind either as readers, or as potential pilgrims.

That Richeome narrates no examples of dangers specific to women, and tells no tales about specific women experiencing danger on the road is perhaps not surprising. Even when counselling against their travelling he does not want to give the practice bad press. That *no* pilgrims and very few other travellers narrate such tales is surprising, however. The dangers the journey presents to women are present as an imagined, anticipated fear; they are rarely, if ever, narrated in terms of exemplary, lived experience. Indeed the few women who do merit mention figure as demonstrating the positive, usually healing power of this or that (usually Marian) shrine. So, for instance, Maignan celebrates the Queen's travels to Liesse on 5 October 1575 in search of fertility, and Villamont celebrates the return, at Loreto, of a French nobleman's wife from a state of semi-conscious 'folie' which had plagued her and her husband for a number of years.[74] Each of these instances speak *of* and not directly *for* the women whose histories they narrate. The cure in each case is narratively represented by means of an exchange of information between men about the power of a given shrine. Maignan's text is addressed to the king, and Villamont hears the story (which he narrates in Italian) from the French woman's husband; she herself is mute until cured, and is then hurried home.

Rather than telling us more about the women to whom they refer, or indeed anything about their motivations and their needs, these instances give us pause. The fact that the shrine is in each instance Marian, and that the malady cured is represented as specific to women does not make these into women's stories. The accounts are *about* women pilgrims; they speak of women as the objects of representation. But what of their own stories, what of women pilgrims' experience: can we locate instances of women exercising the choice to act as objects of their own representation within the lived narratives of pilgrimage? The immediate answer to this last question is no. Röhricht—the most comprehensive bibliographer of pilgrimage

---

[73] The seventeenth letter was edited (but not, as mentioned, translated) alongside the second, in 1605.

[74] See E. Maignan, *Petit discours de l'utilité des Voyages ou Pelerinages* (1578), 'Au Roi'; and Villamont, *Les Voyages du seigneur de Villamont* (1611), pp. 121–2. The nobleman is named Pierre d'Argent13y; his wife, unnamed, is from Grenoble.

writing—does not mention one pilgrim account authored by a woman in the years 1490–1615, and I have found none to supplement his list. Some pilgrims do record the presence of women in their company. So Possot, for instance, names two 'soeurs pelerines' subjected to unwelcome sexual advances on their arrival in Jaffa. Yet even these women are 'representative' rather than present in their own right; their fate demonstrates both the wickedness of (some) locals ('Mores et Turcs') and the goodness of others ('chrestiens de la ceinture') who come to their assistance.[75]

Within the accounts of other pilgrim men, it is hard to recognize actual women behind the flurry of word games and figurative play through which they are, on rare occasions, presented. Fabri, once again, seems both to anticipate and best represent the kinds of language used about women fellow-pilgrims later in the Renaissance. He mentions women on three occasions, each of which frames them as medical and moral 'cases': the first are, 'through old age, scarcely able to support their own weight'; the second is revealed as being pregnant on board ship.[76] The last, a Flemish woman, travelling with her husband, is castigated for making her fellow pilgrims' lives a misery by embodying the twinned vices of 'curiositas', and 'garrullitas'. Fabri concludes his brief textual treatment of her with a redirection of the misogynist tropes he has marshalled so far, and by way of an ironically rewritten Pauline gloss: 'She was a thorn in the eyes of us all.'[77]

Even these rare women do not figure in the German vernacular version of Fabri's travels printed by Feyrabend: yet more women are erased from the printed history of Renaissance pilgrimage. It becomes all the more important, then, to notice that Geiler's prisoner still moves; that the girl in the *Garden* reads in such a way as to make a Jerusalem of Venice. For each might find in such redescription of his or her enforced home both physical pleasure and spiritual consolation. To deny either the possibility of this pleasure, this consolation, is to argue that they cannot work out a kind of freedom within the policed borders of home. To say, in Foucauldian vein, that the conditions of this possibility are not really there, that they are denied by the structure of the power relations which determine her subjectivity as a woman reader at this juncture of the Renaissance, for instance, is to play along with a fantasy of power even more elaborate

---

[75] D. Possot [*Description du*] *Voyage de la Terre Sainte* (ed. C. Schefer), pp. 154–5.
[76] Fabri, *Wanderings*, i, pp. 11, 41.   [77] Ibid., pp. 166–7.

than that of her spiritual director. For the author of the *Garden*, like Geiler in his sermon, knows that we can always read, in Certeau's terms, as poachers.[78] That they know this is evident from the degree of phenomenological detail with which they structure their imaginary trajectories. Both the spiritual director and the preacher know that agile readers can use a guide-book to take them on journeys of the mind beyond the reach of the law, of literal Jerusalem, or of the author's own imaginings.

Not all poachers are caught; and perhaps Certeau's terms are no more proper to this context than Foucault's. Perhaps neither Geiler nor the *Garden* writer thought of themselves as gamekeepers, policing the dangerous forests of readerly desire. It remains the case that their texts can usefully be read as early moments in the history of pilgrim subjectivity described in this and the previous chapter: a history written, above all, in polemical mode. The tone of polemic is hard to get out of your voice when you speak as a pilgrim in the Renaissance. It is the voice of the (church) Fathers, and it is they who taught you how to speak. Thus, whether you are arguing for the validity of the journey proper, or arguing that the proper journey is one which takes you nowhere other than inside yourself, you are still arguing. You cannot help but take up a position on whether men and women should be either on or off the road, within walls or free from suspicion and murmur.

It is this insistent tone of argument that frustrates the attempt to hear and listen to other voices. If we do want to know more than the polemical texts directly reveal, then we need to attempt further, differently formulated, questions, and interrogate the nature of the tropes which take the place of those whom our authors silence. Such questions begin with basics: what is the referential status of the bodies obsessively mentioned in these texts? They might develop as follows: is it really women the writers fear, or is it that the female body has become a privileged site of anxiety for pilgrimage writing? Perhaps the pilgrim's body—male or female—is less really present in our texts, than a point of cathexis at which the discourse of spiritual direction agonises about its own effectiveness? Certainly such a reading of the place of the body at the conjunction of desire and language does recur in the Christian tradition. And perhaps nowhere more

---

[78] See M. Certeau, *L'Invention du quotidien: 1. Arts de faire* (1990), p. xxxvi: 'Le quotidien s'invente avec milles manières de braconner.'

powerfully than in the pollution anxieties and fantasies of late Renaissance men as their minds and pens turn to the matter of pilgrimage.

Perhaps. But there is also an important sense in which to read the body in this way is to mime the evasions and collusions of some of the texts under study. In particular, the move to hypostasizing 'the body' from the initial question about certain women's bodies shadows the troping moves of Fabri, Gregory, and Richeome, and repeats that performed by Castela in his *Guide* and Granada in his *Vray chemin*. For it reinscribes women as woman, and woman as *the* figure for seduction. If we ourselves repeat this gesture, we also deny the resistance to just such metaphorizing displacements to which these texts at certain points bear witness. Gregory, like Grandgousier, insists on referring to women as embodied people, whose material, physical needs produce problems on the road: hence the anxiety about 'mixing' in the hostelries and with monks at home while the pilgrim is away, or the concern as to how a woman is to be helped on to a horse.

But even this plea for real reference has a tendency to collapse back into figure. For there is a sense in which even Gregory's, Castela's and Lipsius' women's bodies are not truly the women's bodies (proper to the women) so much as men's fictions of the same. Certainly they are unthinkable to these men except in relation to their own bodies, and they are, as a consequence, unknowable to us except in the men's terms. And the resonances of these terms often elude the men's conscious understanding. Are we to act as their Father confessors, or their analysts, creating the space for them first to betray and then to forgive themselves? And will they forgive us for forcing them to reveal things they never knew? There is little to be said for a historically attuned cultural poetics conceived of as dialogue, if, in the end, we allow *them* only to say things they never quite knew they meant. We may well, in doing so, acquire, by using our skills in forensic interrogation, more 'knowledge' about them, but we risk never quite acknowledging that their voice lives on in ours. This is to echo Richeome's own strategy: it is not dialogue but ventriloquism.

Menedemus: The Stay-at-Home

We saw in the previous chapter that *Guide* writers tell pilgrims not to look at, or over, the walls of the places they visit. In this chapter, we have seen that even those who argue the worth of the literal journey can never quite look over the metaphorical walls of polemic which surround them even on the road. Some try to look through these walls: they construct puns, apply pressure to the terms to see if there is space between the rocks, they displace the words into different languages, or rearrange the stones into different shapes. But they find they are still building walls, between each other, and between themselves and the others they left their families to find. And even Utopia has walls. Rabelais has Frère Jean imagine that his French Utopia, Thélème, will be without 'murmurs' because there will be no 'murs'. But the French foundational language game relies, of course, on there being a 'mur' on both sides of both the pun and the place it seeks to found. He has the place built, walls and all, anyway, and hangs these walls later in the history with 'marchandises peregrines'.[79]

The 'marchandises' on the walls of Thélème—tapestries of Achilles' exploits and other such things, woven on islands beyond the pillars of Hercules—bear witness to journeys into other worlds. In this, they are like the texts we will explore in the remaining two parts of this book, as we move from texts *about* pilgrimage to accounts which are *of* pilgrim journeys. The worlds which actual pilgrims and their fictional counterparts encounter may be found at the distant centre of the earth; or they may be in an 'arrière boutique', a secret self not disclosed either to the reader, or fully to the writer. Some travellers—Zuallart among them—move and write as if there were few walls around them; they are the Mandevilles and the Panurges of pilgrimage writing. Others, such as Regnaut, Balourdet, Dublioul, and Cuchermoys, appear *not* to see what is really there, and notice only those things which other pilgrims have noted before them; they are too concerned to conform to Castela's ideal pilgrim figure to acknowledge that they are on foreign ground. Others still—such as Thevet, Villamont, or Valimbert—climb up on to the metaphorical walls of pilgrim discourse, they go on a literal pilgrimage and use pilgrim terms in their texts, the better to see what is happening beyond the scope of their habitual immurement, and to write things beyond their inherited imaginings. Whichever narrative model the individual traveller adopts, the terms in which the 'lesson' of pilgrimage is imparted ensure its survival. For it is the writing, rather than the

---

[79] *Gargantua* 52; *Quart Livre* 2. I return to Rabelais' walls and the 'marchandises peregrines' below, Ch. 7.

lesson, which maintains the possibility of the play, and allows for the noise of other worlds to be detected in amidst the rustle of pilgrim language.

One last detail: what Richeome terms the '*noises et inimitiez*' of pilgrims' inns. As noted above, Gregory's most telling displacement of the terms of pilgrimage is to render home more sacred than away. This is his 'lesson'. It is taught by way of a linguistic game, whose rhetorical force derives from the fact that the same term is used for the infected inns which the pilgrims must pass through and for the chambers of the heart which Christ may visit: both are, in the Latin translations which survive, *diversoria*. By arguing that the true pilgrim should be more concerned to ensure the cleanliness of his or her internal *diversoria*, so as to make the 'chambers of the heart' ready for Christ's visit, Gregory encapsulates the kinds of moves we have been tracing here. First, the place on the road is internalized and the need to travel away from home is rendered obsolete. Secondly, the now static pilgrim is given a new activity, and a new identity: that of cultivating their internal house and garden. Thus the shift of this one term anticipates both the domestication of pilgrimage and the opening of the space for discursive play within pilgrimage writing which accompanies this move. It is a move rehearsed and repeated in relation to other, similar terms in the course of pilgrimage history: for many, the last move in the dance is Erasmus' dialogue, the *Peregrinatio religionis ergo* with which we began. We return to Erasmus, and to the details of how the pilgrim's place and the terms of pilgrim subjectivity converge, in conclusion to the first part of this book.

Ogygius tells of his pilgrimage as a series of stages, which he terms *stationes*. This is a term which came into Latin—and then vernacular—pilgrimage writing only late in its history. Egeria, in the earliest extant pilgrimage account proper, and one of very few to be written by a woman, never writes of *stationes*; nor yet does she mention *diversoria*, indeed she seems oblivious to the material conditions of the pilgrimage and to those perilously indiscrete inns in which she must have mixed with all kinds of travellers. Her word for the stopping points in her journey is *mansio*. Initially a term of measurement rather than value, *mansio* refers in the early part of her text to the distance travelled in a day's journeying. In that it represents a unit of progression towards Jerusalem, it has implicit spiritual value, but it is not glossed as such. Within Jerusalem itself, *mansiones* are the points of liturgical supension along the way which retraces Christ's actual steps; at each *mansio* the appropriate passage is read from the Bible, and an appropriate prayer is said.[80]

The cognate term *mansion* survives into early French pilgrimage accounts as a term similarly signifying, initially, a unit of measurement, a pause in the journey. So, Huen, in his early vernacular account of the Jerusalem pilgrimage, notes: 'Revoluz xliiij Jours que mansion avons faicte en venise, desirans tous les Jours notre expedition.'[81] Huen, though he does suggest that French pilgrims should stay at a particular inn while languishing in Venice, does not complain about the state of the inn, still less represent this, or any other hostel as morally suspect. Like Egeria, he seems disinclined to speak of the material calculations of the journey in these terms. If specific inns are indeed dangerous, and if travelling is especially dangerous for women as the *Guides* suggest, it is not in pilgrims accounts that instances of danger are recounted.

Within Jerusalem itself, Huen's structuring unit of physical progression is the term *item*; the devotional pauses on the journey are marked by signs denoting the number of indulgences to be gained in each place. Unlike Egeria, in other words, Huen does not take the term *mansion* with him to Jerusalem; it does not occur again in his text after Venice, except once on Mt Sion, where it appears to be a misprint for the 'maison' of the monks.[82] The sacred places themselves are either referred to by name, or, generically, with reference to the vernacular version of Ogygius' (rather than Egeria's) Latin term: *station*. 'A chescune station estoit predication ou declaration de ses dignitez: ou tous excitez estions a escouter.'[83]

These terms—*item*, typographic signs for indulgences, and *station*—thus displace Egeria's repeated use of *mansion*. Three different terms for one; the linguistic inflation represents the new economy of pilgrimage, as people travel to collect indulgences, and earn remission from the time spent in purgatory atoning for their sins (a motivation for pilgrimage altogether foreign to either Gregory, or Egeria). The terms of this inflation, and the effects it will have on the construction of new pilgrim identities later in the Renaissance are made clear as Huen returns to Rome, where his three terms converge. His

---

[80] For more on Egeria, see L. Spitzer, 'The Epic Style of the Pilgrim Aetheria', *Comparative Literature* 1:3 (1949), pp. 225–58, and Campbell, pp. 15–33.
[81] Huen, *Le grant voyage*, fol. viij[r].   [82] Ibid., fol. xvj[r].   [83] Ibid., fol. xviij[r].

compendium of pilgrimage material concludes with a series of lists, detailing the *stations* of the churches of Rome, each of which is signed with an *item*, and each of which gains a set number of indulgences, duly marked with a cross in the margin of the text.

Huen explains to the reader that he has listed these points as a kind of appendix, and marked his text in this way because of the Holy Father's recent decree: pilgrims no longer need to travel all the way to the Holy Sepulchre to gain plenary indulgences: 'Celluy ou celle [*sic*] quil pour cause de devotion oraison ou pelerinage parviendra a nostre siege de sainct jehan de latran il est absolut de tous ses pechez.'[84] Jerusalem is displaced from the centre of the world; Rome is—in part to fund the building of ever more splendid church walls—decreed to be (equivalent to) the City of God. This is, perhaps, some way from Gregory's displacement of the 'sites of contagion' into the chambers of the Christian soul. But one translation, one displacement, does lead to another: Egeria's fourth century Latin *mansiones* move from being units in a day's devotional travel, to being vernacular *stations*, first on the road, and then imagined in early Renaissance Venetian hearts. They are then externalized once again, painted, or engraved, and hung on those splendid walls, which late Renaissance pilgrims will marvel at as they make their way to Jerusalem; and to which cultural travellers today make pilgrimage.

For of course this process of translation between the road, and representation, and then back again does not end with Huen, or with the invention of the stations of Rome. As we noted above, Ogygius uses what had become a cherished pilgrim term when he describes his journey as a series of 'stations'. But Menedemus has also been on a journey of sorts while his neighbour has been away: he has risen in social status, and has also acquired mastery of the language games of the learned. He is thus able to effect a further displacement of the terms of pilgrimage, albeit to a less than devotional end. In conclusion to their discussion, Menedemus explains to Ogygius why he is such a stay-at-home by advising the pilgrim to keep his house in order and to understand *stationes* in a particular way. Rather than treading along the road to Compostella, Menedemus has, he says, 'enough to do with [his] stations of Rome'.[85] Ogygius protests that Menedemus has never been to Rome:

---

[84] Huen, fol. cxciij[v].   [85] Erasmus, *The Colloquies*, trans. C. Thompson, p. 312.

Men[edemus]. I'll tell you. Here's how I wander about at home. I go into the living room, and I see that my daughter's chastity is safe. Coming out of there into my shop, I watch what my servants, male and female, are doing. Then to the kitchen, to see if any instruction is needed. From here to one place and another, observing what my children and my wife are doing, careful that everything be in order. These are my Roman stations.[86]

Egeria, the unmarried woman pilgrim and ascetic, is taken off the pilgrim road and sequestered at home, lest she become a thorn in the eyes of male pilgrims. Gregory's chambers of the Christian heart are translated first to the walled Venetian garden, and then the Flemish husband's household. A unit of devotional progression is redescribed as an item of capital: spiritual, financial, or cultural. Bodies also become transfigured into commodities. The bodies of women and other subalterns become the pilgrim's business, are imaged as lock-up shops, whose doors and windows need to be bolted at night: Menedemus defines the truly modern pilgrim as one who best attends to his own body by securing others, and so properly husbanding his resources. An inversion of a kind has taken place which extends Gregory's earlier inversion of pilgrim terms. The body—male or female—is here neither travelling in search of the holy other, nor prepared in quiet meditation for the entry and indwelling of Christ; rather it measures its movements, controls its emotions, and counts its blessings at home.

The spiritual guides of Granada and others explored in the last chapter take this image further and give it body and movement within the home. True to the methods of pilgrimage, each morning's meditation, for instance, refers to, and begins with a reading from, scripture. So Wednesday morning concerns those sections of the gospels which tell of Christ's presentation to Annania, Caiphas, Herod, and Pilate, and conclude with his being tied to the pillar and whipped. The text quotes the passages, in translation, and then, through direct address, impresses on the reader the extent to which this entire scenario was staged for him:

faut que face [ce jour] plusieurs stations en la compagnie de ton Sauveur, si ne veux t'enfuir avec les disciples, ou si tes pieds ne sont trop pesants, et paresseux, pour aller par le chemin que feit notre Seigneur pour ton salut. Cinq diverses fois il est à ce jour mené devant divers juges, et en la maison de

[86] Ibid.

chacun il est mal traité pour toy, et par tes debtes et demerites. En l'une des maisons il est souffleté, en l'autre craché, en l'autre mocqué, en l'autre fouëtté, et couronné d'espines, et en fin condamné à mort. Regarde si ces stations ne meritent pas qu'on y aille pieds nus, et le sang en decoulant, et si ce n'est pas pour nous crever le coeur, et nous induire à compassion. Allons donc à la premiere station.[87]

There follows a set piece description of ecphrastic bravado, in which each of the 'stations/maisons' are placed before the eyes and further senses of the reader. The five stations here are characterized as 'maisons', although the gospels do not group these places in this way; this has a dual edge.

In the first instance each 'maison' represents a 'mansio' on the route towards the cross, a unit of both real distance and devotional travelling. Referring to 'maisons' further locates the series of events as taking place indoors, and specifically within the household of each of the men to whom Christ is led. The analogy with the 'maison' in which penitents read, bringing Christ then into their own house as they do so, is thus reinforced. In the process, the potentially aleatory bodily movement of pilgrimage is translated to the rhetorically ordered space of the home church and the devotional handbook. The intimacy of the address and location finds corresponding intimacy in the physical detail with which Christ's sufferings are described. Through the technology of the imagined stations of the cross, the descendants of Menedemus, his wife, his daughters, and his servants—whether they are of the Reform or the counter-Reform—learn to make a Holy Land of their home.

Menedemus' words have become the most quoted in Renaissance pilgrimage writing. They have passed for some long time as the last word on pilgrimage in the sixteenth century. Yet Erasmus was himself a pilgrim and, as we have seen, his texts say different things about pilgrimage in different contexts.[88] At times he is sharply critical of the practice, while at others he relies on the discursive inventiveness of those—such as Ogygius or Folly—who argue its worth. The same is true of Rabelais. On occasion he has Grandgousier point out to the hapless pilgrims in *Gargantua* that men should not leave home, in case the women wander while they are away. The old king's aim here seems to be to turn all pilgrims into little Menedemuses, but this is not Rabelais' last word on pilgrimage. Panurge and Pantagruel

---

[87] Granada, *Le Vray chemin*, fol. 40^{r-v}.   [88] See above Ch. 1.

describe themselves in the *Quart Livre* as 'amateurs de peregrinité', buy 'marchandises peregrines', and more importantly, tell tales which in both structure and intent belong within the pilgrim tradition, while the narrative itself casts doubt on the possibility of ever truly returning home.[89]

Arguments about Gregory of Nyssa's letter sustained pilgrimage polemic through the Reformation and counter-Reformation, as we have seen here. Like the *Guide* writers discussed in the previous chapter, and Augustine and Fabri in our opening chapter, the polemic shifts often uneasily between literal and figural meanings, between celebration of metaphor, and anxiety about where metaphorical language might lead. It makes little sense to make any of these writers, still less Erasmus or Rabelais, mean one thing when their texts say several, for to do so is simply to perpetuate polemic. It is to build more walls around both of them, to circumscribe once again the space for play they open up within the field of pilgrimage writing. The same is true of others later in the long century, and Erasmus and Rabelais are no more nor less alone in their times than Montaigne in his. For in becoming the subjects of physical and narrative seduction in the course of their travels and in their writings, these canonical authors, as we have seen, are coming to terms with problems encountered by, and inherited from, a host of fellow pilgrims from Late Antiquity to late Renaissance. They also join the company of those to whom we turn in the chapters which follow: the innumerable pilgrims on the sixteenth-century road.

---

[89] Rabelais, *Gargantua*, 53; *Quart Livre*, 2, 5, 52.

PART TWO

BEING THERE: THE EXPERIENCE OF PILGRIMAGE

Behold him now come from the Italian frontier, and a good fresh tale all about pilgrimage or captivity, entering the house with humbly bowed head, and lying hard till all the poor host's poverty goes into the pot and on to the table; that host will be a well-picked bone in a day or two.

(Cited, Waddell, *The Wandering Scholars*)

C'est abus d'y aller principalement pour brinber ou camander, ou pour son plaisir, et passer son temps, moins pour folastrer et faire dissolutions. Sortant et rentrant au logis prier Dieu par les chemins garder silence, ou prier, mediter, tenir des bons propos, chanter chansons spirituelles, endurer patiemment les difficultez du chemin, supporter et ayder, consoler, soulager l'un l'autre avec grande charité et concorde, donner a tous bon exemple. Voila en bref le devoir d'un bon pelerin.

(Halin, *Brief Dialogue d'un homme passant son chemin, et d'un honeste et scavant Prestre qui conduit des pelerins à Maestrecht, auquel est montré le proffit des Pelerinages, et la manière de les bien faire*)

CHAPTER FOUR

'Where His Feet Stood':
Describing the Centre

'Pour Consoler le Lecteur': *Pilgrim Style*

Pilgrims are distinct from other travellers insofar as they travel consciously 'juxta scripturas' (accompanied by/joined to the scriptures).[1] This produces within them, and in their accounts, a specific relationship to the rhetoric of personal description. Everyone travels within the bounds of language, through the library of the world; as we walk, so Paracelsus suggests, we turn the pages 'pilgrimly' with our feet.[2] Palestine pilgrims' accounts differ from those of other travellers—merchants, explorers, poets, and the rest—because of their heightened awareness that they are engaged in the hermeneutic project of 'reading' the land as they pass over it. Most are, furthermore, clear as to the collectively—rather than personally—validated terms of this hermeneutic. The journey has value, and the pilgrim has an identity, insofar as he conforms to patristic models of conduct; their descriptions have value insofar as they confirm the truth of the scriptures.

Thus, when, against the strictures of both priestly legislators and non-pilgrim critics, pilgrims persist in writing their own descriptions

---

[1] This phrase inaugurates the earliest extant Jerusalem pilgrimage account, Egeria's *Peregrinatio*. It is a fragment and so begins thus by happy chance; but the phrase is repeated again and again, each time the pilgrims stop, to look, and pray, at a site. See Egeria, *Journal de Voyage*, pp. 120–1; H. Ziegler, 'Die "Peregrinatio" Aetheriae und die heilige Schrift', *Biblica*, 12 (1931), pp. 162–7.

[2] See E. R. Curtius, *European Literature and the Latin Middle Ages* (1972), p. 322.

either of the journey, or of the place, they are rarely self-consciously innovative. On the contrary, most stress the continuity of their experiences, and, crucially, of their narrative style, with those of pilgrims who have gone before them. This need not, however, be thought of as evidence of unthinking or unoriginal mimetic effort. Nor should we imagine that pilgrim writers knew nothing of the attacks levelled against them. Indeed it is possible to see the simplicity of pilgrim accounts of being 'in the place' as a decisive attempt to offer some measure of narrative 'consolation' to those at home who experience themselves to be in times of sceptical crisis. This will be my argument here, as it is throughout this book.

Nicole Huen, writing during the early French Renaissance, sets consolation as one of his primary objectives. All pilgrims write, he knows, 'pour consoler le lecteur'; Jerusalem pilgrims seeking to effect such consolation face, however, a particular, and extraordinary, representational challenge:

Si nous avons par droit en reverence des glorieux martyrs non seulement les precieuses reliques ou cendres: mais seulement les ymaiges ou pourtraictures: et de nos bouches humblement les baisons: que ferons nous ou que devons nous faire a icelle tant precieuse terre toutes les aultres dignement excedant: duquel millieu nostre salut procede en la mort doloreuse de nostre redempteur?[3]

Huen expresses the challenge in the form of a question. Its answer he finds less in his own personal account, than in the proliferation of texts he reproduces by way of a history of Christian contact with the Land. He does not produce a consolatory description by looking for new or different things to do or say, nor even by finding different ways to say the same thing. His method is less to innovate than to collate, and even the 'description de la Terre saincte' which forms a signalled, separate part of his text is a compendium of commonplaces which hardly betrays the fact that he himself has seen the things he is describing.

In effect, Huen responds to the specific representational challenge of describing the centre of his world by *not* describing what he sees. He anticipates, and as it were extends, the logic of inattention which underscores the advice from the manuals and dialogues discussed thus far. Not only does he not tell of others, he does not tell of himself and his own sense of what it is like to travel to, arrive at, or leave

---

[3] Huen, *Le grant voyage*, fol. vʳ. See also the conclusion to Ch. 2, above.

the place he had so longed to visit. Even the pilgrim's first person voice is given over, in large part, to the voice of his guide. For despite having experienced the journey himself, Huen narrates the *grant voyage* by way of an adapted translation into French of Breydenbach's earlier Latin pilgrimage, which serves as his—acknowledged—guide throughout. The difference between his own experience and that of Breydenbach, or the French kings, crusaders, and pilgrims listed in appendices to his own brief narrative, is not the important issue for him. It is rather the continuity of experience that matters. The roll call of precursors is part of the 'consolatory' pose introducing his work, a means of sustaining a tradition perceived to be under threat, and thereby gaining the reader's attention and goodwill. But it is also more than this, and Huen's textual procedures draw on the original, strong senses of consolation within epideictic and panegyric rhetoric: his text is both a display and a solemn, festive gathering around a sacred centre.[4]

In staging a self-conscious dialogue with tradition and gathering together those who have gone before, Huen celebrates a certain pilgrim style defined, as it will be a century later, in terms of its difference from others:

querrant briefvete de langaige, pour eviter aulx lecteurs grant ennuy: en langaige des pelerins usité: le grant stile laissant aulx gens de court . . . delessant le langaige emprunte rompu ou faint qui faict scabrosite: ou qui demonstre de son acteur la curiosite; qui quiert ambages qui sont obscurite.[5]

The key term here is 'curiosité'. As in Granada's writings, and those of the priestly *Guides*, so too in Huen, curiosity is grasped as not just a question of moral intention but also of textual style. As Castela will stress at a later stage in the style wars, the pilgrim infected with curiosity is no pilgrim but an 'acteur'—dangerously close to becoming an author.

'Sans fiction', Huen continues, 'diray ce que jay veu non pas en querrant grande fasson de dire: mais seulement verite.'[6] Through such insistence that pilgrimage narrative is a form 'sans fiction', pilgrim writers throughout the sixteenth century are able to develop new forms of textual attention and to elaborate new and sanctified forms of description. Under the sign of 'le langaige des pelerins usité', even those who have never travelled on a literal pilgrimage find

---

[4] See Curtius, pp. 69 n., 80–2.   [5] Huen, *Le grant voyage*, fol. xjʳ.
[6] Ibid.

themselves able to respond to the challenge of representing the Holy Land. In particular, they experiment—as this chapter will show—with the rhetoric of consolation so as to elaborate new ways not so much of seeing the place for themselves, as of bringing Jerusalem 'home', and making their readers, like them, see with pilgrim eyes.

Defining Description

Description se faict quant plusieurs propositions dependent reallement ou apparentement les unes des autres, comme: se la justice estoit faillie le peuple sentretureoit chascun desroberoit et cent mille aultres maulx l'on feroit.[7]

Description is a difficult term to define, as, even within pilgrimage writing, it inhabits a number of different discursive fields. Its scope encompasses not only a wide range of French vernacular texts, but also the writings of a number of German, Spanish, and Latin devotional authors, including Feyrabend, Pascha, Adrichomius, and Loyola. The term, its cognates, and the rhetorical procedures they enact, change shape between these contexts and languages. The vernacular rhetorician Fabri's account of 'description' within judicial and deliberative oratory cited above has little immediately to do with, for instance, the term as it appears in the earliest printed French pilgrimage narrative, the anonymous *Voyage de la saincte cyte de Hierusalem avec la description des lieux, portz, villes, citez et autres passaiges,* first published in 1480. This 'description' amounts to a list, a traveller's log, written under the sign of utility, and seems to share little with either the propositional rhetoric of Fabri, or the ecphrastic 'descriptio' of educational manuals on poetics and style.[8] It certainly has little to do with vivid representation of the place, let alone realism.

It would be difficult likewise to deduce from Postel's extraordinary *Description et charte de la Terre Saincte, qui est la propriété de Jesus Christ* that its author had spent some considerable time in Palestine.[9]

---

[7] Fabri, *Le grant et vrai art de pleine réthorique* (1534), fol. cᵛ.

[8] See T. C. Cave's discussion of *descriptio* in relation to the new ascendancy of *enargeia,* in *The Cornucopian Text* (1979), pp. 3–18, and 27–34. He draws on M. Baxandall, *Giotto and the Orators* (1971) (as he notes, p. 27). The movement I am tracing in this chapter is part of that larger shift towards intimately connecting ways of seeing and ways of reading—and thereby constructing a particular sense of interiority to the act of reading—which both these studies detail.

[9] Postel's *Description* is appended to his *Concordance des quatre evangelistes.*

Postel charts a journey around a Palestine which is a utopia of a certain kind of reading: a place devoid of the co-ordinates and accents of subjectivity, outside of history, and consequently timeless. It is the authority of scholarship and exegesis that matters to this description, appended not to an account of his own life, but to a life of Christ, and a concordance of the Gospels. Postel uses the form of the description neither to tell his own story, nor even, like Huen, to recount those of previous pilgrims. Others, however, will do otherwise, and will describe a very different place from that of Breydenbach, Huen, or Postel.

Once the coordinates of time and movement, and with them subjectivity, have been introduced into the rhetorical space of description, vernacular *Descriptions* cover a host of narrative kinds. Pilgrims begin to allow themselves to report not simply on the truth of the Gospel texts, but also the texture of their own experiences. To some extent this development is reflected in the titles of vernacular pilgrims' accounts. Description moves from being advertised as something within the narrative (*le voyage . . . avec la description de . . .*, cited above) to being the substance of the narrative itself, and its primary attraction as, for instance in Possot's *Tresample et abondante description du voyage de la terre saincte*.[10]

In vernaculars other than French, description is similarly advertised as a substantive feature of pilgrims' accounts, and is often qualified with approving adjectives. So, for instance, the vernacular version of Fabri's travels, published in Ulm, 1556: *Eigentliche Beschreibung der hin und wider Fahrt zu dem Heyligen Land gen Jerusalem*. In later sixteenth-century German usage, this term, *Beschreibung*, extends its reach and worth still further, encompassing the work of both those who travel, and those who do not. It becomes the standard term both for giving an account of one's own journey, and also for telling of others' journeys. Witness the German name given to Münster's *Cosmographia, oder Weltbeschreybung* (Basel, 1550), to Feyrabend's *Reyssbuch des heiligen Landes, das ist ein grundtliche Beschreibung aller und jeder Meer un Bilgerfahrten zum heligen Lande* (Frankfurt, 1584), and to the individual titles of many of the travel narratives within these collections, including that of Fabri cited above.

---

[10] It remains the case that most French Renaissance pilgrims' accounts are published as some or other form of 'Le Voyage', with the term 'description' included somewhere on the title-page.

Like its cognates in French and Latin, 'Beschreibung' calls upon mimetic representation to explain itself. Feyrabend characterizes the experience of reading his 'grundtliche Beschreibung' as that of looking at the world 'als in einem hellen Spiegel'. Like the similitudes of devotional literature and the sentences of commonplace books, the 'Beschreibung' is of moral worth, as it uncovers true 'Reichtumb unnd Guter' in the form of 'allerhand Exempel . . . Lehr | Warnung und Ordensregel'.[11] It also, finally, joins utility with pleasure. For, thanks to the efforts of those who 'selbst mit augen gesehen | observirt und wol ingenommen | auch eigens fleiss auffs Papyr bracht', the reader is presented with descriptions which are 'nicht allein zu wissen nutz und notig | sondern auch zu horen lustig und lieblich'. Feyrabend's claim is that his is 'zweifelsfrey' a text more profitable still than Münster's, for it contains riches greater than those revealed by either the ancients (he names Herodotus, Xenophon, Plutarch, Thuycidides, Polybius, Livy, Tacitus, 'und andern') or the moderns (Columbus, Vespucci, Magellan). This is all prelude to an assertion of the enduring worth of pilgrimage, as witnessed by those texts found in his collection: 'Beschreibungen der Reysen | Wallfahrten | Expeditionen und Herrzuge zum H. Grab und in das gelobte Land.'[12]

Feyrabend still prizes pilgrimage above other forms of descriptive writing. This may, as mentioned, in part be the editor-publisher's own publicity for his encyclopedic work over that of the still popular Münster. But even if Feyrabend does see the Cosmographer as a rival, he shares his great precursor's understanding of description. Neither recognizes any real rivalry between authorship and collation, since both understand 'Beschreibung' in the sense of a collocation of different works whose authors' hands are still visibly present, their names and personalized style woven into the texture of the writing.

The question remains as to what relation, if any, such a definition of description bears to that of lay French pilgrims, or that of the later priestly *Guide* writers who anathematise narration. And even though they use the same term, do rhetoricians and poets who seem to encourage the art of descriptive narration in fact mean something quite different by it again? Certainly, there are substantial differences

[11] S. Feyrabend, *Reyssbuch des heiligen Landes* (1584), 'Vorrede', fol. iij^r.
[12] Ibid.

in the contexts in play here. But I want to suggest that the repetition of the term across different languages and different discursive fields does none the less point to important connections. These become clear if we are prepared to do the kind of detailed work which gives them sense. For the long life of these terms, and their displacement across languages and contexts reveals how description in pilgrimage writing bears, in both function and form, on concerns which are at once historical, theological, judicial, and poetic.

Within narrative accounts, pilgrim description is less part of the picturesque, than a sanctioned way for pilgrims to account for the features of the terrain, and to express their emotions. Like Petrarch's steps up Mont Ventoux, the material contours of the pilgrim's journey are invariably mapped on to moralised coordinates. To indulge in description without moralisation is to fall prey, yet again, to the entangling lures of curiosity. So, where the title-page of the anonymous 1480 *Voyage* text tells us that this is a 'description faicte et compillee curieusement', the adverb advertises not the singularity of the writer's style, so much as the care and due attention (the 'cure') he has paid to the biblical resonances of the places he describes. It connotes also that he has kept the needs of the putative future traveller— rather than his own lust for narration—firmly in view. This is close to pilgrimage account written as *log*. It is little more than parataxis, a barely animated list of place names and distances between. The 'description' of towns on the journey amounts to a list of notable churches, and relics, with details of which indulgences can be had in which places. Such writing bears little trace of the pilgrim's subjectivity, and the account is not written to establish his identity as an author, rather, it is conceived under the sign of usefulness to a community of readers. The point is made explicitly in the prologue to the *Voyage*: the returned pilgrim writes 'pour esmouvoir les devots chrestiens a voyager et visiter les saints lieux . . . non pas par maniere de cosmographie ou aultre description artificielle mais simplement et ainsi que les choses se sont offertes à mon entendement pendant ledict voyage'.[13] The publisher advertises his work further; it is useful 'pour tous chrestiens qui vouldront entreprendre ledict voyage', and was written 'par un pelerin qui fist ledict voyage; a commencer depuis le partement de Paris jusques au retour en icelle'.[14]

[13] *Le Voyage de la saincte cite de Hierusalem* (n.d.), fol. aii^r.
[14] Ibid.

The clause following the semi-colon stresses that this is a text with integrity ensured by closure: it will take you away, but will make sure you, like its author, remain a pilgrim, and it will bring you home.

The anonymous pilgrim denigrates cosmography as a 'description artificielle'; France's most celebrated cosmographer would reverse the terms. Thevet throws off what he considers the artificial, restrictive pilgrim habit in order to give free reign to his discursive desires. For him, the authority of his description rests on the rhetoric of autopsy, not that of consolation. He trumpets his first-person experience, defined in opposition both to the inexpert errors of bookish pilgrims, and of others who have been in the place before him. When in Jerusalem—as we shall see in Chapter 7, below—Thevet is keen to point out new things, and to assert that earlier travellers have misread the signs. In this context, however, it is clear that his real criticism is directed not against fellow travellers—who are simply less good at observation than he—but at the sedentary scholars who are fool enough to believe them. He refuses to accept the prevailing cosmographic definition of description, determined by cabinet geographers and publishers: a cartographic projection of a way of seeing the world without having to travel oneself.[15] His name-calling of other writers as shop keepers, peddling second-hand goods, is countered by their characterisation of him as an itinerant purveyor of trifles, a trader in literally far-fetched fictions. This latter accusation is to turn Thevet's argument against him, and to claim, with Montaigne, that if you describe what you have not seen, you are writing fiction, and deserve to be locked up.[16]

The argument turns, once again, on the definition of description. And the debate has considerable bearing on the development of the language of testimony in travel accounts. The central question is whether to describe as a pilgrim is the same as to inscribe the

---

[15] For statements of this method see S. Münster, *Cosmographey*, p. 1752; A. Ortelius, *Theatre de l'Univers* (1598), sig. *2–3; G. de Terraube, *Brief Discours des choses plus necessaires* (1569), fols. 3ʳ–4ʳ. See also M. Pastoureau, *Les Atlas Français* (1984), *passim*; M. Simonin, 'Les Elites Chorographes ou de la "Description de la France" dans *La Cosmographie Universelle de Belleforest*'; M. Böhme, *Die Grossen Reisesammlungen des 16 Jahrhunderts* (1962); G. Strauss's more specific *Sixteenth Century Germany: Its Topography and Topographers* (1959); M. Korinmann's immensely useful 'Simon Grynaeus et le *Novus Orbis*: Les pouvoirs d'une collection', in *Voyager à la Renaissance* (1987), and F. Lestringant, 'The Crisis of Cosmography', in *Humanism in Crisis*, pp. 153–80.

[16] See Montaigne, *Oeuvres*, I, xxxi, p. 203; III, ix, p. 923.

contingencies of one's own peculiar journey or viewpoint. Or whether it is rather, to present a series of propositions about a place in such a way as to gain assent, or conjure up an image in the reader's mind. Is a text more authoritative for being the product of one who bears witness to things he has seen, or is authority rather a question of rhetorical expertise, right reading, and the due exercise of judgement? And can it really be that if you can write and describe (as Thevet does) 'from experience', you cease, in some important sense, to be a pilgrim?

Thevet's whole project is to deny that Huen's opening question about the representational challenge of Jerusalem can be answered with reference to traditional forms of description. He argues for the replacement of inherited similitudes with the authority of autopsy (seeing for oneself), and with the rhetoric of *testatio*.[17] Thevet's innovative efforts in this regard we shall return to in more detail below; for others, description of the Holy Land must be undertaken in what Huen termed the 'langaige des pelerins usité'. Huen himself argues that just as the pilgrim used the Bible as his guide, so the reader will use the *Description*; pilgrim readers are led on a tour of the sites, and so learn to see, 'par les yeux de la pensee', first Christ's body enwrapped, and then the empty grave; they learn to hear 'le doulx Jhesus preschant tres doulcement comme sil fut present'.[18] The pilgrim's truth is not a question of 'what it was like'; he does not say 'jay veu' in the way that others do. For he writes not so much in order to produce a representation, as to enable participation in a drama: the drama is that of the incarnation on the page, and it is not the traveller, but Christ himself, who occupies centre-stage. The central, enduring claim of such description is that it effects a communion, whereby both pilgrim and reader bear witness, not to their absence from the place, but to their sense of the real presence of Christ, and to the voice they hear speaking from the page.

We need now to examine this claim with respect to descriptions of the Holy Land written some fifty to eighty years after Huen. Distant

---

[17] Thevet refutes, on the basis of his own experience on pilgrimage, a number of tenets of scriptural geography—including that which is central to the descriptions of this chapter, namely that Jerusalem is the centre of the world—in both his *Cosmographie de Levant* (pp. 172–6) and the *Cosmographie Universelle* (i, fols. 177^{r-v}). For this he was accused of blasphemy, and comprehensively vilified in turn, by his rival Cosmographer, Belleforest. See on this 'duel', Lestringant's excellent analysis, *André Thevet*, pp. 189–230.

[18] Huen, *Le grant voyage*, fol. v^r.

in time, these texts are also different in kind to his account, for they extend into a separate genre what is simply one of the many sub-genres within Huen's compendium. The 'Description de la Terre Sainte' as it comes to fruition in the counter-Reformation devotional exercises of Adrichomius, Pascha, and Loyola, does not represent scenes in which the protagonists are present; they do not stage encounters on the road, either fictional or real. For the most part they are predicated on a dual absence, being produced not by pilgrims, but by cabinet geographers who have no more seen the places they describe than have their untravelled readers.

But rather than apologize for this, most of the writers to be discussed here argue that autopsy is not the only way to describe a place; calling on *testatio* might not be the most telling or effective descriptive method. Indeed, as writers as dissimilar as Erasmus and Belleforest will argue, the proper deployment of certain other rhetorical figures can conjure up in the reader's mind a far more powerful picture than that produced by the disordered ramblings of the 'mere' witness. For the rhetorical procedures and techniques of *descriptio*, allied to *enargeia*, and amplified by the technology of the printed page, can produce the effect of real presence. One of Erasmus' responses to Huen's question 'what can I do with these bones?' is pure provocation: 'Ignore them, and read the Bible.'[19] His critique of the material focus of pilgrim devotion soon modulates in the writings of others, however, into devotion for a new kind of pilgrim artefact: the printed book. Counter-Reformation writers will argue that with the Erasmian rhetoric of presence transplanted back into pilgrim soil, the Holy Land will flower once again. Sacred description can be so effective in bringing the place home to the reader that the words seem to smell as sweetly as relics once did, and the page itself can be heard to speak. With pilgrimage redefined as a mode of attention, rather than a particular journey, reading itself can be thought of as the 'vray' pilgrimage. The journey is once again supplemented by its representation; the place proper is displaced by its own description. The careful measurement of Christ's steps, and his wounds, can—to the greater consolation of the reader—materially translate the precise contours of the Holy Land and of Christ's body on to the page, and from there to the reader's cell, or chapel, or room.

[19] Erasmus, *Enchiridion,* fol. xxvi^v; see above, Ch. 1.

'Rapporter': *Villette's Description*

> *Rapporter.* To report, relate, recount, recite, rehearse, tell,
> deliuer; also to referre, compare, apply one to; to match, to fit,
> equall one with, another; to lay peece by peece, or one close by
> another; also to beare, yeeld or bring forth fruit; also to bring,
> or carrie, backe; also to represent, as formes, unto the thoughts,
> to imprint them therein.[20]

In a work dedicated to the 'freres de la confrerie du S. Sepulchre' and
written for the 'instruction et consolation de tous Catholiques',
Claude Villette, a priest, undertakes a *Description des lieux de la
Terre Saincte, ou nostre Sauveur Jesus Christ a cheminé: et les jours
des années de ses oeuvres en ladite terre Saincte.*[21] Following the dedicatory letter to the confraternity, Villette opens with a text from the
Psalms: 'Adorabimus in loco ubi steterunt pedes eius.' This, the first
of many scriptural quotations in his description, serves to remind the
confraternity members what they—like Huen and Thevet, but unlike
Villette, who has never been to Jerusalem—have in fact already done:
we shall worship in the place where his feet stood.[22] Villette's text is in
form and substance thoroughly different both from the pilgrimage
accounts we have looked at thus far in this chapter, and from the
guides of the last. In several important ways, however, his 'description' and others of its kind share a similar understanding of the
ostensive, inclusive force of the language of pilgrimage. They also
share a sense of the importance of the role, and the place, of the
reader in pilgrim discourse. Indeed the genre of 'description' as
exemplified here by Villette's text was instrumental in developing the
kinds of exercises extending the reader's mental representation of
place which had been the focus of the *devotio moderna*, and were to
prove central to counter-Reformation pilgrimage.

In the dedicatory letter to his description, Villette stresses that he
has written 'pour faire voir comme à l'oeil les lieux qu'avez visités'.
The first part of this phrase is, as we have seen, a commonplace of
enargic rhetoric, but its conclusion points to the peculiarity of Villette's position. For he writes to 'tous les pellerins' he has read, and

---

[20] R. Cotgrave, *A Dictionarie of the French and English Tongues* (1611).

[21] C. Villette, *La description des lieux de la Terre Saincte* (Paris, Bourriquant, 1608).
I have found record of only one surviving copy of this short text.

[22] The text is Psalm 131: 7. Membership of the confraternity of the Holy Sepulchre was
at the time open only to returned Jerusalem pilgrims.

more particularly the members of the confraternity from which he is by definition excluded. They have actually seen the holy sites, and his description is composed of the tales they have brought back—'rapportez' is the term he uses—from their journey. They report, bear witness, bring back . . . and he sits, transcribes, edits, draws together analogies, collates similar passages, and themes; they travel, witness and tell, while he listens, reads, and writes. The opposition between pilgrim travellers and stay-at-homes could not seem clearer than in this instance. And yet, in the same opening address, Villette describes the activity involved in composing his description as follows: 'je les ay rapportez icy au bref par l'ordre de la carte de la terre saincte verifiée.'[23]

What, then, is the sense of this privileged and repeated term: 'rapporter'? As Cotgrave's dictionary confirms, both the pilgrim's narration of things seen on the journey, and Villette's composition of a text made up of things narrated by pilgrims returned home, could be encompassed by the same verb.[24] Indeed, the sense of Villette's description, a kind of limit case of the 'description' genre which it obtusely represents, depends on maintaining both directions of the term 'rapporter'. We must understand 'description' neither as a pretense to bearing witness, nor yet as collocation by way of substitute pilgrimage. Rather, it is to project a way of seeing which is a function, above all, of the collocative, collective act of worship which is meditative reading. With description defined in this way, Villette can indeed describe, for he can place propositions about the sacred territory in careful relation to each other. He can project a way of seeing which leads the reader to a series of conclusions or beliefs about the places and propositions in question.

If the function of pilgrimage is defined in terms of narration and reading, what becomes of the pilgrim's body? Does the pilgrim kneeling before the shrine, and kissing a relic, have no role to play in the future of the institution so defined? The questions arise, because, although Villette's text initially appears odd in its confession of being written from a position of physical absence, it also crystallizes certain clear changes which took place in the last quarter of the sixteenth century. The changes have, as we have seen, to do with how rhetorics of experience and description relate, and they shape a

---

[23] Villette, p. 4.

[24] 'Rapporter' would seem to harness the force of the German 'beschreiben' better than its more immediate cognate 'descrire'.

common problem, that of how best to bring together the potentially conflicting projects of forming the pilgrim person and representing the holy place.

Villette's is neither the most rhetorically complex, nor the most inventive elaboration of the kinds of description he exemplifies: descriptions to be used for devotional, rather than travelling purposes, written by those who had never seen the place itself. But it is one of very few such texts to be written originally in French: little of the experimental mimetic work in this field is first done in the French vernacular. Many texts, such as Pascha's influential *Pèlerinage spirituelle*, are composed in Flemish or Italian before being translated into French.[25] They are often rhetorically richer than Villette's *Description*, and some present typographically elaborate alternatives to seeing the place proper, by means of images, borders, and the like printed on the page. Nicolas de Leuze's French edition of Pascha, for instance, displays an exquisite series of engraved borders, in which each day of the year is made into a visually separate unit of progression towards Jerusalem. Here, with the help of engravings, themselves framed within engraved borders, the pilgrim can read of:

toute la vie et conversation de nostre Seigneur . . . disposée selon certaines journées de toute l'année . . . ensemble aussi toute l'histoire du chemin pour aller en Jerusalem et retourner: et ce pour faire tant mieux en ce monde journellement peregrination spirituelle vers nostre païs d'enhault, qui est la sainte Cité de Jerusalem celeste.[26]

Within the first decade of the new century, however, French vernacular writers develop, along with the form of the *Guide* explored above, their own, often still more elaborate, meditative pilgrimages. Richeome once again exemplifies the kind of rhetorical pleasure that can be derived from pilgrimage polemic in his bizarre, long, and exquisite devotional novel *Le Pelerin de Lorette*.[27] Perhaps most rhetorically extraordinary of all such descriptions is the baroque textual feast laid out before the reader in the anonymous *Pèlerin véritable*.[28] This text displays several engravings and figures taken from

[25] J. Pascha [van Paesschen], *La Peregrination spirituelle vers la terre saincte* was first published in Flemish, and then translated into French and published in Louvain in 1566. See Gomez-Géraud, 'Contempler Jérusalem'.

[26] Prefatory Dedication to Margaret of Austria, *non. pag.*

[27] L. Richeome, *Le Pelerin de Lorette* ([Bordeaux, 1604], in *Oeuvres*, ii, pp. 193–360).

[28] *Le Pèlerin véritable de la Terre Saincte auquel soubs le discours figuré de la Jerusalem antique et moderne est enseigné le chemin de la Celeste* (Paris, 1615).

Zuallart though its author had no more been to Jerusalem than had Villette or Pascha. He none the less disposes his material in such a way as to be read as a journal of the actual journey to Palestine. Loyola's spiritual journey takes weeks, Pascha's takes all year; the anonymous 'véritable' pilgrim takes an indeterminate time, lingers lovingly over details, and moralises each of the material necessities of each day of his meditational progress.

Villette is heir to the stresses on the physicality of meditative reading in Granada, Pascha, Zuallart, Richeome, and others. He cites none of his precursors by name, however, preferring to acknowledge the anonymous pilgrims who make up the confraternity whose stories he collates, and to whom he dedicates his work. This gesture represents description as pure gift; less of value in itself than in the relations of interdependence it generates, or confirms. For the gift of description bestows shared order on the individual pilgrim's otherwise scattered, perhaps ill-remembered experience. The one who describes attains the role of the priest listening to confession, or the director of conscience: creating the space for a narrative of one's own within the protective frame of a tradition. To describe thus becomes less to give an account of a place, than to provide a topical and temporal structure for the telling of experience, to offer it shape, and thus significance. It is to provide a sanctified, figural frame within which to represent the scattered reality of the journey proper.

We need to see in detail how this space for narrative recall is created, and to do this we must read Villette's description closely. The broad structure of the description is twofold. The first half, a kind of gazetteer, is taken up with description of places alone. The second half details Christ's own travels around all the places thus far located. Here the description becomes recognizably a spiritual exercise, shifting from a spatial to a temporal structure: 'Les jours des années de la vie et oeuvres de nostre Sauveur Jesus, en son humilité en la Palestine' takes up the final twenty-eight pages of Villette's text. The places described in the first half of the text are, and are only, scriptural. The journey advances by way of quoting and remembering events from the Bible, Villette's only named source. Direct quotations are always given in Latin, and the margin notes where they can be found in scripture. The first quotation is from the Psalms; it stands, as noted above, as an epigraph to Villette's entire project: 'Adorabimus in loco ubi steterunt pedes eius.' The French text begins as follows:

La Terre Saincte, le scabeau et marchepied de la sacrée humanité de nostre Sauveur Jesus-Christ en terre, est assise au milieu des trois parties du monde, l'Europe, L'Afrique et l'Asie.[29]

Given the scrupulous margin notes which run alongside Villette's description, it comes as some surprise to note the missing reference to the text of which this opening sentence is in part paraphrase, Ezekiel 5: 5. 'This is Jerusalem: I have set it in the midst of the nations and countries that are round about her' had underscored descriptions and depictions of the world with Jerusalem as its actual centre, from the earliest 'T-O maps' to their more elaborate realizations in the Peutinger map, and the Hereford Mappa Mundi. The biblical text oriented map-making projection for many years, and Feyrabend, for instance, cites it in support of his claims for the worth of pilgrimage narratives over those which tell of far-flung corners of the earth.[30] Many pilgrims, in their accounts, note that they have been to the centre of the world. Beauveau is one traveller who is initially disbelieving. There is a hole, he says, which priests tell you goes 'jusques au centre de la terre' [*sic*]. This is already a displacement of the claim—it is not itself the sacred centre, but leads to the geological middle. Once alone in the place, however, Beauveau finds himself unable not to sense its force; he measures the width of the hole, though—he tells his readers, gaining their confidence by the curious trope of the lack of witnesses—no-one saw him do it.[31] Another pilgrim, Giraudet, actually places his finger in the hole; his self-representation as Thomas-like in his doubts is but prelude to confirmation of the truth of the place. He notes, with Latin authority concluding the otherwise vernacular description of his actions: 'Hic est medium mundi.'[32]

Villette does not tell of such experiences; nor even, in this case, does he quote the scriptural text which authorizes their telling. More surprising than the absence of the conventional reference to Ezekiel,

[29] Villette, p. 7.

[30] Feyrabend, *Reyssbuch*, fol. ii^v. See also D. R. French, 'Journeys to the Center of the Earth: Medieval and Renaissance Pilgrimages to Mount Calvary', in *Journeys Toward God* (1992) and, more extensively, P. Alphandéry, *La Chrétienté et l'idée de la croisade*, 2 vols. (1954), esp. I, pp. 9–56.

[31] H. Beauveau, *Relation Journaliere du Voyage de Levant* (1608), pp. 128–31.

[32] G. Giraudet, *Discours du voyage d'outremer au saint sepulcre de Jerusalem* (1575), pp. 38–9. Others who speak of this place in similar terms include F. Fabri, *Evagatorium* ii, pp. 306–8, Hault, *Le Voyage de Hierusalem* (1601), fol. 65^r, and Villamont, pp. 414–15.

is—given the date of this text, 1608—the continuing convention of dividing the world into three parts. But the symbolism of ternary structure is more important to Villette's descriptive method than verisimilitude or the detail of the 'invention' of America. Having opened with the tripartite division of the world, he continues: 'Ceste saincte terre est divisée et composée de trois Provinces [Daniel 19, reports the margin]', within which are three lakes, two in Galilee and one in Judea.[33] The river Jordan, '(riviere sanctifiee sur toutes les rivieres du monde par l'attouchement de nostre Sauveur en son baptesme) passe au travers de ces trois Provinces, comme s'il servait de mesure à la terre saincte du costé d'Orient'.[34] The three lakes in turn 'contiennent la longueur de la terre Saincte, depuis le Septentrion jusques au midy, que le Jourdain toise de son cours, depuis les monts Liban jusques à ce lac d'Asphalte, mer morte'.[35] It is within this measured and contained space that Christ walked, and performed his miracles.

A microcosm of the world in three parts, the land is both divided into, and composed of tripartite units. As organized by Villette, and invested with the presence of Christ, the geographical features of place are both sanctified and figural. Note the (slightly bashful) figurality of the river's constructive purpose—'comme s'il servait de mesure'. For those whose descriptions are accounts of their own pilgrimages there is no need for such bashfulness. Immersion in the Jordan forms an integral part both of the drama which they perform and the narratives which they subsequently produce. It is a tradition validated by, for example, a late thirteenth-century *Descriptio de Terra Sancta*, in terms identical to those of Villette: 'These are the very waters which came into contact with the body of Christ.'[36]

Certain early modern accounts, such as those collected in Feyrabend's *Beschreybung*, more anecdotal still in style, will give examples of the ways in which the waters heal, or protect. Fabri, for instance, tells of how the knights who accompanied him dived into the Jordan, fully clothed, in the belief that their clothes would become impenetrable to the weapons of their enemies.[37] Given the waters' powers, those who are told that the Jordan excursion is too far, or too dangerous that year are justly indignant.[38] Some who do

---

[33] Villette, p. 7.   [34] Ibid., pp. 7–8.   [35] Ibid., p. 8.

[36] Philip, *Liber de Terra Sancta* ([1377] 1871), viii, pp. 64–5.

[37] Fabri, *Evagatorium*, ii, pp. 36–7.

[38] Voisins notes that 'personne ne les osa conduire', p. 35; Villamont, ill on the day of the

make this trip carry water home in a phial in order to afford children baptized with it protection from sin; others record resistance to the marketing of these transportable tokens of presence. The anonymous pilgrim reports that anyone found with such phials on them risked being treated like Jonah, or at very least having the bottles thrown overboard.[39]

Villette has neither place nor time for such anecdotal material within his description. He does on occasion mention the present location of certain relics, especially those which have been brought back—'rapportez' again—to France. So, for instance, the 'doigt de l'Agnus Dei [qui] ne peult brusler, qui est en France, à nostre Dame du Puy, en Velay'.[40] And his pilgrim sources may well have told him of such things, or even shown him their own tokens of having been in the place. But these are incidental to his purpose, and rare in the text; for the *Description*'s sense of the transportability of Christ's presence is not dependent on the material translation of objects. Indeed its generally applicable force would be compromised by details of experience which are proper only to certain individuals. The Jordan is less 'really there' (wet, swimmable in, bringable home in a bottle) than a sign of the limits of sacred space. Above all it 'sert de mesure', marking the boundary of the territory of sanctified description, that territory which is marked by Christ's footsteps, the edges of the space in which pilgrims can legitimately travel—and add their own details at will.[41]

Having set the bounds to his description, Villette proceeds to detail the features of each of the three provinces in turn.[42] Initial scriptural references are given at the head of each section, others enclose the text as it progresses. Samaria calls on 'Luc 17. Jean 4. Gen. 12.'; Galilee on 'Esay 9. Matt. 2. Luc 7. Matt. 22. Jean 6.'; Judea

excursion, made his companions wait an extra day after he recovered so that he could go there alone, p. 495; cf. the tale in H. de Marsy, *Les Pèlerins normands en Palestine* (1896), p. 19.

[39] Anon, *Le Voyage de le Sancte Cyté de Hierusalem* (1480), pp. 101–2. See also Fabri, *Evagatorium*, ii, pp. 20–1. This tradition regarding the water's powers lives on, though in displaced form: a friend was christened, in Northern Ireland, with Jordan water brought home by her Grandmother on an El Al flight. Her bags were searched for suspicious articles, but the water, it seems, presented no real danger.

[40] Villette, p. 9.

[41] For a contrasting account of how to speak about the Jordan, see Postel, *Description*, pp. 34–5, 92.

[42] First Samaria, p. 9; then Galilee, pp. 9–11; and finally Judea, including Jerusalem, pp. 11–25.

on 'Josué 15. Reg. 15. Num. 3. Hier 31. Ezec. 43. Neem. 9. Matt. 21. Luc 1. Luc 10. Act. 9.' Such are the direct scriptural references which bound the text; others, indirect, structure the movement through the land. There is, in other words, very little narrative movement in the text, and the information in which it deals is rigorously static. Collocation, rather than narrative, ensures the continuity of reading, and the connected passages are animated by means of nothing more complex than a list, with the simplest possible structure: that of successive inclusion.

Just as the Holy Land is the microscosm of the whole world, so within this central emblem there is another: 'Hierusalem, le centre du monde', a city which itself is further enclosed: 'bastie sur costes de montagne, et ceinte de deux murailles [Josué 15].'[43] Names and numbers are crucial to this stage of the description, as it projects a toponymic grid in detail: so Villette notes that there are eight gates, each of which has a number, and also a name. The gates are then located with reference to other local features of the land—such as valleys and rivers—themselves also named. Neither reasons for the names, nor events which might have occurred at these places concern Villette as yet; this naming of parts is not a prelude to narrative, or history, or travel. It is pure enumeration, and it is dull. Reading the description of last gate, for instance:

La huictiesme porte estoit entre les monts Moria et Sion, entre Midy et l'Occident, et se nommoit la porte Siloé pres la valleé de Gennon, où toutes les eaux des torrens de Cedron, fontaines et piscines se rendoient. [Neem. 9][44]

The enumerative dullness of the text is the point. Other writers— most notably Adrichomius as we shall see—make it their business to develop enumerative collocation to an art. With ecphrastic bravado they seek to satisfy those readers 'possessed by a desire to picture to their minds those things which they are not able to behold with their eyes'.[45] And with a proper sense both of the grammar of narrative, and of the politics of history, they will conjugate back to the verbs and persons of action which produced these proper nouns: why this place-name, when was it imposed, and by whom, and when was it changed, and why?[46]

---

[43] Villette, p. 11.   [44] Ibid., p. 15.
[45] Brocardus, *Descriptio Terrae Sanctae* (1536), p. 4. The same turn of phrase is used by Adrichomius in his *Descriptio* (1584). We return to Adrichomius in detail below.
[46] For a sense of how many *Descriptions* were published in the second half of the

Villette has other addressees than those concerned with the political history of Palestine. Rather, he writes to encourage the narrative recall of his readers' own experience of the place, within the apparently timeless biblical frame. The first half of his description outlines the topics needed to facilitate them in their invention; the second orders the *loci* in the space and time of Christ's Life, and so provides an exemplary model of disposition. Villette, however, never having been a pilgrim himself, cannot provide the *elocutio*, cannot perform the final, narrative act.

The point can be clarified by reference to differing accounts of one particular place in the descriptions of Villette and Feyrabend. Villette describes, at one point in the first half of his text, the following series of propositions: 'si vous entrez en la Galilée, vers le lac Genezareth, à six lieuës de Nazaret, vous y trouverez Bethulie, ville delivrée du siege par Judith, tuant Holofornes.'[47] What the reader is given here is pure scriptural reference. We are not shown Bethulia a pleasant town, with several well-preserved monuments, good hotels, and varied night life as a modern guide might have it; nor even Bethulia, where 'warzeichen der belagerung Holofernis und das Thal darinn Judith sich bey Nacht weschet' can still be seen, as one of the accounts in Feyrabend does have it.[48]

We need to be clear about these differences in description, for they are not so much of chronology, as of kind. The German description cited above is Feyrabend's edition of Johann zu Solms' *Beschreibung* of the pilgrimage he undertook with Breydenbach. The detail about Judith washing herself might appear to be an eye-witness detail, available only to one who had been there. But this is not so, for Brocardus' far earlier *Descriptio* is as likely a source as actual travel: he, like Solms, mentions 'traces' of Holofernes' camp and the valley where Judith 'washed herself', all of which, he writes, 'I examined as diligently as I could, for I abode in Dothan for one night.'[49] It will thus not do to say that descriptions grow more personal, or more subjectively accentuated with the growth of the individual in the Renaissance. Brocardus' *Descriptio* predates Renaissance descriptions by centuries, and may be the source both for zu Solms, and for Villette.

---

sixteenth century and how many different ways there were of composing such texts, see the bibliography Adrichomius appends to his *Descriptio*, pp. 222–8.

[47] Villette, p. 20.   [48] Feyrabend, p. 68.   [49] Brocardus, p. 40.

We are often tempted to ask: what enables this particular pilgrim to tell, or not tell, of a night's stay in a certain place, a place which they describe in identical terms to those who stayed nearby one night centuries earlier? What authorizes, or motivates one writer to say 'I did this, here, for this long, and it was like this', and another to remain silent on all such details? We may never find the answer to such questions, though they nag away throughout this study, and are central to the chapters which follow this. What is clear from the *Descriptions de la Terre Sainte* is that they are questions which cannot be answered in terms of either chronology or genre alone; their answer lies rather at the conjunction of history, form, and the functions of genre.

There is, of course, something akin to a narrative subject in Villette's *Description*. The text is not altogether static. Verbs of movement do introduce an element of subjective agency into the space of enumeration, and consequently the beginnings of narration: 'Sortons, hors la ville, le païs voisin sont montaignes [Matt. 21].'[50] This invitation, 'sortons', does in a sense produce an event, within a sort of history: it takes us, readers included in his first person plural, to the top of a mountain, where we stay, looking, like Petrarch, first one way and then the next, for some few pages. It also leads to changes in perspective: we turn our eyes first eastwards ('de l'autre costé de ceste montagne') at the top of page sixteen, and then westwards. We see as far as Hebron in one direction, and as far as the Terebinthe tree in the other. All of this could seem like a point of view; it could suggest ways in which the rhetoric of description produces both a narrative subject and a self-consciously fictional sense of 'being there' in the reader.

But the final note added to Villette's description of things visible from the mountains stops such speculation short. It underlines the fact that Villette represents this not as a fictional point of view, but one grounded in reported experience. He himself has never climbed this mountain (referred to in Matthew 13), neither in body nor disguised as a character actor, or author, and when describing the location of things not specifically located in scripture, he can see only as far as he has read. If there is an embodied voice telling of this experience, it is a voice and body borrowed from others, as Villette confesses with neither regret nor bravado: 'Là est le Therebinthe, arbre y planté dès le commencement du monde, qui vit encores: tous les Pellerins le rapportent ainsi.'[51]

Villette's description exploits the trope of textual movement in part to remind his dedicatees of the course of their own travels, and in larger part to impress on them the reality and significance of the places they have seen. This is true even when, shifting from first to second person verbs, he deploys the directly instructional tone of the guide: 'Descendez du Liban à la mer de Sirie ou Mediterranée, vous y trouverez sur le bort pour port de mer, la grand[e] ville Sidon, loing de Hierusalem de 80 lieuës.'[52] When Villette speaks as a guide, he speaks as one directing readers to the *sense* of place as determined by Scripture: '[Sidon] C'est d'où estoit Jesabel femme du Roy Achab, où s'adoroit l'idole Baal, et où le plus loing nostre Sauveur ait esté de Hierusalem.'[53] The precise, ternary, nature of this description merits examination; we shall take the sentence in three parts. Firstly, the place name, Sidon, is reinforced with two other names, Jezebel and Ahab. What might be termed a mnemonic topography here collocates and so facilitates the simultaneous recall of the biblical characters and the place in question. In fact *Jesabel-et-Achab* functions as one name, and can be more easily remembered alongside *(Tyr-et-)-Sidon* as such.[54] Secondly, the place and name(s) are aligned with a further name, that of Baal, and all three elements are brought together. *Tyr-et-Sidon*, *Jesabel-et-Achab*, and *Baal*; all now are in place, the same place. Thirdly, this place is named as the furthest that Christ travelled from the centre. With this last item of information comes a retroactive recognition of the figural limit which *Tyr-et-Sidon*, *Jesabel-et-Achab*, and *Baal* represent in the Old Testament. The place, the demonic pair, and the false god they worship are at the triple edge of unbelief within sacred territory. It is to this edge that Christ's own travels took him, and to this edge Villette's pilgrims have themselves travelled.

The first part of Villette's *Description*, through such precise, concise location, at once reveals the *locus* to be a palimpsest, and confirms to his readers the multiple meanings of the place in which they have stood. In the second half of his text the peculiar *temporal* force of this layering of the pilgrims' travels on to those of Christ, themselves charting the borders of belief, is measured. There the pilgrim is explicitly enjoined to think of Christ's travels not only in terms of place, but also with reference to calendar time, so as to (re)cover the land of the Old Covenant, and inscribe it with the properties of the New. The story begins with Christ's birth, in Bethlehem, 'à trois lieuës de Hierusalem, selon l'ordinaire supposition l'an du monde 5200'.[55] What follows is not a *Vie*, does not account for all the days of Christ's life. There are, narratively speaking, empty spaces, months, and years not detailed, and of course most of the available narrative material relates to the last four years. The text is consequently divided into four: the first three 'Pasques Juifves', and the 'Quatriesme Pasque Juifve, et premiere Pasque Chrestienne'.[56]

The effect of this temporal ordering is twofold. Christ's life becomes narratable for the reader, in real time, across the course of the entire year. And the central time-frame of pilgrimage—the day-by-day commemoration of Christ's life over the Easter weeks—is translated and extended into each day of the year.[57] On the first of April, for instance, Christ feeds the five thousand, on the third he walks on water, and on the first of May he arrives in Nazareth. Here he reads in the synagogue the prophecy from Isaiah 61 ('*Spiritus Domini supra me etc*') which relates, as he is aware, to himself.[58] On the fifth he climbs Mount Thabor, 'où il publie la loy Evangelique, l'extinction de celle de Moyse'. On the sixth he arrives in Capernaum, where he performs a number of miracles, and so on.

To say 'this is where something happened'—the tag line of pilgrimage—is to tie an event to a place in the world. To say 'it happened on the third of May'—the innovation of Villette's *Description* within pilgrim discourse—ties it to a particular day in human time. That much is obvious. But to tie an event to a date on a calendar is also to place that event within a narrative which is not only reiterable, but also commemorative. The function of the calendar is to imagine the possibility of meaningful repetition. It makes events part of a story, susceptible to commemoration, rather than random, subject to mere chance.

Villette is involved here in the creation of a new kind of relation between daily time and the Passion narrative. He is translating the

---

[55] Villette, p. 26.   [56] Ibid., pp. 28–9, 29–35, 35–43, 43–8.

[57] Might this be seen—at least in narrative, if not pictorial emphasis—as counter-Reformation appropriation of the *Calendriers historials* which were the staple of Reformers' printing houses for some long time? See N. Davis, *Society and Culture in Early Modern France* (1987), p. 204.

[58] Villette, p. 31.

events of Christ's last days into terms which make contemporary, daily, sense for his readers. And, true to the rhetorical strategies of the counter-Reform, he teaches them how to tell their days in time to the rhythms of the church calendar. On 25 January, for instance, Christ preached penitence for the first time, 'à mesme jour que S. Paul fut converty pour prescher penitence aux Gentils [Luc 4. Marc 1]'.[59] This temporal ordering of the description makes explicit a process of collation which implicitly structures the entire text. Through precise placing on the calendar, these two central ecclesiological events are effectively identified with each other, and the reader is identified with Paul's original public. In this way, time and place are made to converge on the act of reading and on the person of the reader. For it is for us, Gentile readers, that Christ and Paul preach together on this day of which we read.

As we saw in the opening circumscription of the Jordan and the lakes, Villette suggests that the ordering designs of his composition of the 'carte verifiée' are already inscribed in the land. The same is true of the stations of the cross, which work on the inherited tropes of Christian pilgrimage so as to effect the ritualisation of the everyday and render the home sacred. The first use of the ubiquitous trope of rhetorical movement—'sortons'—led in Villette's *Description* to the Mount of Olives, and there was found 'la premiere station de sa Passion où il a laissé engravée la figure de ses genoux suant sang et eau'.[60] This is a recurrent stopping point in pilgrims' own accounts, but few talk of 'stations' when describing this place. Villette, however, reads their texts, and reads the ground they speak of, as bearing not only the marks of Christ's presence, but also representing, in figures naturally engraved on the rock, the 'stations' of his passion. The land, he says, prefigures the liturgical procession of 'stations' in the home church, which it in turn authorizes. This is the rhetorical charmed circle which is Villette's world. With Jerusalem still firmly located at the actual and rhetorical centre, and no 'nouvelletez' such as America to speak of, devotional attention to the distant place gives an order of physical locality to worship at home. The liturgy thus colludes with description to bridge the gulf between those who have travelled and those who merely read. And reading with the liturgy in mind can translate the special, sacred collusion of time and place evidenced in the Holy Land into the space of home.

<hr>

[59] Ibid., p. 29.   [60] Ibid., p. 15.

This process of collapsing then to now, there to here—'c'est le lieu
où | à mesme jour que'—is constitutive of Villette's descriptive
method, as it is of the spiritual pilgrimage as defined by the counter-
Reform. It is what Nietzsche will term monumental history: history
which commemorates things, places, and people by producing
analogies in such a way as to refer them to the problems of the present.[61] Thus Jewish and Roman stories, people, and places are subsumed to the Christian masterplot, and the land is reinscribed as
sacred through, and for the sake of, Catholic memory and future nar-
ratability. About this, Villette makes no bones in his concluding
remarks on his own method: 'Ce que dessus se trouve aux escriptures
de la vie en terre de nostre Sauveur: l'ordre du temps et des lieux le
rend facile à retenir.'[62]

And yet Villette's description, for all its enargic rhetoric and careful placing in time and location, is grounded on several kinds of
absence. He cannot truly hope to fulfil the promise of pictorial representation which his title and his allusions to ecphrastic rhetoric
offer.[63] Indeed, in pictorial terms, this *Description* is offered doubly
in vain: not only will it not show the confraternity members anything
they have not seen before, but also, if the general reader chances on
this text, all he will learn is that he cannot really see these 'lieux' at
all. The point is stressed when Villette speaks, in his prefatory letter,
of those who have been given the gift of experiencing the physicality
of the place 'en personne':

Afin que le Lecteur voye la devotion qu'avez euë, et contentement qu'avez
receu de les voir [les lieux] de vos yeux, les baiser de vos levres, les toucher
de vos mains, et d'y joindre et flechir vos genoux.[64]

The general reader may well be shown things, but the physicality of
the rhetoric here only serves to emphasize that readers are all, and
only, eyes. The reader is not Gregory of Nyssa, Huen, or Castela; he

---

[61] See F. Nietzsche, 'Vom Nutzen und Nachteil der Historie für das Leben' in *Werke*,
(1984), esp. pp. 219–25.

[62] Villette, p. 48.

[63] Nor can he support the rhetoric with the image even to the extent of his Protestant
precursors, the *Calendriers historials*, since no one has invested in his text to the extent of
producing illustrations, bordered pages, or indeed images of any visual kind. His publisher is less prepared, or less able, to take the kinds of risks taken by Feyrabend, Nicolas
de Leuze, or those who published Breydenbach, Zuallart, the *Pèlerin véritable*, and
Adrichomius.

[64] Villette, pp. 4–5.

has no body, has not kissed with lips, nor touched, nor knelt, nor connected intimately with the sacred earth. Bodiless he can only give names—'devotion, contentement'—to the things others have felt and received:

Et afin aussi que le mesme Lecteur, qui n'a point eu ce don de Dieu d'y avoir esté en personne comme vous, juge et recognoisse par ceste lecture la joye spirituelle qui vous accompagne, et qui ne vous quittera point, desirant par vos saincts voeux estre faict participant des merites qui vous suivent, devots Pelerins de ce sainct Paradis terrestre, la terre saincte, pellerinage le plus precieux et meritoire qui se puisse faire par un Catholique.[65]

Villette's prefatory dedication identifies a gap between orders of reader which the body of his text works to close. The difference between literal pilgrims and readers at home is revealed by the verbs which describe their actions relative to holy ground. 'Rapporter' initially stretches to encompass and so unite the different actions of writer and pilgrim, as both are joined in the act of narrative description and recollection. But the reintroduction of the body into the space of description accentuates differences once again, and opens up a space between the meanings of verbs and the modes of reading the land. The pilgrim reads *with his own body*, he participates in the Passion, and his are actions of physical contact with the place proper. The non-pilgrim, by contrast, reads, at best, with a surrogate, represented body. As Villette notes, the reader 'juge et recognoisse'; rather than being part of a pilgrimage proper, the reader 'desire estre faict participant'. These are verbs which have distance written into them, they are all figures of desire, and carry absence with them.

What, then, of that deeper 'rapport' which only the collating writer can bring to light, to print, and to readers? A valorization of the experience of travel over that of reading is what Villette's preface offers his addressees. But if we distinguish between the confraternity who are his official public, and his imagined readers—anyone who chances on the text—a different set of relations between narrative and experience emerge. Indeed, once the preface is past, Villette's text, as we have seen, argues for a different reading of the relations between a place and its description. It also fantasises a different kind of desire in readers of descriptions. The original addressees of a text may well not be the readers the author most desires; and, as Villette

---

[65] Ibid., p. 5.

seems to recognise, even these addressees may read differently at different times. His returned pilgrim narrators may, in becoming readers of the text, surrender the position of the witnesses, the ones supposed to know, in order to relive, and recount, the experience as if for the first time.

Once again it comes down to a reading of the conjunctions of time and place represented by Villette's verbs of movement: 'Sortons . . . Descendez . . . vous trouverez'. These verbs point to the heart of Villette's method. The future tense they imply is—for the returned pilgrims—false time: his public has already done what it is being told to do. But this future is only as false as the future of the 'adorabimus' in the text from the Psalms which heads Villette's *Description*; only false, then, in terms of actual, past travel. If we recognize that this rhetorical description is structured in two temporal directions—in commemoration of the actual journey now completed, and in anticipation of narrative recollection still to come—the future remains full. It is a future full of potential, defined according to the time and place of narration, worship, and ritualized reading.

Description as Theatre: Adrichomius

To write a *Description de la Terre Sainte*, Villette suggests, is to substitute syntax for creation, composition for innovation. In terms of its *style*, pilgrim description negotiates a place for the body and for writing somewhere at the conjunction of articulation, ordering, and theatricalization.[66] Writers of spiritual descriptions and exercises know that prayer must pass through language, and must affect the body, but, unlike those who travel to Jerusalem, they are not themselves physically engaged in the drama of pilgrimage. They are, rather, its scenographers, and having written the script and told the actors what gestures to perform, they watch and wonder at the forms of subjectivity their theatrical descriptions have produced. Though they themselves are aware of the kinds of physical absence on which their texts are predicated, the theatre they produce within the *writing*

---

[66] See R. Barthes, *Sade, Fourier, Loyola* (1971), pp. 45–80. I use Barthes' tripartite scheme as it seems more profitable for a stylistic reading of these particular texts than that of 'composition', 'analysis', and 'affective prayer' elaborated by L. Martz in *The Poetry of Meditation* (1962).

sustains an illusion of presence which makes the reader seem to see the place as if before his eyes.

This is most dramatically clear in the last of the writers of descriptions of the Holy Land to be considered in this chapter: Christian Adrichomius. It is Adrichomius' writings, not translated into French within the time of our study, but influential in French devotional practice, and quickly English'd, which are most commonly, and convincingly, credited with fixing the stations of the cross in the European imagination. The *Jerusalem, sicut Christi tempore floruit, et suburbanorum insigniorumque historiarum eius brevis descriptio* [*Descriptio*], first published in Cologne in 1584, is a description composed of 270 numbered descriptive units (*loci*), ordered alphabetically.[67] The *Theatrum Terrae Sanctae et biblicarum historiarum* [*Theatrum*], published first in Cologne in 1590, presents a series of commented maps of the land divided into twelve tribes.[68] Both texts were authoritative and striking in their scope and method. Their reception, by both Protestant and Latin communities of readers, effectively confirmed the most decisive displacement of the terms of pilgrimage effected in the Renaissance.[69] They made into method what Menedemus had imagined long before: the translation of sacredness from 'elsewhere' into the 'home'.

To underwrite this move, Adrichomius employs both visual representations of the place, and the *topoi* of enargic rhetoric which others have marshalled in their cosmographies, descriptions, or narratives. This is what will allow readers of his *Descriptio* to see Christ's sufferings 'quam iam ante oculos'.[70] As readers we are to be led 'as it were by the hande' by the book in our hands, such that 'with the eies of faith and of our minde [we] looke upon the same sonne of God, and inwardly behoulde him'.[71] Like other writers of

[67] The English text is *A Briefe Description of Hierusalem and of the Suburbs therof, as it florished in the time of Christ . . . Translated by Thomas Tymme Minister* (London, 1595).

[68] The *Theatrum* has, to my knowledge, yet to be translated. It is a far more expensive publication than the *Descriptio*.

[69] For more on the Church's adoption of Adrichomius' measurements for the way of the cross (which he says he has from pilgrims, whose names are noted in his margin), see H. Thurston, *The Stations of the Cross* (1906), pp. 96–108. This is still the best study of its kind in English.

[70] Adrichomius, *Descriptio*, p. 18.

[71] Adrichomius, *A Briefe Description* (Preface, *non. pag.*); for the Latin, see *Descriptio*, p. 20.

descriptions, Adrichomius calls on the scriptural passages which
praise Jerusalem in conclusion to the preface of the *Descriptio*; and
standing guard in the margin at the outset of the *Theatrum* is
'Hieroyn, in Ezech 5'. The *Theatrum* proper opens with the quotation which Villette will also use to inaugurate his *Description*: Palestine has been selected by God to be his 'home, his dwelling place . . .
to serve him as a throne for sitting, a footstool for praying, a mattress
and a pillow for sleeping'.[72]

The force of Adrichomius' style lies, however, more in its difference from the descriptive tradition, than in these prefatory connections. In particular, it is his powerfully articulated understanding of
how to compose his text in terms of a drama which deserves attention. Adrichomius' sense of the imaginative reach of description for
readers who cannot undertake pilgrimages themselves is more fully
developed than that of either Feyrabend, Villette, or indeed Loyola.
He tells us in the *Theatrum* that he too has never been to Palestine; he
tells us also that he has his information from the 'memoria' of the
best sources.[73] The best of these is Brocardus, 'perlustrator et descrip-
tor' of the land, and Adrichomius admits no shame in imitating
others. Indeed he prides himself in having done so: 'I am not ashamed
to imitate . . . indeed it could hardly be otherwise, since it will be
plain to all that nothing is said here that has not already been said.'
Safe in this knowledge, the reader can read in good faith, and will
find no digression into novelty. For Adrichomius has written 'for no
other reason (dear Reader) than to group together these texts in such
as way as to make the truth plain to you'.[74] The central term in the
Latin here—'hac collatio' is the group of texts—carries, as we saw
with respect to Augustine and Erasmus, the sense of 'dialogue'. What
the *Theatrum* stages is a dialogue of consolation between the reader
and tradition, with Adrichomius as prompter, reminding us all of our
lines.[75]

The *Descriptio* sets itself an equally precise, and similarly theatrical, task, signalled in the margin by 'operis huius ratio':

---

[72] Adrichomius, *Theatrum*, sig. *3[r]. Translation mine.
[73] As noted above, Adrichomius lists these in a bibliographical index, giving author's
dates and details of recent publications of Late Antique and medieval texts.
[74] Adrichomius, *Theatrum*, sig. *4[r].
[75] For more on *collatio*, see C. Leyser, 'Lectio divina, oratio pura: Rhetoric and the
Techniques of Asceticism in the "Conferences" of John Cassian', in *Modelli di santità*
(1994).

first [to] portray and set forth the true and lively Image of Jerusalem ... as it florished in the time of Christ ... Secondly rightly [to] dispose the places of Christ his passion, and represent everything which he suffered, in every place, even as if they now were donne before our eies, and so represented that I might explain it with plainenesse and brevity.[76]

The efforts at *enargeia*, careful disposition, and, once again, dialogue with tradition are brought into play in order that Christ's sufferings might be 'both more plainely understood, and also more profitably remembered'.[77] These elaborate gestures of explanation suggest that people need to be told how to read the text, and are an indication of both the novelty and the devotional usefulness of such forms of description. They also clarify the extent to which Adrichomius conceives of reading as a form of 'theatre'; an imitative scenario modelled on the drama which is the pilgrim's physical enactment of the life of Christ. He fully understands what Barthes will recognize to be the seductive power of the Ignatian schema: 'on divise la matière imitable (qui est principalement la vie du Christ) en fragments tels qu'ils puissent être contenus dans un cadre et l'occuper entièrement.'[78] Such is successful synecdoche at work; a holy arithmetic which, through the medium of the printed word, adds up to a powerfully consoling sense of presence.

Adrichomius makes no bones about the need for methodological rigour in devotion. Indeed he develops certain textual and typographical effects which are peculiar to him—no other writer in this field exploits these effects—and which place extraordinary demands on his devotional readers.[79] It is these we focus on in conclusion, with particular reference to the point which most amply exemplifies Adrichomius' method: description of locus 118, the way of the cross.[80]

---

[76] Adrichomius, *A Briefe Description* (Preface, *non. pag.*); for the Latin, see *Descriptio*, pp. 17–18.

[77] Ibid.   [78] Barthes, *Sade, Fourier, Loyola*, p. 51.

[79] See Barthes on how only 'une méthode extrèmement rigoureuse' can counter 'l'éparpillement des images, qui marque psychologiquement, dit-on, le vécu mental', ibid., p. 73.

[80] Locus 118 straddles pp. 124–7 in the Latin; it is 117 in the English, pp. 57–60. The English is frequently shorter than the Latin text, and the difference in numbering occurs because Veronica's house (no. 44 in Latin) is missing altogether. The gaps, in this Protestant rendering, are telling. Later in the sequence, for instance, 198 the sepulchre of Mary, 197 in English, is a few lines compared to over a page of Latin, and, crucially, does not bear the witness of the Latin pilgrims—such as broc[ardus], brei[denbach], sal[ignac], and pasc[ha]. Also omitted is the Latin 203 'tugurium s. pelagiae', based as it is only on 'in vitus Patrum, brei, Iul, sal. and pasc', with neither scripture nor Josephus in support.

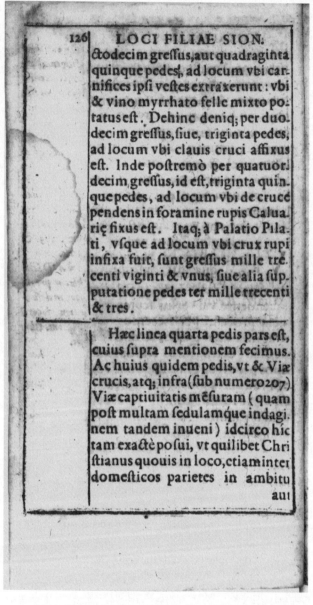

Fig. 4.1. Reproduced by permission of the Bodleian Library, Oxford, shelfmark Opp. Add. 8° 11.257, p. 126

The *Descriptio* is structured not in terms of a journey so much as according to a process of scriptural framing of *loci* as 'legenda'—things to be read. This framing is akin to the visual organization of Jerusalem as represented in the *Theatrum*. It is also a visual feature of the typographic organization of the text on the page of the Latin *Descriptio*.[81] The text with its numbered paragraphs of print is bordered on four sides, and within this rectangular page-within-a-page is another discrete rectangle. This contains further numbers: those of the page, to which the lengthy index refers, and—in italics—the textual references which supply the authority for Adrichomius' own words, themselves framed by a large rectangular border. Such is the format of the page.

Locus 118 at first appears no different to any other. It is located within the external frame of 'places within Jerusalem', and the internal frame of 'places on the daughter of Sion', one of the hills of the City. The 'Via Crucis' follows alphabetically from the 'Vallis Cedron', and precedes the 'Via introitus equorum' and the 'Xystus porticus'. The many accompanying references are framed within their italicized place to the side of the description proper. All this is standard for this text. Less so, however, is the exhortation to picture Christ walking each step of the way. On turning the page we find the *place* in which Christ walked similarly marked as different, both in terms of the rhetorical mode of description appropriate to it, and with respect to its typographic arrangement on the page.

The place begins as pure topic: 'VIA CRVCIS'.[82] But the gloss already invests the *topos* with desire: 'THE WAIE OF THE CROSSE, by which Christ having received his judgement to be crucified, went forward with painefull and bloudy steppes to mount *Calvary*.'[83] The desire is for detail, and is marked by the adjectives attached to the 'steppes'. It is a desire for an intricately imagined scenario, invested with the details of measurement and movement, and it propels the text forward in careful, extended sequence. I quote the English translation:

For beginning at the Pallace of *Pilate* he made six and twenty steppes (which make threescore and fiue foote) vnto the place where the crosse was layde vpon him.

[81] See Fig. 4.1.   [82] Adrichomius, *Descriptio*, p. 124.
[83] Adrichomius, *Briefe Description,* p. 57. The Latin is similarly emotive.

From whence (all the cittye gazeing on him) carying his crosse on his sore
shoulders, hee came towardes the Weste, or rather North-weste, fourescore
steppes, which make two hundred foote, to the place, where men say, that
hee fell downe vnder his crosse . . .

Taking his way hence by one hundred ninetie and one steppes, and half a
foote, (which commeth to foure hundred and seuenty foote) hee came to the
place where . . . once againe he fell with his crosse.

Frome thence hee ascending faintely a very heard and stony way
towardes the North, hee gained three hundred and forty and eighte steppes
and two foote (the summe eight hundred seuentye and two foote) . . . hee fell
downe the laste time, at the foote of the mounte CALVARIE. From thence hee
wearilie and faintingly went forward eighteene steppes . . .

Then he went on twelue steppes, or thirty foote euen to the place where he
was nayled on the crosse. . . .[84]

This is passionate writing; articulate and theatrical. Its force lies in the
adverbs, and in the detail: the gaze of the parenthetical crowds, the
translation of steps into measured feet, the computation of these feet
connecting paragraphs and amplifying the affective mode as the
journey progresses. Clearly, when the desire for narrative enters the
bounded space of pilgrimage, a locus becomes a journey. This particular journey is itself a *topos*, to be sure—'The Waie of the Crosse'—but
precisely by being dramatized in such detail, it becomes an endlessly
reiterable scenario. Thanks to the obsessive accuracy of a priestly
accountant, the steps Christ took to the cross are made both *legenda*,
to be read, and theatre, to be reproduced in exact imitation.

The measured movements can be repeated, anywhere, and precisely, at will. Round your house, round your garden, between the
kitchen and the bedroom, you can take as many steps as Christ took
between the stations on his way to the cross. If you know the exact
measurements, know how many feet there are in a step, you can walk
exactly as far Christ walked, and perform your own precise pilgrimage. Thus locus 118 concludes with the following computation:

So that from the Pallace of *Pilate*, vnto the place where Jesus was crucified,
the distance is a thousande three hundered and seuen steppes: or by another
accoumpt, three thousand two hundred sixtie and eight foot,[85]

---

[84] Adrichomius, *Briefe Description*, pp. 58–9.   [85] Ibid., p. 59.

DAVGHTER OF SION. 59

laboring forwarde threescore steppes and one and halfe a foote, (which make foure hundred and foure foote) hee fell downe the laste time, at the foote of the mounte *CALVARIE*. From thence hee wearilie and faintingly went forwarde eighteene steppes, or fortie fiue foote to the place where the hange-men drewe off his cloathes, where they gaue him to drinke wine mixt with mirrh and gaule.

Then hee went on twelue steppes, or thirty foote euen to the place where hee was nayled on the crosse on mounte *CALVARIE*. So that from the Pallace of *Pilate*, vnto the place where Iesus was crucified, the distance is a thousande three hundered and seuen steppes: or by another accoumpt, three thousand two hundred sixtie and eight foot,

We haue made such exacte descripion and demonstration of the way of the crosse (as also the way of the Captiuity hereafter expressed vnder the number of two hundred and seuen) to the ende that euerie Christian man, in all places, euen in the doores of his house, or walking often times in his garden, or being in a iourney, or in the Temple, either lying in his bedde, may by the Imagimination of his minde conceiue the like way, and with godly affection of the hearte may meditate vpon the passion of Christ: the which no doubt is both acceptable vnto God, and for our owne soules health moste profitable as the holy Scriptures, and the writinges of good men by their often exhortations do testifie.

I 2   THE

The printed line is important. In the English, where the margin references are not bound within a rectangular frame, it simply marks a pause, albeit the only one, in the alphabetical and numbered sequence which otherwise articulates the text.[86] It serves to distinguish the Passion narrative, in paragraphs as shown, from the explanation for the change in descriptive mode which follows it:

We have made such an exacte descripion [*sic*] and demonstration of the way of the crosse (as also the way of the Captiuity hereafter expressed vnder the number of two hundred and seuen) to the ende that euerie Christian man, in all places, euen in the doores of his house, or walking often times in his garden, or being in a journey, or in the Temple, either lying in his bedde, may by the Imaginination [*sic*] of his minde conceiue the like way, and with godly affection of the hearte may meditate vpon the passion of Christ.[87]

Both key terms in this explanation are typographically mis-set; it is as if the typesetter could not quite bear to 'conceive' the clarity of Adrichomius' method here. Indeed the English edition further confuses and obscures the clarity of the Latin in other, more significant, respects. In particular, it ignores the true purpose of the printed line.
In the Latin the line is this long, and has this shape:

'_____   _____   _____ __ ' .[88]

Here, as mentioned, the references are framed within their own discrete border alongside the text, the line traverses the border to the left of the text, and consequently cuts into the space of the references.[89]
This is no mistake; indeed, badly printed though it be, it must have taken some considerable effort on the part of the printers to achieve its effect. The Latin line does not serve either as a pause, or to a mark a distinction between description and explanatory reference, as it does in the English edition. Nor yet does it pass, as in the English, unmentioned in the text. Rather it both breaks the typographical borders of the texts thus far in play, and is drawn attention to as an integral part of the description. Below the line the Latin reads:

Haec linea quarta pedis pars est, cuius supra mentionem fecimus. Ac huius quidem pedis, vt et Viae crucis, atque infra (sub numero 207) Viae captiuitatis mensuram (quam post multam sedulamque indaginem tandem inueni)

---

[86] This is the only such typographic marker within in the text proper. See Fig. 4.2.
[87] Ibid., directly below the line.   [88] Adrichomius, *Descriptio*, p. 126.
[89] See Fig. 4.1.

idcirco hic tam exactè posui, vt quilibet Christianus quouis in loco, etiam inter domesticos parietes in ambitu aut horto saepius circumeundo, vel iter replicando, possit similem sibi viam ordinare, aut in templo seu cubiculo mentis imaginatione similem concipere; et pio cordis affectu Christi passionem meditari.[90]

We need to be clear about what is being said here. The first sentence above translates as: 'This line is the fourth part of that foot which we mentioned above.' This detailed measurement and self-reference is suppressed in the English edition, which exhorts the reader to conceive the like way in his Imagination, but does not offer the exact means by which to do so. It urges him to read the book and, leaving the book behind, to reproduce mentally, and physically, the space just traversed in reading. The Latin seeks to establish a different relationship both to the book, and to the 'way'. It suggests that the line, as represented on the page, offers the literal measure by which the steps to Calvary can be translated, in the exactest detail, into the reader's home. The ambiguous formulation 'iter replicando'—to perform the journey, or to come back to it, or even to turn it over and over again in the mind—stresses the point. With not only *loci* and numbers as reference points, but also the broken line explicitly referred to as a literal yardstick, the way of the cross is made more than either legend or theatre. The steps Christ took are measurably brought home to the reader, and to his holy household. They are 'rapportez', not through physical pilgrimage, nor as a synecdochic relic, but by way of a technology of reading as itself a means to the more exact imitation of Christ; an imitation made more real by the artful devices not only of rhetoric, but also, and especially, of the printed page.

Describing Ideology as Prayer

La plus part des occasions des troubles du monde sont Grammariennes . . . Combien de querelles et combien importantes a produit au monde le doubte du sens de cette syllabe *hoc*![91]

One of the guiding principles of this study is that the changing uses of pilgrimage discourse throw light on the larger changes in the metaphors we live by. Another is that these changes, whether within languages, in translation from Latin to the vernaculars, or across

---

[30] Ibid., pp. 126–7.   [91] Montaigne, *Oeuvres*, II, xii, p. 508.

generic kinds, can be seen to be at work in the smallest, seemingly unrelated details. Adrichomius' line is one such detail; as are Geiler's computation of the number of times a man would have to walk around his cell to reach Rome, and Menedemus' punning reference to his nightly pilgrimage around the locks and bolts of his house.[92] Villette's assertion that his 'rapport' of a place he has never seen might reveal a deeper 'rapport' of text and place to the faithful reader, even the reader who has stood in the place proper, is another. What we are witnessing in such instances is the gradual translation of the pilgrim from the one who went away, who took on the burden of exile, into the pilgrim as devotional householder. In the terms of one early modern dialogue 'auquel est monstré le proffit des pelerinages', the pilgrim moves from being figured as a 'passant' into a peculiarly pious 'bourgeois de ce monde'.[93]

This is a reading of pilgrimage not so much as an occasion for a journey, an encounter with others and otherness elsewhere, as a means to establishing coordinates of identity. As Adrichomius and Villette have shown, pilgrim *description* can, rather than accounting for having been away, provide a sanctified and measured way to describe a place as home. It is tempting to tell this as a confessional story, and to recuperate these details to the plot of the History of the Counter-Reformation. It is possible to give the 'details' cited above greater resonance by relating them to the pilgrim's persistent anxiety about how properly to represent the sacred place as we have done, following Huen, in this chapter. We can also usefully understand the changes in descriptive method as bearing on early modern arguments concerning the host. The pilgrim's performative utterance—'hic est locus'—might be thought of as analogous to the 'hoc est corpus' of the mass: the 'est' changes aspect, and the deixis ('hic/hoc') becomes more specific in direction. The change can be linguistically determined as a shift from ontologically associative to metaphorically syntagmatic, from being a relation of identity to one of equivalence. So, as the doctrine of transsubstantiation is codified even as it loses universal assent, 'hoc est corpus meum' is taken to shift in meaning

---

[92] See above, Chs. 2 and 3. For an analogous instance of a telling 'detail' in a patristic manuscript tradition, see C. Leyser, 'Long-haired Kings and Short-haired Nuns: Writing on the Body in Caesarius of Arles', *Studia Patristica*, 24 (1993), pp. 143–50.

[93] See J. Halin, *Brief dialogue d'un homme passant son chemin, et d'un honeste et scavant Prestre qui conduit les pelerins* (1623), fol. 3ʳ; cited above in epigraph to part II of this study.

from 'this is my body', to 'this is [a representation of] my body'. Within the confessional History, this change would be occasioned over the course of the Reformation, and Marburg might be thought of as the place where the argument became at once articulated and polarized.[94]

By becoming subject to relations of equivalence, the body becomes subject to representation; as does the 'locus' of pilgrimage. The counter-Reformation then 'reacts' by affirming the relations of identity, both in relation to the mass and to pilgrimage. This in turn encourages the elaboration of various forms of substitutional equivalence for the act of standing and speaking in 'the place proper'. Copies of the Holy Sepulchre are placed on church altars, the stations of the cross are developed. The Church becomes the place proper.[95]

The story can also be told in terms of rhetorical developments. An early Erasmian critique of relics—'they should not be mistaken for the real thing, namely scripture'—hardens into more stringently wholesale Calvinist condemnation of pilgrimage as grounded in a misprision of sacred synecdoche—'it seduces the faithful into idolatry, as they mistake the part for the whole'. Counter-Reformers then sanctify just this seductive power, by allying it to representation properly directed: the spiritual exercise is elaborated, and the devotional, figural pilgrimage gains imaginative focus and strength. In the process, it becomes increasingly possible not only to use places as parts of a memory theatre, but also, through the properly directed use of the forces of *enargeia*, to use description as a kind of narrative, to guide the reader to an imagined Jerusalem.[96] Arrangement of places not only in space, but also, in time, makes of the city of Jerusalem largely an object of fantasy, and of meditation. So Villette changes the focus of his description from spatial disposition to temporal relevance to the time of reading. In time the technology of the

---

[94] This is, of necessity, a hasty sketch. For differing, but more detailed accounts of this change, see E. Cameron, *The European Reformation* (1991), pp. 157–67 and J. Z. Smith, *To Take Place*, pp. 97–100. The classic account of the Marburg colloquy remains W. Köhler, *Das Marburger Religionsgespräch 1529: Versuch einer Rekonstruktion* (1929).

[95] For more on how stone and wooden sculptures in churches came to stand in for the holy places, see Thurston, pp. 45–50, 76–95, and Smith's discussion, *To Take Place*, pp. 87–95.

[96] A powerful poetic development of this idea is Chassignet's *Le Desir qu'a l'Ame de parvenir en la Supreme Cité de Hierusalem*, in his *Le Mespris de la Vie*, pp. 136–9. For discussion of memory theatres, see J. Spence, *The Memory Palace of Matteo Ricci* (1984), (pp. 12–22 in particular), and F. A. Yates, *The Art of Memory* (1969), though Yates says little on their devotional uses.

printed word makes it possible to stand in one's own room, and, within the exactly measured space of Calvary, to say 'this is the place', and in doing so to transfer to the home the holiness of Jerusalem.[97]

This imagined, theatrical trajectory which leads to the expression of desire, a structure common to Loyola, Adrichomius, and Villette, crystallizes the changes we have been describing here. Jerusalem gradually ceases to exist as a primarily real place in the European imagination, a place to be seen, witnessed and described *in situ*. It is gradually replaced by an imagined Jerusalem conjured up by description; less a place than a topic, part of a narrative or devotional sequence: a means to prayer and a prelude to the expression of desire.

There is a clarity about such an argument which is persuasive. It connects with much recent historical and theological debate concerning the changes occasioned by the Reform and the Counter-(or Catholic) Reformation. It also connects to the development in recent years of 'humanistic geography', that discipline which—following the Kantian geographical programme—reads place less as being 'out there' to be described, than as a function of the imagination. The key term in such an understanding of place is 'cognitive mapping', a term which has itself migrated from geographical discourse to cultural criticism.[98] The explanatory force of cognitive mapping as an idea is due in part to its use as an analogy for the workings of ideology: both offer an imagined relationship to the real relations in which the subject lives. The elaboration of the devotional pilgrimage, the spiritual exercise, and the descriptions of an imagined Jerusalem, thus seem to be a part of the development of an ideology of prayer centred on the holy household. From the *devotio moderna* to the Catholic Reformation, the focus of the 'cognitive map' is the individual's cultivation of the self, in private, and according to regulatory systems of medita-

[97] The pivotal point of this development in Renaissance devotional writing is sometimes represented as Loyola's *Exercitia Spiritualia,* composed in Paris in 1535. Much of what I have to say is a gloss on work done on Loyola, as the notes make clear. But I have not read the *Exercises* in detail here, as they were not translated until 1620, and even in Latin their impact on the French field seems to have been far less significant than, for instance, the work of Granada, discussed above in Ch. 2. See p. 81, n. 76. For more on the Ignatian tradition in general, see H. Rahner, *Ignatius the Theologian* (1990), pp. 181–213.

[98] For brief accounts of different approaches to this shift, see F. Jameson, 'Cognitive Mapping', in *Marxism and the Interpretation of Cultures* (1988), and C. Taylor 'The Moral Topography of the Self', in *Hermeneutics and Psychological Theory* (1988).

tion, articulated by means of directed reading. Erasmus' game, and his genius, is to make explicit what others merely imply, to anticipate what others will take time to develop: that the real rituals are now those of sexual and material ownership, as exemplified by Mendemus' nightly performance of the 'Roman Stations' around his home.

There is, as mentioned, something rather seductive about such a history, connected as it is with the development and modulation of a specific textual genre. Problems arise when we try to establish the precise contours of historical change. The mistake is to try to locate a moment at which description became allied to ideology in such a way as to render Jerusalem itself pure figure. It is more a question of how particular pressure came to be placed on the relation between literal and figural modes of understanding at particular times. Exploring the dynamic relations between a static, topic, or place-centred model of description, and one which is temporal and tied into the calendar, offers one way of glimpsing such alterations in pressure. Description was, of course, always already a political matter, in that it has always been about how to invest common places with particular significance, and how to correlate events with their significant consequences: 'Se le pasteur dort le loup a plus temps de venir aux brebis [.] Se levesque nenseigne ses subjectz ils pourront facilement entrer en heresie.'[99] Such are the rhetorician Fabri's illustrations of propositional description at work, and they show that the politics is already there in the examples: 'Se vous ne pugnissez cestuy vous serez cause de ce quil se fera pendre et gastera tous les filz des bourgoys de ceste ville parqouy juge conseillez vostre honneur et le salut de tous.'[100] This is description in its topical, rhetorical sense; it takes narrative order—the order of an Adrichomius, a Loyola, or a Villette—to animate this rhetoric, to breathe personal life into its dry bones.

Description did not need to wait for the counter-Reformers to find ideological and personal direction; but it did gain from them a focus for the direction, and perhaps distortion, of readers' desires. Both Geiler and the author of the *Garden of Prayer* already understood that life is found in the details: it is the adverbial details of the way Christ walked to the cross, and the time he took to do so, that direct the penitent's attention to the time and place of reading. The narrative structure inscribed in the pilgrim journey, itself modelled on the

[99] Fabri, *Réthorique*, fol. cᵛ.   [100] Ibid.

Passion narrative, acts as a means to lead the penitent to translate an imagined set of coordinates into the terms of daily life. In this way temporal power affects the reader's spiritual and unspoken desires. Erasmus, Geiler, and the *Garden* author do something rather different, however, from simply anticipating the future. Having seen how descriptions develop, we can look back to the Garden and to early sixteenth-century pilgrims such as Huen and Ogygius, and see elaborated in their stories a mode of attention in which both the literal and the figural Jerusalem are fully and simultaneously present in the act of reading. As the century progresses and pilgrimage discourse is allied to polemic, it becomes increasingly difficult to maintain this balance. You have to decide (for a time), whose side you are on, and, depending where you stand, Jerusalem is either a real place in a distant land, to which one should or should not travel in order to gain holiness, or it is a figure for the imagination, a secret place of meditation and release from the distraction of the real.

Of course it can be both, as it possibly was for most people throughout the time of our study, and still is for many. For a few, and for a time—the few who wrote, and the time of polemic—it would seem that it could not. Huen's invitation to lead his reader 'par les yeux de la pensee' is an invitation to a journey, one which, for all the polemical ballast of his preface, leads away from the kinds of narrow definition of politics which polemic fosters, and into a different space. It is in such a space that Villette wished to place the readers of his description: a place of both 'instruction' and 'consolation'. To arrive at this place involves a journey of reading, and the effect of imagining a way into a better country. The scene of such reading involves not only internal vision, and not only the imagined presence of Christ, but also the material sight and presence of the pages in the book. The book in your hands, Huen tells the reader, works its effects 'par maniere moult merveilleuse: car par escript et par figures le [the voyage] congnoistres: non seulement par vostre entendement: mais par les yeux corporelz: dont des hommes sont fort refocilles: et leur esperis doulcement consolés'.[101]

Adrichomius, even as he renders the literal journey to Jerusalem redundant, reads Huen's 'figures' literally as numbered paces within a holy arithmetic, and a carefully measured line on a printed page.

---

[101] Huen, *Le grant voyage*, fol. iii^v. I have written about this in a different form elsewhere. See S. Trangmar and W. Williams, 'Contemplation', in *Reading the Glass* (1991).

For his part, Villette has recourse to the formulae of scriptural prayer. To close his text he adopts once again the Latin voice of the Psalmist: 'Adorabimus in loco ubi steterunt pedes eius.' Again it is the first person plural which unites readers and writer; it is also the first person plural of the pilgrim tradition. The Psalmist's hope had been expressed time and again as the motivating desire of pilgrims from Late Antiquity to Villette's own time. But we need to attend closely to the tenses of the text, for it is in the tenses and mood of such verbs that ideology works its effects and changes.

'Adorabimus in loco ubi steterunt pedes eius': We shall worship in the place where his feet stood. The Psalmist's first, future, verb (adorabimus) is now our present, given that his second verb, a past acting as a prophetic future (steterunt), is now, for us as readers, Christ's past presence on earth. The status of the verb of devotion is also altered by this shift in eschatological tense. 'Adorabimus' becomes in effect performative in the moment that we read it. Reading Villette's text so closely, and in particular, reading of the Psalmist's prophecy with careful reference to the places where Christ has in the meantime stood, we find ourselves already in that position of worshipful attention which characterizes the kinds of reading we have been conducting here: a combination of philology and close reading. In contexts other than that of literary criticism, such attention goes by the name of prayer.

CHAPTER FIVE

Narratives of Experience I

The Confusion of Kinds:
Pilgrimage Accounts, 1490–1584

Almost a century separates the two pilgrims at the centre of the two chapters which follow, but more than the passage of time distinguishes one from the other. From these texts it will become clear that the material conditions of pilgrimage changed considerably across the century; clear also that the pilgrimage accounts themselves undergo transformation. We have seen in previous chapters that those who write *about* pilgrimage in the Renaissance express an intense concern regarding the physical and spiritual motivations of the pilgrim. Curiosity, 'mixing' with others, and becoming one of the 'errans' emerge as threats to the pilgrim's integrity. These anxieties are both inherited from Late Antiquity and intensified by the contexts in which Renaissance pilgrims travel. It is the effects of this intensified anxiety on the writing of pilgrims who do not so much write about pilgrimage, nor yet read their way to Jerusalem within their homes, but who take to the road themselves, and attempt to tell of their own travels, that I want to explore here. I shall do so in relation to two pilgrimage narratives in particular.

In attempting to establish the ways in which pilgrimage accounts represent the experience of the journey, we need to understand such 'experience' as the product of just that physical and generic contamination most feared by the writers encountered in previous chapters. For experience is produced as a function of a struggle at the crossroads between 'domaines de savoir, types de normativité et formes de subjectivité'.[1] The debates which took place in the 'domaines de savoir' of theological argument were explored in earlier chapters; as were the normative types legislated or fantasized in the devotional and instructional literature attaching itself to pilgrimage. In the close readings which follow, I shall seek to measure the impact of these debates on the texts and the subjectivities of those who undertook the journey to Jerusalem themselves. It is the relation between inherited narrative forms, the modes of subjectivity which they offer, and particular pilgrims' accounts of their experience of the road which is of interest here. As we shall see, the experience of pilgrimage across the sixteenth century alters almost beyond recognition, and yet still turns about certain unchanged and unchanging axes: it both conforms to inherited norms, and changes the shapes of subjectivity.

Neither of the accounts central to the two chapters which follow sits easily in the context of the writing outlined thus far in this study: the pilgrim tradition as it is received and renewed in the Renaissance. For neither pilgrim directly cites Augustine, nor Gregory of Nyssa, nor Erasmus, nor Richeome. Neither wrote guide-books to accompany their journeys; nor even do they appear to be travelling as envoys of others.[2] More story than argument, their texts are, in a sense, pilgrimage narrative in the raw, and so represent a significant change in direction from those we have discussed in earlier chapters. The first was written by Jehan de Cuchermoys, in 1490, and appended to his version of a romance which he began translating in the course of his own pilgrimage to Jerusalem.[3] Cuchermoys' pilgrimage account is short, sparsely written, and, for the most part,

[1] This is Foucault's working definition of experience (and I have yet to find a better). See *L'Histoire de la sexualité* (1976–84), ii, *L'Usage des plaisirs*, p. 10. His characterization of research as a journey driven by 'la curiosité' remains both a method and an inspiration: 'la seule espèce de curiosité, en tout cas, qui vaille la peine d'être pratiquée avec un peu d'obstination: non pas celle qui cherche à s'assimiler ce qu'il convient de connaître, mais celle qui permet de se déprendre de soi-même' (p. 14).

[2] In contrast to many other pilgrims, whose accounts are often stuffed full of incident and detail, as if telling a good story—and agreeing or even arranging to have it printed— were part of the pilgrim's contract. See for instance the accounts of Hault, Thenaud, Thevet, Postel, and Terrelle. Terrelle was (one of a number of people) sent by François I to collect Byzantine manuscripts from the East. He was, when Montaigne met him and talked to him of his travels, keeper of the treasures and relics at Meaux cathedral. See Montaigne, *Journal*, p. 4. For more on those named above, and some of the others who will appear here in due course, see Rouillard, pp. 37, 43–7, 189–95, and 229–38.

[3] Cuchermoys' account is appended to his translation of *La tresjoyeuse plaisante et recreative hystoire . . . du chevalier Guerin par advent nommé Mesquin* (Lyons, 1530).

distinctly impersonal. Written under the twinned signs of utility and exemplarity, his story is at the centre of this chapter. The second narrative, at the centre of Chapter 6, is that of Jacques de Valimbert, and is a world away from Cuchermoys. Valimbert takes notes on the journey, copies down many other texts, snatches of dialogue, official documents, and incidental details. He then forges the whole into a narrative on his return home, styling himself as something of a romance hero: a pilgrim more exceptional than exemplary. His account was never published in the Renaissance (and remains unpublished); but it was transposed by Valimbert's friend, the devotional poet Chassignet, into a poem against literal pilgrimage. In making of his exceptional friend a negative example, one of the 'errans', Chassignet repeats the argument that the metaphorical is the true pilgrimage. Valimbert's rambling, unfinished narrative proves to the devotional poet that pilgrimage is best performed at home, away from the body, and in meditational preparation for death.[4]

These writers present us with pilgrimage narrative in the raw, but they also demonstrate the different ways in which pilgrims cooked the books—selected, seasoned, and served up 'experience' both to their readers and themselves. For both were read at the time, and need to be read now, in relation to orthodox pilgrim discourse as elaborated in previous chapters on the one hand, and to non-pilgrim kinds of writing on the other. The 'other' genres attached to pilgrimage—romance, devotional poem, and so on—seem at times to describe the pilgrims' experience better than the pilgrimage account proper is able; at other times they disguise the pilgrim to the extent of making him unrecognizable.

Cuchermoys and Valimbert are 'mere' lay, vernacular pilgrims and their accounts themselves carry little pre- or counter-Reformation polemical baggage, little desire to reveal the inner workings of either their enemies' minds, or the Turkish court. Both present their narratives as actual, lived experience, and from their opposite ends of the century they serve here as markers of the chronological and generic boundaries of our study. They also serve as guides to the narratives of

---

[4] The manuscript, which survives only in an eighteenth-century copy, is in the Bibliothèque Municipale at Besançon: Ms. 1453, fols. 46–67. Its existence was signalled by G. Gazier, 'Le pèlerinage d'un bisontin en Egypte et en Terre Sainte en 1584', *Doubs*, Xe série, 2e volume (1932), pp. 35–64. The poem, 'A Jacques de Valimbert, Besançonnois, Chevalier de Hierusalem', is in Chassignet, *Le Mespris de la Vie et Consolation contre la Mort* (pp. 121–31).

other pilgrim writers whose accounts we cannot read in detail, but which contribute to gaining some sense of the ways in which the experience of the Jerusalem pilgrimage is described in French texts of the time. Alongside detailing the specific movements of Cuchermoys' and Valimbert's journeys, we will gesture towards these other texts, and in doing so we should be able to see how often the same places are written about, the same routes followed, the same difficulties encountered, and the same kinds of prejudices and pleasures aroused. What becomes clear is the degree to which imitation under-scores both the practical and the narrative conditions of pilgrimage; it is an exercise in the imitation of others as much as it is *imitatio Christi*. The pilgrim's experience may be defined in terms of differ-ence from Others, but rarely is it altogether different from that of other pilgrims, as the two chapters which follow make plain.

The difference between the two narratives to be isolated here is thus in part a question of pilgrim kind, in part due to their relation-ship to non-fictional textual forms, and in particular a function of their relationship to the rhetoric of pilgrim exemplarity. These are by no means the only surviving pilgrimage accounts from the long six-teenth century. Many more survive in both print and manuscript, and several of these are both more expansive and clearer than either of the texts chosen for close reading here.[5] But I have isolated these accounts not least *because* of the degrees of mediation involved in their sur-vival. They represent the pilgrims' experience all the more directly for being so subject to rewriting and distorted transmission.

From the readings conducted in this study so far, it is clear that the ideal Pilgrim is one who travels towards the visible trace of a now absent person, whether the bones of a saint or the marks of Christ's footsteps. The place is a sign at once of an absence ('He is not here', the angels said), and of presence ('This is where he was, and look, there's the mark', the guides say). Sites of pilgrimage are tangible fig-ure: scripture made flesh and bones, and language made local. On arrival at the place where the trace of the body can be found, the pil-grim gazes upon it, touches it, and then heads for home. Some pil-grims wonder how else to enter into contact with the body here present by way of sign; they may try to do so *in situ*—to kiss the

---

[5] In the two chapters which follow, I shall, given the frequency of references, cite pil-grims' texts in notes by author's name and page reference only. For fuller references, see bibliography.

bones, or the stones—, or they may try to take pieces away so as to maintain contact when they have returned home. They will be stopped by officials in attempting to do either action, for each destroys the object of desire, threatens to erase both the trace proper and the figural importance of the place. Too close or too personally enduring a possession of the sign is both denied and impossible. It seems that pilgrimage has to be about being there for a time, and for a time only; about registering the charge of presence, and then leaving.

This becomes a problem of literal erasure when pilgrims give expression to the desire literally to mark their presence in the place by inscribing their name or initials on the sacred rocks. Hault, for instance, notes that he scrawled his name on several rocks and walls, including those of the room in Bethlehem in which Jerome translated the scriptures: 'je croy que mon nom si [*sic*] trouveroit encor escript.'[6] This is an act central to pilgrimage: you mark your name in the place where others have already marked theirs. And adding to the graffiti, you make further pilgrimages—those of later generations of readers, translators, and writers—at once possible and harder to perform. Your journey uncovers the significance of places which have hitherto been only textual in your mind, it makes them real; your signature on the rocks defaces them, buries them under yet more writing. But it also adds to the body of texts which incites others to make, or read of, the journey in turn, and so ensures the enduring cultural survival of those steadily disappearing rocks.

In admitting to writing at all while in the Holy Land, both Cuchermoys and Valimbert are consequently both breaking the rules, and conforming to the habits of pilgrimage. Alongside the argument that pilgrims should not be (caught) writing *in situ*, ran another which claimed that pilgrims' texts, since they were composed in the place proper, carry the charge of presence all the more directly to the reader's home. Possot, for instance, is said by his editor to have travelled 'toujours . . . la tablette en main', and this is what has made his *Description*, with its 'belles painctures', such a singular account.[7] For the most part, pilgrim narrators argue that their texts need little ornamentation, and can admit of few textual paintings of places or things. When they themselves admit to having written while on the

---

[6] Hault, fol. 37^r.

[7] See the editor's prefatory letter to Possot's *Description, non. pag.* For more on the rhetoric of description in Possot and other literal pilgrims, see Ch. 4, above.

road, they do so in order to plead with rhetorical humility for generous readers, given the circumstances of the text's production. Balourdet echoes the terms of many in the century preceding him when he
writes: 'Vous plaise [Madame] excuser le rude stile, et peu d'ordre
qu'y trouverez: ayant esgard, que sur les champs, et mer, on n'a le
moyen d'escrire si proprement qu'en l'estude.'[8] Hault, although he
stresses that his narrative can be trusted, since it was written 'sur [s]es
tablettes tous les jours durant [s]on voyage' and has remained unpolished since its return, nevertheless warns subsequent pilgrims not to
follow his example, for fear of being 'caressé comme on faict les es-
pions'.[9] Castela, ever the legislator, expands on this theme, confirming how, by virtue of a certain rhetorical ascesis—figured as a *diktat*
imposed by Others—the subjectivity of the majority of Christian pilgrims is best confirmed through narrative silence:

> Ceux qui sçavent peindre en pourtraiture soient bien advisés de ne des-
> seigner rien, ou coucher autrement par escrit, tout le long du chemin, à la
> mesme peine que les espions ont accoustumé de souffrir auparavent qu'ils
> ne s'eschappent des rigeurs de leur justice.[10]

The silent pilgrims, the majority, are the ones we can know little of in
detail, those we cannot attempt to speak with, or resurrect. Some
sixteenth-century pilgrims, however, do write of their experience,
often in response to the requests of those to whom they have narrated
their stories on their return. You must put your experiences down on
paper, transfer your notes to print, is what many pilgrims are told.
Hault is one who finally, reluctantly, agrees to the demands of his
uncle (and patron), and fixes the terms of what happened from when
he left to when he arrived home. As if acknowledging that he is doing
so by way of contract, he concludes with a list of what—financially—
the journey cost him. If Hault does not say what it cost him to write
the account, he does none the less acknowledge that it was not easy.[11]
    The pilgrimages narrated by Cuchermoys and Valimbert are
thus—in that they became narratives—more exceptional than typ-
ical. Which is to say, we read them in the first instance for what they

---

[8] Balourdet, 'Epistre Liminaire' to Princess Renée de Lorraine, *non. pag.*
[9] Hault, fols. 1ʳ–2ᵛ. Hault also notes that both Zuallart and Villamont, who were on
the same pilgrimage, have written 'si curieusement avec un tant bel ordre' that he cannot
match them. In Hault's case this is, I think, genuine modesty, but the terms are charged,
and in any other pilgrim's preface would amount to damning with faint praise.
[10] Castela, *Guide*, fol. 62ʳ.
[11] For a list of how much money things cost him, see Hault, fols. 82ᵛ–87ʳ.

tell us about themselves, and about the details of the material conditions of the journey to Jerusalem as they develop and change across
the long sixteenth century. We also read them as exemplary in that
they reveal the narrative conditions of Renaissance pilgrimage. But
the modern reader looking for elaborate descriptions, adventurous
tales, and the expression of emotion by pilgrims must either read the
texts signalled here in the footnotes, or search in languages other
than French. Reiter and Tucher (1479, German), Fabri (1489, Latin),
Casola (1494, Italian), von Harff (1499, German), and Guylforde
(1506, English) are all more expansive and complex in narrative form
than either Cuchermoys in his terse account, or Valimbert in his
truncated, imperfectly copied manuscript notes.[12] Why then should
we choose these texts for close reading? The answer lies in their position midway between kinds, and their understanding of the pilgrim
as a character who travels through confusion.

The translation of the pilgrim into a Pilgrim, or a voyage into a
Sainct Voyage, is, for some, as difficult as that of a body to Palestine
and back. As our two texts make particularly clear, in composing
narrative accounts of their journeys, pilgrims can find that the initial
desire for recollection of 'what it was like' comes up against a number of obstacles. The desire to recreate the immediacy and intimacy
of the conditions on board ship, the emotions felt at night in the
woods, or mountains, or hostels, the look of the chapel in Bethlehem . . . is not always fulfilled by the means of representation available to them. After confronting contagion with Others of all kinds,
including the Turk, the heretic, death, and images of their own hitherto unknown desires, they can find themselves lost to the procedures
of representation, diverted away from their general pilgrim integrity,
and subject to the particular tricks of writing and memory. The pilgrim becomes confused in his text with the trickster, the trader, the
cosmographer, or the simply curious.

As the individual narrator alternately encourages and resists identification with these figures, and that of the representative Pilgrim,
his narrative becomes a confusion of kinds. It 'mixes' perilously with
forms of writing which share pilgrim territory, and the peculiarity of

---

[12] The dates of the above travellers seem to give the lie to the idea (put forward by
Howard and others) that pilgrimage cannot accommodate the subjective voice. But it is
important to note that none of the above were printed in their fullest digressive form in the
Renaissance (neither was the text of Fabri, which Howard relies on to make his point; see
above, Ch. 1).

the pilgrim experience is threatened with erasure. It is, then, the often confusing challenge of representing the experience of a Jerusalem pilgrimage in the sixteenth century, and, in particular, the effects of generic 'mixing' on the integrity of the pilgrim narrator, which are the focus of our readings in the chapters which follow. Each text narrates a number of journeys and in our reading of them we will follow them at the pace they set—now laboriously slow, now perilously fast, now rich in explanatory detail, now oddly unconcerned to make the connections we might expect. The purpose of reading in this way is to gain some measure of what it was like, at the time of telling, to be a pilgrim, and to tell a pilgrim's story.

1490—The Example of Jehan de Cuchermoys

Reading Romance

On Wednesday, 23 June 1490, in the town of Ragusa on the Dalmatian coast, Jehan de Cuchermoys began translating the romance of 'Guerino, detto Il Meschino', from Italian into French. Cuchermoys, aged about 25 and a native of Lyons, had set out from home six weeks earlier, on the eighth of May, with his friend Pierre Filz-de-femme, 'maistre de la monnoye de Bourges', bound for the Holy Land.[13] The romance the pilgrim translates far extends the geographical boundaries of his own journey, taking in places, people, and things Cuchermoys will never see. For it tells of the far-flung travels of one Guerin, rightful prince of Albania and son of Millon, himself one-time companion of Charlemagne, who is separated from his parents at the age of 2 months by a usurper, rescued by his nursemaid, and then taken from her and his homeland by pirates. These then sell the boy, 'ensemble daultre marchandise', to a passing merchant who takes him to Constantinople and there raises him as his son, teaches him Greek, Latin, and 'plusieurs langaiges pour lutilite de la marchandise et pour le navigaige', and renames him Mesquin.[14] The learning of languages and the disguise of a new name does not so much train the boy to be a merchant like his adoptive father, as equip him to fulfil the role of Trickster hero in the quest which will lead him back to his first name, his parents, and his home.

---

[13] Cuchermoys, fol. Oi^v.   [14] Ibid., fols. Aiii^v Aiiii^r.

While still in Constantinople Mesquin comes to the attention of the Emperor's son, Alexandre, who makes him a free man, loves him as a brother, and introduces him to his 15 year-old sister, Elizene; with whom Mesquin falls in love. A joust is declared for her hand, but Mesquin is unable to compete. For the Emperor has prohibited all but the noble from entering, and, as the ladies of the court know and frequently discuss—amid much shaming laughter and scorn— Mesquin is ignorant of his true father. Alexandre takes Mesquin's part and together the two men:

se retirerent en une chambre et veillerent toute la nuyt a deffournir une tunicque qui estoit de drap alexandrin a celle fin quelle fut claire et quelle ne fut point congneue pour couvrir luy [Mesquin] son cheval et escu et en couvrirent la nuyt le cheval. Et firent tant que celle nuyt peu ilz dormirent.[15]

Just as Mesquin's adoptive father had taught him the principles of linguistic disguise, so here his adoptive brother teaches the young man how to conceal his face and body from others. The passage is, in both incident and vocabulary, an eloquent staging of the erotics of disguise. It also sets the initial frame of the romance, which turns on the material, sexual, and rhetorical senses of 'couvrir'. The one mutually adoptive brother covers the other, in secret, and with a cloth which both conceals and bears his name: 'drap alexandrin'. In diegetic terms this is done in order that the adoptive brother may make a wife of the sister of the blood brother. The young prince, like the nursemaid and the adoptive merchant father, disguises Mesquin in order to fantasise the creation of family ties not based on class, ethnicity, or blood. Romance will have blood, however, and in generic terms, these teachers of disguise are themselves being used by the plot first to love the boy, then to teach him, and then to lose him as he continues his quest for home.

Mesquin enters the joust, duly disguised, and wins. A dispute ensues between the myriad knights who have assembled; the ladies at court also want to know: who was that man? Before things can develop between the potential lovers, the court is besieged, and everyone grows anxious under the Turkish threat. Everyone, that is, except Mesquin, who 'se sentoit de tant de valleur qu'il navoit nulle paour'. Elizene, unaware that Mesquin is the winning 'chevalier blanc' to whom she has lost her heart, misreads his valour as a sign of

---

[15] Cuchermoys, fol. Avi[r].

something else: 'Pour certain tu dois estre Turc qui nas nulle honte et ne ten chault de nostre affaire vaten et te oste de devant moy serf et esclave que tu es.'[16] Misrecognized in this way, Mesquin finds his love turning to hate. Elizene's final jibe—'et encores ne scez tu qui tu es'— silences the young man, and he turns away. He cannot bear to look at the princess, and will never forgive her. Neither does the narrator: 'Et pource toutes meres doivent enseigner leurs filles de bien et honeste-ment parler. Car Elizene par sa langue et legiere parolle perdit a mary celluy qui plus elle aymoit en ce monde.'[17]

The jousting tournament is followed by a battle on a larger scale in which, now fighting for the city of Constantinople, Mesquin is again triumphant. He delivers Constantinople from the attack of the Infi-del, and marriage is again the projected prize: 'l'empereur et sa femme serchoient de donner au mesquin elizene pour femme mais ce n'estoit que peine perdue.'[18] For this time Mesquin will have none of it. He is unable to settle down a heroic husband, wounded as he is by the shame of not knowing his 'generation'. In this shame world of claims and accusations, Elizene could have been right about his iden-tity. After all, he has no way of proving her wrong without breaking the covering frame of having been disguised at the jousting. To do this would implicate Alexandre in the disguise plot which contravened the father's initial law. Such disloyalty to his adoptive brother and prospective father-in-law could neither guarantee recognition of a new identity, nor recover the truth of his history.

In fact, of course, it is Elizene who has been framed: the disguise pact made between the two men, ostensibly to ensure Mesquin's pos-session of Elizene, sets her up to misrecognize him. Like the others who want to stop the Romancer's travels, her desires are denied by the plot. The narrative thus imprisons her, as much as it does the former captive Mesquin, within the thematics of deception which ensure that the Law of the Father remains in place (even if the individual father wishes it otherwise), and that brother (even adoptive brother) will not marry sister. This triangulating thematics of kinship, dis-guise, and taboo is one from which Mesquin will spend the remain-der of the romance trying to escape. Telling Alexandre that he has been metaphorically placed 'dedans une navire de fortune qui ne peut arriver au port de mer', he pledges allegiance to the quest. Redemp-tion is to be found only through acting out, in the plane of the real,

---

[16] Ibid., fol. Aviii^v.   [17] Ibid., fol. Bv^r.   [18] Ibid.

the conditions of our metaphorical enslavement. 'Je dois', he explains, 'cercher de ponant en levant. Et par tout le monde je doys aller pour scavoir qui est mon pere.'[19] It is with a similar, if more teleological, understanding of how literal journeying may be the condition for release from our metaphorical enslavement in the flesh that the pilgrim sets out from home.

First published in Italian in Padua in 1473, then in Venice in 1477, 1480, 1498, 1508, 1512 . . ., *Guerino Meschino* was a popular romance.[20] Cuchermoys perhaps bought, or was given, his copy on his way through Venice on his way to Jerusalem. We do not know how he came to have it in his possession, nor what motivated him to start translating in Ragusa—the coastal town which he terms 'la plus forte petite ville de chrestiente', and which now bears the name Dubrovnik.[21] We know only that he translated the romance: his translation, the only one extant in French, was published in Lyons, albeit not until 1530, forty years after the journey. Cuchermoys' pilgrimage account, in which he notes having begun to translate Mesquin's story, is bound together with the romance, taking up the last six of 106 pages. The translation, he declares to his 'nobles lecteurs ou auditeurs', was undertaken 'par maniere de passe temps . . . c'est un livre de bonne foy'.[22]

It is on the question of 'bonne foy' in relation to the thematics of 'couvrir' as outlined above that the romance turns. As Mesquin travels in pursuit of the truth about his origins, so the reader responds to the hero's constant recourse to the proscribed arts of divination, deception, and disguise. His journeys take him first to the East in Alexander's footsteps, then to the deep South in search of Prester John and the source of the Nile, and then due West to St Patrick's cave and the mouth of Purgatory. We cannot follow him in detail here. We need rather to focus on certain pressured moments in the text at which Mesquin 'mixes' with others, and at which his story courts that of pilgrimage. For though Cuchermoys only acknowledges his

---

[19] Cuchermoys, fol. Bvᵛ.

[20] The romance is now attributed to Andrea da Barberino. There were eight surviving manuscripts in Italian at last count (1908), and it was often printed: there were seventeen prose editions before 1555, more in verse, and another spate of editions in the early 1800s. There is no modern edition in either Italian or French.

[21] The pilgrim course along the Dalmatian coast remains a locus of conflict. Dubrovnik's impregnable walls once again helped to save many lives in 1991–2, now mostly of a different faith.

[22] Ibid., fol. Oiᵛ.

connection with romance at the one point in his pilgrimage account (when he notes that he had started the translation), Mesquin encounters several pilgrims of various kinds at several points in his journey. It is the relation of these moments to the larger movement of the plot which may teach us something of how the pilgrim's journey and that of the romance hero intersect.

Following the directions of an Egyptian necromancer, Mesquin first sets out, in the company of two guides, for India and before long they reach the territory of one King Paciffero, whose court (like that in Constantinople) is awash with suitors for the hand of a young girl. Once again the romance principle of repetition is in play; but for all the similarities, there are important differences here. Mesquin finds the King's black skin 'si estrange' that he is not sure how to look at him; the King finds Mesquin's fair face 'si bel' that he cannot take his eyes off him. King Paciffero ask the newcomer if he is 'masle ou femelle' and despite Mesquin's 'honteulx' answer to the effect that he is a man, keeps him in a richly furnished room to await his pleasure.[23] The King tries to force himself on Mesquin (and earns criticism from the narrator for his 'sodomie et luxure contre nature' for doing so), but he quickly relents when Mesquin resists. He then tries to marry the young man to his daughter, and again Mesquin resists, only this time his refusal results in his being imprisoned in a foul dungeon. By this stage, however, the King's daughter (who is never named) is in love, and agrees to free Mesquin both from the prison and from her father's desire in exchange for satisfaction of her own. Mesquin consents to the contract and loses his virginity. But the princess is—like Elizene—the most deceived in this encounter. Her tale is not told; rather, like all those who attempt to divert the Romancer from his quest, she is punished by the romance. Mesquin leaves, she is left holding the baby, and there is every expectation that the child, a boy, will one day repeat his father's movements, leave his mother, embark on his own quest, and discover the truth of the falsehood behind his generation in turn.[24]

Following further adventures, Mesquin arrives in due course at the trees of the sun and the moon, to see if they will tell him what he wants to know. They do not, and so he returns due West in anger, haranguing his fellow passengers, a group of 'pellerins chiens sarrazins qui alloient aux arbres du souleil par devotion'.[25] These are the

[23] Ibid., fol. Ciii^r.   [24] Ibid., fols. Ciii^v–Ciiii^r.   [25] Ibid., fol. Cviii^v.

first pilgrims he encounters in his travels and his anger is in large part directed at himself for having taken on the 'false' identity of the (non-Christian) pilgrim, erring East beyond Jerusalem. But travel, even digression, is a pretext for an encounter and for further shifts in the shape of Mesquin's identity. He next finds himself fighting for the Persians at Persepolis; he also finds another young princess. She is 14 years old, 'belle comme ung bel ange de paradis', in tears when first seen, and 'reallement vestue'. She is not, then, in disguise. The double sense of 'reallement' (meaning both royally and properly) confirms her identity: she is the Persian Princess. Her father—once king of Palestine and other places—has been killed by the Turk, and his absence alleviates the need for disguise, either linguistic or material. There is consequently no danger of Mesquin becoming entrapped in the triangulation of the desire between daughter/son, father, and himself which has haunted him thus far. Indeed the encounter with the 'bel ange' opens up the space for a new discourse between the lovers, as the erotics of disguise are displaced by those of open contract. Her father's death has left Autiniche, as she is called, rich beyond measure, but deprived of speech; unable to tell her own story, she is dumb with grief. The men who accompany her—and Mesquin becomes one—tell it for her. One of these men, the one who recaptures her land and converts her grief into bliss, stands to win the dowry.[26]

Mesquin momentarily sets aside his quest for legitimacy and 'pour lamour delle entreprint la guerre'. He is duly victorious, and Autiniche, for her part, shows herself to be neither always silent, nor altogether powerless. She moves from being the object of the quest, to an active subject in the new discourse of contract which follows the war. Their stories become interwoven as she commits Mesquin, before he leaves to pursue his quest, to a negotiated oath. She will wait for him for ten years, and he must keep himself for her; crucially, he must return to her even after he has completed his quest and found his own father, mother, and identity. This is a canny contract. For if what unites the two lovers is their grief at separation, and their need to recover a certain property—Mesquin's is his proper name, Autiniche's her land—then Autiniche is anxious to ensure that Mesquin's recovery of the objects of his desires will not cut short hers. In this way she ensures that both she and Mesquin will together

---

[26] Cuchermoys, fol. Diiii[r].

escape the triangulation of the desire of another; it keeps alive the possibility of their survival (as a married couple with children) beyond the end of the romance.

Mesquin leaves Autiniche, recaptures Jerusalem for the Sultan, and swears on the Holy Sepulchre that if he is given the grace to find his parents he will keep his promise to return to the princess. This he swears, along with the oath to convert her, 'secrettement'. For although kneeling a full night before the Holy Sepulchre, Mesquin does not do so openly as either a pilgrim, or a crusading knight; he is fighting for the Persian princess and the Sultan, and is still in disguise.[27] After travelling (too far) East and returning to Jerusalem, Mesquin heads (again too far) South, past Sinai to Ethiopia. Here, he meets Prester John, and is told that he is still in error. Truth is not to be found in the desert: he must go the Pope, gain his blessing, and travel to Purgatory, due West. If he survives this he will find that the end of the romance will figure both a return to home territory (the recovery of parents), and a return to a domesticated foreign space: marriage with, and conversion of, Autiniche. Before these multiple reunions, however, there is, of course, further entanglement in error, further twists of his own tale, and further separation to be endured.

Mesquin encounters and saves the life of a fellow-traveller on the road. He, unlike Mesquin, knows both who he is and where he is going: he is an English noble, named Divoyne, and is on pilgrimage to Jerusalem. The two travellers endure a number of trials and battles together in Africa before, eventually, they both leave the continent in the same way that Mesquin had arrived: in a boat full of pilgrims. This time the pilgrims are Christians and the text, rather than ridiculing their devotion, celebrates their piety.[28] But this reunion of romance with pilgrimage is also prelude to further separation. Divoyne joins the pilgrim company, and so leaves the romance, whereas Mesquin must continue his quest due West.

He is propelled further on his journey, now westwards across Europe. In effect this move serves both as a change of geographical direction, and as a shift in narrative mode. The strange beasts and peoples of the East are replaced by the allegorical temptations and triumphs of the Christian West.[29] So Mesquin makes his way to

---

[27] Ibid., fol. Ei[r].   [28] Ibid., fol. Gviii[v].

[29] In complementary contrast, the woodcuts which accompany the romance change from those depicting battles and jousts involving humans in early-Renaissance clothing, to those depicting naked men, women, and beasts involved in orgies of several kinds.

Ireland. He enters the opulently, and above all complicatedly, erotic caves of the Sybil, and then wanders through the complementary caves of St Patrick, through the seven circles of Purgatory, and up the Mountain of Delights. As well as meeting the ghosts of those monsters and enemies he had killed in the first half of the romance, Mesquin speaks with the shades of characters from stories other than his own. He converses with Enoch and Elijah; he battles with a number of vices, embodied as snakes and monsters. Following this he is given a glimpse of his parents, as if through a glass darkly. He is able to see that he is of royal blood, and can now leave the Hibernian caves. At the mouth of Purgatory, he is met by Divoyne, who offers him a wife and half his lands. Mesquin knows his quest is not over, not yet. He must return to Autiniche, return due East to Albania, free his parents, and win back his own lands from those who are in league with the Turk.[30]

This return from the living death of Purgatory to the troubles of Europe is a return to the arena of contemporary history: a space neither East nor West, neither monstrous nor allegorical. It also marks a return from the thematics of exile to the folds of the family romance. For, travelling back from the periphery to the centre, Mesquin is reunited with Alexandre and receives a letter of encouragement from Autiniche. He soon finds his true father and mother languishing, releases them from prison, and restores them to the throne. The romance is (almost) over; like the early anonymous pilgrim log, it has taken readers away, but it has brought its hero—and its readers—home.

Clearly the Pilgrim and the Trickster cross ground which is geographically and even metaphorically similar. Perhaps they connect in that, on occasion, Cuchermoys must have wondered what sort of a world he had come to. He and his fellow pilgrims must also have been the object of some curiosity for people they encountered on the way. We don't know this for sure. Cuchermoys rarely mentions nonpilgrims in his text, and rarer still his own emotions and dreams. In terms of its narrative style Mesquin's adventure could not be further removed from the pilgrimage Cuchermoys pursues as he translates. The romance stages two central meetings with pilgrims, and Mesquin, like the pilgrim Cuchermoys, kneels a full night at the Holy Sepulchre to confirm the vows which motivate his journey. And yet he does so in disguise, while fighting to regain the land for the love of another.

[30] Cuchermoys, fol. Kii^v.

We return to the thematics of property, desire, and disguise, and find them centred on the Sepulchre in Jerusalem even in so far-flung and far-fetched a romance as Mesquin's. But there are also more material connections between the reading of romance and pilgrimage. It is, as mentioned, only because he translated the romance that we know of Cuchermoys' own journey to Jerusalem and home again. As if following the Persian princess Autiniche's example, Cuchermoys ensures that his own story is told after the end of the romance. His account of the pilgrimage follows the tale, occupying the (albeit small) space beyond its conclusion.[31] In gothic print with woodcut illustrations, the pilgrimage account opens with a bordered page, headed by an image of a pilgrim leaving a fortified town—a woodcut which had already accompanied Mesquin's peregrinations earlier in the text, peregrinations the pilgrim had begun translating from within the most fortified little town in Christendom. The reading and indeed the iconography of romance and pilgrimage connect, in this text, in material, thematic, and metaphorical ways.

Whereas Mesquin produces versions of himself, as if by accident, the pilgrim travels with the express purpose of losing his individual subjectivity in the physical translations of the story of another (Christ). He travels in search of signs not of his own origins, nor of things counterfeit and strange, but rather for confirmation of the truth of scripture, and an encounter with Christ in the 'place where he stood'. And yet this particular pilgrim, Cuchermoys, also read and translated Mesquin's story as he travelled. Pilgrimage narrative should not, the rule books say, be the place to tell your own story; your life is mapped on to, and subsumed to, that of Christ. Cuchermoys submits, in the narrative of his own journey, to these pilgrim norms. But he also tells of a very different kind of journey, and binds the two narrative kinds together without further comment. Might romance, and the translation of romance, be the place to explore, and tell of, things unspoken in the pilgrimage narrative proper? A way of both telling your story and keeping the faith? The coincidence of these narratives bears still closer reading, as does exploration of closer points of kinship between the particular moves of these two characters, and of the more general question regarding the 'formes de subjectivité' which they represent.

---

[31] Ibid., fols. Oiʳ Oviᵛ.

It has been argued that the enduring attraction of the romance plot—which underscores both Cuchermoys' and Valimbert's pilgrimage accounts in exemplary ways—is due to its recursive nature. Literature returns to the *topos* of the journey and to the polytropic ruses of the travelling hero with such regularity in order to raise questions regarding the status of literary discourse itself. In being about apparently leading readers astray, the better to lead them home, romance is said to be the paradigm for all story-telling. Among the most influential and eloquent statements of this position in our own time is that offered by Northrop Frye. He explains how romance first creates a fictional world, and then reveals that we have been looking at our own world, disguised as another, all along: 'the conflict takes place in, or at any rate primarily concerns, *our* world, which is in the middle'—as opposed to the 'upper' or 'lower' worlds.[32] In our romance, this is translated into Mesquin's more lateral East and West. The hero's quest represents that of the reader of literature in search of the truth there disguised: 'the quest-romance is the search of the libido or desiring self for a fulfilment that will deliver it from the anxieties of reality, but will still contain that reality.'[33]

The Trickster travels on behalf of, and in the time of, the individual reader whose understanding of his own story re-enacts Mesquin's recovery of his own name and identity. This is the measure of Frye's— at once Freudian and theological—claim for reading romance which resists the troping of the journey into pure trope:

The culture of the past is not only the memory of mankind, but our own buried life, and study of it leads to a recognition scene, a discovery in which we see, not our past lives, but the total cultural form of our present life. It is not only the poet but his reader who is subject to the obligation to make it new.[34]

In our perspective, this is to make of reading romance an orthodox form of pilgrimage in itself. It is to read all literal movement as figure, and all apparently novel kinds of meaning as in fact versions of always already known—if dimly, and buried—cultural norms and forms.

This is a compelling account of what fiction is and does. But to make of the romance voyage (only) a locus of literature's own critical self-reflection is to foreshorten deliberation as to how pilgrimage and

[32] N. Frye, *The Anatomy of Criticism*, p. 187.
[33] Ibid., p. 193. See also Frye, *The Secular Scripture*, pp. 28–31.
[34] Frye, *Anatomy*, p. 346.

romance connect. It is to ignore both the politics and the history of forms, to avoid engaging with the ways in which pilgrimage and romance intersect with the rhetoric of crusade, and how these forms variously negotiate the terms of an experience which is now in large part lost to us. Only the enslavement of critical thought within its own professionally charted territory makes of any journey a rite of confirmation, and makes of all reading a kind of orthodox pilgrimage, structured as an exercise in recognition by, for, and on behalf of the metaphysically posited Reader. For no pilgrimage account, romance, or crusade is ever only orthodox, and it is in the cross-fertilisation and confusion of kinds that critical thought is propelled beyond its own already charted borders.

Returning to the romance, we find that, for all its centrifugal ex-centricity, it ends on a note of severe implosion: Mesquin's father and mother die not long (in the time of narration) after their recovery, and Autiniche soon dies giving birth to a son. Suddenly Mesquin is both doubled by a legitimate other—his proper son who bears his own name, Guerin—and alone. Once again he readies himself to leave. 'Estant en bonne disposition de son salut par ung tresgrand vouloir et ferme proupos de despartir', he heads now not for the edges of the earth, but to 'quelque hermitaige' to die 'finablement'.[35] This 'finablement' reads, in this context, as an ethical as well as a temporal adverb: Mesquin has learned to die well.

Read in this way, even independently of the pilgrimage, the romance traces a course back from the dangerous asocial realm of figure into that of socialized forms of referential narration. Far more than just an exotic package tour, it appears to be a powerful affirmation of the laws of poetics, family, and property. But as we shall see now in moving first to the pilgrimage narrative attached to this particular romance, and then to the later pilgrimage account of Jacques de Valimbert, there are other, equally compelling, ways of reading romance. These become especially clear when romance is reunited with its often forgotten twin: pilgrimage. For when the twinned journeys of romance and pilgrimage are placed alongside each other, they reveal ways in which the norms and forms which are central to our culture are a kind of 'barbarism', an aggression towards, fear of, and desire to deny or obliterate, others.[36] Furthermore, when read in

---

[35] Cuchermoys, fol. Nviii^v.

[36] See W. Benjamin, *Illuminationen* (1977), pp. 258–9; see also, from a different perspective, F. Lestringant, 'Catholiques et cannibales: Le Thème du cannibalisme dans le

active conjunction, these narrative forms suggest that our cultural barbarism—etymologically: 'langages pellegrins'—can on occasion give rise to the articulation of a contradictory desire to that of erasing otherness: losing oneself to alterity, 'mixing' with others, with their lives, their shapes, and their stories, and returning home altered oneself. It is, our texts teach us, this doubly determined desire—to remain self-identical and to open oneself up to the indwelling of an Other—which animates both pilgrimage and romance, and which in turn determines to no small degree the forms of subjectivity to which we are today obligated.

Reading Pilgrimage

Jehan de Cuchermoys and his companion Pierre Filz-de-Femme set out from home on 8 May 1490 as true and orthodox pilgrims: 'tous deliberez de ung bon et ferme proupos de aller.' Unlike Mesquin, they are headed neither for the retreat of a hermitage, nor the death which releases him from this self-inflicted immurement. The Jerusalem journey they have ahead of them is measured, in the logbooks they have consulted and which serve as their narrative model, in miles and days travelled, not in the allegorical advance of obstacles overcome, oracles disproved, or origins recovered. The *Voyage* that Cuchermoys writes alongside his romance translation is, in its structure and intent, true to pilgrim form; but it does, as we shall see, have significant recourse to the 'three-day rhythm of death, disappearance, and revival' which Frye discerns pulsating at the heart of romance.[37]

Following three days' business in Lyons the pilgrims crossed the Alps, sold their horses in Turin, took the boat from Chieri, and arrived in Venice on 23 May. After shopping around, they drew up a contract with one Bernard Boldu for a passage to Jaffa and back; the price agreed was forty ducats 'd'or et de poys' each.[38] They were

discours protestant au temps des guerres de religion', in *Pratiques et discours alimentaires à la Renaissance* (1982), pp. 233–45. I return to this theme in Ch. 7 below.

[37] Frye, *Anatomy*, p. 187.

[38] The main agents for the Jerusalem package were Boldu and the Contarini brothers, although they ceased to operate in the time of our study. For details of this and other costs see: Affagart, pp. 22, 24–6; Balourdet, p. 11; Beauveau, p. 114; Castela, pp. 44–6; F. Fabri, *Evagatorium*, i, pp. 13–14, 87–90; Hault, fols. 4ᵛ, 17ᵛ, 78ᵛ, 82ᵛ–87ʳ; Lesaige, fol. iiiᵛ; Giraudet, pp. 7–10, 29; Marsy, *Pèlerins normands*, p. 19; Possot, p. 87, 146, 195; Regnaut, p. 16; Salignac, fol. Ccᵛ; Villamont, pp. 367–8, 387–93; Röhricht and Meisner, *Deutsche Pilgerreisen*, pp. 11–14; Sumption, *Pilgrimage*, pp. 185, 189–92, 203–10; F. Braudel, *La*

obliged to wait in Venice for eighteen days before a boat was prepared to sail, but this gave them time to be drenched by a storm in which stones fell, large as eggs, leaving no pane of glass in the city unshattered, and to see several saints' bodies, 'naked and complete'.[39]

The two pilgrims, now part of a larger group, made their way along the Dalmatian and Istrian coast, arriving at Ragusa on Tuesday, 22 June. Moving on from Ragusa to Modon, Rhodes, and Cyprus, they disembarked in Jaffa on 4 August. In Jaffa, Cuchermoys had his possessions stolen, and was obliged to return in disguise to the ship, to collect enough money and clothes to continue the journey. They were subjected to further delay in Ramleh, during which a German pilgrim died from the exhaustion of the journey. This is the first mention of a pilgrim dying in the text; he does so on sacred ground, not at sea. Others on the return journey are less fortunate, as we shall see. The surviving company of pilgrims arrived in Jerusalem on the tenth: three months and two days after leaving home.[40]

Within Jerusalem, and beyond it, further pilgrimages were made, to Bethlehem, Judea, and Bethany. The pilgrim mentions little of the land except those sites which carry biblical resonance, many of which are underground. Only those places which are also scriptural *loci*—glosses on Christ's Life as written in the gospels—drew his attention. As in Villette's description, so here too, the land is made up not so much of places, as 'places where'. Places had existence for Cuchermoys—as for the earliest pilgrims whose accounts survive—only as a function of their sacred significance. *Imitatio* motivated the pilgrim's every step, and the process of increasing identification with Christ culminated in the initiation into the order of the Holy Sepulchre, a ceremony which took place after the second of three days and nights spent in the tomb. For Cuchermoys this occurred on the night of 14 August 1490. He writes the date into his account: it matters.

This is no journey of discovery, still less one of allegorical

---

Méditerranée (1949), i, pp. 212–52. Bernard is simply incorrect in saying that no pilgrims give such detail (*L'Orient du XVIe siècle*, pp. 95–7).

[39] 'Comme le corps saincte Barbe, saincte Luce et saincte Helaine', Cuchermoys, fol. Oi[v]. The epithets 'entier et nu', which Cuchermoys—in common with other pilgrims—uses with reference to relics which merit especial mention, mean 'not encased'. See Lesaige, fols. iii[r]–hi[r]; Voisins, p. 21. Montaigne, in the 'Au Lecteur' to the *Essais*, uses the same terms to refer to his posthumous self (*Oeuvres*, p. 9).

[40] Cuchermoys, fol. Oii[v].

abandon; it is more a rite of confirmation. When Cuchermoys and his companion are not inside churches, or tombs, they stay indoors, sheltering from the heat and the perceived threat of the locals. Part of the deal struck with Boldu in Venice was being guided and guarded in the Holy Land, and it is agents who talk and pay taxes to the authorities on the pilgrims' behalf. This is noted by Belon who, as well as detailing the fruits and flowers to be found on the hillsides of Jerusalem, tells us that pilgrims are guided by a 'droguement' who is always present 'pour parler aux gens du pays et respondre pour les pelerins'.[41] His formulation 'pour les pelerins' rather than 'pour nous' is a mark of Belon's difference from pilgrims. It need not necessarily mean that interpreters literally spoke for pilgrims, and so prevented them from speaking themselves. But as we saw with respect to the debate around Gregory of Nyssa's letter, as the guide books and catechistic pamphlets make clear, and as pilgrims themselves state in their texts, they were strongly advised not to address the locals, on pain of death. It is one of the strongest taboos ensuring the propriety of the normative type of the pilgrim in text and language, mouth and body, and soul.

Mesquin, as we saw, speaks, eats, and sleeps with many people and beasts on his travels; and he pays no taxes.[42] By contrast, when Cuchermoys meets the local people, the experiences are almost all bad. Arrival in Jaffa had begun a series of distressing encounters; leaving Jerusalem and returning to Jaffa, the pilgrims are again held hostage. Boldu's agents, for an extra fee, negotiate their release. Cuchermoys remarks how pilgrims—in being held hostage, not being able to speak for themselves, and having to give several ducats to both parties—pay the price of the exchange of words between the locals and their guides.

The importance of the role played by guides, and the reasons for the pilgrims' habitual aggression towards the locals are made more

[41] Belon, *Observations*, fol. 250ʳ.

[42] Nor do Belon, nor Beauveau, both travelling in the train of ambassadors. Nor indeed does Regnaut who, by chance, meets ambassador Aramon and his train (including Gassot, who left his own account, and a certain Pierre de Cochart) at the door, and so is let in for free (p. 67). Beauveau notes that ambassador de Brèves negotiated a lower tax for pilgrims, and that he himself entered without paying (pp. 114–18). Balourdet too had documents which exempted him from the fee to enter the Sepulchre (p. 5). For the regulation and use of the taxes levied on pilgrims, see O. Heyd, *Ottoman Documents on Palestine, 1552–1615* (1960), pp. 174–84. This book offers valuable perspectives on Christian pilgrimage seen from the point of view of the local authorities.

explicit in the texts of more lettered pilgrims, such as Huen, whose reworking of Breydenbach's account includes several appendices in support of the 1517 call to crusade. From his account it is clear that early modern pilgrim subjectivity is both bound together with the romance, and besieged by memories of crusade. And the rhetoric of crusade has a long life: Giraudet's *Voyage*, frequently published in the 1570s and the 1580s, includes in its liminary material an eloquent lament by Palestine, figured as a woman pleading to be delivered from captivity. As 'late' as 1608, Beauveau, on arrival in Jerusalem, regrets that he comes pen and not sword in hand; on leaving, he laments the fact that he had not been there in the crusading company of Godefroy de Bouillon and his kind. He concludes by ironically suggesting that since he cannot occupy the land, he can at least capture it in writing.[43] In these more polemical and learned texts, the ideological connections between pilgrimage and crusade are clearly marked. But questions remain as to how these are represented as experience by pilgrims such as Cuchermoys in their narratives of the journey. Does Cuchermoys' romance relate to his pilgrimage account in the way that the calls to crusade found in the treatises, liminary poems, and ironic remarks of the priestly and diplomatic writers relate to theirs? Can we look for clues to his understanding of pilgrimage in the deflected voice of the translator of Guerin's travels? Does the romance speak volumes about pilgrims' concerns, or do the sparsely written sentences of the pilgrimage account proper tell us most, and most clearly, about the pilgrim's experience on the road?

After three weeks in Palestine, narrated in a number of paragraphs, Cuchermoys tells how on 31 August he and his fellow-pilgrims set sail for home once again, singing 'Te deum laudamus etc.'.[44] The return journey involved a storm, in which the ship was blown off course; at this point, illness and discontent at the appalling conditions on board, which had rarely been mentioned on the outward journey, struck both crew and passengers. Cuchermoys' companion Filz-de-femme almost died, but recovered; others were not so fortunate and many, many pilgrims died on the return home.[45] They were often buried at sea, contrary to the terms of the contract which stipulated they be buried in Christian ground. Friends made on the

---

[43] Beauveau (1608 edition), pp. 116; 156.   [44] Cuchermoys, fol. Ov[r].

[45] Ibid., fol. Ov[v]. Hault makes a rare mention of near-fatal sickness on board ship on the way out—he puts it down to melons (fol. 22[v]). Those who give details of the circumstances of death on the return journey include: Lesaige (his companion Jehan de Bos, of fever),

journey were useful in many ways, not least of which was ensuring your body was returned to sanctified ground; or, in rare instances, to bring home your account, to supplement the absence of your body.

The way home is the route to Jerusalem in reverse: Cyprus, Rhodes, Corfu. Here the pilgrims leave the galley and board a smaller ship (a 'grippa') to Ottranto, a passage which costs each pilgrim a ducat. Boldu's agent refuses to accede to a discount, despite the fact that the pilgrims do not return with his galley all the way to Venice.[46] In Ottranto there is the further expense of a horse to take them to the relics of St Nicolas at Bari. Eventually the pilgrims reach Rome, arriving on 1 December. It takes nine days to complete the pilgrimage of the seven Roman churches, and, having named them all and listed the indulgences to be had in each, Cuchermoys heads for home. The pilgrims arrive back in Lyons on 1 January 1491, 'environ midy. Deo gracias.'[47]

Departure: Lyon, 8.5.1490, environ XXV ans, dieu aidant.
Return: Lyon, 1.1.1491, environ midy, deo gracias.

The journey has taken some thirty-four weeks. Thirteen weeks from Lyons to Jaffa; eighteen weeks to get back to Lyons from Jaffa. This leaves three weeks in the Holy Land itself. Having travelled across the surface of the earth to get there, once in the Holy Land, the pilgrim constantly walks away from the local people and ignores virtually everything which is to be seen on the surface of the ground. He walks downwards, deeper into the earth, measuring the steps, as if in search of a deeper, quantifiable sense of what it means to be there. But for all the measured details of time and place, a number of questions remain. They are questions we want to address to the pilgrim himself, for his text does not provide the answers. A total of eight days and nights you are kept against your will in caverns underground and under guard. And still you choose to spend three of the remaining thirteen nights locked underground in a tomb—the Holy Sepulchre—and yet another in the room in Bethlehem, enduring the cold, in your own terms, 'merveilleusement'.[48] Why this flight from the surface, from the conversations and coordinates which we might now

fol. Ci[r]; Hault (several pilgrims, including a young man, who fell overboard on the night of 23 Oct. 1593 while relieving himself), fols. 80[v]–81[v]; Villamont (several more, of plague), pp. 563–4, (more still, with fever), pp. 691–2.

[46] Cuchermoys, fol. Ovi[r]. For similar complaints see Voisins, p. 39 and Possot, p. 100.
[47] Cuchermoys, fol. Ovi[v].   [48] Ibid., fol. Oiv[v].

take to be those of the experience of elsewhere? And what of the romance? When and where did you translate Mesquin's story; and what things might it tell us of your own journey, which your *Voyage* keeps silent?

When reading the romance we focused on those moments in which Mesquin encountered pilgrims. If we want to gain some sense of the pilgrim's voice, we must do the reverse, and isolate the points at which Cuchermoys meets with the non-pilgrim stranger. In doing so, we find that they intersect with the only other points in Cuchermoys' text at which the first person intrudes into the otherwise vigorously impersonal account: 'on/nous' becomes 'je' at points of anxious pressure. To establish the status of these 'personal' intrusions, we need to read carefully, to place them in context, and to pause at two specific stages on the pilgrimage—first Modon, and then Jaffa.

Ragusa and Modon: Translators and Others

Cuchermoys himself begins to answer our earlier questions in a rare intrusion of his own voice into the text. This, the pilgrim's first use of the first person singular is marked as a moment of writing; but it is not that of writing his own account, rather one of translation: 'en celle ville de Raguse je commencay a translater le livre de Guerin Mesquin de langue Italyenne en langue Francoyse.' Set in the context of the sentences which frame it, this apparently personal record reads:

Che xxii jour de Juing veille de la sainct Jehan arrivasmes au royaulme de esclavonie en une ville nommee Raguse ou gist Monsieur Sainct Blaise. Lequel ilz tiennent pour leur patron et est une seigneurie commune et de celle ville de Raguse nya que demie lieue jusques au royaulme de Boscine, qui est ung des xvii royaulmes Crestiens mais a present il est au Turc. Raguse est la plus forte petite ville de Crestiente jacoit que Rodes et Genes soient fortes villes et inespugnables en celle ville de Raguse je commencay a translater le livre de Guerin Mesquin de langue Italyenne en langue Francoyse et le vendredy dudit moys passasmes par devant Corso une ville qui est en Grece. Laquelle est au Venisiens.[49]

If it is significant that Cuchermoys translates a crusading romance to accompany his own pilgrimage, then it must be even more so that the pilgrim begins his romantic (self-) translation into a crusader from

---

[49] Ibid., fol. Ōiᵛ.

within what he terms the strongest, most fortified little town in Christendom. For in generic terms this is to register his own experience, in the first person, only in relation to the fortified genres of romance and crusade. But these significances are not explicitly offered by the text itself, any more than it offers exegesis of the geo-political coordinates of the journey: the apparently ever-present threat from the Turk, for example, and the fact that the Jerusalem pilgrims' route is predicated on, and functions as confirmation of, Venetian trading hegemony in the Mediterranean.[50] These things are not explicated in the text, only suggested by juxtaposing frames of reference, and occasional shifts between persons within the course of single or adjacent sentences.

Cuchermoys does not use the first person singular again until he arrives in Jaffa. From the moment of the inception of his translation to that of arrival in the Holy Land he returns to the plural identity of 'we, the pilgrims'. In this company he pursues the journey, arriving in the next paragraph in Modon. The text marks the date and day: Sunday, 27 June, the eve of Greek Easter that year. Here the pilgrims encounter another potential model traveller. 'Chimbres que on appelle Boysmes en france, qui sont povres gens et mal conditiones' are said to originate here, as another of the pilgrims also in Modon that same day, similarly remarks in his account.[51] Ragusa had provided Cuchermoys with a figural travelling companion in the person of the romance hero Mesquin, and we might reasonably expect him to recognize in the figure of the Gypsy the romance hero's non-fictional counterpart. Like Guerin Mesquin, the Bohemian/Gypsy has a 'false' double name, is suspiciously polyglot, and of doubtful direction and origin. But, in common with many other pilgrims, Cuchermoys denies any commonality—romantic or actual—with 'Boemiens', whom he defines as 'ceulx qui courent par le monde'.[52]

Other pilgrims react with articulate aggression to the narratives of origin which attach themselves to the Gypsy: von Harff gruffly dismisses the claim that they are 'little Egyptians', and Carlier de Pinon proves to himself they are not from Egypt by talking Arabic at the

[50] After Lepanto, pilgrims take a different route, usually straight from Venice to Rosetta in Egypt.

[51] Voisins, p. 22. We return to this account in the next chapter.

[52] Cuchermoys, fol. Oi^v. Gypsies are a particular problem also for cosmographers, whose task is to place people where they belong; see, for instance, Münster/Belleforest CU ii, p. 880.

group he meets on the road; he is pleased to note that they do not understand him.[53] Cuchermoys does not record speaking to Gypsies, but he undoes the myths of origin by locating the source of their name, first at a precise distance from the pilgrim route, and then within the context of fable and 'Poeterie':

et viennent de cinq lieues de la de une petite ville nomme Gipte et a ceste cause sont ilz nommez Giptiens et nonpas egiptiens et a un traict darc de celle ville de modon est lisle de Sapience ou laristote par sa disputation reconsonna la Poeterie et le dernier jour du mois de Juing passasmes par devant lisle de Sirygo qui se souloit appeller Lythurcee et est celle ysle ou Paris print et ravit la belle Helayne femme du roys Menelaus pour laquelle Troye la grant fut arse et destruicte.[54]

Cuchermoys' brevity is tantalizing. The allusive way in which he refers to those narratives and items of knowledge which attach themselves to places on the journey raises as many questions as it resolves. What, for instance, does this reference to Aristotle on the island of Wisdom signify in this context? Who knew of the *Poetics* in France, Venice, or indeed Modon at the time? Is this a touristic gobbet, specific to this overdetermined island, and with no greater reach; or is Cuchermoys saying—to those that know, and if so, who are they—something about the connections between the pilgrim, the gypsy, and the poet?

Within the next few sentences Cuchermoys takes in a host of other tales and places, travelling from Crete to Patmos, and on past Rhodes. In the course of the paragraph we are informed of Jason, who hunted the golden fleece, Tiphus, who invented navigation, and John, who saw and wrote the Apocalypse; we are, briefly, introduced to the Argos, Daedalus, and the Minotaur. It is as if the journey teaches the pilgrim to read in preparation for the reading of places in Palestine. He does not learn to read in detail; rather, as in Jerusalem, each stop on the journey records a 'place where' narratable things occurred. As well as an initiation to modes of reading sacred places, the pilgrimage, like a quest romance, but, crucially, in a less digressive form, also amounts to a recovery of lost narratives.

The point is itself staged in the final port of call before arrival at Jaffa. With reference to Cyprus, Cuchermoys tells a more recent

---

[53] Von Harff, pp. 80–1; Carlier de Pinon, p. 161; Walther, p. 82; Fabri, iii, p. 338; for images of Modon, see H. W. Davies, *Bernard von Breydenbach and his Journey to the Holy Land* (1911), plates 17, 18.

[54] Cuchermoys, fol. Qi^v.

story than those collected and alluded to so far; it is the first of the stories told on his journey which relates directly to pilgrimage. An English Queen on her way to Jerusalem had been abducted by the King of Cyprus, who, desiring her, had offered her shelter in his castle, and had raped and killed her. The English King, learning of this, sent a crusading force to destroy his castle, which was, like 'Troye la grant' in the previous paragraph, 'destruicte'. Cuchermoys makes no explicit links between the crusading story and the Trojan narrative in miniature which he presents, but it seems clear that the story of the English Queen brings that of Helen up to date, and more firmly into the territory of pilgrimage and crusade. Clear also is the fact that the two stories are read each through the lens, and in the terms, of the other. The English Queen's experience doubles that of Helen: it both repeats and renews the dangers of travel, and in so doing confirms the enduring truth represented by the ancient, authoritative fiction. The two stories are mutually accrediting, and through their adjacent and echoing narration in Cuchermoys' account, both are brought into relation with pilgrimage. No women pilgrims are mentioned as being on board Cuchermoys' ship; like Autiniche when first met, they are spoken for. Their place is taken by stories such as this.[55]

Other, later, pilgrims will have more to say about women, and about themselves in directly contemporary relation to the people and places on the journey. So, for instance, at Cyprus, rather than translating romances or collecting allusions to ancient fictions, certain pilgrims tell of more recent tales, and, by extension, of their own experience. Hault stayed in Cyprus for several weeks, and became Godfather to the daughter of a man he befriended there; Villamont, for his part, met a Greek orthodox priest on the island who asked him—in Italian—if he was a Lutheran, and on discovering he was not, took him on a tour of the island while telling him the inside story of the janissaries' revolt. Beauveau, finally, relates the story of a reclusive monk who having lived in a grotto for years had died just the week before; on his death, he turned out to have been a woman all along.[56] The point is that all these are personalized tales, connected explicitly in the moment of narration with their tellers: Cuchermoys

---

[55] Cuchermoys, fol. Oii[r]. Possot also tells this story in similar terms, p. 145. He is also one of the few to mention women pilgrims, p. 153. See also Fabri, i, pp. 11, 26, 41, 166. See Röhricht and Meisner, pp. 6–7, who say the Pope forbade women to travel and that some overcame this by cross-dressing. I have found no direct evidence of either point.

[56] Hault, fol. 79[v]; Villamont, pp. 355–61; Beauveau, pp. 127–8.

has no such stories—or at least he tells none in this account. His text confirms not so much the singularity of this or that traveller's experience, told by way of the exchange of stories with the locals, as the pilgrim's generic sense of belonging, confirmed by studied ignorance of local people and recent narratives attaching to the places on the pilgrim route. Thus, rather than proleptically gathering new tales for future readers, Cuchermoys' pilgrim narrator traces a recursive, analeptic course of remembering and collecting ancient, authoritative fictions. Pilgrimage, when figured in this way as an exercise in both imitation and collective remembrance, counteracts the alienating movement away from home.

Cuchermoys classes himself as 'natif de Lyon' and bound for Jerusalem from his opening sentence onwards. He is, in other words, neither epic hero, nor romance quester, nor gypsy wanderer. The texture of his writing suggests that he courts proximity with all three, but never quite surrenders his identity to any of these other travellers, keeping always a measured distance between himself and them. It is a distance which is also, however, a closeness of sorts. For Jason, the English crusader, Mesquin, and the Gypsy are all essential to the pilgrim's self-understanding as one who recollects stories on behalf of others, but is neither a wanderer, nor a soldier himself. And it is the Gypsy Other who binds the heroes of romance, epic, and pilgrimage together in close communion. For, unlike the 'coureurs du monde', all three share the idea of rest, their narratives project the hope of one day telling their tales on their return home.[57]

Jaffa: The Theft of Belongings

Arrival in the Holy Land brings the second instance of Cuchermoys' use of the first person in the course of his account. It also—at the point which should promise confirmation—brings the greatest threat to the integrity of his text and the clarity of his self-identity as a pilgrim. The threat creates anxiety, expressed in the return of the repressed counter-identity of the 'Boemien'. Cuchermoys and his companion arrived in Jaffa on the morning of Sunday, 25 July. They were not permitted to go ashore until 4 August, and even then were held for three further days in 'cavernes a porceaulx comme Boemiens'. The sentence reads:

[57] It takes a Baudelaire to put pilgrim and Bohemian back in the same boat: 'Bohemiens en Voyage', *Les Fleurs du Mal*, p. 21.

Le Mercredi iiii jour Daoust nous descendismes en terre et fusmes comptez et escriptz lung apres laultre par les Seigneurs Mores et fusmes mis dedans des cavernes a porceaulx comme Boemiens ou nous demourasmes troys jours et demy et deux heures devant mon departement me fut desrobe tout mon petit cas par ung traystre More parquoy *je fus contrainct* de aller en gallere en habit dissimule pour avoir ce que besoing mestoit.[58]

This move into the first person singular occurs on the threshold of arrival, and is, like the previous instance in which the pilgrim writes 'je', explicitly marked as a moment of writing. It is on leaving the ship and becoming subject to the economy and writing of the other ('nous fusmes comptez et escriptz') that the pilgrims first experienced misrecognition of their true identity. This is an experience common to all pilgrims. The fact that to enter the Holy Land is to become a subject of foreign authority is a shock registered in many accounts, and is articulated in others' texts with real aggression, with learned and legal reasons as to why they deserve better, and why crusade should be undertaken to recover the Land.[59] For Cuchermoys the experience has the specific charge of a particular misrecognition. The ghost of Modon—the threat of being taken for a 'coureur du monde' and so confined to a pigsty, rather than being recognized as a true pilgrim, and so led to the Holy Sepulchre— haunts him even as he lies incubated for three days on arrival in the Holy Land.

All pilgrims are subject to this delay, since it takes time for the authorities in Jerusalem to be informed of their arrival, and to send guides to accompany them on the road. These three days can be read as initiating pilgrims into the mythic rhythm of death, disappearance, and resurrection. More specifically still, it could read as a proleptic moment of *imitatio Christi*, anticipating the three days and nights pilgrims spend in the Holy Sepulchre. As such, we might see the Jaffa experience as further testing and confirming the pilgrim's identity on arrival. But this move, which makes an allegorical luxury of the literal conditions of captivity, is one which Cuchermoys cannot perform. For him there is only further distress. Rereading:

---

[58] Cuchermoys, fol. Oii[v] (my italics).

[59] See for instance Giraudet, p. 27; Hault, fol. 22[v]; Possot, pp. 152–4; Balourdet, p. 5; Voisins, pp. 26–8; Beauveau, p. 135; Villamont, pp. 380–6; Palerne, p. 229; Carlier de Pinon, pp. 243–4.

et deux heures devant mon departement [de Jaffa] me fut desrobe tout mon petit cas par ung traystre More parquoy je fus contrainct de aller en gallere en habit dissimule pour avoir ce que besoing mestoit.[60]

It is when his belongings are stolen that Cuchermoys singles himself out from his fellow pilgrims by taking on foreign clothes, and with them the first person singular. Several further allegorized readings of this moment suggest themselves here. The pilgrim resents being mistaken for a 'coureur du monde', but himself courts proximity with romance in his efforts to overcome the situation. For in using the dramatic and costumed first person in his narrative, in representing the Turk as treacherous, obliging him in turn to adopt disguise, Cuchermoys is imitating not Christ but Mesquin. Is it more than coincidence which dictates that the second moment at which Cuchermoys' text says 'je' is another point of entry to the writing and thematics of romance? In what ways is the theft of Cuchermoys' 'cas' analogous to the theft of Guerin's proper name and inheritance? Certainly, both force the 'desrobé' figure into disguise.

If such an analogy between Mesquin's and the pilgrim's disguise does seem legitimate, what force should we give, in the context of Mesquin's subjection to King Paciffero's advances, to the sexual sense of 'cas' in Cuchermoys' account? Von Harff hints at sexual humiliation when he was imprisoned in Gaza, and warns future pilgrims not to resist demands made on them; but he neither details what happened though it 'would be a wonderful history', nor writes a romance to accompany his account, arguing instead that 'it would take too long to write'.[61] Is the 'wonderful history' of Guerin's romance the place where Cuchermoys is able to speak of experiences 'too long to write' in a pilgrimage account? Certainly Cuchermoys does seem, albeit indirectly, to address issues regarding the lessons of romance and to point towards connections between fictional example and actual experience, but he does not resolve any of these issues in direct terms. Nor does he offer more than clues as to how one is to be read in relation to the other. Rather, his text obliquely raises a number of questions concerning *imitatio* and the terms of intertextual, sexual, and intersubjective appropriation; and then moves on with the pilgrimage.

His brevity is, at it was throughout the journey to the Holy Land,

---

[60] Cuchermoys, fol. Oii".   [61] Von Harff, p. 186.

tantalizing. The coincidence of the shift into the first person ('je fus contrainct') with the pilgrim's sense of being robbed of his identity ('me fut desrobe tout mon petit cas') does seem to stand in relation to the lessons both of romance and crusade: that subjectivity, like property, is a function either of exchange or of theft.[62] Whatever sense we give to 'tout mon petit cas', it is clear that what is stolen along with Cuchermoys' material belongings is his sense of intersubjective belonging, and in particular his sense of belonging to a self-evident community of pilgrims. Certain also is the fact that this initial theft, causing a rupture from the community of pilgrims, occasions the recurrence of a form of singular subjectivity—the 'je' which Cuchermoys has used at only one other point so far, that of initiating the translation of the romance. And the enigma of arrival in the Holy Land, with all its cross-generic resonances, matters because after this point, Cuchermoys' newly obliged sense of singularity never quite leaves him alone.

Continuing to read his journey we find that on regaining the shore he regains his friend Pierre: it will be possible to write 'nous' again. But the two friends are not so much reunited as forced together: 'Et lorsque je fus en terre je trouvay tous les aultres pelerins montez sur asnes. Et ung More me print par force et mon compagnon et nous fit monter sur deux chevaulx.'[63] Once again subjectivity is experienced as a function of subjection. There is an uncomfortable irony here in that pilgrims traditionally rode on asses in imitation of the humility of Christ on entering Jerusalem.[64] Being forced on to the animal which in other locations would be the chosen mount denies the pilgrim the chance to experience humility in its proper place; rather they are singled out for humiliation. The point is stressed in the conclusion to Cuchermoys' sentence, where, at once proud and anxious, he acknowledges that he has been both physically singled out and forced to use the first person singular. He is thus obliged to mark his difference from the norms of pilgrim behaviour and narration: 'ce quil ne advint long temps a nul pelerin.'[65]

---

[62] See the lesson of linguistics as articulated by Benveniste in, 'Le Langage et l'expérience humaine', 'Structure des relations de personne dans le verbe' and 'La nature des pronoms': 'Le langage est ainsi organisé qu'il permet à chaque locuteur de s'approprier la langue entière en se désignant comme je' (Problèmes de linguistique générale (1974), ii, p. 262).

[63] Cuchermoys, fol. Oiiᵛ.   [64] See Hault, fol. 23ʳ; Voisins, p. 28; Possot, p. 161.

[65] Cuchermoys, fol. Oiiᵛ.

Rome: The Narrative Cure

There is no more personally engaged a reader than the pilgrim, yet few early pilgrims speak of themselves as individuals. The use of the first person singular in Cuchermoys' account is rare and somewhat forced, as we have seen. The coordinates of time and space in the text coincide less with the vectors of the pilgrim's own past journey than with those of future narrativity. The crucial unit of space–time travelled is the *narreme*; a place is a pretext to the narration, a commonplace story, or it is not a place. Which is to say, rather than mimetic, Cuchermoys' account is mnemonic: a party to the arts of memory and an aid to future narration. What is implicit in the journey to Palestine becomes explicit in the land itself. Cuchermoys' account of what he did and what happened to him in the Holy Land is almost entirely subjectless. It is a pure litany of places and rituals, ready for reading as one of the 'rapports' which Villette or Adrichomius will use in their *Descriptions*.[66] The moment he says 'I' is the moment when he realises he is becoming part of the story of another culture, another authority—those of the powers that occupy the Land.

A condition of the talking, walking cure which is pilgrimage is the bringing together of the body and the word. The pilgrim walks across the world in order to place his feet in the footsteps of Christ, to place his own body quite literally 'alongside the scriptures'. This is reading with the body, linguistic *imitatio Christi* experienced as physical experiment. The Jerusalem journey remembers stories in relation to travel, its dangers, and its pleasures; the account of the place proper, and of the experience of being there, is succinct and unaccented. 'It is', as Mary Campbell writes of the earliest extant pilgrimage account, 'an experience only to the degree that being present at the consecration of the Host is an experience, an infinitely repeatable one in which the participant is absolutely equivalent to all his fellow participants, an experience as nearly as possible independent of its subject.'[67]

As nearly as possible; part of the pain registered by Cuchermoys' account of his time in Palestine is that, for the early Renaissance pilgrim, this surrender of the coordinates of individual subjectivity was not altogether possible while in the Holy Land itself. On the return journey, however, the pilgrim regains his sense of shared self, his representative anonymity. As a more extended reading of the text

---

[66] See above, Ch. 4.   [67] Campbell, *The Witness and the Other World*, p. 22.

would show, the trials endured and the miracles witnessed on the way home both confirm Cuchermoys' place as a member of the particular, pilgrim, confraternity, and see him recall a series of narratives which bear on the meaning of home. One example—what the pilgrims experience in Rome—can stand in for many.

In a Roman church, Cuchermoys and his companions see 'guarir ung demoniacle contre ung des pilliers de marbre contre lequel nostre seigneur preschoit en hierusalem'.[68] This miracle underlines the theme of the 'narrative cure', underscored itself by the rhetoric of topical displacement which lies at the heart of pilgrimage. For it is a miracle which takes place by virtue of what we might call sacred contagion. What heals the sick man is a metaphorical contagion of word and thing made possible by pilgrimage's literally physical conception of reading and translation. Egeria's 'juxta scripturas' specific to the Holy Land is translated in Cuchermoys' text by the specific moment of this collocative cure: '[juxta/]contre ung des pilliers [. . .] contre lesquels nostre Seigneur preschoit.' The geographical displacement of the pillars of the church (Jerusalem to Rome), reveals itself to be a condensation at once literal and metaphorical (ruined stone becomes edifying pillar) of the terms of pilgrims' *imitatio*. If it is 'contre' the pillar that Christ preached, then it is by placing his body 'contre' the same pillar that the possessed man can be cured.

To return and witness this miracle is to experience a homecoming. For it is to experience a confirmation of the rites of pilgrimage, the physical understanding of representation on which it is predicated, and the reading of experience in relation to authorized narrative on which it relies. And it is to do so not at the centre of the Others' world, but at what you take to be the centre of 'Chrestienté'. For the Jerusalem pilgrim, for whom being in the Holy Land was, as those scenes we have isolated suggest, to be subject to a kind of possession by the Other, this is a powerful consolation. It underlines the value of pilgrimage narrative as a place in which even things which appear to be beyond representation may be seen, experienced, and recounted, because they are recuperable to Christ's spoken word.[69]

---

[68] Cuchermoys, fol. Ovi^v.

[69] For moments similar to that told here by Cuchermoys, see Lesaige, fol. Eiii^r–v; Possot, pp. 208–10; Villamont, pp. 121–2, and Montaigne, *Journal*, pp. 138–43. See also C. Bené, 'Humanistes et pèlerinages au XVIe siècle: Montaigne à Lorette', in *Montaigne e l'Italia* (1991), pp. 597–607; and W. Williams, ' "Rubbing up against Others": Montaigne on Pilgrimage', in *Voyages and Visions* (forthcoming).

Cuchermoys' account consequently bears little trace of his own spoken word; it bears witness not to emotions, feelings, or actions unique to him, but rather to the fact that the 'déjà lu' was the defining mode of experience for early vernacular pilgrims. Like the 'acteurs' of allegorical devotional poetry, Cuchermoys and his fellow pilgrims are not so much authors and finishers of their own travels, as representative readers of the pilgrim way. With their bodies, and with their stories placed alongside those of Christ, they recover on behalf of an imagined community of readers a now largely lost shared territory of significance, and shared modes of narrativity. This understanding of pilgrim identity is, as we have seen in previous chapters, placed under extraordinary pressure in the course of the Renaissance. As we shall see in the chapter which follows, late Renaissance pilgrim writers could sustain neither this representative role, nor the peculiar faith in representation it demands.

CHAPTER SIX

Narratives of Experience II

1584—The Example of Jacques de Valimbert

Besançon to Chieri: Legitimacy and Translation

Almost a century after Cuchermoys, Jacques de Valimbert, probably also aged around 25, set out, in March 1584, for the Holy Land. The eighteenth-century manuscript which is the only surviving copy of his pilgrimage account opens with fourteen lines of Latin, glossed in the margin as 'copie de l'attestation de messieurs les Gouverneurs de la ville Impériale de Besançon donnée à Jacques de Valimbert à sa sortie de Besançon, partant à Jerusalem'.[1] Following the Latin attestation, Valimbert opens his French account in the first person singular: 'Sortant de Besançon avec volonté, aidant Dieu d'accomplir mon voyage de Jérusalem, je passai le St. Bernard pour aller à chyers en piémont.'[2] The opening, subjectless, dependant clause, and the 'aidant Dieu' are pure pilgrim-speak; the 'je passai' is not.

From the outset, Valimbert's first person singular marks this text as different from Cuchermoys' pilgrimage, and from others of its kind. We read Cuchermoys' *Voyage* as that of a representative who travels, writes, and remembers on behalf of a community. Valimbert, for his part, seems both to speak more directly in the first person, and to suffer from a mania for documentation which proves his attachment to a number of communities: certificates testifying to his status

---

[1] Valimbert, fol. 46ʳ. The manuscript has, as noted above, yet to be published; all references here to 'Valimbert' are to this pilgrimage account.

[2] Ibid.

as a member of several cities, universities, countries, classes, and chivalric orders are transcribed into his account. As we shall see, walking alongside him as he travels and writes, Valimbert's experience of the pilgrim road is quite different from that of Cuchermoys and the pilgrim community he represents. Indeed the very plurality of literal and written proofs in Valimbert's account, and the absence of a singular pilgrim purpose which they betray, served only to reinforce both in him and in his contemporary readers the sense that the literal pilgrimage was now not only more difficult to perform, but also probably a waste of time, or worse.

Valimbert's first stop on the journey is Chieri, which he visits, he writes, in 'reconnaissance de mes parents', and because the town is 'l'origine de mon père'.[3] To attest to the 'qualité de [s]es prédécesseurs', Valimbert asks the magistrates for proof: 'que jeus telle', he writes, before copying the Italian text—more an official document than a Guerin-like romance—into his own. The document attests to the 'nobilità' of the family, to their goods and worth in Chieri before they moved to Besançon, and, crucially, to Jacques' being Bertini di Valimberto's legitimate son. This is vital information for the traveller to share because Jacques is nowhere recognized as his father's son in municipal documents surviving in Besançon. Although other sons—Luc and César—are mentioned as following their father into the position of 'maistre monnoyeur', and becoming part of the governing establishment in Besançon for some long time, Jacques never occupies any positions of municipal authority.[4]

The official documents attest to Jacques' historical existence, but they offer little information about him (apart from the fact that he was imprisoned for heresy later in life), still less record his views and his vote on municipal matters, as they do those of the family who seem not to recognize him. The extant copy of his manuscript is similarly tantalizing. It attests to his having travelled, and records his first person voice, but is not an autograph. The narrative of his journey is incomplete, and has not survived well: the ink has seeped

[3] Ibid.
[4] The information in Gazier, 'Le pèlerinage d'un bisontin' should be supplemented by the many references to the Valimbert family, and the rare mention of Jacques to be found in the Archives Communales at Besançon. See in particular HH. 41–3 (concerning the 'maistre monnyeur' dynasty); MSS Chifflet 4, fols. 68 and 105 (on Jacques' machinations in Rome, in the year following his pilgrimage, on behalf of Ferdinand de Rye, seeking to gain him the lucrative bishopric of Besançon); see also A. Castan, 'La Rivalité des familles de Rye et de Granvelle, *Doubs*, 6e série, 6e volume (1892), pp. 1–130. See also next note.

through both sides of the paper, such that many passages remain indecipherable.[5]

Nor does the mediation stop there. As we noted above, Valimbert's account is usurped to polemic effect by the devotional poet Chassignet, who makes an example of him in order to question the legitimacy of travel, and in particular pilgrimage, as a proper means to devotion. The material history of the text's transmission, the generic proximity of the narrative to both romance and devotional poetry, and the stuffing of the personal narrative with official documents all act to question the integrity and self-sufficiency of the pilgrim's voice. For Valimbert, writing as a pilgrim was both a material risk and a narrative adventure.

To guard against the material risks, Valimbert seems to have as many official documents and attendant identities as there are official checks on his identity. The sense of narrative adventure is represented by the fact that, in contrast to Cuchermoys, whose romance is marked as separate from his pilgrimage, and who uses the first person singular only rarely, Valimbert's records a constant process of redefinition of the travelling self, in response both to the conditions of the road and to the challenges on pilgrim identity from a host of others. The plethora of documents and the cross-references to other narrative models in his text do not so much amplify the lay pilgrim's voice within the discourse of late Renaissance travel, as demonstrate its near-inaudibility. But the pilgrim never travels alone, even when he is not in the company of others. And rather than seeing the pilgrim's voice as having been distorted beyond recognition by the poets, priests, officials, and copyists, we need to recognize that these others are instrumental to the transmission of Valimbert's story—both on a material and a metaphorical level. Moreover, as the earlier chapters of this study have shown, these narratives cannot properly be considered as somehow separate from the oppositional contexts in which they are articulated. For such a view not only distorts the history of their survival, but also misrepresents the moment of enunciation, and with it the texture of pilgrim experience.

---

[5] AC. BB. 45, 1597–1599, fol. 243—not noted by Gazier—refers to Jacques' imprisonment for 'propoz scandaleux mal sentans de la religion', on 30 June 1599. Besançon was a town repeatedly gripped by anxiety on this score, and the archives give details of frequent and severe punishment exacted on heretics. Jacques' will was dated 1601 (by U. Robert, *Inventaire des testaments . . . de Besançon* (1891), 1, p. 58), but it does not seem to have survived.

Chieri to Cairo: The Agony of Egypt

Leaving Chieri, Valimbert made his way to Pavia, where he studied for three days, 'affin d'etre matriculé et reconnu escholier'. He then moved on to Ferrara, where again he was matriculated, and finally to Padua, where again he studied '12 ou 15 jours', securing thereby another matriculation certificate.[6] This apparent mania for fast-track learning reveals itself to be a practical consideration: the documents enable him to 'passer seurement sur le vénétiain et ne payer daches'.[7] Practical considerations also explain his detour to Genoa, as he needed to obtain letters of credit from Genoese bankers before setting off to Jerusalem. On arrival in Venice he discovered that finding a boat proved harder than he had anticipated. It was surprising how few other pilgrims were waiting for the galley. Whereas, as we saw above, earlier pilgrims complained that even after having signed contracts with Boldu or Contarini they had to wait in Venice for weeks at their own expense before being allowed on board, Valimbert's complaint is of a different order. It is only from a town crier that he discovered that, since the capture of Cyprus, the Venice to Jaffa galleys no longer plied their trade, and that his best option was to board the boat to Egypt, which was leaving very soon.

Before boarding, he met two French noblemen from Monceaux, who suggested he ensure possession of a number of further documents. The first was an attestation that he was a 'gentilhomme francese et servitore di sua majesta christianissima' (which he was not). This certificate would serve to confirm not only his newly authenticated noble identity, but also the new bond of friendship with the Frenchmen: 'ainsi je passa[i] pour françois avec ces Seigneurs pour la seureté de la personne, cas advient que fussions pris.' Valimbert also procured a 'passeport' from the French ambassador ('que j'eus tel'), and a letter proving that he had sufficient money to make the journey there and back ('pour ce faut-il être reconnu et avoir attestation que j'eus du nonce à Venise tel que suit').[8]

---

[6] Valimbert, fol. 46ᵛ.

[7] Ibid. Gazier points out that 'les fils des parlementaires et de bourgeois vont poursuivre leurs études dans les grandes Universités, telles que Louvain, Paris, Cologne, Pavie ou Padoue', 'Le pèlerinage d'un bisontin', p. 1.

[8] Valimbert, fol. 46ᵛ. This protective bond is a firm one, and is maintained throughout Valimbert's journey, until the Frenchmen go on from Aleppo to the Embassy at Constantinople, leaving Valimbert to wait for a return ship to Venice. Many French travellers, including Postel, Belon, Thevet, and a host of others less known, passed through this

These documents are all duly transcribed in his text; they increase the pilgrim's sense of safety in numbers. From the Church authorities' perspective, as the explicit threat of excommunication for those who do not have such documents on them on arrival in Jerusalem makes clear, they insure against the pilgrim depending on the Franciscans in Jerusalem to fund his return trip. But they are also, as the vocabulary of recognition, disguise, and witnessing suggests, existential issues.[9] For Valimbert cannot simply join the company of pilgrims—such a self-evident company no longer exists. He must rely on other networks of allegiance, on the good faith of other travellers, and on the kindness of strangers, forging and reforging the terms of pilgrim identity as he travels.

Before leaving Venice, Valimbert wrote a letter to one of his sisters, explaining his reasons for the trip, and outlining his will should he die.[10] Up to this point, his personal narrative had referred to, and often transcribed, a host of other documents—imperial passport, letter of credit, student passes, certificates of nationality, papal permission to travel—all exemplifying the kinds of writing generated by the journey. The letter home was not copied into the text, and has not, it seems, survived.[11]

Valimbert's account summarizes the crossing of the Mediterranean in a single, brief, sentence, listing simply the names of places passed. His journey towards Jerusalem was not a slow process of initiation into pilgrim rhetoric by means of landings in those places which have legends and stories attached to them—such as Ragusa

Embassy. Some are listed in Simon Sauget's *Album amicorum*, a collection of signatures and notes gathered in Constantinople in 1589, and now in Besançon, A. D. Doubs. MSS. 34. 1589 (see L. Febvre, *Philippe II et la Franche-comté* (1911), pp. 330–1). Much has been written about this Embassy, and this is not the place for detail; from a pilgrim perspective, the business of passing oneself off as a 'Franc' does seem to have been helpful on occasion: see, for instance, von Sedlitz's account of his capture in Constantinople and subsequent release thanks to the French ambassador, Feyrabend, fols. 262ʳ–269ᵛ.

[9] Other French pilgrims who mention similar documents, though less extensively, include Villamont, p. 637; Giraudet, pp. 9–10; Possot, arriving in Jaffa with no papers is almost sent home, pp. 146, 195; see also Zrenner's discussion, *Die Berichte der europäischen Jerusalempilger*, p. 93.

[10] Valimbert, fol. 47ʳ.

[11] I looked for it, of course, in the Besançon archives, but no letters from Valimbert himself are noted as surviving, nor are any of his sisters' letters noted as being on file. 'Letters home' is a genre absent from this study. Hault is the only other pilgrim I have noted as saying when and where he writes letters home (to his brother), fol. 14ʳ; he also has certificates from the Pope and several others, fols. 6ʳ–9ʳ.

and Modon—and which pilgrims such as Cuchermoys collect and repeat within their accounts. It was, he notes, something of a relief to arrive in Rosetta, and to have the crossing pass so unremarkably. Less comforting was the fact that once in Rosetta, he and his companions were forced to 'marchander à des mores pour nous conduire seurement en alexandrie'. Like Mesquin before him, he notes that people here are 'tous noirs', but, unlike the romance hero, he adds that 'le chemin est plein de voleurs et tueurs'.[12] The travellers were, however, unmolested until they arrived in Alexandria, where 'un juif' searched their bags, looking to rob them, but they were wise to it, and had sown their money into the 'buscs des pourpoints'.[13]

The journey as Valimbert represents it is not so much a process of encounter and dialogue, dispelling or reconfiguring preconceptions, as a series of practical difficulties, which appear to confirm the travellers' suspicions about all sorts of Others. It is, in many ways, a sadly predictable business. But there are also moments of surprise, expressed, if not by the pilgrims, then by those who encounter them. One César de Paolo, whom the travellers meet at the 'fondique des Francs', where they stay in Alexandria, comments that they had 'pris une étrange route pour aller en Jérusalem'.[14] Once assured of the pilgrim travellers' noble status—they have the documents to prove it—Paolo offers them 'bonne chère', and shows them the sights: the Needles, one standing, the other fallen; Pompey's column, preserved entire, is, he writes, 'la plus grosse colonne et merveille du monde'. Alongside remarks concerning the ancient marvels, Valimbert takes care to note the presence of Christian sites and relics: Joseph's granaries; the rocks on which St Mark and St Catherine lost their heads; neither rain nor dew falls in the place where Christ lived for seven years, and this had allowed him to sleep 'à l'air seurement'. The pulpit John the Baptist used when preaching in the Egyptian desert is here; it is in pieces, but it is here.[15]

It is thus in Egypt—which Cuchermoys never visits—that Valimbert first notes his response to things foreign, things visited beyond the bounds of Europe. It is here that he learns to read place as a pilgrim does, and to echo other pilgrims in articulating distinct forms of response to different Egyptian sites. The sights of antiquity are of the order of the marvellous: a function of craft, size, and perhaps also distance from home territory. Those of the Biblical story are mostly of the order of the miraculous: things out of the ordinary which happen within domestic space.[16]

Still carrying their documents, Valimbert and his companions travel down the Nile towards the mountains of the moon. They are headed for Cairo at the insistence of César de Paolo, who arms them with further documents, letters of introduction to Paolo's uncle, one M. Vante. From the safety of the boat (a 'djerme'), Valimbert passes the time watching the janissaries shoot at the people and other animals they see both on the banks, and in the water around them. The equivalence of the human and other 'riverains' is established in his text by virtue of the fact that the 'gens nuds' are 'assemblés comme bêtes . . . criants et urlans de nuit, voyans ou sentans autres que des leurs'.[17] Once again—as with Paolo's expression of surprise at the pilgrims' 'étrange route' in Alexandria—Valimbert's text seems to acknowledge its difference, its estrangement both from conventional narratives, and from conventional forms of pilgrim behaviour. And yet—once again—this sense of difference is expressed not in his own voice, nor in those of his fellow pilgrims, but in the voices and cries of those they meet on their journey. The remarkable sentence concerning the 'riverains', quoted above, even as it equates the local people with animals, imputes to them (and *not* to the passing pilgrims) the understanding that the people shooting at them from the boat were fundamentally, dangerously, 'autres'.

To move his narrative down river, Valimbert has recourse to the degree zero of travel writing: 'on voit . . . on voit là . . . on voit aussi.'[18] After nine days the travellers reach Cairo, where Paolo's uncle, M. Vante, shows them 'bonne chère', and gives them further letters of introduction to traders they might meet in the course of their journey to Sinai.[19] They leave Cairo armed with these letters, with some

---

[16] For the 'merveilleux' as a register of awe at size, see Possot on Mont Cenis, p. 44; Lesaige in Florence (fol. Ciii[r]), Rome (fol. Di[v]), and Venice (fol. Fiii[r]). For the marvellous in poetics needing to be well away from home, see T. Tasso, *Discourses on the Heroic Poem* (1973), pp. 50–1. In commonplace form, this becomes 'celuy peut impunément mentir qui vient de loin'—see the letter in conclusion to Étienne Pasquier's 'Sommaire description des terres que l'on appelle neuves' (*Lettres*, iii, 3, p. 84). The prime locus for the domestic response to the miraculous is Loreto; see Possot, pp. 208–10; Lesaige, fols. Eiii[r–v]; and Montaigne, *Journal*, pp. 138–43.

[17] Valimbert, fol. 48[r].   [18] Ibid.

[19] He was making a bid at the time to be recognized as 'consulat des chrestiens' in Egypt, and Valimbert is clearly impressed: 'il ne pouvoit rencontrer de plus braves témoins pour s'autoriser du roi de France.' He seems to have been successful; see Villamont, pp. 637, 663.

guards, and with the final blessings of one of the fathers from the newly established Jesuit college: '[il] pensoit que ne reviendrions.'[20] On arrival at Suez (where, according to the margin, the Israelites crossed the Red Sea) there is, on presentation of the letters of introduction, more 'bonne chère' in the company of Venetian merchants, served by twenty-seven servants on their knees.[21] The Venetians were on their way to sell grain to pilgrims at Mecca, and Valimbert's response to this conjunction of Venetian traders and Muslim pilgrims merits attention.

Later in the text, when wandering in the steps of the Israelites through the desert, he expresses an aggressive relation to Muslim pilgrims, whose pilgrimage to Mecca doubles and shadows his own to Jerusalem. He claims that after meeting those 'venant de Mecque' the Christian is lucky to escape alive.[22] On the road and in the desert, there is the fear and aggression towards others which had characterized the accounts of Guerin and other earlier French pilgrims. In Venetian space, by contrast, which is to say not only in Venice, but anywhere in the company of Venetians, Valimbert's relations to Muslim pilgrims are subject to the mediated violence of diplomacy and trade.[23]

Travels in Egypt can, Valimbert learns, form part of the plot of pilgrimage in both contemporary and historical terms: 'imitatio Israeliti' is what recuperates all the 'bonne chère' in Egypt from being too literal a variant of Granada's 'viandes et ails d'Egypte'.[24] In the city of Tor, by the Suez, for instance, Valimbert sees the twelve springs of Moses: the biblical city, with its still living waters, establishes a continuity of biblical and present experience. But not everything Valimbert encounters can be reconfigured as sacred or useful to an understanding of pilgrimage. Even at sacred sites, profane acts can be witnessed. In the margin, 'comme s'il en avait honte' as Gazier notes, Valimbert tells us that the locals at Tor:

se pêchent les sirènes cum quibus cocunt piscatores, puis les tuent et mangent ils font des semelles de souliers de leurs peaux liés sur les artois pour fermer.[25]

The syntax is disjointed, and the manuscript possibly corrupt: we cannot be sure that these notes were either incomplete, in the margin,

---

[20] Valimbert, fol. 48ᵛ.   [21] Ibid.   [22] Ibid., fol. 50ʳ.
[23] Diplomats' and traders' accounts have a different relation to Islamic pilgrimage altogether, see Bernard, pp. 245–6; cf. Nicolay, pp. 201–6; Giraudet, p. 87; refuted by Palerne, pp. 323–4; Carlier de Pinon, p. 140; Villamont, pp. 418–19, and Georgiewitz, fol. B4ʳ.
[24] See above, Ch. 2.   [25] Valimbert, fol. 48ᵛ.

or in Latin, in Valimbert's original, for this is, to repeat, a later copy. But it is clear, none the less, that the competing discursive frames of trade, diplomacy, and pilgrimage lead to generic, syntactic, and lexical confusions being inscribed in the text. The pilgrim's confusion as to the true nature of his journey is perhaps mirrored in the confusing contiguity of differing forms of linguistic, mythological, biblical, and sexual reference which describe moments of pressure such as these.[26]

This confusion progresses as the pilgrims press further into the desert; notes about sumptuous 'bonne chère' are replaced by examples of sirens, sexual violence, 'vestiges' of others' bodies marked in the ground, and stories about the dead. The Greek monks at Tor, for instance, tell Valimbert that they had not seen white-skinned pilgrims for seventeen years, and that the last group had been burned to death by the sun. They advise travelling by night, and as the pilgrims travel on through the sand and the dark, they see, unlike in the Nile waters or in the Tor springs, 'aucune bête, pas même une mouche'.[27] The desert produces a host of anxieties which are both mediated and expressed by the violence and rituals associated with the very soles of the pilgrim's desert shoes.

This is the world's worst journey; it both affects the texture of Valimbert's account, and marks his body. The corresponding monotony of the narrative is broken only by occasional changes in syntax as the rhythm accelerates and as anxiety, momentarily, is given voice. This is especially evident when Valimbert adopts the tone of the guide, thereby allowing himself to speak of anxieties largely suppressed in the account of his own experience. So he tells his readers they must go in the summer, despite the intense heat, 'affin d'éviter les vents en ces déserts sabloneux, qui agités font des ondes, c'est à dire des tourbillons qui soubterrent hommes et chameaux, c'est à dire les couvrent et enveloppent et aveuglent et renversent'.[28] The accumulation of the verbs of action, themselves in the urgency of the present, mimes the effect of the wind, sweeping along all in its path. Even the repeated

---

[26] Gazier reads the passage just quoted as referring to turtles, but states only that sailors do strange things with them, 'Le pèlerinage d'un bisontin', p. 12. He refers the reader to C. de la Roncière's, *Histoire de la nation égyptienne* (1937) (i, p. 31), rather than explain. Roncière writes in fact not about turtles, but a certain Nile fish, which can be blown through one end, like a bag, and then used as a ball, or deflated again to simulate (what he cannot quite call) farting sounds. He says nothing about sailors having intercourse with these turtle-sirens, as the manuscript implies, and as is, (I am told by an officer of the RSPCA) common legend/practice.

[27] Valimbert, fol. 50ʳ.   [28] Ibid.

gesture of clarification ('c'est à dire'), which attempts to control the pace of the sentence, and describe, and so arrest, the force of the wind, only leads to another, longer string of verbs. Nor, when Valimbert speaks of his own body, does he seem able to do so in clarified sentences; it is not only turtles who risk losing their skin:

Il nous falloit enfermer dans les chambres sur le chameau qui nous secouoit et nous faisoit quasi étouffer, j'y fus tellement brulé pour ne pouvoir endurer la chaleur que nous ressemblions à des éthiopiens, et moi more toute ma peau tomba de brulure.[29]

The sentence is all over the place and Valimbert writes in fear of falling apart. Plural rooms on a single camel, plural verbs following on from singular pain, and the curious formulation 'moi more toute ma peau . . .' The 'chambres' on the camel offer an encapsulated image of containment in motion, an exemplary representation of the pilgrim on the road.[30] The pilgrim is protected from external contact with others, but not from the fears which his sentence translates: like a passenger in a boat, enclosed and buffeted on board this ship of the desert, we are so out of place, suffocating, I can't bear this heat, I'm burning so much that we look like Ethiopians, and I a Moor my skin is falling away.

The fate of the sirens which Valimbert had seen skinned alive before being turned into the soles of his shoes now threatens the pilgrim himself. Beyond the agony of the desert, the material conditions of the heat, heaviness of the air, and excruciating sunburn, is a deeper anxiety. It is the fear—articulated through the broken syntax of the sentence—that he has already passed beyond the pale, that the pilgrim has turned native.

This pollution anxiety had haunted the earliest, fourth-century Christian pilgrims, as we saw above in relation to Gregory of Nyssa's letter, and its terms were revived with the letter's edition and translation in the Renaissance. It bears also on the rhetoric of both positive and negative 'contagion' which structures much of what Montaigne has to say about travel and our relation to others.[31] Although Valimbert makes no mention of either Gregory of Nyssa or Montaigne,

---

[29] Ibid., fol. 49ᵛ.
[30] Von Harff draws a diagram of what such 'chambres' might have looked like. He calls it a 'box . . . a wooden chest, covered with coarse pelt on account of the great heat of the sun' and says it cost him two ducats (p. 135). His moving account of the journey to Sinai is more polished, and also more gruesome in detail, than Valimbert's.
[31] It will later become a central theme in the fantasy and fears of colonial rhetoric in

writers who occupy the canonical 'domaine de savoir' of his time, as his friend Chassignet knew well, his narrative clearly offers perspectives on this wider context. But we betray the experience of the pilgrim if we do not allow this broken, syntactically confused sentence its specific, dislocated space on the road. It is something which neither Gazier, who quotes the sentence in a syntactically and racially clarified form, nor indeed Chassignet, who recuperates such moments in the journey to the rhetoric of meditational poetry, is willing or perhaps able to do.[32]

Guerin, the romance hero, left Egypt in the company of pilgrims. Travelling in search of legitimation of his family origins, Valimbert finds that his pilgrimage through Egypt is at once a romance, articulating deeply felt anxieties about others and elsewhere, and an epic of providential domestic provision. The 'place where' Moses struck the rock for water is just one of many *topoi* which serve to recuperate his own travels, and in particular his insistently enjoyed 'bonne chère', to the Biblical desert narrative. He finally leaves Egypt through a romance trope in the form of a tree. For the last obstacle he faces is what seems to be all too overdetermined a domestic miracle: the fig tree which had opened to allow Mary and the Christ-child to enter Egypt unhindered, but which does not permit 'illégitimes' to pass through it. It is a tree visited by many, many pilgrims, and, like most obstacles in romance, is there to be overcome. Valimbert walks through it unharmed.[33]

'C'est le lieu où': *Valimbert on Holy Ground*

As if by magic, the one tree opens, and then leads directly to the open tomb beside the tree which is the cross. The next page of script has Valimbert standing at the opening of Christ's tomb, waiting to enter

India, mediated through disguise, espionage, and pilgrimage in, for example, Kipling's *Kim*; or again in North America, as in Cooper's *Last of the Mohicans*.

[32] See Gazier, 'Le pèlerinage d'un bisontin', p. 15. Chassignet's skill in imitative appropriation with respect to Montaigne's *Essais* is well documented. His introduction to the *Mespris* echoes Montaigne often and at length, as do many of the poems themselves. See R. Ortali, *Jean-Baptiste Chassignet: Un Poète de la mort* (1968), pp. 38–44 and R. Leake, 'Jean-Baptiste Chassignet and Montaigne', *BHR* 23 (1961), pp. 282–95.

[33] Valimbert, fol. 52ʳ. For other accounts of experiences at this tree, see Beauveau, p. 168; Villamont, p. 659; and Castela, who narrates a cautionary tale about the 'Dragoman' whose own son (or so he thought) got stuck in the tree: 'laissant à son pere un marteau en teste, et dequoy rougir de honte, d'avoir luy mesme experimenté à ses despens, ce qu'il avoit dict de la propriètè de l'arbre susdict' (p. 415).

and be initiated into the Order of the Holy Sepulchre. If arrival in the Holy Land was a shock to Valimbert, if he was obliged to endure the common ritual of initiation and inscription at Jaffa, if this was a singular experience for him in the way that it was for Cuchermoys, he does not say. His account is longer and more digressive than that of Cuchermoys, and in this respect, as in its quest for legitimacy, his story seems closer to that of Mesquin than that of the early pilgrim. But, in truth, Valimbert's Jerusalem is the same as that of the earlier pilgrim. His journey and his text move along the worn paths and in the measured structural paces of Cuchermoys a century before, and Egeria centuries earlier. He writes of his journey 'according to the scriptures', noting not simply places, but 'places where':

C'est le lieu où . . . tout près est le lieu où . . . un peu plus loin ya . . . là, auprès de la maison de pilate . . . nous fusmes de là en la maison de . . . auprès de la porte on voit . . . puis nous allasmes voir une église, où . . . on y voit . . . aussi . . . en ce meme lieu, on nous montra au coin . . . à la droite est la prison où nostre Seigneur. . . .[34]

By means of such a structure of accounting, Valimbert first records the inherited pilgrimages around Jerusalem, and then extends the model to the entire Holy Land.[35] He reads traces of Christ's presence everywhere: in the walls, the roads, the houses, and the rocks. The land, he wants to argue, is paradise itself. If few flowers survive in Damascus, the specific location of Eden, it is because the Flood 'emporta toutes ces bonnes plantes et apparences du paradis'.[36] But he cannot help noticing that paradise is now alien territory; and certain providential signs prove to have been subject to a specific, and disturbing, form of literal translation. The sweeping away of flowers in the Flood is one thing; the theft of one of Christ's footprints is another.

The 'vestiges' of Christ's footsteps are in a sense the paradigmatic signs of the pilgrim's own journey. Mentioned in every pilgrimage I have read, ancient or early modern, they serve as a literal representation of the psalmist's prophecy about pilgrims, reiterated from Jerome to Villette: 'we shall stand in the place where his feet stood.'[37]

[34] Valimbert, fol. 53ʳ.   [35] Ibid., fols. 52ᵛ–54ʳ, 56ʳ–60ʳ.   [36] Ibid., fol. 60ʳ.
[37] These include Egeria, pp. 43–5; Brocardus, p. 83; Hault, fols. 43ᵛ, 70ʳ; Beauveau, p. 155; Guerrero, pp. 39–40; Castela, pp. 284–5. See also Hunt's discussion *Holy Land Pilgrimage*, pp. 113, 161. The image on the cover of this book is taken from Breydenbach's gloss on this text *in situ*. The Psalmist's text and its translation in pilgrims' accounts was the focus of Ch. 4, above.

They are iconic signs and their forcible translation—experienced by Christian pilgrims as a theft—carries all the more force as a result. Valimbert writes:

il y a au milieu et au sommet du mont une eglise, lieu meme d'où Jesus notre Sauveur monta aux cieux et on y voit encore le vestige d'un de ses pieds gravé sur une pierre . . . l'autre pierre avec l'autre vestige est au temple de salomon les turcs en font une mosquette et n'y laissent entrer sans argent.[38]

Where the displacement of the footprint is disconcerting, Nazareth is a shock. The town is full of beggars and thieves, and Valimbert notes: 'nous fumes obligés de marchander aux voleurs memes, de nous garder cette nuit en une caverne.'[39] Here again—as in Venice and Rosetta with respect to the pilgrim galleys—trade with non-Christians is represented as a necessity forced on him because the institution of pilgrimage is in ruins. Cuchermoys, remember, had been obliged to stay in a 'caverne' in Jaffa, but once the formalities of arrival were over, he was hosted by priests wherever he went in the Holy Land. The early pilgrim was 'protected' from Others and from the kinds of contact which come of trade. Valimbert, by this stage of his journey, is used to trade, and has managed to recuperate (most of) it to the plot of his own particular pilgrimage. But 'marchander' here carries little sense of exchange. The obligation to (pay to) enter a mosque to see the footprint of Christ, and the need to do a deal with some thieves so as to find somewhere to sleep, have far more to do with what Valimbert experiences as a form of blackmail.

There is of course a way of reading Valimbert's Nazareth experience as part of a pilgrimage narrative: like Cuchermoys' being obliged to sit on a horse when he would have preferred a donkey, Valimbert is here being forced into a kind of displaced imitation of Christ. It's the right gesture—finding no room at the inn—but it is performed in the wrong place—Nazareth, not Bethlehem. But in truth it is not 'performed' at all: Valimbert does not stage his difficulties. They happen to him, and he writes about them. In common with later French pilgrims such as Villamont, Beauveau, Castela, and

---

[38] Valimbert, fols. 56ᵛ–57ʳ. Castela notes that it is to the Muslims' credit that they honour the footprint, which they know to be that of Christ; he also says that Christians cannot get in to see it, but, exceptionally, he did; it was bigger than his own foot (pp. 284–5). I am told by a traveller recently returned (from a conference on Montaigne held in Haifa) that it is still shown for substantial sums of money as one of the Prophet's footsteps.

[39] Valimbert, fol. 59ᵛ.

Hault, he dwells on the agony of the road, and so fills the space between reiterative *loci* with the particular conditions of the journey. In doing this he, to paraphrase Montaigne, makes of himself the matter of pilgrimage.[40] Like the poet Chassignet, he makes a character of the individual, recuperating his particular journey to the rhetoric of life's *Voyage*. And if we read Valimbert's text as an exemplary dramatization of the late pilgrim's troubled journey, we do more than follow in his footsteps as he followed in those of the pilgrims before him. Because he makes of himself the matter of pilgrimage, we, as readers, make an example of the man.

Aleppo to Baghdad: Sites of Contagion

The trade and the agony of the desert, the double dealing and occasional doubt as to the worth of sacred signs in the Holy Land; these can all be recuperated to the master plot of Christian pilgrimage. Even the insistence on the ruinous and parlous state of the buildings which once offered pilgrims shelter serves to stress the good faith and enduring heroism of this particular pilgrim. Valimbert's travels beyond Jerusalem first north to the markets of Aleppo, and then east to Baghdad cannot, however, be made part of the pilgrim plot. With the change of place, so too comes a change of narrative style. It is difficult to derive a sacred sense from, for instance, Valimbert's remark that a certain Mgr d' Hausperge proved in the market at Aleppo to be a greater Seigneur than Valimbert had thought, 'me menant avec lui acheter des tapisseries indiennes et turquesques, vaisselle de porcelaine, et autres belles marchandises, en quoi il employa plus de dix mils sequins'.[41] These are 'marchandises peregrines', goods exotic and temporal, rather than spiritual. Still less can pilgrim motivation be detected in Valimbert's remark that he followed an Englishman and a Venetian to Ormuz because he was bored with Aleppo.[42] Even the terms for travel that Valimbert begins to adopt at this point mark his departure from pilgrimage: 'En notre *séjour* en Alep, nous alasmes voir *en promenade*, en deux petites journées Antioche.'[43] True, they go to Antioch to see St Peter's Square, but being on pilgrimage is an altogether different mode of being from that of being 'en séjour' and 'en promenade'.

---

[40] Montaigne: 'je suis moy-mesmes la matiere de mon livre', 'Au Lecteur', *Oeuvres*, p. 9.
[41] Valimbert, fol. 61ʳ.   [42] Ibid.   [43] Ibid.

The French nobles Valimbert had first met in Venice leave him at Aleppo, as they are headed first for Constantinople, then Poland, Germany, and home. Valimbert cannot afford to return overland, and so awaits the boat to Venice, passing the time wandering the streets: for the first time in his account he writes 'je me promenois'.[44] From this point on the manuscript sees him lose his way several times, taking him eventually to Baghdad (ostensibly looking for a way to get back to Christendom). The pilgrimage is far behind him, but in the market in Baghdad Valimbert encounters a compassionate Jew who reminds him of his true identity. In words which recall César de Paolo's on finding a pilgrim in Alexandria, he is told that 'je m'éloignois beaucoup'. Here, however, there is the added information: 'que j'étois en danger.'[45] Valimbert is advised to return to Aleppo with the next caravan in order to secure passage back to Venice. The Jewish merchant arranges for him to undertake the twenty-four day journey in the service of a passing Armenian Christian. The trade routes which carry him away from the pilgrim road are, then, the same as those which will lead him back home. The point is stressed by the seemingly over-determined information that the very caravan which Valimbert had grown bored of waiting for in Aleppo had just arrived in Baghdad on its return journey.[46]

Valimbert can, it seems, recuperate the error of the journey away from pilgrimage and on to the East in its entirety: like his namesake Jaques in Shakespeare's *As You Like It*, he has 'gained experience' for having gone astray.[47] But there is a condition to this form of return. Shakespeare gives Jaques a generically perfect understanding of the spiritual pilgrimage which comes after romance: like Guerin, he retires to a hermitage.[48] Valimbert has no such plans, and, still imprisoned in the plot of disguise, he must lose more of his own lands before he can return home. In order to join the Armenian Christian's caravan, he was, he writes: 'obligé de me déguiser en arabe, esclave.'[49]

'Moi more': Valimbert's transformation, at once feared and fantasized back in the Sinai desert, is complete. He is once again part of a camel train, but the space between the enclosing 'chambres' on the Sinai camel and the folds of the cloth of the slave walking alongside

---

[44] Valimbert, fol. 61ʳ.   [45] Ibid., fol. 61ᵛ.   [46] Ibid.

[47] *AYLI*, IV. i; see also Ch. 7, below.

[48] In this he follows not only Romance heroes, but also the exemplary 'convertites', Charles V (1555) and the Duc de Joyeuse (1587, 1599). See *AYLI*, V. iv.

[49] Valimbert, fol. 61ᵛ.

the camel from Baghdad to Aleppo is unbridgeable. The first protect the pilgrim's identity, if not his skin, the second save Valimbert's skin by disguising his pilgrim identity. This difference witnesses to the increasingly acquired practical skills of the traveller: the Arabian clothing must have offered some measure of protection from the suffocating heat and from the sunburn which had earlier torn off his skin. But Valimbert has also travelled some considerable symbolic distance in his relation to the non-pilgrim Other.

Remember the boat in which he sailed, expressing surprise not so much at the fact that his guards shot at the figures swimming in the Nile, but at the humanity which their screams revealed; remember also the monstrous figures Guerin encounters both east and west of Jerusalem; remember finally Cuchermoys' silence regarding the customs of the locals, and his need to disguise himself momentarily in order to recover the requisite pilgrim clothing stolen from him at Jaffa. These are moments of contact with others which speak of fear and incomprehension, emblematized in Valimbert's fear of becoming Other himself: 'moi More'. Here, however, Valimbert writes: 'nous les suivismes, mon armenien et moi.' This is in sharp contrast to earlier anxieties, and stresses the possibility of transformation through dialogue: 'mon armenien et moi, qui me fit bonne aide et compagnie . . .'[50]

There is a similarity in our two pilgrims' experience of subjection in relation to disguise, expressed in the very terms they use to explain the transition from pilgrim clothes to others: 'je fus obligé de me desguiser en . . .' But the difference between Cuchermoys' disguise and that of Valimbert is a sign of their different relations to the language of pilgrimage, and the place, within that language, for self-description. Cuchermoys does not describe his disguise, does not transfer the shame of having to be Other into his account in such a way as to be able to picture the pilgrim in a non-pilgrim costume. Valimbert does, and he enjoys the description: '[j'estois] habillé en arabe, avec ma robe, une chemise bleüe et un toupot de laine rouge à long poil en forme d'un Greau [?], avec mes grands souliers éperonnés pour aller sur les chameaux.'[51] The 'éperons' here are not those of his hard-earned knightly identity; but he would seem to be happy to wear them, and certainly takes pleasure in describing both them and the figure he cuts in disguise.

[50] Ibid., fol. 62ʳ.   [51] Ibid.

The journey back from Baghdad to the Mediterranean is long and gruelling. At its end, in Tripoli, Valimbert sees a flock of birds block out the sun for a full quarter of an hour: 'Ils voloient sur le chemin d'où je venois et je crois qu'ils alloient aux indes.'[52] The birds retrace the journey he has just completed, but are headed—perhaps like his winged thoughts—beyond it, for Valimbert never reached India. Instead of following the birds in body, he waits for a boat home, only to fear drowning even before boarding. For the ground turns to water beneath him during the days of rain which follow the cloud of birds, and so as not to drown, Valimbert clambers up on to some bales of straw. Here, fearing that he will be pushed off them, or that he might, as he puts it, 'tomber de soi', he binds himself to a tree. Within the compass of the narrative, he never comes down from the tree and never makes the boat home. The text breaks off leaving him suspended, and in fear of '[s']enfoncer en la terre qui estoit marécageuse'.[53]

'Nous Autres Pèlerins'—*Sensing the End*

The Holy Sepulchre: 14 August 1490–24 September 1584

In comparing these two pilgrimage accounts, we are evidently not comparing like with like; neither their textual history nor their internal logics are identical. Yet for all their differences and their differing degrees of mediation, certain thematic and structural points do connect them: a concern with family, name, legitimacy, and property; the transcription or translation of Italian texts by way of authorization, shifts in voice and person; contact with non-pilgrim Others, cross-fertilization of genres, and anxiety about losing one's identity, or skin. These different concerns are articulated in terms of the triangulation of disguise, kinship, and taboo. And all three travellers—Guerin, Cuchermoys, Valimbert—resolve the conflicts and confusions of their journeys with reference to the geographical and rhetorical centre of their world: the Holy Sepulchre. For all three, the tomb is the locus of resurrection, the place where release is to be found from those entangled desires which have brought them to this point.

Guerin Mesquin, disguised as a Persian soldier, participates in the

---

[52] Valimbert, fol. 62ᵛ.   [53] Ibid.

recapture of Jerusalem, and on arrival kneels a full night in the Sepulchre, where he secretly vows to convert Autiniche and start a new
family with her once he has recovered his own parents. The pilgrim
translator of Guerin's romance mentions none of the other members
of his family, but notes that he was himself secretly translated, during
the night of 14 August, into a member of the chivalric order of the
knights of the Holy Sepulchre:

En celuy jour a souleil couchant nous entrasmes dedans le sainct sepulcre et
demourasmes fin a souleil Levant et celle nuytee furent faictz les chevaliers
de lordre de Hierusalem.[54]

Alongside the text at this point the printer has placed a woodcut
image of the resurrection; this is a visual image used only once in the
book.[55] Like the experience it marks, the image is both conventional
and unique; the event repeated with each new company of travellers
to Jerusalem, but central to the individual pilgrim's journey. For this
centre holds for many, many pilgrims, whether they kneel there alone
and in disguise as does Guerin, in pilgrim's habit as does Cuchermoys, or in the regalia of a knight as does Jacques de Valimbert. On
24 September 1584, at the entrance of the tomb, Valimbert paid the
requisite fee (nine gold ducats), declared 'au Bascha' first his own
name, and then that of his father, and provided evidence that he was
a legitimate son. Once inside, he was questioned again, this time by
the 'Patriarche ou Gardien', who asked first if he was a legitimate son,
and then signalled the end of Valimbert's quest: 'Quid quaeris? je
lisois ma response dans un livre de parchemin et répondis effici miles
sanctissimi sepulchri domini nostri jesu christi.'[56] With the authority
of the documents he has collected on his journey, and through the
practice of imitation proper to this place, Valimbert is duly initiated
into the order, some ninety-five years after Jehan de Cuchermoys.

   Like all the Jerusalem pilgrims whose accounts have survived,
Valimbert spends a good deal of his journey towards and away from
this centre reading (scripture, guide-books, the land), and writing
(letters, his own account). He spends more time than most collecting
documents and transcribing them, but the ceremony at the Sepulchre

[54] Ibid.
[55] Cuchermoys, fol. Dvʳ. Both the image of leaving a castle which opens the account,
and that of the boat on the high seas which occurs towards the end also accompany the
romance.
[56] Valimbert, fol. 54ʳ.

affirms that these moments of writing represent no real digression from pilgrimage. Rather, they are means to the end of making the journey run more smoothly: as we saw above, Valimbert notes that students are exempt from taxes in Venetian territory, and those who cannot show that they have paid the Franciscans in advance risk excommunication. Most importantly of all, that certificate which names Jacques as Bertini de Valimberto's legitimate son had to be produced before the guardian of the Sepulchre before Valimbert could be given the certificate sealed with a resurrection which confirms his chivalric and pilgrim identity. The ceremony brings Valimbert's own particular romance to an end. He describes the scene by alternating between the Latin which was spoken in the Sepulchre, and his own French commentary, written after the event. He represents the occasion as one of real dialogue, between languages, between the celebrants, and with tradition:

cela fait il me mit en main deux éperons dorés qu'il me fit chausser étant toujours à genoux, puis, il donne l'épée dorée nuë, disant accipe jacobe sanctum gladium in nomine patris et filii et spiritus sancti, et utavii [*sic*] eo ad defensionem tuam et sanctae dei ecclesiae et ad confusionem inimicorum crucis christi ac fidei christianae.[57]

While nearby monks were heard to sing 'Veni creator spiritus etc.', Valimbert took the sword and spurs, and a great golden cross was hung around his neck. Another, final, certificate is here copied into the account, one which the margin glosses as 'Lettre de ma chevalerie'. It is, like the opening attestation from the governors of Besançon, in Latin, a language which both starts and ends the quest: 'Cela fait fut expediée la lettre de chevalerie bien signée et sçelée du grand sçeau, qui est une resurrection. . . . Puis il me licentia de ne porter ma croix s'il ne me plaisoit jusqu'à ce que je fusse en notre pays.'[58]

This painfully won and officially certified identity as a Christian knight is, as we have seen, constantly at risk for the remainder of Valimbert's journey. Before he is able to put on his golden spurs and

[57] Valimbert, fol. 55ᵛ. There are many other accounts of this ceremony in pilgrims' texts. Amongst the most richly evocative are those of Possot, pp. 178–80 and Villamont, pp. 444–50 (Larjot, his publisher, adds a number of texts concerning the ceremony and on the 'ordonnances' of the order, pp. 817–44).

[58] Ibid., fols. 55ᵛ–56ʳ. Cuchermoys' text, as noted above, places a woodcut of the resurrection at this point.

wear the cross 'en nostre pays', he finds himself obliged to wear the 'souliers eperonnés' of the slave, simply to save his skin. On arrival home, though he does not know this yet, he will find that fashions have changed, that the pilgrims' gaudy golden cross and spurs are now thought of as proof of overliteral attachment to signs, and are something of an embarrassment.

The Confusion of Persons

Articulating the past historically does not mean coming to know it 'the way it really was' (Ranke). It means seizing hold of a memory as it flashes up at a moment of danger.[59]

Cuchermoys' first significant port of call had been Ragusa, a point of suspension between Christendom and Jerusalem, the last fortified position on the edge of alien territory. Here, he noted: 'here I began translating a romance', as if inviting us to read the pilgrim as a romance hero. Such a reading is difficult not to indulge in the case of Valimbert, though he himself accompanies his text not with a translated romance, but with a host of largely untranslated official documents, signed and sealed by the authorities. Moreover, his account was first unearthed—and perhaps first copied—because of its having been travestied in Chassignet's poem arguing that the romance conception of pilgrimage is an error whose time is now past.

  Both narratives speak, I have argued, of the pilgrim experience all the more directly for being subject to contagion with adjacent forms of representation—documents, romances, poems, marginal notes, dates, times, and costs, scriptural quotation, foreign words, visual images, and so on. To focus on moments of enforced disguise is to gain a sense of the particular and real fears of the pilgrims on their journeys. But these points can also be read as generic *gnorismata*, moments of danger which flash up before the reader, not so much indices of 'the way things really were', as marks of the enduring and illicit narrative kinship of pilgrimage with romance. It is important, precisely because of the degrees of mediation involved in these accounts, to respect the trace of the will to reference which each pilgrim marks in the ground of their texts. These are events which the pilgrims are at pains to represent as having actually taken place. And it is also important to recognise that the generic kinships which these

[59] Benjamin, *Illuminationonn*, p. 255 (translation mine).

narratives reveal are a shaping part of the history of pilgrimage, both as event and as representation.[60]

Cuchermoys' pilgrimage is printed as an appendix to, but in other respects is defined by its difference from, the romance; there is little generic contamination (and no Italian) in his account, and his journey bears little plotted relation to that of Guerin. But—and this is crucial—neither traveller's journey ends in Jerusalem. Pilgrims, across the long century, do narrate their return journeys. More importantly, romance and pilgrimage can—at least in the early Renaissance—co-exist; a condition of co-existence is acknowledgement of generic difference, of their difference each from the other.[61] Cuchermoys' account brings him home safely, and his narrative bears witness to a kind of homecoming which escaped Valimbert. He can in the same move and at the same time travel, write a pilgrimage account, translate a romance, and go home. This he can do without substantive fear of losing his way, losing his integrity as a pilgrim, or having Guerin's romance contaminate his own story; and he can do so publicly, and in print.

It does seem that this is not an option for the later pilgrim, though this has less to do with his allegiance to a specific literary form, than with the confusion of generic kinds within his account; that and his desire to represent himself. The structural similarities between the romance paradigm and that of pilgrimage are constant. What changes is the nature of the relationship between these paradigms, and their relation to something called personal experience. The later pilgrimage reveals its desire to be a narrative of just such personal experience (rather than a collective affirmation of faith) through its *anxious* relation to romance. The anxiety is itself not altogether new: Cuchermoys' account of his experience in Jaffa suggests that the production of a discourse which says 'I' was always already anxious. But for Cuchermoys, the use of either romance or pilgrimage as a frame for the narration of the details of personal experience is an aberration. When he is forced into the first person, into writing about

[60] I owe the term 'will to reference' to A. Jefferson, 'Realism reconsidered: Bakhtin's Dialogism and the "will to reference" ', *AJFS*, xxiii, 2 (1986), pp. 169–84.

[61] *Pace* Howard, who, identifying what he terms 'a real difference between the medieval mind and the modern', argues that the homecoming scene is proper to romance, and to 'practical and worldly voyages of exploration or commerce or diplomacy . . . which were almost never likened to a pilgrimage', *Writers and Pilgrims*, pp. 48, 50. See Ch. 1, above and Ch. 7, below.

himself as an individual, he regrets the circumstance, and narrates it as the result of subjection. For Valimbert it would seem to be the point both of the journey and of the narrative.

The comparison of two further contrasting points of suspension on the journey which the accounts of Cuchermoys and Valimbert offer, two snapshots (*clichés*) of themselves in disguise—Cuchermoys in Jaffa, Valimbert in Aleppo—suggest how this is so. For Cuchermoys presents himself as a pilgrim who has had his goods stolen, returning on board ship in disguise. He needs to collect another set of pilgrim clothes in order properly to re-enter the Holy Land. Valimbert, by contrast, has by the time he reaches Aleppo for a second time, long since lost his pilgrim clothes. Having been through several self-transformations, he binds himself to a tree in the midst of a storm in order save his skin one more time. Each image is a translation into pilgrim discourse of the romance *topos* of disguise; each is also represented by the pilgrims as resulting from contact with the non-pilgrim Other. In Cuchermoys' case the disguise is momentary, and instrumental; for Valimbert, by this stage in his journey, it has become a habit. Measuring the distance between these two moments in the context of the pilgrim's relations with the non-pilgrim, with self-presentation in the first person and with self-preservation in disguise, we are able to understand more clearly what happens to pilgrimage writing in the course of the sixteenth century. We should also gain some sense of the force of certain broader questions which relate these images of translation, imitation, and disguise to the binding of others and of ourselves to the narrative shapes which we now give to experience.

The digressions and diversions of Valimbert's journey speak of a generic contamination which leaves the pilgrim almost unrecognizable and the pilgrimage account incomplete. Does his image of a man suspended from a tree, as if in imitation of the crucifixion, represent Valimbert's last attempt to wrest his text back into the frame of *imitatio Christi*? Perhaps it is purely practical skill: anyone with common sense would do the same. Or, lastly, is it perhaps a ruse, another cross-generic gesture, in which Valimbert–Odysseus bids for epic status in tying himself to the mast-like tree in a storm? Both Christ and Odysseus inhabit the 'domaine de savoir' of Renaissance travel writing. They, along with the—by this time—somewhat dated hero of romance narratives such as *Guerin Mesquin* represent competing normative types of traveller. We may allegorize Valimbert's experience, and his body bound to the tree, as suspended between these types. In doing so, however, we need to acknowledge that he makes explicit reference to none of them in this specific context; not least since other, more lettered pilgrims—Thevet and Castela in particular—will more consciously fashion themselves, in sentences at once more ornate and more directly referential, as heirs to all three.[62]

It is in this context that it is important to note that most verbs in Cuchermoys' account are motivated by the first person plural. In the first instance he is saying, 'I and my companion, Pierre, we.' Pierre eats, sleeps, sees, and reads as part of Jehan's story; he is included in his verbs and actions. Like Cuchermoys' account, that of Philippe de Voisins, who travels in the same year as Cuchermoys is also written primarily in the first person plural. Both narratives make extensive reference to one other named companion who is thereby involved in the process not only of the journey but also of its narration and accreditation. For these writers the pilgrim is primarily someone who travels with, rather than towards, others. True, the Jerusalem pilgrimage is a journey to somewhere other than the home community, but others from home accompany the pilgrim on the journey, and pilgrims consciously carry the people and the values of their community with them across the world.

Of course Cuchermoys' pilgrimage is bound—in both a material and metaphorical sense—to be read as an appendix to romance. But the nature of his text, its verbs, and its distinction from the translation, motivate away from entanglement in narratives of individual worldly detail, and move its readers towards an understanding of pilgrimage as a collective experience. This is most clearly demonstrated when the pilgrim is separated from his companions and obliged to conjugate events in the singular. It is also clear in the manner in which Cuchermoys narrates his return home:

Le ix jour dudict moys de decembre ainsi que nous voulions despartir [de Rome] ung gentilhome de Piedmont qui escuyer estoit du cardinal Allerie nous fit parler a nostre sainct pere le pape lequel nous donna sa benediction et a chescun ung confessional et trois agnus dei et lors de luy prismes congie et montasmes a cheval et chevaulchant par maintes journees passasmes par les alpes de bouloigne et les montz de Savoye ou maintes froidures nous endurasmes mais la mercy dieu nous arrivasmes a bon saulvement a Lyon le premier jour de lan mille iiii cens iiiixx et unze environ midy.[63]

[62] We return in detail to Castela and Thevet in Ch. 7, below.
[63] Cuchermoys, fol. vj^r.

You meet the Pope, you are granted the right to choose your confessor; granted these are important. But what about your wife, your friends, and your lovers, your children, your house, your work? What of the people and things Menedemus defines as making up his pilgrimage? Had they changed? Had you changed? The romance you translated is eloquent about these things, and yet you are silent. Is it right that 'we' moderns cannot read in your sentence a recognisable story of the pilgrim's return; and does this, your last documentary gesture, which may have confirmed your return to your own community, only represent to 'us' an active resistance to being recuperated, or recognized?

If we cannot read a proper return into Cuchermoys' sentence then we must recognize that we cannot inhabit the pilgrims' first person plural. 'Our' kinship is less with the pilgrim or romance hero, than with Menedemus, and with what the counter-Reformation pamphleteer terms the 'bourgeois de ce monde'.[64] For Cuchermoys' 'we' refers to an altogether more specific order of person, one bound to another kind of collectivity. In saying 'nous [autres pèlerins]' the pilgrim articulates a sense of how the journey makes him at once a representative of his own family, village, town, and culture, and also 'autre' to the community, precisely by becoming recognizably its representative. Cuchermoys' 'we' refers initially to 'My companion and I'. More collectively, it speaks of 'Me, my companion, Pierre, and our fellow travellers, who risked our sense of self in the course of the experience which is pilgrimage, we saw, witnessed, and now write. . . .' And most importantly of all, it bespeaks a collectivity which is a function of the journey itself, grounded in the terms and the practice of Christian imitation: a peculiarly theological sense of the individual in relation to history.

Valimbert, in writing 'je', knows that he has already lost something of his pilgrim self. It is the movement towards this loss of a specific pilgrim identity, grounded in a certain collectivity, that in their different ways, Zuallart, Castela, Villette, and, I am suggesting, Cuchermoys long before them, resist. For the pilgrim's collective understanding of experience is predicated not so much on the collation of distinct and recognisably subjective responses, as on that of the one pilgrim, the companion, and the third traveller on the road. The voice of this third party is translated, either consciously or

---

[64] See Halin, *Brief Dialoguo*, fol. 2ᵛ.

unconsciously, by pilgrims in the course of their accounts. The ghost writer of first person pilgrimage can be variously figured: the priest, the trickster, the trader, the renegade, the reader at home, or Christ: 'Pierre, and I, and Christ, we. . . .'

It is the often unacknowledged, and sometimes unrecognized, presence of a third party which makes it possible for pilgrims to speak of their own experience. And it is in relation to such a presence that Valimbert's mania for documentation makes sense. For his pilgrimage suffers from his having no-one to write about him in the third person, to seal the worth of his experience, and to assure his text a safe passage home. The official documents he transcribes are so many attempts to create for himself at once a constant travelling companion, and the necessary third party. The point is made, and the generic worth of these documents as gestures of verification confirmed, by another Jerusalem traveller, who says he has no need of such things. Belon writes: 'Le gardien des cordeliers du mont de Sion a de coustume bailler une certification aux pelerins qui ont esté envoyez par quelqu'un afin que ce leur soit tesmoignage qu'ils ont esté là.'[65] For Belon, of course, what matters is that he does *not* need such documents, any more than he needs the 'droguements' pilgrims use to speak for them. He stresses their absence in his text so as to certify his own professional and independent identity. His words speak, he hopes, for themselves; they mark the fact that he is *not* a pilgrim and, with an almost cavalier curtness, he passes over the place pilgrims move earth to visit: the Holy Sepulchre, he writes, 'contient toutes autres choses par le menu, que n'avons pas specifié en ce lieu à cause de brieveté'.[66]

Belon suggests the documents are created for (those who have funded) pilgrims who travel by proxy. But Valimbert travels on his own account, and thus for him they must have a more personal significance. Perhaps they can be seen to anticipate any lone traveller's photographs, taken by others: 'I have been there, look there, that's me, someone took the photo for me, look, in the corner, there's the date, I was there.' Others perhaps, are more personal deictic gestures of verification, taken with a camera set on self-timer: 'this one's me in front of the pyramids, on Mount Sinai, on the back of the camel in the desert.' Valimbert writes of himself, not least because he has

---

[65] Belon, *Observations*, fol. 254ʳ.   [66] Ibid.

no-one else to write about him. The incomplete pictures he paints of himself as hero of his own journey are not the polemical, exemplary first person of an Augustine, or, in Valimbert's time, of a Léry in Brazil, or a Castela, or a Balourdet in Palestine. Still less are they the self-aggrandizing professional confessions of a Thevet, or a Belon. Unable to sustain a meaningful dialogue with either pilgrimage or romance, Valimbert anxiously tries produce a discourse of the self which is neither one nor the other, but might encompass, as if by accident, and in the course of the journey, both. Forced into the habit of first person narration, Valimbert insistently shifts into others' voices; it is these moments which are a refracted mirror image of Cuchermoys' rare moves into the first person. It is neither the person of the verbs they use, nor the nature of the documents they cite which binds these pilgrims' narratives together. What matters, rather, is the alternation of repetition and innovation, quotation and direct speech, of translation and the vernacular. It is these different voices that tell us of the changing relations between pilgrimage, romance, and experience.

Valimbert speaks often, if fragmentedly, of his own body, and of the pain, displacements, and disguises to which he is personally subject. But he does so at a cost to the generic integrity of his account. His search for his own personal legitimacy in the course of his pilgrimage, his mania for documentation, and the eventual incompletion of his narrative, all distinguish it from pilgrimages proper. This lack of narrative closure, and the uncertain authority of the manuscript text, find response in other aspects of Valimbert's story. Back home in Besançon he never quite enjoyed the fruits of his return as he had anticipated: he faced litigation contesting his right to inherited properties, found himself in prison for heresy, and found that his text never made it to print, despite his having collected enough documents to fill a library.

Back on his pilgrimage, he remembers, things had appeared more hopeful. He had walked through the middle of a miraculous tree in Egypt, and worshipped at the foot of another in Jerusalem. Perhaps fearing the loss (once again) of his precariously balanced sense of self, he had bound himself to yet another in Tripoli. We can read these three trees as sharing hermeneutic kinship: the Holy Family tree certifies his own legitimacy, the cross redeems him and seals the effect of the earlier tree, and the last, though personal to him, bears the weight of epic legend, even as it saves his life so that he can tell his tale. Such a reading, however, runs the risk of framing Valimbert as a romance figure, or at least a man of letters. We translate the strangely sparse lexicon and syntax of his narrative into a more recognizably symbolic set of tropes. We risk once again making an example of the man, and translating the 'langages pellegrins' of his text into traces of our own hermeneutic desire.

For, at the crossroads of digressive fiction and sparsely written itinerary lies the experience of pilgrimage in the Renaissance. Like the irruptions of the first person into Cuchermoys' account, Valimbert's rigorously impersonal documents signal both the generic confusion of persons, and the will to reference which pilgrimage narratives articulate. Our texts, in their very different ways, are at once examples of that textual hybridity which is the effect of a tradition in the process of change, and attempts to register the real; not as effect, nor by way of nostalgia, but as actualized presence: 'non pas un souvenir, une imagination, une reconstitution . . . comme l'art en prodigue, mais le réel à l'état passé: à la fois le passé et le réel.'[67]

Coming Home, In a Poem

If this is so, then the question arises as to what we, now, are doing when we follow these traces inscribed in manuscript or in print. Are we pilgrims, looking for signs of the real presence of people at once recognizable—*nous*—and other—*autres*—to ourselves? If so, do we, like Castela's ideal pilgrim, take the values of our community across time and place, and in doing so fail to engage in an encounter with the otherness of these texts, or the people who wrote them? If pilgrims are readers, what sort of pilgrims are readers?

The transmission of Valimbert's text is the result of three different moments of historical investment, or faith, in the value of travel writing. The first is that of Enlightenment cosmopolitanism, which ensures that the autograph manuscript is copied as part of a collection of still unpublished texts relating travel to a wide range of places from Baghdad to Louisiana. The second is that of the local patriotism which the Annales school exemplified earlier this century, and which brought and still brings many such texts to our notice: Gazier, for instance, entitles his article signalling the existence of Valimbert's

---

[67] This is Barthes on the 'tel' in *La Chambre claire* (1980), p. 130. Cf. *Fragments d'un discours amoureux* (1977), pp. 261–4. See also A. Jefferson, 'Roland Barthes: Photography and the Other of Writing', *JIRS* I (1992), pp. 293–309.

narrative: 'Le pèlerinage d'un bisontin.' And he opens by citing Feb-vre's contention in his 'beau livre sur *Philippe II et la Franche-Comté*' that the Comtois, 'loin d'avoir été sédentaires, des gens d'horizon borné . . . ont au contraire aimé et pratiqué beaucoup les voyages'.[68] The third is my own interest in pilgrimage as a surviving, changing discourse in the Renaissance, an interest which has taken shape in response to the critical schools and movements of recent years—such as New Historicism, and the efforts of Foucault, Greene, Cave, and others to effect dialogue between history and poetics.

Even placing our own, and others', work in context does not, how-ever, tell us what motivates the critical search for the anecdotal trace of a real presence, rather than, say, the apparently formulaic gestures of authentification which vehicle the pilgrim's journey. In more exist-ential terms, what motivates the desire to read a singular, recogniz-able person inhabiting the verbs of history, rather than, say, an author-function, or even a fictionally fashioned self? To read these texts as non-fictional accounts of actual journeys, narratives of lived experience, it seems imperative, at the level of the sentence, to privilege the singular and active verb over passive or plural verbs. But this is to avoid one of the central questions which these pilgrim-age accounts present to their readers. How much does a (first) person (verb) weigh; and what force does a date, a time, a place convey?[69]

The question as to the value ascribed to autopsy, to the eyewitness report, is an insistent one in Renaissance travel writing as has been shown in relation to the 'duel des cosmographes'.[70] It was discussed above in relation to writers of sacred descriptions in chapter four, and I shall return to this issue in relation to other travellers—Georgiewitz, Thevet, Castela, and Panurge—in the concluding part of this study. From the discussion thus far in this study, it is clear that

---

[68] Gazier, 'Le pèlerinage d'un bisontin', p. 1. See also, as noted above, the articles by de Marsy (before Gazier) and Major (after him).

[69] The best discussion of this problem remains J. Derrida's *La Carte postale* (1980), par-ticularly 'Envois', pp. 7–273. For an altogether less generous critique of attempts to read the reality principle at work in places you would least expect (exemplified by Greenblatt's essay, 'Fiction and Friction'), see J. Fineman's 'The History of the Anecdote: Fiction and Fiction', in *The New Historicism* (1989), pp. 49–76, itself a mixed bag of essays on similar themes to those I am addressing here.

[70] See the magisterial work of Lestringant, *L'Atelier du cosmographe*, and *André Thevet*, pp. 189–230, in particular. For a brief account, see his 'The Crisis of Cosmog-raphy at the End of the Renaissance', in *Humanism in Crisis*.

having set out with a desire to get some measure of the pilgrim experience, we come to an understanding that 'experience' is itself a contested field within pilgrimage writing; and that the contest is as much over verbs, nouns, and persons, as it is over places and people. As I suggested above, there is no more personally engaged reader than the pilgrim, and reading pilgrimage must be similarly engaged. The engagement is at once political and theological; for theology is about how we inhabit sentences, and politics about how we get from one sentence, or narrative paradigm, to the next.

The issues at stake here are exemplified in the textual afterlife of Valimbert's account within the Renaissance itself, prior to the histories of reading outlined above. I have suggested that Valimbert's last words in the manuscript are difficult not to read as the emblem of the instability and inconclusiveness of his dialogue with narrative tradition. The material incompletion of the manuscript seems to figure the late pilgrim's inability to give his journey the sense which comes of ending. This kind of allegorizing with its emphasis on the problematic status of the pilgrim's return home may seem a peculiarly 'modern' reading of Valimbert's travels; but it is not. It forms the basis of the devotional poet Chassignet's poem, 'A Valimbert', which figures the poet and traveller in conversation about the journey and its worth; listening to this dialogue will conclude our own discussion here.

Chassignet opens with direct, and apparently laudatory, reference to Valimbert's new-found state as knight and author:

> Chevalier que le ciel en Bourgogne a fait naistre
> Comme un autre Postelle, afin de reconnoistre
> Les pais lointains, soit qu'ore en ton recueil
> Tu lises de nouveau les choses que ton oeil
> En Egipte arrivé peut n'aguiere comprendre.[71]

This is ironic encomium, for Valimbert is no Postel; and the rhyme 'recueil | ton oeil' draws on the rhetoric of autopsy only to prepare for the argument of Valimbert's inadequacy as a witness to the truth of travel. The 'de nouveau' suggests that reading from his notebook is something that this traveller—like one who returns with too keen a desire to show off his holiday slides—has done too often. The structure of the poem, especially clear in the beginnings of the lines, continues as follows:

---

[71] Chassignet, 'A Valimbert', in *Le Mespris*, pp. 121–3; here p. 121, ll. 1–5.

> Soit que les vieus tombeaus fais en pointe de flamme
> Où les cors entassez confis dedans le basme,
> Tu dises à tes amis . . .
> Soit que des chaus desers . . .
> Soit que
> Ou . . .
> Où . . .
> Ou . . .
> Ou ce que tu as veu en la ville celebre
> Où le Sauveur souffrit sa passion funebre.[72]

The structure of the first thirty-four lines of Chassignet's poem represents Valimbert-come-home as the archetypal travel-bore, telling and retelling the anecdotes of his journey. The point is stressed lexically in the anaphoric repetition of 'Soit que', and in the mocking alternation of 'C'est le lieu où' with the purely enumerative connective 'ou'. The phrase all pilgrims use to introduce significant places is thus likened to that which simply introduces items on a list, indifferent to their significance and quality. So too with the magic of the place-name; for Chassignet it is clearly something of a wilfully self-defeating game to tick off events and places in a pilgrim litany. So, following Christ's 'passion funebre' comes a list:

> Bethlem, Nazareth, Antioche, et Nain,
> Humps, et le bourg, où l'eau fust convertie en vin,
> Soit que Rhode, Corfou, et les Isles d'Espaigne,
> Cypre, Malthe, Candie, et Corsique et Sardaigne
> Te plaisent à compter et tant de lieus divers
> Qu'on ne pourroit comprendre en mille et mille vers
> Escoute, je te pries. . . .[73]

The repetition of 'comprendre' (lines five and thirty-two), and the attendant alteration in its sense over the course of the journey, summarize the poem's central criticism of the traveller: you start by wanting to understand, but you end up being unable to contain the amount of things you have to say. Even since getting home you have not stopped rambling on.

As the break in rhythm sounded by the imperative 'Escoute, je te pries', suggests, it takes a friend and poet to bring the story to an end. And, as is indicated by the image of narrative exhaustion which precedes the imperative—'mille et mille vers'—it takes a particular kind

---

[72] Ibid., p. 122, ll. 9–26.   [73] Ibid., pp. 122–3, ll. 27–35.

of poetry to convert the expense of the journey into a profitable lesson. What Chassignet goes on to offer his friend is a lesson in sacred, normative poetics, transposing the hesitancies, peripeties, and agony of the road into a scene of narration recollected in the ordered tranquillity of the devotional alexandrine. For the Catholic devotional poet, the procedures of usurpation are clear, as clear as they are to Reformers in their criticism of pilgrimage: Valimbert, in leaving home at all, had gone beyond the pale, and his literal journey—too literal a reading of the terms of pilgrimage—can only be redeemed through returning his experience to the field of metaphor. The poem thus refigures Valimbert's journey as error, the pilgrim as wayward sinner; the real disguise is that of the body, and that must be thrown off to arrive at the true Jerusalem. Physical pilgrimage is but a dangerous diversion from the Christian's 'vrai pelerinage'—to celestial Jerusalem.[74]

Valimbert does not bring the fragmented body of his prose narrative home in the sense of giving it the closure of recognizable form. This absence of closure is unacceptable to Chassignet, whose poem reassembles the pilgrim body in fragments and returns the pilgrim soul home to the living death of exemplary narrative framed by a carefully crafted devotional poem. Following a summary of the pilgrim's wanderings, narrated in order to be classed as worse than worthless, the poem outlines the course of a profitable, figural pilgrimage to death and beyond. In death, Chassignet promises, Valimbert will be provided with the constant companion denied him on the road, and with the joy of conversation and contact which, on the literal pilgrimage, proved so elusive.

This promise made, Chassignet's poem shifts the action away from the literal earth and up to the metaphorical skies, from the actual present to a future moment of retrospection. With this movement, a space opens up: that of (self-) representation. The interlocutors, as if in the future, look down from heaven and see themselves acting, as if in a drama, in the present. The two companions see that they will one day cease their arguments about things—property, legitimacy, the body—which once moved them so much, and that they will smile at themselves and each other:

---

[74] A recurrent theme for Chassignet: sonnet CXVIII: 'Ce cors material n'est l'habitation | Ançois l'hostellerie, ou l'ame non mortelle | Ses thresors precieus ne cache et ne recelle | Mais pour un seul moment y fait provision' (p. 112). See also, for an extraordinarily eroticized account of this journey, 'Le Desir qu'a l'Ame de parvenir en la Supreme Cité de Hierusalem' (pp. 136–9).

> Qui, pour un point de terre ensemble s'entrebattent
> Et comme les enfans de cholere s'esclattent
> Pour moins d'un raisin vert;[75]

This imagined drama, and the resources of simile, offer them the ability to see themselves as other; they are 'comme' wilful children, and should know better. It also offers the chance to reconfigure their particular argument as a generalised debate between body and soul, flesh and spirit, passion and reason. The line continues:

> bref, nos ames alors
> N'auront plus de débat contre nos propres cors,
> Car la chair, se mourant, lairra la raison vive,
> L'esprit en liberté, la passion captive.[76]

The pararhymes and paradiastole are mischievous; the semantic pairs and verbal echoes fantasize a future silence beyond argument. A progression is charted from 'point de terre' to 'raisin vert', and from there to 'chair . . . [qui] lairra la raison vive . . ., la passion captive'. These verbal games echo within the sound-box of the poem and silence the 'débat' between the two friends. They also, crucially, dispossess Valimbert of the terms in which he attempted to make sense of his own efforts at pilgrimage.

For this celestial and sublimated vision of human action is all future, all metaphor. It resolves the tensions of actual existence, the coordinates of experience, by means of an equation between speculation and the metaphorical pilgrimage. Which in turn relies on a prior equation of reading and actualized futurity. For of course the 'vision' of the dead friends is already available to readers of the poem in the moment of reading. We do not have to wait until we arrive in Jerusalem—actual or celestial—to see the pointlessness of our efforts to get there by our own volition. The preacher in Chassignet is using the poetry to teach lessons which the pilgrimage narrative, entangled in time, events, and places, and in its belief that travel is worthwhile, cannot. To 'stand where his feet stood', we need only kneel, read, and pray.[77]

The ironic argument of the poem, and the measure of its bitter success, is to offer Valimbert the companion he so missed on the road, on

---

[75] Ibid., p. 130, ll. 255–8.   [76] Ibid., ll. 258–60.

[77] The force and scope of this phrase from the psalms is explored in relation to the rhetoric of pilgrim description in Ch. 4 above.

condition that he figure himself as a particular kind of pilgrim: the silent, static, contemplative, waiting to be translated into death:

> Là puissions nous tous deux aller faire demeure,
> Genereus Valimbert, et quittant en peu d'heure
> Ce monde desloyal, contempler l'unité
> De ceste alme, ineffable, immense TRINITE.[78]

The prospect of a shared, significant future is created by means of projected collectivities which Valimbert never knew while wandering abroad. The first is the image of the two friends looking back at their earthly travels from the perspective of heavenly Jerusalem, with wonder and with a smile. The second is of devotional readers in the present, reading this poem with—Chassignet hopes—similar wonder at the wisdom of its lesson, and perhaps a smile at the skilled sweetness with which it is preached. The third is that of a unity beyond either subjectivity or companionship. The dialogue between the two friends is replaced by silent contemplation of the third traveller: their individual souls are sublimated, or subsumed, into that 'alme ineffable, immense' which is the Trinity.

The enfolded, litanous, phonic, and semic patterns of the final two quatrains enact Chassignet's translation of Valimbert's literal journey into the resonant terms of orthodox figural pilgrimage: the spoken, written dialogue between literal travel and its figural sense is over:

> Là puissions nous voir en telle conference
> Que voyant L'ETERNEL en sa magnificence
> Hautement sublimé, tous en luy nous soyons,
> Nous sçachions tout en luy, tous en luy nous voyons,
> Et vivions tous en luy; tu jugeras adoncque
> Si jamais tu receus en province quelconque
> Tant de joye en un an que tu recevras
> En moins d'un bref moment quant tu l'appercevras.[79]

In such redirection of the terms of pilgrimage, neither the physical 'noises' of the journey which Richeome so feared, nor the noise of debate can be heard. The primary sense in play here is sight, and even

---

[78] Chassignet, 'A Valimbert', in *Le Mespris*, p. 130 ll. 267–70.

[79] Ibid., pp. 130–1, ll. 271–8. Line 271—crucially concerned with dialogue and eliding sight and sound—is inexplicably missing in the *TLF* edition. I have completed it with reference to the original edition held in Besançon library (Besançon, 1594), p. 94.

the 'conférence' is seen, rather than heard: the sublimation of place to *topos* is complete. Chassignet, like Menedemus, or Granada (or Grandgousier, as we shall see in the next chapter), refigures the attempt to place experience somewhere 'out there', on the road, as error. Once again the reader at home triumphs and recuperation is aligned with appropriation.

But there are crucial differences in these pilgrim stories told here with respect to the issue of recuperation. As Augustine and Petrarch demonstrated in their use of the terms of *peregrinatio*, pilgrimage is concerned with locating a sense of a real presence which is not so much 'prior' to usurpation by the everyday dispossessions we experience, as intrinsic to the very notion of experience. The pilgrim's story has always already been usurped, before the trumpeted arrival of the reader. The Guerin romance about being stolen as a child is powerful not least because it suggests that there was a beginning, and therefore will be an end, to loss. There will be recovery, and a recognition both of place and persons; for a time. Pilgrimage as Cuchermoys experiences it—through insistence on literal movement as a function of the cure—shares a similar sense of ending. It argues the worth of pilgrims' exposure to the dangers of elsewhere and others, because it is predicated on the possibility of their return, either to the home community, or to the Jerusalem located in the undiscovered country beyond death.

Postscript

[C]'est que un plus un font au moins trois . . . *Expérience* a toujours designé le rapport à une présence, que ce rapport ait ou non la forme de conscience.[80]

Pilgrims' relation to recuperation, and to the location of that place called 'home', is the central difference in the narratives and descriptions isolated in this, the second part of this study, and in the norms and forms of subjectivity which they exemplify. Cuchermoys has his sense of belonging stolen on arrival in the Holy Land, and in this he is like Guerin: robbed of his proper name before he reaches consciousness of his identity. Subjection and theft have forced him into knowledge of his own subjectivity; but, for the pilgrim, as for the romance hero, there is a cure for this knowledge, a cure which consists in continuing on the journey which first took them away. For

[80]   J. Derrida, *De la Grammatologie* (1967), pp. 55, 89.

this is the journey that ensures their return home, and allows them, perhaps, to see its significance for the first time.

Perhaps, because if this is the case, they do not tell us themselves. Cuchermoys, like Villette, the composer of the *Description de la Terre Sainte*, is largely silent about himself. When either writer speaks as a witness, it is to the experience of others: Villette's 'rapport' is akin to Cuchermoys' brief account of the cure of man possessed in Rome. Perhaps, again, the miracle cure in Rome bears witness to the fact that the pilgrim returns home possessed of a sound body, mind, and soul. Certainly, for Cuchermoys, the experience of return is *part* of the pilgrimage; it does not come after, it is not a subsequent gloss, and it is not the work of another. It does not need to be narrated in the first person singular, or cast as a recognition scene for the reader to be effective, still less experienced.

It in this sense that Cuchermoys' sense of his narrative labour is akin to Villette's understanding of his representative role with respect to the pilgrims he has heard and read. For Valimbert, by contrast, there is no experience of either cure or community within the terms of his own travels and writing. He cannot seem to escape the reading of the alienated terms of pilgrimage which the poet Chassignet exemplifies. The literal and figural seem, even within the compass of his own account, to have been mapped on to the 'faux' and the 'vrai' respectively, and his cross-generic identity reads less as part of the pilgrim plot, than as a sign of secular confusion. Valimbert has much to say of himself, but little to say within the terms of collectively formulated experience grounded in imitation. As a consequence, he cannot use the rhetoric of witness to report on the cure of another and read it as a sign of his own health. Even as he binds himself not to a pillar in Rome but to a tree in a foreign land, Valimbert betrays his overliteral understanding of the terms of pilgrim return, the conditions of the pilgrim cure. The pilgrim body in his narrative and in Chassignet's poem is no longer sanctified and transformed through *imitatio* (*Christi*), through the ceremony in the Holy Sepulchre, anonymous communion in the mass, or the rituals of meditative reading. It can only be celebrated as a thing to be lost.

That pilgrimage has to do with loss has been the argument of this book throughout. The sense of loss is most acutely sensed in relation to the rhetoric of self-representation within pilgrim writing. It seems—almost—axiomatic that the pilgrim must die in order for the Author to be born; or at least appear to do so. But this death is not absolute, nor final. It does not stop pilgrims travelling—by all accounts, early modern pilgrims are 'innombrables' (and still they move); nor does it stop pilgrims writing. Rather, it reinforces the process whereby pilgrim experience becomes expressible only in terms of polemic, figure, or example. The referential details of pilgrim experience are rendered 'readable', but only at a cost—the cost, precisely, of the surrender of the coordinates of experience to confessional, literary, or historical doxa. From early to late Renaissance, pilgrim style develops; but it does so at the cost of pilgrims' writing.

One last detail; one last version of an early Renaissance pilgrim's homecoming. Also present in the Holy Sepulchre on the night of Cuchermoys' investiture in 1490, though Cuchermoys does not mention his being there, was one Philippe de Voisins, Seigneur de Montault. We know Voisins was present because of the survival of a manuscript account of his journey, written by his secretary and companion Jehan de Belesta.[81] This account is different again to that of either Cuchermoys or Valimbert; its sense of the worth of pilgrim narration is different to that of either Chassignet or Villette. It is, in a sense, a purer vernacular pilgrimage, in that it is written only in French, there are no foreign words, nor any 'foreign' forms, neither preceding romance, nor subsequent poems. As it is written by Voisins' secretary, for the most part in the first person plural (unlike Montaigne, Voisins never takes over the narration, never seeks to register his own voice), the particular problems of voice and subjectivity we have explored here do not arise in quite the same way. The plural verbs sustain the collective sense of pilgrim writing; the personal pilgrim's style is not at stake. By way of postscript to the explorations of this chapter, and as a gesture towards the many, many other similar

---

[81] *Voyage à Jérusalem de Philippe de Voisins*. The autograph has not been found. A copy was, however, made in the seventeenth century, and edited by Tamizey de Larroque in 1883 for the Société Historique de Gascogne in an effort to demonstrate the intrepid character of Gascon travelling knights of the Renaissance. The romance which was Orientalism accounts in large part for the few modern bibliographies and editions of these pilgrimages. A study complementing and complicating Said's *Orientalism* with specific respect to French and German Palestinography could usefully start with Marsy's editions and articles (he edited Cuchermoys), with the German work of Röhricht and Meisner, and the English EETS and PPTS. It is a story which bears comparison with the plethora of 'New World' writings researched and edited now. For a recent hasty reading of Voisins, again proudly 'gascon' in tone, see Major, 'Vision externe sur l'empire venitien: Les voyageurs meridionaux au XVe siècle', *Le Moyen Age*, 2, XCVIII, 5th series (1992), pp. 213–26. Cuchermoys notes Voisins' presence on the return journey, when the pilgrims transfer on to the *grippa* and head for Ottranto.

pilgrimages here unread, we pause to read the moment of Philippe de Voisins' homecoming. It is narrated as follows:

Et partismes dudict Avignon le secund jour apre Noel en tirant a la citte de Nysmes et a la ville de Montpellee, et a la citte de Besiers; et de la au lieu de Confolens pres la citte de Carcassonne, ou est l'une des maisons dudict Philippe de Voisins; et ne fault pas dire ne demander s'il y feust a grand joie et plaisir, veu que c'estoict la fin de son voyage. Et y a dudict Avignon jusques audict Confollens 38 lieues.[82]

This, the final sentence of the account, is closer to Cuchermoys' conclusion than to Valimbert's return in Chassignet's poem; it leaves many questions hanging. So this is how Philippe de Voisins arrived (at one of his) home(s). What about you, who wrote this? Was this also your home? And who, if anyone, was waiting for you; what did they say? Or you, when you saw first saw them, or later, as you ate, or before you slept, what did you say of your experience? The secretary's response to such questions is contained in that curious phrase which is at once an invitation to recognition, and a refusal to engage: 'ne faut pas dire ne demander.' What recognition there is derives from the distance of the narratorial voice: it is a moment in which the secretary takes himself out of the story, the better to comment on, or perhaps even articulate the emotions of the traveller come home. The formulation 'ne faut pas dire ne demander' perhaps states, even as it declines to do so, the self-evident sweetness of return which comes with closure: 'Heureux qui, comme Ulysse . . .'[83]

But the secretary's account also declines to give the details which would make of the pilgrimage a story, a narrative of experience. Frustrating certain readers' expectations either for echoes of epic, or for anticipation of the poetry of exile, the pilgrimage here adds one last piece of *useful* information, by way of log: the last of the distances listed in his text. The detail of the thirty-eight leagues between Avignon and Confollens is not absolutely unrecuperable to figural pilgrimage. There will always be people determined, or condemned, to translate the traveller's miles into paces around a walled garden, a house, a cell, or a mind. The details of distance are, however, also an invitation to direct attention away from the recognition scene, the 'lisible', the ideological closure of literary or devotional form; and in so doing, to return the pilgrimage account to the measured pace of the road.

[82] Voisins, p. 45.   [83] See du Bellay, *Les Regrets*, xxxi, p. 98.

PART THREE

FORMS OF RETURN: THE AFTERLIFE OF PILGRIMAGE

Dieu m'ayant inspiré de faire le S. Voyage, de retour que j'ay esté, me suis hazardé de le coucher par escrit, y ayant reserré comme en un tableau, ce que j'ay peu remarquer de mes yeux.

(Castela, *Le Sainct Voyage de Hierusalem*)

These are the pilgrims. Children of a sublimer realm, members of a greater commonwealth than any on which the sun has ever looked. Foreigners may mulct an Englishman of all his spending money; but he can well afford to lose it if all his capital is safely invested at home in the Bank of England. How can a dukedom in some petty principality present attractions to the scion of an empire, who is passing hastily through the tiny territory, as fast as steam and wealth can carry him, to assume the authority of a mighty monarchy?

(Meyer, 'The First of the Pilgrim Fathers', in *Abraham, or The Obedience of Faith*)

ROSALIND A traveller! By my faith, you have great reason to be sad. I fear you have sold your own lands to see other men's; then, to have seen much and to have nothing is to have rich eyes and poor hands.

JAQUES Yes, I have gained my experience.

(Shakespeare, *As You Like It*, IV. i)

CHAPTER SEVEN

Other Men's Lands

He went on, telling the men in his company that to give an account to the Sovereigns of the things that they saw a thousand tongues would not suffice, nor his hand to write, for it appeared that it was enchanted; he desired that many other persons, sober and of credit would come there and of them he says he is sure that they would not praise these things less than he does. The Admiral says more and these are his words: 'I do not write how great will be the benefit to be derived hence. It is certain, Lord Princes, that where there are such lands there should be profitable things without number; but I did not stay long in any harbour, because I desired seeing the most countries that I could, to give the story of them to your Highnesses, and also I do not know the language, and the people of these lands do not understand me, nor I them, nor does anyone on board'.[1]

Pilgrims' Characters and Occupations

Columbus: The Pilgrim as Explorer

The above quotation is from Columbus' journal of the first journey, dated 27 November 1492, as transcribed and commented by Las Casas. Having already sighted land and made initial contact with the inhabitants, Columbus reflects on his mission. In particular, he glimpses its potential failure (he has yet to find either gold or Jerusalem), but forestalls consideration of these facts by displacing

---

[1] Columbus, *Raccolta* 1, vol. 1, p. 50. For the English (which I have slightly altered) see *Journals . . . of Christopher Columbus*, pp. 103–6.

his royal readers' interest on to the details of the process of discovery. To do so he employs the rhetorical figure which will be the focus here: *occupatio*, defined in a contemporary French rhetorical handbook as follows:

occupation, c'est quant on fainct vouloir passer oultre et ne vouloir point dire ce que on dit clerement, comme . . . je ne vueil pas dire comme tu as deceu tes compaignons et desrobé leurs chevaulx. Je ne diray pas tes larcins; je ne revelleray pas tes homicides; tu n'as garde que je die les trahysons que tu as machinees contre le roy; j'en pourroye ennuyer les auditeurs.[2]

The rhetorician's list of examples—there are more, and they all have to do with deception, betrayal, or dispossession—concludes: 'Et est ceste maniere moult compendieuse et abregee, et rend les auditeurs suspens a escouter.'[3]

   This chapter is neither about Columbus nor suspense. It concerns modes of narrative translation and exchange between discovery, fiction, and available forms of religious belief in the Renaissance. Following Fabri's definition, it pursues the workings of *occupatio* into writings adjacent to pilgrimage, texts which point towards a wider world than that of the 'narration particulière' which has been at the centre of this study thus far. It consequently takes the form of a collocation of displaced 'scenes', encounters from each of the various genres we have explored in this study: literal pilgrimage account, guide-book, theological treatise, and fictional narrative. All of the texts in play in this chapter deal with either pilgrimage, discovery, or trade; or all three. The theoretical underpinning for such *bricolage* is borrowed from anthropology, which, as we have seen, itself led to the serious study of pilgrimage from a rhetorical perspective.[4] The general method—familiar from other areas of cultural criticism—involves reading anecdotes as synecdochic indicators of greater truths about a culture, and so uncovering hidden structures of kinship between apparently diverse groups of texts. In particular, linguistic and rhetorical paradigms are assigned revelatory value, as though, to recoin a much circulated phrase, culture were structured like a language.

---

   [2] P. Fabri, *Réthorique*, fol. 174. Erasmus also has fun with *occupatio* both as a form of 'subiectio', where his examples have to do with the violation of vestal virgins and social climbing, and as a kind of 'correctio', where he plays with the anxiety of digression; see Erasmus, *de Copia*, pp. 347, 409–10.
   [3] Fabri, *Réthorique*, fol. 174.   [4] See above, Ch. 1.

Exploiting the figure *occupatio* allows us both to adopt and to question this alignment of anthropology and rhetorical analysis with respect to Renaissance writing. To focus on rhetoric at work in pilgrimage writing is to demonstrate the enduring relevance of pilgrimage discourse to Renaissance culture. This has been the purpose of this study throughout. In this final chapter we explore the way in which this relevance proves to be due in large part to the pilgrim's uneasy relationship with his traditional—and newly ascendant—travelling alter ego, the merchant, and anticipates the birth both of the anthropologist and what has been called the literary pilgrim.[5] It is the shifting shapes of these characters in Renaissance travel narratives beyond the field of pilgrimage which I trace in the scenes which follow.

Tracing a journey back to Rabelais, I want here to raise a number of questions about critical investment in 'literature' in relation to the apparently old-fangled forms of experience elaborated in pilgrimage writing. Most of the texts to be read here in detail were written after Rabelais, but they will be discussed before revisiting first the pilgrim chapters in *Gargantua*, and then the discussion of 'marchandises peregrines' which animates the second chapter of the *Quart Livre*. In the first, we find pilgrims swallowed in a salad, dislodged from between the giant's teeth, almost drowned in a flood of urine, captured as spies, freed again, and finally sent safely home. In the second, the travellers are no longer pilgrims in any strict sense, but the objects they buy are given pilgrim names, and prove, on closer inspection, to be relics of a pilgrim world.

If it is true that pilgrimage is about the joining of heaven and earth and the role in that joining of dead human beings; if pilgrimage writing begins with the desire to speak with the dead; if pilgrims leave home in order to undergo the therapy of distance and to experience a sense of release from the pain of individuation by imitating the Life of Christ down to the measured detail of the steps along the via dolorosa; if pilgrims resist translation into the languages of romance in order to translate their own movements into the obsessively rehearsed terms of scripture; then it is also true that early modern pilgrims set out from home in fear of filling with their own bodies some distant and unmarked grave long before they set eyes, hands, and lips

[5] See Howard: 'the best of [these pilgrimage narratives] deserve to be called literature', *Writers and Pilgrims*, p. 53 For more on this see above, Ch. 1.

on the mouth of Christ's empty tomb. As we have seen, fear accompanied the Jerusalem traveller each step of the way. He was only entitled to leave home having made due provision for his dependents in case he should not return, and it was his moral duty to keep his mortality always in mind. As we shall see further now, the pilgrim's return offered some the chance for a new life as an author.

Cuchermoys and Valimbert each in their way demonstrate how the journey is an exercise in *imitatio*, how the outward trajectory teaches pilgrims how to read the Land. The logic of this reading, and of the pilgrim's identification with Christ extends, as Villette in particular demonstrated, to the very centre of the earth. There, if of a certain class or standing, pilgrims were initiated into the Order of the Holy Sepulchre, and received a Latin certificate, which had a status akin to a relic: a transportable token of having 'been in the place'. Many pilgrims print these certificates as appendices to their accounts; others use them to stand in for the entire journey.[6] Valimbert's marginal note alongside the seal on the copy of his certificate confirms both his own survival, and his membership of the order: 'c'estoit une resurrection.'[7] So too, Renaissance allegorists argue, was Odysseus' homecoming. His falling asleep before reaching the port figured death, and the return to Ithaca signified arrival in the celestial Jerusalem. This mode of reading pilgrimage into classical texts structures the accounts of a number of later pilgrims, as we shall see here. Valimbert is not alone in finding such deflected ways to speak of the pilgrim's fear in images drawn from 'langages pellegrins', or—to use another resonant formulation—terms which are doubly 'unheimlich': far from homely, and distinctly uncanny.[8]

In essence this chapter recounts ghost stories, attempts by writers and pilgrims to speak of various kinds of return from the dead. But there is also an argument here: while the pilgrim's *elocutio* may appear insufficiently styled for the moderns to merit the name 'literature', Rabelais' chronicles can be seen to draw on the pilgrim hermeneutic, and on the pilgrim's peculiar powers of narrative inven-

---

[6] John Lok, an English traveller to Palestine in 1553 'does not record his actual pilgrimage about the holy places, being satisfied to present an official certificate in Latin from one of the custodians to the effect that he had made it.' (E. G. Taylor, *Tudor Geography* (1930), p. 24.) Lok's diary was printed by Hakluyt, 1589. See also Villamont, pp. 817–44.

[7] Valimbert, fol. 55ʳ. See above, Ch. 6.

[8] I borrow the term from Freud's 'Das Unheimliche', in *Gesammelte Werke*, 12, pp. 229–68. It has been translated as 'The Uncanny', in *Art and Literature*, pp. 336–76.

tion and organization, in ways which are frankly nostalgic. The tales generated by many pilgrims, albeit non-fictional, share the tri-partite structure of the encounters narrated in Rabelais' chronicles: the anticipation of physical voilence (incorporation or dismember-ment), its endurance (actual or imagined), and its resolution (through repression, displacement, or representation). The fiction writer's indulgence of pilgrims' ways of reading the world seems ini-tially to pay due recognition to the passing of a particular way of gaining experience. In truth, however, it can serve to mask the appro-priation of pilgrimage discourse by other, burgeoning, forms of writ-ing. In rereading Rabelais we can gain some sense of what happens to the terms of pilgrimage writing in the discourses of Panurge's kin-folk, those 'amateurs de peregrinité' who are said to have dislodged pilgrimage and established their own hegemony. We shall see that if pilgrimage is, already in the mid-sixteenth century and again now, represented as belonging to the salad days—the happy days before the war, exploration, colonialism, tourism . . . —this is because of a nostalgia for the sacred experienced less by the pilgrim than by those other professional travellers: merchants, missionaries, and men and women of arms and letters.

Georgiewitz: The Pilgrim as Slave

Following Columbus, the second scene, a street-scene, takes place in the souks of sixteenth-century Constantinople, on an extended and enforced detour from a pilgrimage to Jerusalem.[9] A 'Turc', a mer-chant by trade, invites a 'Chrestien' to converse with him in his nearby house, and there seems no reason to refuse what is presented as a seductively rare opportunity for dialogue. In fact Islamic trad-itions of hospitality probably afforded many such opportunities. Such at least is the impression given by the frequent injunctions in pil-grims' guides, as we have seen, to avoid discussion with the Turk at all costs.[10] Contact brings contagion, they are all involved in trade, con-stantly looking to trap you, body and soul: 'Le meilleur sera de con-trefaire avec eux l'homme aveugle, sourd et muet.'[11]

---

[9] Georgiewitz, *La maniere et ceremonies des Turcs* (Anvers, 1544), fols. Eiiii^r–Fi^v.
[10] 'Turc' here means, as the opposition to 'Chrestien' makes clear, the non-Christian local; the etymology of the term was glossed by some travellers as 'cut off from God'. See Thevet, *CL*, p. 45; and Postel, *République des Turcs* ii, p. 34.
[11] Castela, *Guide*, fol. 60^r. See above, Chs. 2 and 3.

Georgiewitz's conversation, printed in conclusion to his pilgrimage account, presents a rare instance of a pilgrim breaking this interdiction. It is one of the few openly confessed, that is to say recorded, conversations with a Turk in Renaissance pilgrimage writing. One of fewer still attempts at bilingually transcribed exchanges located in the Old World, this text gives each phrase first in Turkish (transcribed into Roman script), and then in French. Other pilgrims, as we have seen, had already written foreign words into their accounts. Following Mandeville, Breydenbach's *Peregrinatio* printed Arabic script in a near-authentic form for the first time. Huen, in his translation and extension of Breydenbach, copied down the alphabets of all the peoples of Palestine, and was the first to print them in a French text. One of the earliest surviving sets of phrases in anything like Turkish is that given by von Harff in his pilgrimage, and both Villamont and Palerne will later conclude their accounts with a phrase book in a wide range of languages.[12] But Georgiewitz alone treats the foreign language as language, as something other than singular, decontextualized objects displayed in the cabinet of his text. He alone teaches the French reader 'la maniere de compter Turquois', and how to negotiate with the locals, by means of an exemplary conversation. Like the rest of the text—which has survived in an unusually large number of different versions and editions from 1544 to 1670, and was translated into several European languages—this conversation is one of the first attempts to present, and explain, Ottoman society to a European readership in this way.[13] It might be thought to mark the beginnings of anthropology due East.

And yet the conversation, like the text, is written under the sign of *occupatio*. No sooner has the merchant initiated dialogue, inviting the foreigner to enter his house, than the Christian grows suspicious and anxious. In other words, no sooner is the offer made to enter

[12] See Breydenbach, fols. H4ᵛ–5ᵛ. For Mandeville's alphabets, see Letts edn., pp. 151–60. Von Harff copies many of his alphabets from others (pp. 76–9), but also adds his own, including Albanian, some Basque which, Letts tells us, 'still eludes the ingenuity of students of that difficult language', and some phrases in Turkish (pp. 244–5). Palerne's *Peregrinations* end with an (unpaginated) phrase-book in French, Italian, Greek, Turkish, 'Moresque' and 'Esclavon'; see also Villamont, *Voyages*, pp. 544–7, 582–90.

[13] For more on the print history of Georgiewitz's different Latin and French accounts, see Rouillard, pp. 189–95, and M. Heath, *Crusading Commonplaces* (1986), p. 103. For a discussion of Georgiewitz's contribution to translation history, see W. Heffening, *Die Türkischen Transkriptionstexte des Bartolomeus Giorgiewitz aus den Jahren, 1544–1548* (1942).

Turkish space freely—contractually, rather than as a captive, or in disguise—than it must be declined:

Au departement.

Chr. [Chrestien] Allahatsmarlahadoch tseni, *Je vous recommande a Dieu.* ben oraagitmezom. *Je nyray point par la.*

Tur. [Turc] Bre neden korkartson, *He qu'est ce que tu crains*, nitcie gelmetson? *pourquoy ne viens tu?*

Chr. Benum iolum oraa deghelder, *mon chemin nest pas par la.*

Tur. VVargeth tsaglogla eier ghelmetson *va ten a la bon heure, si tu ne veux venir.*

Chr. Gegsien hair oltson, *Dieu vous doint bonne nuict.*

Tur. Aghbatehair oltson, *et a toy aussi.*

Chr. Ben kurtuldom tsoch succur Allaha. *Je suis delivre soit loué Dieu. AMEN*[14]

This final line gives the game away; it suggests that no dialogue has really taken place. For why should the 'Chrestien' express his evident relief on escaping from captivity, and from having to enter into Turkish conversation, in 'Turkish'? With the veracity of the translation rendered questionable, so also is the status of the speech act itself. To whom are these words in 'Turkish' addressed, and did the event they represent ever take place?

Georgiewitz's account is, as the title-page stresses, predicated on individual experience of foreign places: *La maniere et ceremonies des Turcs. Par Bartholomieu Hongrois Pelerin de Hierusalem. Lequel aiant este illecque esclave, a cogneu par experience tout ce qu'est contenu en ce present livre. Avec beaucoup de motz, aussi la maniere de compter Turquois, Salutations et Responces des Perses.* And yet, consistent with that reticence to indulge in narration which characterizes the text as a whole, the pilgrim carefully avoids recording this conversation as an event, marked by his presence as both actor and author. Rather, he presents a scene which is pure threshold, all about never quite going on stage to talk Turkish, but which none the less ends—even in the absence of the other character—in the forbidden language. What initially appears to be a snapshot image of a real street encounter thus turns out to be virtual reality, an early anthropological fiction. And the dialogue is thus a potential event, an exemplary, reiterable language exercise: 'I have been there, learned the language, and so, by staging a conversation in Turkish involving an

---

[14] Georgiewitz, *La maniore des Turcs*, fols. Eiiii^r–Fi^r.

exemplary Christian who is (not) me, can teach you how (not) to talk
to others, how (not) to enter their language, their houses.'

The '(not)s' are central; they reveal how the refusal to enter foreign
territory is a hoax, the dialogue with the other a bluff. They are the
means by which the escaped slave exploits the phrases he has learned
in captivity to capture those who hijacked his pilgrim identity. He
makes of the dialogue with the Other a scene of reading staged in
proof of his good faith before the reader at home. In so doing, he is
able simultaneously to justify his diversion from the pilgrim road,
and to satisfy a desire peculiarly acute among pilgrims as they leave
their parishes for Palestine: to indulge curiosity on the journey and to
tell of what they have seen, without running the risk of contagion of
the heart, and consequent loss of identity, or the soul.

Several points arise from this truncated Turkish/French encounter
and its further translation into other languages, English in particular; points at once personal to Georgiewitz's case and representative
of the ways in which pilgrims across early modern Europe represent
contact with others as perilous. For other travellers—the trader, the
missionary, and the anthropologist—some acquisition of the local
language is essential. Hence, for instance, Columbus' painful admission in his letter to Ferdinand and Isabella of his failure to narrate
'cosas de provecho', profitable things.[15] For the pilgrim, the development, and more importantly the increasing legitimation, of these
other forms of travel pose a real threat. As we have seen in the *Guides*,
this threat is felt at the level of language. The two forms of temptation—physical abroad, narrative at home—are connected. For the
pilgrim priests are anxious to preserve the integrity of the true
pilgrim both from foreign bodies and lands, and from the dangers
hidden in the wide seas of travel writing which stretch on all sides:
'it is only vain curiosity which takes us to new lands to see new
peoples, and to feast our eyes on the variety of creation, so as to

---

[15] Brazil was in this, as in other ways, a new Eden for French writers. Thevet copies and
uses many Tupi words in his *Singularitez de la France Antarctique* (1557) and his *Cosmographie Universelle* (1575) although he avoids transcribing dialogue. Léry is an exception.
His 'pilgrimage in reverse' (Certeau), the *Histoire d'un voyage faict en la terre du Brésil*
(1578) transcribes a model conversation, by way of demonstrating the convertibility of the
locals. In the process he inaugurates the long life of French anthropology due west (see
C. Lévi-Strauss, *Tristes Tropiques* (1955), pp. 74–8). Greenblatt, in 'Kidnapping Language', has interesting things to say about the relative needs of missionaries and traders to
learn local languages (*Marvelous Possessions*, pp. 86–118). He says nothing here of
pilgrims.

boast, after the event, of having seen this or that rare or singular thing.'[16]

We must be careful not to misrepresent the kind of historical change taking place here; the above advice, taken from Granada, already warns late fifteenth-century pilgrims as to the manner in which they should travel.[17] But the argument here is not so much about absolutely new terms for the pilgrim, as how pilgrim terms come under new pressure, and so take on a different force. The Turkish merchant with his offer of hospitality does not know that the passing foreigner is trying hard to present himself to his readers as an incurious pilgrim in times when such a performance is increasingly difficult. Nor can he know that his offer is more personally mistimed: Georgiewitz is only able to speak Turkish as a result of having been captured and held as a slave for thirteen years as he was on his way to Jerusalem. Having finished the tale of his years of captivity—the bulk of the narrative—he must reassert his pilgrim identity, must steer his text home.

In contrast to Columbus, Georgiewitz claims a hatred of travel and a desire to tell no stories.[18] His experience—so a later edition of his narrative suggests—has been such that it does not bear narration: 'La quelle misere j'ay l'espace de treize ans experimenté. Et ne scauroye racompter les calamitez de telle maniere de vie.'[19] And yet rather than defer narrative detail, he—in all the versions of his travels subsequent to the 1544 edition—in fact indulges it copiously. The text grows and grows, and the experience which cannot be spoken of is spoken of at ever greater length. But one thing remains constant throughout these various editions and additions to Georgiewitz's story. The same character is being produced: the traveller who has more experience and knowledge of others than he intended to possess. For this character to be formed, Georgiewitz needs to deny that he came by the knowledge which he shares with his readers by choice. Rather than admit to having wilfully broken the rules of pilgrim conduct, spoken with others, eaten with them, slept with them, served them in their own houses, the would-be returned pilgrim retrospectively stages a

[16] Granada, *Istruttione*, p. 13. Translation mine.

[17] See Santo Brasco, *Viaggio* (1481), which has a brief guide for putative pilgrims, fols. 48ᵛ–49ᵛ. Much of this anticipates Granada's *Istruttione*, verbatim.

[18] In this respect he anticipates the pilgrim lament of the reluctant anthropologist: 'Je hais les voyages et les explorateurs.' Lévi-Strauss, *Tristes Tropiques*, p. 3.

[19] Georgiewitz, *Discours de la maniere de vivre des Turcs* (Liège, 1600), p. 70.

refusal to engage. This is a very different linguistic confession to that of Columbus referred to above; it is less a frank admission of the inability to communicate with others, than a denial of having really spoken to them at all.

Perhaps such a reading of the character who speaks through Georgiewitz's text is unfair to the man who, if he is to be believed, was captured, held slave, and subjected to a miserable existence for thirteen long years. Perhaps he really did have no choice in whether or not to enter into foreign houses and learn such (to him and his readers) strange tongues. The texts which bear his name are not the kinds of document which tell us beyond doubt. And indeed what is important in the context of this discussion is the insistence that the true nature of the experience Georgiewitz relates is beyond traditional forms of telling:

> Ce n'est riens de la servitude d'Egypte, ny de l'exil babilonicque, ny de la captivité Assyrienne, ny de la destruction faite par les Romains, au regard de ces miseres icy. La ou on peult ouyr tous les jours les lamentations de Hieremie, qui se font journellement, non pas de parolles, mais d'effect.[20]

And yet this rhetoric of impossible narrativity, underpinned by *occupatio*, is complemented by detailed descriptions of the conditions in which captured Christians lived, and the indignities to which they—particularly women—were subject. Georgiewitz distinguishes, for instance, between the concubinage into which those who were 'belles' were forced, and the things which the 'moyennement belles' were made to do. These last he terms 'aucunefois si deshonnestes, qu'on n'en scauroit parler assez honnestement', before going on to do so: 'Elles sont constrainctes de suyvir leurs maistresses avec un pot plain d'eauë, quant elles vont vuyder leurs ventres, pour laver leur derriere.'[21] Even here, however, the rhetoric of witness and of *occupatio* is used to frame the pilgrim's experience as useful both as a negative example to others, and as an incitement to helping those who have themselves been captured but have not yet escaped.[22] The point is further exemplified in the translation history of Georgiewitz's

---

[20] Georgiewitz, *Discours de la maniere de vivre des Turcs* (Liège, 1600), p. 81.

[21] Ibid., p. 69.

[22] The text is often bound—as in the Mazarine copy—into collections of pamphlets supporting the work of the Holy Trinity order who repurchased captives from the Ottoman authorities; it was also published as an appendix to Bourgeois' treatise *Institution et fondation de l'Ordre de la tressaincte Trinité et rédemption des captifs* (Douay, 1606). For more on this order (though next to nothing on Georgiewitz) see G. Turbet-Delof, *L'Afrique barbaresque* (1971). M.-C. Gomez-Géraud, 'Récit de pèlerinage et

account, and in particular by its survival and translation into English.

The early French version of Georgiewitz's narrative concludes with a gesture from the renegade to the reader: 'Le mesme Pelerin au Lecteur Salut.' The narrator here reminds the reader that he has exercised restraint and has not written of all the things he has seen. For to do so would be to 'contaminer nostre papier', and would involve telling of things 'non seulement laides descripre ou lire, mais aussi douyr lire'.[23] This rhetorical purity, expressed in terms of a physical cleanliness of method, emblematized that pollution anxiety which we have encountered often in pilgrimage writing, and found both expressed and repressed in the remainder of Georgiewitz's account.

Later English versions of his story take these images further, explicitly addressing the notion of language itself as polluting. Attention is drawn, in the first English translation, specifically to the Turkish writing, which has been added 'not of necessitie, but for delectations sake: that thou mayst understand.' What the reader is to 'understand' is that the Turkish language itself—rather than customs or lives of others—is a sign of 'how grosse and barbarous they be'. The fact that they speak this other language, carefully reproduced on the page as spectacle, reveals their dangerous otherness. It is also a comforting sign of the reader's membership of a linguistically self-sufficient community: 'The ever liuing God graunt, that they may haue more neede of our speche, then we of thers. Farewell.'[24]

A still later English version lists in an index all the 'rarities' advertised in its title: *The Rarities of Turkey, gathered by one that was sold several times a Slave in the Turkish Empire.* This translation both extends the slave's experience in time and domesticates its lessons, for these are rarities said to be 'newly printed for the author' (in 1661!) and now 'exposed to view for the benefit of his Native countrey'.[25] This process of domestication to late seventeenth-century

---

modèle: Le Cas de Frère Pantaliao d'Aveyro', *Littérales*, 7(1990), pp. 71–83, tells of another pilgrim's encounter with renegades. For more on the history of renegades, see B. and L. Bennassar, *Les Chrétiens d'Allah* (1989).

[23] Georgiewitz, *La maniere* (1544), fol, Fiii^{r-v}.

[24] *The Offspring of the house of Ottoman . . . whereunto is added Bartholomeus Georgieviz, of the customes, Rytes, Ceremonies, and Religion of the Turkes* (London, 1570?) fols. Giii^{r-v}. This is the first English translation; I return to others below. There is no mention of the 'otherness' of the French from which this text must have been translated.

[25] Georgiewitz, *The Rarities of Turkey* (London, 1661).

England extends also to altering the body of the text, amputating in particular the foreign language, and with it the terms of pilgrimage. For the dialogue in Turkish is missing, as is the insistence that the author is first and foremost a pilgrim. This version does include a 'narration of a dispute' with a Turk on matters of religion, described as having taken place 'in the *Arabian* [*sic*] Dialect', but the dispute is printed entirely in English, and concludes with the Turk asking for instruction in the Christian religion.

The French-speaking Hungarian pilgrim turns English missionary. He still needs the Other's language to do so—though now it is 'dialect', and it is '*Arabian*', not Turkish—but the reader need not learn it, nor, in this late English version, even see it printed. The pilgrim's original story becomes a cabinet of curiosities, a pretext for a collection of gathered rarities, 'exposed to view'. The visual emphasis is similar to the rhetorics of enargic presence which led readers to believe they might, in reading, see the place 'as if before their eies'.[26] But there is a world of difference between these texts and those of Huen, Adrichomius, and Villette trying to bring Palestine home to their readers. The 'as if' of self-conscious mimesis—central to the 'description' genre—is here forgotten; as is the earlier pilgrim-Georgiewitz's declared hesitancy to represent the detail of his experience of otherness. Gone too is the voice of dialogue, for no one goes to look at the 'rarities' displayed in the English text in an effort to hear Huen's 'doulx Jhesus' speaking 'comme s'il fust present'. Still less are they attentive to the invitations of those who stand at doorways in the souks of Constantinople.

Pilgrims' Fantasies and Fears

Castela: Fearing Dismemberment

Trescher amy, tu m'estimeras en l'entreprise de ce S. voyage d'un coeur presque Herculéen d'avoir prins les armes contre tant de Geants, et tiré en champ de battaile tant de grands personnages confis en toutes sciences. Car s'il advient que j'en contente quelqu'un, ce me sera dompter le Lion Neméen, esteindre par feu le serpent Hydra, percer dans les nuës à coup de traicts les oyseaux de Stymphale, suffoquer entre mes mains Antée, planter les colomnes dans la mer Oceane.[27]

---

[26] See above, Ch. 4.   [27] Castela, *Le Sainct Voyage*, 'Au Lecteur', *non. pag.*

This is Castela, the fiercest critique of physical 'mixing' on the journey, expressing his anxiety in the liminary material to his own account. What he fears most is the reception of his text by readers. As Fabri and Georgiewitz knew, and as Castela discovers when he sits down to write, the hardest thing of all is to come home. This displacement of fear is significant, for his anxiety does not bear on his own body on the road or at sea; he has after all returned alive and relatively unscarred. His fears are rather for the body of his text, which he knows will be dismembered by professional readers in the marketplace of contesting discourses. They will take to pieces the narrative which he has constructed out of the disparate, aleatory incidents of his journey:

[A]pres tant de perils que j'ay evité au travail des chemins, je retente une autre fortune . . . Les Poëtes s'animeront contre moy: les Historiens ne manqueront à me donner quelque coup de langue: Les Cosmographes y treuveront à redire: Les Geometriciens, Ingenieurs et Architectes y treuveront à reprendre. Voilà (Lecteur) de combien d'ennemis je me voys menacé.[28]

This is not the only way to tell of the return journey, or to bring a text home to readers. Indeed over the course of the Renaissance pilgrims work hard to find generically and theologically acceptable ways of doing so. Many, like Georgiewitz, establish ways not only of recounting the journey as a form of therapy or pleasure for themselves, but also of making this narrative act *useful* for others. They frame their texts not simply as an incentive to others to leave, not simply as guides, pre-texts for further departures, but as a way to come home, a means of reintegration into the home community.

This is not easily achieved. The models for telling of return are not immediately available within pilgrim literature; as Howard suggests, they are more likely to be found in romance or epic. What he ignores, along with others who draw historically inapposite boundaries between genres, are the kinds of generic cross-fertilization which I hope to have shown to be instrumental to the survival of pilgrimage writing as a living, changing force in the Renaissance. Survival comes at a cost, however: as Georgiewitz demonstrates, the price you pay is that of generic purity. Castela, intensely aware of the dangers of physical mixing on the journey itself, seems to acknowledge the risks in

[28] Ibid.

generic mixing in his narration. As if conscious of the critique that pilgrimage cannot properly accommodate the epic traveller, he characterizes not the journey itself as Herculean, but the labour of writing a text which goes by the name of pilgrimage.

It is of course possible to read all this as liminary self-publicizing. An inflated humility *topos* is deployed, the better to impress the worth and integrity of what is being said on the lay reader. I propose, however, that we take this desire for integrity on Castela's part seriously; which is to say, take it both discursively and bodily. Repressing the spectre of the diverse and dismembering figures who will bring their professional identities to bear on his text, Castela projects a reader for himself who is, in a strong sense, simple. It is, as it must be, an imagined fellow pilgrim: 'Ce te fera une guide pour te mener en ton chemin, un baston pour te sustenir et une bourse pour te desfrayer.'[29]

In the first instance the reader addressed here is Castela's patron, for like many pilgrims he is funded by another (André de Nesmond, in his case). Liminary flattery—'you too are a pilgrim, though you have not travelled anywhere'—is, like the account proper, part-payment for the costs of the journey. The account is thus a function of an at once financial and narrative contract between pilgrim and patron, which replicates the larger contract between the pilgrim and his home community. The printing of his story is represented as at once an extension of a private conversation, and a public demonstration of a private contract. It confirms that the patron remains in the position of most respect, of greatest knowledge and power: 'Ce petit extraict de mon Voyage n'est qu'un tesmoin occulaire de ce que vostre lecture infinie vous a appris.'[30]

The rewards for pilgrimages performed by proxy could be high. Ogygius travels in response to a vow made to his mother-in-law and is rewarded with a bag full of relics.[31] Catherine de Medicis vowed to send a pilgrim to Jerusalem on foot who would take three paces forward, one pace back. She found a volunteer who 'remplit ses engagements avec une scrupule dont la Reine fut assurée par des perquisitions. Le bourgeois, qui était marchand de profession, reçut

---

[29] Castela, *Le Sainct Voyage*, 'Au Lecteur', *non. pag.*

[30] Ibid. This is a repeated gesture in liminary material to pilgrimage accounts, esp. since so many pilgrimages were performed by proxy. See Hault, p. 4, and Villamont, fol. a4ʳ.

[31] See above, Ch. 1. For Erasmus' mother-in-law joke, see *The Religious Pilgrimage*, p. 13.

une somme en récompense et fut annobli.'[32] For his part Castela too is rewarded; his prize for having risked the journey and the narration is a new sense of his own profession, its pleasures and its dangers:

Tu n'y treuveras chose de grande doctrine, pour autant qu'elles sont couchées et escrites d'un style simple et nud, sans enrichissement de paroles ny aucun attraict de langage, et sans erudition estrangere prinse de la Philosophie: car c'est un discours narratif seulement d'un style simple, selon le deu de ma profession.[33]

Castela's liminary anxiety demonstrates, again and again, his understanding that 'to be a pilgrim' is no longer enough. His body has been preserved, but now that his profession is writing, the value of his labour lies in its style. Working in a professional arena, he understands that for his text to survive in the contest of faculties, he must both stress his own integrity and practise violence on the texts of others.[34] The terms in which he advertises the transfiguration of his own bodily displacement into narrative discourse simply styled are frankly nostalgic: they echo those of an earlier form of pilgrimage writing, the barely animated logs of anonymous pilgrims. Ostensibly, his text gives the reader the place 'as it really is', with little or no interpretative residue. In practice, however, such rhetoric serves to assert the role and place of the author. Castela takes up his position in the market of discourses by embracing the epithets 'simple' and 'nud' only to transvalue them. In relation to his own narrative they connote not so much the spare parataxis of pilgrims such as Possot, as the 'sermo humilis' of the classically learned. Raised onto the plinth of objective narration, enshrined by professional distance from other discursive fields, and, crucially, marking out his difference from the excessive signs, the badges, wax *ex-voto* body parts, shells, and so on of an Ogygius, Castela and his text share a Herculean heart lodged in the statuesque form of a classically styled nude.

All this is consonant with the kind of pilgrim he sought to make of those of his readers intending to perform the pilgrimage and write

---

[32] See H. de Marsy, *Les Pèlerins picards* (1881), p. 19.

[33] This is Castela addressing the reader, not his patron as earlier. In the later 1612 edition the address to the reader is considerably longer, and Castela bemoans the fact that people have pirated his text, translated it, and made it say things he never intended; and have not paid him his financial dues.

[34] S. Greenblatt's discussion of the procedures of self-fashioning is, in this context, difficult not to read as in part a comment on the profession of letters in the late twentieth-century academy as well as Renaissance England, *Renaissance Self-Fashioning* (1984), pp. 3–5.

their own accounts, as we saw above in relation to his conduct manual, the *Guide et adresse pour ceux qui veulent faire le sainct voyage*.[35] But he does not follow his own conduct advice. His *Sainct Voyage* is long, replete with classical allusion, and is one of the most insistently anecdotal, personalized narratives of the journey to survive. He speaks often—and almost exclusively—of his fear, his pain, the fleas, the water, the women, the food, the cost, the sailors, the thieves . . . the conditions of the journey. However, as a closer and more extended reading of his long, long, book would demonstrate, the force of its performance as argument in favour of pilgrimage derives from Castela's insistence on the sacred economy of the narrative. In both the *Guide* and the *Sainct Voyage*, the priest's concern is for wholeness and integrity, asserting the impenetrability of both the pilgrim body and the pilgrim hermeneutic. Castela, like Ogygius, has a seemingly inexhaustible ability to recuperate each event to the plot of pilgrimage, each detail to a sacred design.

One event, signalled in the margin as 'grand accident arrivé a lautheur, miraculeusement sauvé', will have to stand in for many.[36] Castela and his companion have barely left home when they are lost in the mountains. Immediately they recognize themselves to be in the archetypal figural pilgrim's situation: 'plus mors que vifs, ne sçaichant quel chemin tenir.'[37] Their sense of identity is confirmed with reference to the Psalms; Psalm 103 is quoted as directly apposite to their case. This already brings some measure of relief (someone has written about this: someone has been here before, and survived). It also appears to bring help, in the shape of 'quelque homme aux environs', and Castela and companion begin, he writes, 'à adresser nostre voix selon le langage du pays'.[38] Breaking his own rules of conduct the pilgrim invites the local to eat with him and his companion.

They share a meal. But then, suddenly, the stranger makes for the pilgrims 'une hache en la main, avec un cruel et hideux regard'. This—the threat of physical rather than discursive dismemberment—is the first shock which interrupts the friendly feast, the image of travellers' conviviality which the text momentarily presents. A second shock follows immediately, and is one again curiously connected to the pilgrims' initial gesture of generosity, offering food in exchange for direction: the attacker is suddenly convulsed with

---

[35] See above, Ch. 2.   [36] Castela, *Sainct Voyage*, pp. 22–6.
[37] Ibid., p. 22.   [38] Ibid., p. 23.

stomach cramps 'dequoy mon compaignon et moy nous esmerveil-lasmes'. The pilgrims take advantage of this felicitous cramp to escape, and continue on their journey. Castela's narrative moves on with them; he does not tie up all the threads of this encounter, does not allegorize the interrupted feast, nor the stomach cramps, but rather invites the reader to share with him and his companion the sense of pilgrim wonder. This is in part because there is more to come: a voice off-stage:

Dieu encor nous consola, par le chant d'un petit enfant, fort melodieux à nos aureilles *qui ressembloit quasi à la voix d'un Ange*, sans voir autrement personne à l'entour de nous, sinon le voleur avec lequel nous avions prins notre refection, ne se pouvant (ô chose miraculeuse) tenir sus-bout.[39]

The pilgrims ask the angelic voice which path they should follow to reach the inn to which they are headed (it is the *Angelo* inn). The angel (indirectly, 'quasi', named) enters from among the trees and proves to be a young boy, aged 7 or 8, who directs them on to the right path. Once again without explicit comment, the journey and the narrative move on.

The point is clear. Castela's entire trajectory is made up of such moments, each of which provides its own enactment of the terms of pilgrimage's oscillation between error and recuperation, between the literal and the figural, the material and the spiritual journey. Castela's opening anxiety regarding discursive dismemberment is experienced on the road, in the mountains, at sea, always in the valley of the shadow of death. If pilgrimage is an exercise in *imitatio*, and if the reader can also be thought of as a pilgrim, then the narrative of the journey is as much a handbook as the more explicitly pedagogic *Guide*. It teaches how to read experience as a pilgrim; to travel through the valley of the shadow of death is also to travel in the protective aura of the Psalms. Castela's performative, persuasive account of the pilgrim journey demonstrates how the (counter-Reformation) pilgrim has a table prepared for him in the presence of his enemies. It is to this feast that the reader, encouraged to take on the costume and the interpretative habits of the pilgrim, is invited. If we enjoy the meal, if we find it useful—even for our own professional, or ironic purposes—Castela, and with him pilgrimage writing, survive.

---

[39] Ibid., p. 24 (emphasis mine).

Thevet: Escaping Dismemberment

Another tenacious survivor was André Thevet, initially a Jerusalem pilgrim, again funded by, and writing on behalf of, another—La Rochefoucauld. Thevet, whose story has been expertly resurrected by Lestringant in a series of illuminating studies, did not remain a pilgrim. A new-historicist's dream, he sails along the borders of fact and fiction, and converts, on his return from Jerusalem, out of pilgrimage into epic, before going on to invent islands off the coast of Brazil to chart and explore.[40] Writing earlier than Castela, the Universal Cosmographer exemplifies the class of dismembering giants which the pilgrim would come to fear so much.

And with due cause. Thevet's pilgrimage, recounted as the *Cosmographie de Levant*, is followed by a number of travel accounts, culminating in 1575 with his *Cosmographie Universelle*, a compendious encyclopedia held together by the tenuous thread of his own travels. In fact, both Cosmographies are a patchwork of the texts of others, with material gathered by clerks and research assistants such as François de Belleforest. He, scraping a poor living as a devotional writer and translator of tragic histories, never made it to being an Author, not least since he never left France.[41]

The issue is less one of going away, than of the uses of return. To tell of return from Jerusalem in order to authorize further travels elsewhere is to no longer be in *peregrinatio*: it denotes rather a shift out of exegesis and into a different profession, a different mode of reading and writing the world. Two moments from Thevet's writings here illustrate this shift. The first is his arrival back in France from Jerusalem as narrated in the *Cosmographie de Levant*; the second, his narrative recollection of this pilgrimage in the later *Cosmographie Universelle*.

In one of the most textually hybrid homecoming scenes in Renaissance pilgrimage writing, Thevet presents a refracted image of the pilgrim's return. Christ-like, he sleeps through a storm, and in his dream he engages in theological debate. Thus both in his conscious actions and in his unconscious dream-work Thevet represents himself as a Christian traveller, a model pilgrim. He discovers on waking that he is already approaching the port at Marseille:

[40] See Lestringant, in particular his *André Thevet: Cosmographe des derniers Valois*, and his magisterial edition of Thevet's *Cosmographie de Levant* [1554].

[41] For more on Belleforest's pursuit of authorship see M. Simonin, *Vivre de sa plume au XVIe siècle, ou la carrière de François de Belleforest* (1992).

[N]ous arrivames tous bien joyeux, et alaigres: et n'estime point, que Agamemnon fust tant joyeux, quand il vit la ruïne de Troye la grande: ou Electra, quand elle vit Oreste: ou Ulysse, quand il vit le rivage d'Ulichie, que je fus, apres avoir connu, que j'estois en mon païs, lequel j'avois tant de fois souhaité.[42]

He is Christ-like in his dreams, perhaps, but the classical tenor of Thevet's waking *imitatio* only serves to distinguish him from the pilgrim:

Combien que je susse assez, que nous sommes tous en ce monde viateurs, et que l'homme est en son païs, ou il se trouve bien. Si est ce que le païs natif ha je ne say quoy qui nous induit à l'aymer . . .[43]

The Pauline topos according to which we are all pilgrims is exploited in a tone of affected boredom, and 'pèlerins' are displaced by the more generalist 'viateurs'. The 'je ne say quoy' of proverbial (Erasmian) proof confirms his epic status:

tellement que Ulysse preferoit la seule immortaliteé, à l'amour du païs. Dont justement est dit en commun proverbe, que la fumee du païs semble estre plus luisante, que le feu cler d'une terre estrange.[44]

Thus when Thevet steers his text towards the metaphorical significance of his return to Marseille, his port is not celestial Jerusalem, but classical erudition. There follow three pages of allusions to other classical travellers. We should, he concludes, even if we should die at sea (which thankfully he has not), rejoice like Thracians in our arrival at our true port:

Parquoy le divin Platon, ou bien (comme aucuns disent) Xenocrate, ha bien fait, composant un Dialogue intitulé Axioque, ou, du mespris de la mort, ce que Ciceron ha voulu ensuivre en sa premiere Tusculane.[45]

And so he goes on, bluffing his way into the Academy by echoing, unacknowledged, the references which Erasmus adduces to the 'peregrinatio' adage.[46] With the *Adages* rather than the Psalms as his reference book, Thevet is enabled, with a little learning and a lot of style, to make a 'viateur' of a 'pèlerin', a cosmography of a pilgrimage. In the process he displaces the terms of Christian pilgrimage as central to Western modes of coming to terms with the everyday partings of existence and the singular experience of death.

---

[42] Thevet, *CL*, pp. 213–14.   [43] Ibid., p. 214.   [44] Ibid.   [45] Ibid., p. 217.
[46] See *CL*, p. 214, and Lestringant's discussion of Thevet's pilgrimage in *André Thevet*, pp. 33–61. For more on Erasmus' adage, see above, Ch. 1.

This displacement affords Thevet some measure of professional identity, establishing his credentials as both learned and popular traveller. It was a winning combination, and abandoning his pilgrim self, Thevet made his way to Brazil and, on his return, into the court. Ronsard duly sung his praises, in terms which acknowledge Thevet's own epic pretensions:

> Au pris de toy ce Grec [Ulysse] par dix ans ne vit rien:
> Aussi tu as sur luy au double d'avantage:
> C'est que tu as plus veu, et nous as ton voyage
> Escrit de ta main propre, et non pas luy le sien.[47]

Rather than the ostensibly self-effacing 'style nud' of Castela's embryonic poetics of realism, it is Thevet's signature, his own and proper name, which authorizes the increasingly extravagant tales he offers his readers. For Thevet the centrally resurrected figure is no longer Christ, but 'divine Plato or (as some say) Xenocrates . . . or Cicero'; standing behind all three, writing the *Adages*, is Erasmus. The protective dome of the Psalms splinters into the culture of the secular extract. And travel narrative, as Castela will complain, becomes an obstacle course of Herculean proportions, a discursive arena in which the liminal, unlettered, and anonymous pilgrim will have to fight for survival.

Rabelais' giants might represent for the pilgrim Castela the Antaeus he will one day need to suffocate in order to give himself space to breathe and write. Thevet, however, uses the procedures of incorporation to make a giant of himself: for him, Rabelais' textual body is just more grist for the mill of his own self-production. So, for instance, Thevet authorizes his travels by means of several storm scenes, a *topos* which is both an exemplary pilgrim instance of danger, and an opportunity to tell of the working powers of divine intervention.[48] Rabelais re-articulates this *topos* as an occasion for

---

[47] Thevet, *CU*, II, liminary pages; the same point is made by Baif, *CU*, I, fol. eiij'. See R. Le Moine, *L'Amérique et les poètes français de la Renaissance* (1972), and on the Thevet poetry in particular, Lestringant, *André Thevet*, pp. 114–26.

[48] It derives, in the literary tradition, from the *Odyssey* (V, 292 ff.) and the *Aeneid* (1, 34–156). Though these are rarely cited even in the most extravagant pilgrim storms, Anacharsis' dictum that 'those who are at sea cannot be counted among either the living or the dead' is a *topos*; see, apart from Castela above, Fabri, pp. 38–41; Villamont, pp. 692–5; Possot, pp. 132–3, 151–2, and Hault, p. 15 (where the captain cried). See also J. Delumeau, *La Peur en Occident* (1978), pp. 31–41 and M.-C. Gomez-Géraud, 'La Mer: Un espace hors-la-loi? La representation de l'espace marin dans quelques récits de voyage français et espagnols au XVIe siècle', *Revue de Littérature Comparée*, 2 (1990), pp. 385–407.

discussion of motivations for various forms of travel, including pilgrim-age. In doing so, in chapters 18 to 22 of the *Quart Livre*, he incorporates themes and motifs from Lucian, The Acts of the Apostles, Folengo, and Erasmus' *Naufragium*. All this is fair play according to the rules of Christian pilgrimage and classical *imitatio* which Renaissance poets and theorists resurrect and make their own. Thus, as well as a theological allegory within a broadly syncretist framework, we have learned to read the scene as an allegory of reading, an exercise in poetic as well as Christian *imitatio*.[49] In neither frame do we read it as the record of an actual event at sea.

Thevet does, however; or rather, as Lestringant has shown, he makes certain phrases culled from the storm scene in Rabelais' *Quart Livre*, and lines from a poem addressed from Constantinople to a lover at home in France, do the work of recording his own experience at sea.[50] This has important effects on how we understand the texture of what passes for professional experience in the post-pilgrim trav-eller. For Thevet dislodges passages from the mouths of Rabelais' travellers as he does from La Borderie's displaced lover, and makes them speak with his own voice. Undoing the work of poetic incorp-oration, he dismembers the narrative and the poem and presents pieces of both texts, relic-like, encased in the gold frame of his own solidly referential storm.

Panurge, self-confessed 'amateur de peregrinité', returns from near-death, and survives being skewered like a kebab, basted, and roasted at the spit.[51] Other pilgrims are less fortunate; if we are to believe the reports of those who survive, more than one ends up impaled through the rectum, and others are cut to more than a hun-dred pieces. Panurge, mid-storm, makes a vow to 'faire un pèlerin': he means he will send one by proxy.[52] Thevet goes one better than all of the above. He goes as a pilgrim himself, but does so to make of him-self an author. Like Valimbert after him, Thevet is surrounded by water in Tripoli; but this is because he has taken time out to visit the

[49] See M. Screech, *Rabelais* (1979), pp. 341–50; Lestringant, *André Thevet*, pp. 49–56.

[50] See Thevet, *CL*, pp. 46–8. The phrase from Rabelais, and the debt to La Borderie's *Discours du voyage de Constantinoble, envoyé dudict lieu à une demoyselle Françoyse* (1547) are signalled by Lestringant in notes, pp. 263–5.

[51] For fine readings of these adventures, see T. Hampton, ' "Turkish dogs": Rabelais, Erasmus and the Rhetoric of Alterity' *Representations*, 41 (Winter 1993), pp. 58–82, and T. C. Cave, 'Travelers and Others: Cultural Connections in the Works of Rabelais', in *Rabelais* (1995).

[52] Rabelais, *Quart Livre*, p. 113.

baths (don't pay more than three or four aspres, he says) before safely boarding the ship home to Marseille.[53] Their situations could not be more different. Valimbert, as we saw, almost loses his skin in Egypt, has to disguise his identity often, and has his account usurped by Chassignet's poem. Thevet, by contrast, returns home from pilgrimage fortified by the Egyptian spoils he found in Rabelais' chronicles and La Borderie's poem. The spoils of Literature authorize Thevet the renegade pilgrim's own return from the living death of the storm, and the dying genre of pilgrimage. He awakens on arrival in Marseille to his new life as a travelling man of letters.

This is another fall narrative, another oedipal struggle. That the pilgrim must die in order for the Author to be born seems axiomatic, and is part of the story of Modernity as told by critics of pilgrimage. But author and critic are haunted by the pilgrim's ghost to the ends of the earth. The repressed pilgrim returns in the following tale of dismemberment which Thevet presents in the *Cosmographie Universelle*, when reflecting on what had happened to him in Jerusalem in the 1540s. Once again it would seem that nostalgia is not so much a feature of pilgrimage writing, as of the writings of erstwhile pilgrims, anxious to move on elsewhere.

Thevet revisits his own pilgrimage some thirty years after the event. In conclusion to a semi-learned description of Jerusalem he recalls how he had been captured as a spy for having peered inside the Dome of the Rock:

Voyla le progrez de mon histoire de Hierusalem, de sa prise et reprise. Or n'estoit elle pas beaucoup forte. A present on y a faict un fort chasteau, dans lequel j'ay entré, non pour mon plaisir, ains prisonnier, avec deux Chrestiens Nestoriens, et un Cypriot, pour avoir seulement mis la teste dans le temple de Salomon, qui est leur mosquee. Pouvant bien dire une chose, que le plus de tourment que j'ay eu entre ce peuple Barbare, estoit lors que je m'amusois à philosopher et contempler, les entours de leurs riches temples et mosquees, dequoy je ne me pouvois garder en façon quelconque.[54]

From what Thevet could see—'au peu de loisir que j'euz pour le voir'—the Dome itself was 'beau et riche'.[55] The rushed glimpse already tells us that Thevet does not see with pilgrim eyes; the empty descriptive signs betray the scant order of his devotional ecphrasis. The picture he does paint, of himself, of how he was captured for

[53] Thevet, *CL*, pp. 193–6; p. 194 shows the bathhouse interior.
[54] Thevet, *CU*, II, fol. 170ᵛ.   [55] Ibid.

having transgressed Islamic laws, avoids mention of the pilgrim point
to this event: philosophizing and contemplating walls and fortifica-
tions are expressly forbidden in pilgrim guides, as Castela's later classification of the rules makes clear.

But Thevet tells this story not to pay penance for the sin of curiosity, so much as to stress the importance of his own survival, of his
being able to tell the story at all. He was stunned—'je m'esbahis'—
that he had not been put to death on looking into the Dome, given
what had happened four months earlier to a certain Spaniard, a
native of Castille. The Spaniard had dressed up 'à la Turquesque' and
paid a white Moor twelve ducats to escort him in confidence and costume so that he could see the 'simagrees et folies' performed inside.
He was there 'recogneu par quelque renié, et sçachans ceux qui
estoient à l'oraison Mahometane qu'il estoit Chrestien, le mirent en
plus de cent pieces'.[56]

It seems important that Thevet presents this grisly tale as a real life
occurrence, one which he narrowly avoided. Important also, in the
context of our reading of Castela's narrative above, are the connected
thematics of disguise and recognition: a renegade sees the false Turk
for what he really is, namely, a pilgrim. It is his insufficiently expert
deception, unmasked by that professional deceiver, the renegade,
which costs the pilgrim his life. This points to the central recognition
moment here, as the story turns back on itself to read as concerned
with Thevet the pilgrim. The point is that Thevet was not put to
pieces because he had not (yet) disguised himself as anything other
than a pilgrim. He could be taken for a spy, to be sure, but this is precisely what enables him to see further into Islamic territory, while
retaining his pilgrim integrity. Sightseeing under duress ('non par
mon plaisir') and with safe escort ('ains prisonnier') ensures that
Thevet does not suffer the false pilgrim's moral punishment.

This reading is reinforced by the return of the Spaniard's body to
Thevet's text; it is a return which is now explicitly financial, and further underlines the Christian community's rejection of the false pilgrim, even as it confirms Thevet's own election. The cosmographer
relates how two further renegades, 'un jour apres le susdit massacre
commis, apporterent secrettement la teste et un bras de ce pauvre
Espagnol, au monastere du mont Syon, où les Chrestiens Latins

---

[56] Ibid. fols. 170ᵛ–71ʳ. At least one earlier Spanish pilgrim boasts in his own account of
having done exactly this, and surviving to tell the tale. See Tafur, *Travels* (1435), pp. 61–2.

demeuroient'.[57] They wanted twenty or thirty ducats from the Gardien who thanked them for their consideration, but declined to accept 'fort gracieusement', or to pay, thinking that would be the end of it. But the renegades ('ces galans') took him to task:

Disans, Chien que tu es, refuses tu de nous celuy que tu confesses avoir esté ton frere Chrestien, et qui n'agueres demeuroit avec toy? Vous confessez tous, que ceux qui sont mis à mort par les mains des infideles, desquelz vous nous estimez, sont saincts en Paradis, et leur portez tel honneur, que mesmes vous faites enchasser leurs oz en or et en argent: que n'en faites vous autant de cestuicy?[58]

Thus Thevet presents a lucid critique of pilgrimage preached at its central point. His admiration for this argument may be evident in his text. He is careful, none the less, to preach not in his own voice, but in that of the doubly determined Other: the renegade bearer of false relics. His own voice praises the Gardien for his practical common sense, paying the preaching renegades 'de peur qu'autre scandale n'advient', but giving them less than they were asking for—ten ducats: 'à la charge toutefois, qu'ils enterreroient lesdites teste et braz à leur discretion, et où bon leur sembleroit.'[59] The Gardien was right to refuse this exchange, Thevet notes, for had he not done so, he would be obliged to buy any number 'de tels reliquiaires', and all pilgrims would be in danger of 'passer le pas', subject to the same inflationary economy as the commodified Spaniard.

The story thus serves to stress, retrospectively, Thevet's survival to witness the truth as to what happened to pilgrimage: as Calvin and other Reformers were arguing even as Thevet was walking around Jerusalem, the logic of pilgrimage is such that it makes a commodity of the body.[60] Once recognized as a trade, pilgrimage's sacred economy threatened to explode, and Thevet tells this story to remind himself that he did well to sell his shares in it, to invest his identity elsewhere. But, like Calvin and the renegades who lament the passing of the days when things were otherwise, he writes from a position of nostalgia. His exemplary tale marks the return into his later writings of the ghost of Thevet the pilgrim, the ghost of a character the Cosmographer left disputing theology in a storm, in a dream, just off the coast of Marseille.

---

[57] Thevet, *CU*, II, fol. 171ʳ.   [58] Ibid.   [59] Ibid.
[60] We return to these writers below.

Rabelais: Fantasizing Resurrection

Different pilgrim bodies are spoken of, constructed, and dismembered in the texts discussed in this chapter thus far. Georgiewitz, Thevet, and Castela differ significantly in their relations to the textualized and author-centred private body spawned by travel writing, in their articulation of pilgrims' fantasies and fears. Where the character of Georgiewitz develops from generation to generation, Thevet and Castela take up fixed, opposed, and unchanging positions in the contemporary debate over the decorum of travel. Castela's narrative projects itself as impenetrable: deaf, dumb, and blind, a classical statue, an emblem of heroic integrity in response to anxiety. By contrast the newly fashioned Renaissance self which Thevet assembles in the boat off Marseille is adamantly not an anxiously celibate pilgrim. It is, rather, the product of promiscuous reading, of other peoples' labour and other peoples' stories attaching themselves to Thevet's expansive and well-travelled body. What almost happened to him in Jerusalem nonetheless haunts him to the ends of the earth, suggesting that he is nostalgic for that pilgrim soul in himself which he traded in for the body of a paper giant, a man of letters.

How are the incomplete peregrinations of Rabelais' fictional giants to be situated relative to these later bodies, these pilgrim stories? What happens to the pilgrims in *Gargantua* is well known.[61] Their incorporation, regurgitation, and gentle banishment from the text seems parodically to preempt the kinds of violence to which pilgrims are subject in the texts we have discussed so far. Revisiting the 'salad' episodes in the context of our readings here suggests, however, that Rabelais' voracious literary imagination has more than a parodic investment in pilgrimage. Indeed the pilgrim chapters can be read as a discussion of the relationship between the fictional and the non-fictional journey, the stories of the anonymous and the tales of the author. In particular they can be seen to stage an active celebration of cultural indebtedness to pilgrimage in a form which is not (quite) yet that of nostalgia.

Rabelais' corpus is an eating, drinking, pissing, shitting, farting machine of a thing, as Bakhtin, and others such as Jeanneret have since shown.[62] Bakhtin locates the text's privileged site as the market

---

[61] For a fine reading of the pilgrim episode (and others) see F. Lestringant, 'Dans la bouche des géants', *Cahiers Textuels*, 34/35 (1989), 4–5, pp. 43–52.

[62] See M. Bakhtin, *Rabelais and his World* (1968); M. Jeanneret, *Des Mets et des mots* (1987).

place: Jeanneret's is the banqueting table. Both imagine 'happy eaters (and shoppers)', involved in a carnival which valorizes the grotesque as a means of mediating between the bodies social and sacred. In our context it is striking how like these banquet carnivals are to anthropologist Turner's influential characterization of pilgrimage as 'controlled liminality'. Pilgrims experience 'in a mercifully untaxing form the thrill of passing an invisible frontier . . . bridge the cleavage' between men and women, freely circulate between classes, peoples, and languages.[63] So too Bakhtin's Rabelaisian corpus:

> is not in a private, egotistic form, severed from the other spheres of life, but is something universal representing all the people. It is opposed to the severance from the material and bodily roots of the world, it makes no pretence to renunciation of the earthy, no pretence of independence of the earthy and the body.[64]

These are usefully explicit statements of how the liminal figures of a past age are read by our own. It remains, however, difficult 'to disentangle the generous but willed idealism from the descriptively accurate in passages like these'.[65] Such generous idealism is similarly apparent in Jeanneret's recent discussion of the aesthetics and ethics of table talk in Renaissance literature. And whilst *Gargantua* does at first seem to tell a pilgrim story in tune with the Bakhtinian sublime, and Gargantua himself seems to be one of Jeanneret's 'happy eaters', closer reading suggests that Rabelais interrupts the feast of fiction to ask difficult questions. Who does and does not get invited to enjoy the meal, and who is consumed, or lost while the banquet is in progress?

Again the story begins on the pilgrims' return:

Le propous requiert que racontons ce qu'advint à six pelerins, qui venoient de Sainct Sebastian, près de Nantes, et pour soy heberger celle nuyct, de peur des ennemys, s'estoyent mussez on jardin dessus les poyzars, entre les choulx et lectues. Gargantua se trouva quelque peu alteré et demanda si l'on pourroit trouver de lectues pour faire une sallade. Et, entendent qu'il y en avoit des plus belles et grandes du pays, car elles estoient grandes comme

---

[63] For more on Turner, see above, Ch. 1. The quotation here is from P. Brown, *The Cult of the Saints*, pp. 42–3.

[64] Bakhtin. *Rabelais and his World*, p. 19.

[65] P. Stallybrass and A. White (on Bakhtin in) *The Politics and Poetics of Transgression* (1986), p. 10.

pruniers ou noyers, y voulut aller luy mesmes et en emporta en sa main ce que bon luy sembla.[66]

Gargantua performs his own miniature pilgrimage here: he has heard that the lettuces are good, and he wants to experience the truth of what he has heard. The giant's concealed pilgrimage to the vegetable garden leads to his inadvertently swallowing the pilgrims concealed in that garden:

Ensemble emporta les six pelerins, lesquelz avoient si grand peur qu'ilz ne ousoient ny parler ny tousser.

Les lavant doncques premierement en la fontaine, les pelerins disoient en voix basse l'un à l'aultre: 'Qu'est y de faire? Nous nayons icy, entre ces lectues. Parlerons nous? Mais, si nous parlons, il nous tuera comme espies.'[67]

The pilgrims are then swallowed; the text suggests that this happens in part because they dared not declare their liminal status. They have not the words with which to claim their inheritance as privileged travellers enacting with literal bodily displacement the Pauline existential trope whereby we are all pilgrims on this earth. Nor have they the faculty to reason that through their doubly determined liminality in relation to the bodies sacred and social—on pilgrimage and about to become an inverted representation of the host—they in fact serve to reinforce the structural relations from which they are temporarily suspended.

In textual terms the pilgrims' powerlessness is represented through the comedy of scale, perspective, and (mis)recognition. At this stage in the story they have no words for themselves other than questions which betray their fear in what they know to be a time of war. Like both Castela and Thevet they fear being taken for spies. Indeed the next time they appear, the plot has played a trick on them, translating this fear into reality. It takes the Samsonesque slaughtering power of Frère Jean to free them. For the moment they are incorporated both by the giant and by the text which tells his story, and all to slake a little thirst before the real meal begins:

Et, comme ilz deliberoient ainsi, Gargantua les mist avecques ses lectues dedans un plat de la maison, grand comme la tonne de Cisteaux, et, avec-ques de l'huille, de vainaigre et de sel, les mangeoyt pour soy refraischir davant souper.[68]

This no truncated dialogue (Georgiewitz), no shared meal (Castela), and no misfired contractual arrangement (Thevet's Spaniard). Indeed

---

[66] Rabelais, *Gargantua*, p. 217   [67] Ibid.   [68] Ibid., pp. 217–18.

the scene is the negative image of all three of our pilgrim instances: Rabelais' pilgrims are not addressed as they pass by, but go altogether unnoticed; they are not dismembered, but incorporated; they do not invite the stranger to a meal, they are themselves the meal. None of the people involved in this event tells his own story. It is told rather by Rabelais' third person narrator, recounting something similar to that which happened to him by means of his own volition (*Pantagruel* 22). The point is that of authorship and agency.

Incorporation is not always a conscious procedure, and it is important to note that the pilgrims survive. They seem at times unaware of having been swallowed, and certainly Gargantua remains unaware of having swallowed them, even as, true to generic form, the pilgrims return from certain death, plucked from between the giant's teeth. The lettuce which concealed the pilgrims was as large as a 'noyer'; it is with a 'noyer' proper, serving as Gargantua's toothpick, that they are released. There is a pleasing symmetry here, a shift from the apparent to the actual which nicely replicates the pilgrim's hermeneutic. Indeed a similar symmetry, a similar shift, are further evident in the pilgrims' later entrapment and release. All but one of them fall into a wolf-trap, from which the survivor literally disentangles them. They all fall exhausted at the end of their ordeal and Lasdaller reads—disentangles figuratively—the threads of the whole experience as an exercise in scriptural *imitatio*. Thus despite having been literally pissed on, Lasdaller retains the ability, like Castela, to see what has happened to him and his fellow pilgrims as responding to scriptural precedent: it was all prefigured in the Psalms, in sequence and detail.

The text, meanwhile, has done enough violence to the pilgrims, whom it leaves enjoying the appropriately named Lasdaller's phrase-by-phrase explication of the appropriateness of Psalm 124 to their experience: '*Cum exurgerent homines in nos, forte vivos deglutissent nos*, quand nous feusmes mangez en salade au grain du sel . . . *et nos liberati sumus Adjutorium nostrum*, etc.'.[69] The 'etc.' with which the chapter ends, the lack of narrative comment or closure, suggests that the pilgrim hermeneutic has won this battle of attrition: this could go on for ever.

In Jeanneret's terms this resolution reads as another instance of happy eating in that everyone's needs are met. Indeed in an access of

---

[69] Rabelais, *Gargantua*, pp. 219–20.

curative force through narrative symmetry Gargantua's thrust of the toothpick responds to the pilgrim's staff, and cures both the giant of his toothache and one of the pilgrims of a groin abcess which his pilgrimage had left unhealed. The text too is, in this way, nourished: it incorporates the rhetoric of the pilgrim, and so further demonstrates its own cornucopian richness, its ability to feed off a wide range of textual meats and sauces.

But the cornucopian text is not always a happy one.[70] The pilgrims' sense of the rightness of their own reading of events is short-lived, as is the assurance that the text will allow them to continue on the pilgrim road. Witness their last return to the body of the chronicle. No longer comic respite from the war narrative, they had themselves become swallowed by the war, and had in turn engulfed others within it (Frère Jean in particular). Malvolio-like, they now need to be expelled from the text in order for the feasting to begin. Their last entrance, a recognition scene, takes place so they can be banished once and for all.

Once again they return to find a feast about to start (chapter 43). But this time they are not the meal, nor even an hors d'œuvre, as the comedy of scale on which the earlier chapter relies is set aside. No longer taken for slugs, they are recognized as pilgrims, and, in epic terms, expected to tell their story in return for the royal generosity of the meal, to which they are, it seems, invited. The epic signs indicate that the pilgrims' return is achieved at the cost of their pure generic identity. Rabelais, more explicitly than most—and precisely through the apparently liminary incorporation of figures such as the pilgrims—reminds us that culture is a form of cannibalism. The Rabelaisian body, Humanist culture's most fleshy embodiment, is far from generous to those who occupy liminal positions in the nascent discourse of bourgeois self-identity. Gypsies, Jews, vagabonds, the possessed, pilgrims . . . all those who are, to borrow a term from Paul's letter to the Hebrews regarding pilgrimage, 'without the camp', are fair prey to its voraciously incorporating appetite. In amidst all the laughing, the farting, and the shouting, the still small voice can get lost.

Reading in detail, though it cannot always restore the lost voice itself, can at least register the fact of loss. For it is easy, in the fun and fast pace of Rabelais' narrative, not to notice that not all the pilgrims

[70] This has long been clear to readers of Cave's study, *The Cornucopian Text*. It is made most explicit in his conclusion, pp. 332–4.

survive the fictional battles. Six are swallowed, and regurgitated, by Gargantua, but only five are invited to the feast which celebrates Frère Jean's return from apparent death. One is simply swallowed, unaccountably, between chapters. And for those who remain, even the recognition is but a pretext for further loss: that of the worth of their travels, and of their experience. They are spoken *to*, rather than *about*, only in order that pilgrimage can be classified as 'inutiles et otieux voyages'. Appearing as pilgrims for the last time, those who survive the war are not confirmed in their identity by being once again swallowed by the Son in inverse celebration of the host; rather, like Petrarch in our opening chapter, they are castigated by the Father for their folly, and told to go home:

Lors dist Grandgouzier: 'Entretenez vos familles, travaillez, chascun en sa vacation, instruez voz enfans, et vivez comme vous enseigne le bon Apostre sainct Paoul. Ce faisans, vous aurez la guarde de Dieu, des anges et des sainctz avecques vous, et n'y aura peste ny mal qui vous porte nuysance.'[71]

In fact Paul says nothing of the kind. This, like Menedemus' translation of his property into the Church around which he traces his Roman stations, is Humanist damnable iteration.[72] Paul is turned, once again, into politics, and the rhetorically adept Stay-at-homes urge those who wander abroad to look to their homes and inheritance.[73] Unlike Ogygius, these pilgrims concede and abandon their identity—the war of attrition between this literary text and pilgrimage is over. The travellers shake their heads at their own stupidity and head for home, while the retired soldiers go on to found a university.

'Marchandises Peregrines': *Professional Pilgrims*

Figuratively speaking, I travel for the great house of Human Interest Brothers, and have rather large connection in the fancy goods way. Literally speaking, I am always wandering here and there from my rooms in Covent-Garden, London—now about

---

[71] Rabelais, *Gargantua*, p. 256.

[72] Screech here cites a more likely source, [Luther] *La summe de l'escripture saincte*: 'ils courent en loingtain payz en pèlerinage: et laissent leurs enfantz et leurs mesgnye à l'hostel, sans chef et sans gouverneur. Il vauldroit mil fois mieulx qu'ilz demourassent à l'hostel et apprinssent leurs enfantz à la loy de Dieu' (ibid. 257 n. 102).

[73] Grandgousier's way of reading the Pauline passages here cited (1 Tim. 5; 8; Gal. 6: 8) is peculiarly Reformist in tone. See Screech, *Rabelais*, pp. 184–7.

the city streets, now, about the country by-roads—seeing many little things, and some great things, which, because they interest me, I think they may interest others. These are my brief credentials as the Uncommercial Traveller.

(Dickens, *The Uncommercial Traveller*)

Clearly the notion of pilgrims as liminal figures cannot finally be upheld in Rabelais' world. The reformist Humanists of Grandgousier's mobile court have arrogated to themselves the task of saying who is and is not accorded the privileges of liminality; the author has arrogated to himself the role of determining the field of narrative necessity. The Reformers' critique is taken up, as we have seen, by later generations of counter-Reformers, and pilgrims are further banished from the respectable roads. So too both pilgrims and other writers are incorporated by the cosmographer royal, the sales representative for what Dickens will term the Great House of Human Interest Brothers. Perhaps untaxing liminality is only a serious option for pilgrims if they know themselves to be home-owning citizens of the stable city; secure not so much in where they have come from or may one day go, as in where they now belong, and what they themselves can produce.[74]

Certainly, should the pilgrim set off, like Guerin Mesquin, in search of his own 'generation' he risks discovering on his return home that he has missed out on the real family romance. Grandgousier, addressing pilgrims warns: '[les moynes] biscotent voz femmes, ce pendent que estes en romivage.'[75] Such considerations translate also into terms of textual generation and inheritance, as Thevet's figural incorporation of Rabelais and others demonstrates. And they can, finally, as we shall see here, be expressed as an anxiety about the commodification of those very social, devotional, and textual practices which attempt to keep pilgrimage alive.

Calvin: Pilgrims and Merchants

The penultimate 'scene' for reading here has quite different coordinates and concerns from those discussed thus far. It is a text less securely located than those of Columbus or Georgiewitz, Castela or Thevet. It is a pamphlet, published anonymously and without

---

[74] See the Meyer epigraph at the head of this chapter.
[75] Rabelais, *Gargantua*, p. 255.

indication of place or date, some time in the 1530s. Bordering on fiction, being ostensibly authored by the Lord Pantapole (one who can sell anything), 'proche voysin de Pantagruel', it bears a title promising instruction: *Le livre des marchans, fort utile a toutes gens, pour cognoistre de quelles marchandises on se doit garder destre trompe.*[76] In truth, however, this title is no guide but offers only misdirection. For this is no economics textbook, and despite the opening encomium of trade, it soon reveals itself to be a critique of merchants, who have, as the English translation has it, 'occupyed' the world:

Mais ceulx icy ont tout ravy pour toutes choses mettre en vente . . . riens ne leur ont eschappé, dequoy à leur plaisir n'ayent marchandé voire d'hommes, de femmes, de petis enfans nasquis et non point encore naiz, des corps, des ames, et esperitz des vivans, des mortz, des biens visibles et invisibles, du ciel, de la terre et des enfers, des viandes, des temps, et des jours de mariage, de vestemens, rasures, oinctures, acoustremens, de bulles, de pardons, indulgences, remissions, d'ossemens, autres reliques et rogations, expectatives, dispens, exemption de sacremens, et sainstes oeuvres du Dieu. De pain, de vin, d'huyle, de laict, de beurre, de fromage, d'eau, de sel, de feu, de fumigation, ceremonies, encensemens, chans, melodies, de boys, de pierre, de confraries, inventions, traditions, loix, impostures et sans nombre de telles choses.[77]

Enumeration has, as Foucault reminds us, an enchantment all of its own.[78] It takes some time before the reader realizes that the merchants in question are in fact priests, and that the pamphlet is an attack on pilgrimage and the sale of indulgences. The syntax thus nicely stages the Reformist pamphleteer's point, which is that the Church has commodified perception, so that we now read the world no longer as scripture, but as if it were a shopping list. With specific reference to relics the Lord Pantapole stresses that pardoners have made a commodity of vision itself: 'semblables a basteleurs ou mommeurs ils scavent bien vendre la seule veue de leur marchandise et bagages.'[79]

This theme of the commodification of perception is reiterated and

---

[76] It is now attributed to Antoine Marcourt. See G. Berthoud, *Antoine Marcourt, réformateur et pamphlétaire du Livre des marchans aux placards de 1534* (1973).

[77] [Marcourt,] *Le livre des marchans*, fol. 7ʳ. The English translation, [Marcourt,] *The boke of marchauntes right necessarye unto all folkes*, was published, again anonymously, in London, by T. Godefray [1534?]; we return to it below. It here reads: 'their occupyenge conteyneth a hole worlde, there is nothynge escaped them but that they have occupied it at their pleasure', fol. Avʳ.

[78] See M. Foucault, *Les Mots et les choses* (1966), p. 11.

[79] Marcourt, fol. 7ʳ. The English, by exploiting puns, makes explicit connections which the French leaves unspoken: 'these lyke unto juglers or mommers with celling [i.e. con-

elaborated by Calvin, in his later pamphlet: *Advertissement tresutile du grand proffit qui reviendroit à la Chrestienté, s'il se faisoit inventoire de tous les corps sainctz, et reliques, qui sont tant en Italie, qu'en France, Allemaigne, Hespaigne, et autres Royaumes et pays.*[80] Calvin presents his argument through the rhetorical figure whose workings we noted above in the writings of pilgrims and/as explorers: *occupatio*. Calvin exploits the figure on a paragraph by paragraph level, and introduces his own lists and criticisms with such disclaimers as:

Il n'est ja mestier que . . . Combien que je ne puis faire en ce livre ce que voudrois bien . . . il nous faut doresnavant despecher ou autrement jamais nous ne sortirons de ceste forest . . . or pour le present mon intention n'est pas de traiter quelle abomination c'est d'abuser des reliques.[81]

Claiming not to have been on any pilgrimages, Calvin draws up his inventory in a way—to return to Fabri's textbook definition of *occupatio*—'moult compendieuse et abregée'. Resisting the enchantment of enumeration, he takes the reader on what amounts to one of the most exhaustive pilgrimage tours in Renaissance writing. Stressing that there is more to the pilgrimage account than merely naming the places on the journey, he sets out in search of non-falsifiable truth: 'Mais encore le principal seroit de les visiter, et non pas nommer seulement. Car on ne les cognoist point toutes à nommer.'[82]

Calvin's imagined 'visitation' of Europe's holy sites is conducted not with a view to worship, but rather to violence. His is a pilgrimage performed with iconoclasm in mind; he sets out to break the very frame of pilgrimage. Pilgrims typically wonder 'what can we do more than touch, kneel, kiss and gaze' at the relics encountered on the journey? The pilgrim gaze is a stare, beyond history and material questions.[83] Calvin, by contrast, looks, and looks closely at the objects in his critical purview. He constantly subjects the bones to questions about history, translation, travel, and reiteration: 'how did this relic get to be here? who brought it here? how many versions of it exist in Europe today?'

cealing] can sell right derely and sell agayne the onely sight of theyr baggage', *The boke of marchauntes*, fol. bi^r.

[80] It is published in Geneva, by Jehan Girard, in 1543 (I have used Higman's edition). It was soon translated English as: *A very profitable treatise* (London, 1561).

[81] Calvin, *Advertissement, passim.*   [82] Ibid., p. 53.

[83] See Sontag's meditation on the contemporary difference between a stare and a look: 'A stare is perhaps as far from history, as close to eternity, as contemporary art can get' (*Styles of Radical Will* (1994), p. 16).

Not content with allegorical truth, Calvin reads in philological mode. Reintroducing historical space and time into the plot of pilgrimage, he—like Thevet's renegades with their pieces of pilgrim in Jerusalem—finds it wanting. The analogy with the incident in Jerusalem is pre-figured in Calvin's own account. In the last paragraph of his text he comes to his central question:

Car entre tant de mensonges si patens, comme je les ay produictz, où est-ce qu'on choisira une vraye relique, de laquelle on se puisse tenir certain? D'avantage, ce n'est rien de ce j'en ay touché, aupris de ce qui en reste.[84]

Occupatio modulates into *praeteritio* as the trained lawyer waves his papers, and concludes with a flourish. He goes on to note that, even as the book has been at the printers, word has come to him of the existence of another—third—foreskin of Christ: 'Mesme ce pendant qu'on imprimoit ce livret, on m'a adverty d'un troysiesme Prepuce de nostre Seigneur, qui se monstre à Hyldesheym, dont je n'avoye faict nulle mention.'[85]

This is a gesture akin to Columbus' (not quite) mentioning all the gold he has (not yet) seen, and to Georgiewitz's retrospective denial of having gazed upon the monstrous other. It is at some remove from the inverted representation of the host which Rabelais' pilgrims are permitted to figure forth. For there is one scandal which Calvin—for all his obsessively inclusive accounting—cannot quite mention, but on which his analysis rests. It is the notion of Christ's body as monstrous. He can only address the analogy of Christ the monster with several penises by way of an appendix to the print story of his own text. For in order fully to entertain this image, you must stop believing; in particular you must surrender your faith in the body as sacramental, capable of generating in and from itself inexhaustible forms of sacred mimetic capital.

This Calvin cannot quite do. A Moses looking from the mountain at the promised land he knows he will never see, he stands on the margins of both trade literature and pilgrimage. He sees the two in relation to each other, and demonstrates their kinship by highlighting the ways in which the body becomes commodified. The body of the pilgrim and the body of Christ, have, along with the word of God, become subject to the rough and fallen trade of patronage, fallen into the hands of clerical and cultural merchants. Calvin is alive to the

---

[84] Calvin, *Advertissement*, p. 96.   [85] Ibid.

coming ascendancy of the reified, private corpus exemplified by Castela's ideal pilgrim—deaf, dumb, blind to the places and people he meets on the road. As he resisted the connected enchantments of enumeration and recuperative allegory, so too he resists the meta-morphosis of the Christian body in pain into the heroically symbolic neoclassical nude. He seeks to return the torn, mutilated bodies of Christ and of pilgrims to their historical and textual materiality. But the reiterative use of *occupatio*, culminating in the fiction of adding a note to the proofs of his text much as others would add a further fore-skin to Christ's body, betrays Calvin's fear of failure. His nostalgia for a time prior to the age of mechanical reproduction conflicts with an awareness of the burden of debt to the trade on which his own texts so clearly rely for their dissemination and sense. His fear is that he is too late to prevent this trade and its products (the author, the travel book, the novel . . .) from making of the pilgrim body, as of the pil-grim experience, something foreign and strange to European culture, just another 'marchandise peregrine'.

Rabelais: Pilgrims and Tourists

'Historically', Foucault argues, 'discourse was a gesture fraught with risks before becoming goods caught up in a circuit of ownership'.[86] Calvin's similarly structured argument against what has become of pilgrimage is that it now obscures the risk involved in the exercise of faith, and that in the process both the bodies of the faithful dead and the experience of the living have become fetishized. The moment of recognition in both Calvin and Foucault—that (sacred) representa-tion does not escape the market—generates its own retrospective history: not so much, 'there was a time when then this was not articu-lated, or known', as, 'there must have been a time when this was not yet the case'.

It is such nostalgic representations of history that our final scene—a problem of reading disguised as a group of tourists—both indulges and re-evaluates. Pantagruel and his crew in Rabelais' *Quart Livre* set off in search of the Oracle of the Holy Bottle, to discover whether Panurge should marry or not. Under cover of this old-fangled quest, Rabelais raises a number of questions regarding the place of the literary text in history, and in particular the transmission of images of the suffering

[86] M. Foucault, 'What is an Author', in *Modern Criticism and Theory* (1988), p. 202.

body through fiction. He does so in part in order to urge us to tread carefully when we set out to discover truths about 'our own' cultural past.

We begin by retracing the journey so far. For the first three days of their quest Pantagruel's crew see nothing. This is because the route had already been traversed before: they see nothing because there is nothing specifically new to see. This already marks them as different from pilgrims, who, travelling in search of the *déjà-lu*, see only that which they have already seen before, in scripture. On the fourth day they arrive at an island called Medamothy—which the phrase-book appended to this travel account tells us means Nowhere—where they find a market in progress. They set to, buying 'divers tableaux, diverses tapisseries, divers animaulx, poissons, oizeaulx et autres marchandises exotiques et peregrines'.[87]

This scene has, over the course of the last century, lent itself to several readings. All in their way are anthropological allegories, in that they go to the text as a repository of information about a given, foreign culture—Renaissance France. They can usefully be seen to take up two opposing positions: home and away. Those who read Nowhere island as an image of home see in the Medamothy market a satire on the contemporary French court's taste for rich and exotic works of art. The text invites such a reading by judicious reference to the importation of the mannerist style into French painting, the name of the court painter to Henri II, and allusion to existing tapestries on real walls in French palaces, Fontainebleau in particular.[88]

Those of the opposing camp read for signs of otherness. Medamothy is only one of several places on the quest, and it will not do to reduce the impetus of Rabelais' writing to issues of contemporary court taste and patronage. So Pantagruel's journey is compared with those of Cartier—the most celebrated contemporary French explorer—and is set alongside specific references to Canada in the text. Such a reading underlines the travellers' arrival in a specifically French New World, and simultaneously celebrates Rabelais' familiarity with the literature of the 'nouveaux horizons', his personal connections with France's greatest living explorers, and his share in the development of the French Empire.[89]

---

[87] Rabelais, *Quart Livre*, pp. 38–41.

[88] For review of such readings, see P. Smith, *Voyage et écriture* (1987), pp. 167–78.

[89] The most thorough-going analysis of this kind remains A. Lefranc, *Les Navigations de Pantagruel* (1905). He glosses this chapter's relation to Cartier, pp. 290–5. Essential

In each instance—home or away—Rabelais' text clearly has to do with trade, with going to literally or figuratively foreign places, and with opening up new spaces, whether empirical or imagined. It has also to do with techniques of description and the problem of how best to 'rapporter', how best to bring the goods home to France.[90] Rabelais' modern professional readers mime the traveller-tourists in their desire to discover some unexpected bargain at the 'foire' of the text, and, like his narrator, do not baulk at the pairing of the adjective 'peregrin' with the 'exotique'. Any residual traces of pilgrim in the word, and of *peregrinatio* structuring the voyage of Pantagruel's crew, or indeed our own journeys of reading, are erased by the desire to see in the text, and to produce in our readings, things which eye has not seen nor ear yet heard.

This displacement of pilgrimage by the exotic is the movement we have been tracing here, as exemplified by Columbus and Georgiewitz, and feared by Calvin. It is, on Medamothy, confirmed by the fact that none of the goods for sale are relics, or indeed have any Christian religious significance. Rather they are for the most part classical *adynata*—things which are by definition unrepresentable: pictures of Plato's ideas, of Epicurus' atoms, of Echo drawn to the life and so on. A further reading of the market in Medamothy opens up, celebrating forms of discovery which conflate the oppositions home and away, ancient and modern. By parading these particular 'marchandises peregrines', the text suggests that by travelling West and leaving *peregrinatio* and the Levant behind, modern European man was able to break the hegemony of Christian modes of reading and so rediscover classical Antiquity. The spatial movement across uncharted waters to the New World reads as the literal enactment of the intellectual journey across time to the sources of the Old; Renaissance Utopias reorient and relocate the genres and myths of the ancients. Moreover, the fact that classical *adynata* can be bought for trifles at a New World fair would suggest that the rediscovery of antiquity serves primarily to confirm that the moderns can produce goods so wondrous as to bring tears to Alexander's eyes.[91]

---

reading on French America is F. Lestringant, *Le Huguenot et le Sauvage* (1990) (though this book is not directly concerned with Rabelais).

[90] These are problems explored in Ch. 4, above.

[91] Belleforest is the first to apply the *topos* (derived from Plutarch) of Alexander's tears to the sense of wonder evoked by Thevet's travels, in a poem liminary to the *SFA* (fol. aiiij^{r-v}); it is then redeployed by Jodelle (*CU*, I, fol. ellij^{r}), and again by Dorat (*CU*, II, fol. ij^{r}).

If we are to move beyond such (far too) broadly historicist representations of Rabelais' travellers' movements, we need to read more
closely. The text directs our attention by focusing on one wondrous
object in particular, itself part of a story about travel, transformation, and dispossession. 'Gualante et mirifique', it is a painting of
the tapestry which Philomela sent to her sister, Procne, representing
how she had been raped and mutilated by Tereus, Procne's husband,
in the course of the journey from her house to theirs. Rabelais does
not describe the painting, rather he declines to do so, by describing
what it is not. He first alludes to, and then frustrates, the reader's
expectations, arguing that it is quite other to what one might expect:
'Ne pensez, je vous prie, que ce feust le portraict d'un homme couplé
sus une fille. Cela est trop sot et trop lourd. La paincture estoit bein
aultre et bien plus intelligible.'[92]

The painting, described in terms of what it is not, has been taste-
fully executed and wrapped up ready to take home, where it hangs
even now. It has travelled further, returned due East, and come to rest
in a contemporary French household. With an arresting deictic gesture, Rabelais invites us to go and see for ourselves: 'Vous la pourrez
veoir à Theleme, à main guausche, entrans en la haulte guallerie.'[93]

This apparent deixis can usefully be read as a species of *occupatio*.
As with Columbus, the narrator's gesture to go and verify the
existence of the marvellous object which figures his own text reads
as a glimpsed—if here parodic—admission of failure; as with
Georgiewitz, the very gesture which invites us to enter the house
reminds us that we cannot in reality do so. And yet whereas in
Georgiewitz we have in fact already been in the Turkish space for
most of the text, Rabelais arouses the desire for verification only to
demonstrate its impossibility in the plane of the real. What is at stake
again here, in Rabelais, as in Georgiewitz, is the business of reading,
the exchange, circulation, and verification of knowledge about ourselves and foreign cultures. As is evident from the subsequent chapter
of the *Quart Livre*, in which Pantagruel receives a letter from his
father and then sends one home, Rabelais is also concerned with how
we apply what we read, buy, and sell at the 'foire' of fictional example
to our own cultures, our own ways of seeing and being.[94]

---

[92] Rabelais, *Quart Livre*, p. 39.   [93] Ibid.
[94] Not least since this letter mirrors, in position and content, the earlier 'Humanist'
letter of *Pantagruel* 8.

The important point is that the gestures of verification in the *Quart Livre*, even the ones which display their own improbability, *all* work. The signs exchanged between local tradespeople and visiting tourists, like the deixis directed from travelling narrator to reader, reveal the workings of the mimetic trade. The trade fair in Medamothy demonstrates—more clearly than the less fictional texts are able—how news from elsewhere gets filtered home. The clarity of purpose in the fictional text sets the scene for the remainder of the *Quart Livre* in its exploration of the means by which mimetic capital is generated in relation to real places and people. It also further serves to distinguish the *Quart Livre* from the other travel texts discussed here in this chapter.

Occupatio allows Columbus to defer the day of reckoning, the scene of mercantile and narrative exchange at home, by displacing the reader's interest on to the process of discovery. The actual, brute facts of mutual incomprehension with which the letter ends are temporarily relegated to a dependent clause. A trade-off is proposed, which at its most blunt runs: narrative for merchandise, suspense for gold. What Columbus could not yet know was how the terms of this contract, which *occupatio* underwrites from within the discourse of pilgrimage, would be exploited by the travelling sales reps. of the new discourses. But in truth, as his story is read and retold over the course of the Renaissance, Columbus comes to exemplify a particular pilgrim character, one who, rather than defer narrative detail, indulges it the better to show the workings of divine intervention in the traveller's life.

Georgiewitz forges this character on his own account, to prove that he is no renegade, that his story is to be believed, and that he should be permitted back into the Christian fold. But he does so also on behalf of his readers who have followed him inside the Turkish court, have paused to praise its architecture and its political structures, and have given undue attention to its harems, its beliefs, and its language. For he has the pilgrim's awareness that knowledge of others comes at a cost and leaves neither them nor us unaffected. And we readers, travelling as we do after Calvin and Castela, need to sense that reading these texts is both necessary and recuperable. We need reassurance that, for all their generic transgressions, our texts do make up a kind of pilgrimage, and that we too, rather than trading in fancy or stolen goods, are still on course for our own particular Jerusalem of understanding.

The landing at Medamothy cannot, then, properly be read as reluctant anthropology written under the sign of *occupatio*. The invitation to the reader is not (as it was for Columbus, Georgiewitz, and Calvin) 'if you don't believe me, undertake the journey and go and see for yourself'.[95] For such a gesture implies the possibility of falsification; it suggests that the material journey makes all the difference. If Rabelais' deixis is like any of our previous instances, it is close to the persuasive performance of the professional pilgrims Castela, Thevet—and Dickens. For them the text is not a pretext for a journey, it *is* the journey. We are all pilgrims and the metaphor is for real. The reader, meantime, is presented with a gesture of verification which is at once bluff, bravado, and a gift: 'Come and look more closely at what is on the walls of my house—my book—for these marvellous possessions, this island, I have made mine. And—if you take the risk of faith in fictional worlds—they can be yours too.'

[95]   As it is, by contrast, when Rabelais returns later in the journey to the problem of reference and nomination at a distance with respect to the Andouilles: 'Croyez le, si voulez; si ne voulez, allez y veoir' (*Quart Livre*, p. 169).

Moses or China

Literature, then. Literature before and after, if need be. Which does not release me from the demands of tact and humility required for this overdetermined trip. I am afraid of betraying so many contradictory claims.

(Sontag, 'Project for a Trip to China', in I, etc.)

Histoire de la Chine.
Je ne crois que les histoires dont les témoins se feraient égorger.
(*Lequel est le plus croyable des deux, Moïse ou la Chine?*) Il
n'est pas question de voir cela en gros; je vous dis qu'il y a de
quoi aveugler et de quoi éclaircir . . . mais la Chine obscurcit,
dites vous. Et je réponds: la Chine obscurcit, mais il y a clarté à
trouver. Cherchez-la . . . Il faut donc voir cela en détail. Il faut
mettre papiers sur table.

(Pascal, Pensées)

The Nun's Story

One evening, shortly after vespers, a nun enters the church of St-Jean
in Lyons. Thinking that she is alone, she first kneels, and then cries
out her pain to her God. The women she has unwittingly interrupted
in their devotions listen in silence, hidden in the semi-darkness of a
side-chapel (they themselves are there in secret). The nun has broken
the rule of her enclosed order and is passing through Lyons on a pilgrimage to Rome. Without quite understanding how, she has found
herself to be with child; she trusts that the Pope will both understand
how this can have happened, and return to her her lost virginity. One

of the company of women interrupts the nun in her prayers: 'Tell me your story.' She replies that she will speak only to the Duchesse d'Alençon. The woman urges the nun to open her heart to her as if she were the Duchess; but the nun refuses: 'No-one but her can know my secret.' The woman reveals herself to be the Duchess and the nun tells the tale begun above.

We know of this nun, of her experience, and of her faith, because she figures in the last of the stories in the *Heptaméron*, the collection of tales whose author, Marguerite de Navarre, was herself once Duchesse d'Alençon. The story thus at once disguises and names its own author; it is, like the collection which it concludes, in part a story about the difference between authorship and agency. 'La sotte religieuse', 'la pauvre fille', 'la pauvre religieuse', or 'la pauvre femme', as the narrator variously calls the nun before allowing her to speak for herself, is made, like the pilgrims in Rabelais, to play the role of the bad example. Her private story, published by the narration long before she herself gives up her secret to the author disguised as her single, unmarried self, offers the *Heptaméron*'s *devisants*, themselves interrupted on quite other journeys, the chance to lament the abuses of monks and the Church in general, to crack a few jokes at the nun's expense and, in the words of the Duchess, to put 'hors l'entendement le voyage de Rome'.[1]

Pilgrims in Renaissance French literature invariably figure as exemplary bad readers: they misunderstand themselves, their bodies, others' bodies, and the nature of both faith and the world. If they give rise to discussion about the worth of pilgrimage, it is to initiate argument supposedly beyond the scope of their understanding: arguments about property, the proper and the figural purposes of travel, the proper and figural sense of terms. At stake throughout is the status of representation and its relation to the physical coordinates of experience. Those who obstinately travel fail to see that the necessity for physical pain, for financial expense, and for long absence from home can be avoided by the domestication of the pilgrim journey—into a walk around a garden, a house, a church, a cell, or a book.

The cultured folk who comment on the tales which make up the *Heptaméron* are sceptical as to the worth of 'reading' pilgrimage as the practical expression of faith: ' "Croyez, dit Saffredent, que ces pauvres gens ne pensaient point à toute cette théologie!" '[2] But the

---

[1] Marguerite de Navarre, *Heptaméron*, p. 497.   [2] Ibid., p. 498.

apparent failure of pilgrims such as the nun to think of the larger contexts into which others will place their experience is itself telling. For
it discloses that process which the stories in which the simple folk are
overheard in prayer only serves to intensify: a process whereby the
body becomes text, subject to a rhetoric of forensic, narrative detail,
and in which both bodies and books become figured as commodities
in the rough trade of representation, knowledge, and narrative
exchange.

The nun is deprived of her agency as her trust in her priest, her
body, and her story are all, in turn, 'framed' by the narrative in which
they figure; each is made to serve authors', which is to say others',
purposes, of which the pilgrim nun remains, to this day, ignorant.
Like Grandgousier, the Duchess speaks as a good Humanist, and
'sans lui ôter la repentance continuelle de son péché' sends the pilgrim home.[3] She is, however, kinder than the king, and saves her
scorn for the 'religieux scandaleux' who talked his way into the nun's
confidence and body. Even as the text closes and returns the pilgrim
to the enclosure of her order, it evokes her peculiar access to a sense
of real presence in the details of experience, to the effect of the sacred
inscribed in the real.

Thevet, as we saw, also tells a 'foolish pilgrim' tale: that of the
Spaniard. Like the Duchess, Thevet is perhaps in disguise himself
here; certainly, he narrates the story with a similar purpose, that of
establishing his own distance from the pilgrim tradition. And
Rabelais, too, both has his pilgrims get lost, and then himself 'loses'
first one and then all of them, the better to allow his own narrative to
progress. For his part, the pilgrim priest Castela shares the fictional
pilgrim nun's understanding of the order of things. He reads the
events of his experience as being prefigured; they are not contingent,
so much as part of a plot, of which he is less, he confesses, the author
than an agent. As if to prove the point, on the very first day of his pilgrimage, he and his fellow-pilgrims see 'proposé devant nos yeux
pour commencement de voyage, un acte fort tragique'.[4] But, unlike
the nun, Castela maintains his (precarious) sense of agency precisely
by recognizing the stage-play he is in, and engaging in this way with
the problem of authorship. His argument, in the context of the others'
appropriative readings of pilgrims' experience, intensifies into one of
apparent self-evidence: the sense of the drama of pilgrimage is clear

---

[3] Ibid., p. 497.   [4] Castela, *Sainct Voyage*, p. 6.

only to those who confess themselves to be pilgrims; for only the 'personne Chrestienne', recognizable by his faithful reading of the details of experience, can travel the pilgrim road.

'Rich Eyes and Poor Hands'

The texts in this study offer vastly differing readings of pilgrim tradition; they seem, almost, to inhabit different worlds. But all the writers discussed in this book, whether 'literary' or not, are, I suggest, involved in intimately related projects. They in fact live, move, and write within the same world—just—because they share a certain relationship to narrative necessity, to plot. For all those who work within the field of pilgrimage represent as a narrative necessity things which in the plane of the real are neither contingent, nor necessary, but simply the case.

This is in part a historical matter. That the world is the case (rather than a book, a house, a map, or a stage-play) may have been untenable in Rabelais', and even Castela's time.[5] But the idea that the world is indeed the case, rather than a spectacle to be read for the plot, is also untenable for those of us engaged, now, in cultural criticism. The return to history and to discussion of the ethics of criticism have in recent years changed our understanding of the Renaissance in ways that bear on the sense of our own profession. We can now argue more carefully the complexity of connections between fictional and non-fictional writing; we read for the plot of history within the details of textual practice. Reading in detail acts as a form of empowerment to make large claims about the shape of cultural change. The figure of synecdoche combines with the form of spectacle to underwrite the work of the Historicist, old and new; as it does that of the pilgrim.

These tropes cut, however, both ways. They reinstate the importance of the forgotten characters—here, sixteenth-century pilgrims in general, and in particular the emblematically, unaccountably lost sixth pilgrim in *Gargantua*, or the nun in prayer at the close of the *Heptaméron*. But they also threaten to make a stage-play of history, to make characters of individuals. It may be that the world of the

---

[5] This is L. Febvre's famous assertion in *Le Problème de l'incroyance* (1942) (he has next to nothing to say about pilgrimage); it is also asserted by M. de Diéguez, 'Un aspect de la théologie de Rabelais: Le Chapitre 38 du *Gargantua*', *ER*, 21, pp. 347–53. In an otherwise useful essay, he repeats the commonplace view that 'certes, Rabelais avait horreur des pèlerinages, qui étaient florissants à l'époque', p. 349.

sixteenth century is now lost to us; in important respects it certainly is. The temptation is to account for the unaccountable by means of metaphorical equivalence alone: to read the sixth pilgrim or the nun as representatives of other, non-fictional pilgrims; to interpret Thevet's Spaniard as representing his own repressed pilgrim self; to see the stranger with an axe as a figure for the professional readers intent on doing Castela's text violence, and so on. The point is that for history to be a drama, and for synecdoche to be a productive heuristic trope, we have to position ourselves as already knowing the broader outlines of the plot. We risk being deaf, dumb, and blind to the local surprises of the texts we encounter on the way.

The task of reading both in detail and with a long view is Herculean. The critical paths which have opened up (again) in recent years have, however, enabled us to 'gain experience' of forgotten texts, and to come towards a closer understanding of texts we thought we knew very well. These, like the list of goods Ogygius (and Jaques) have on returning from their travels, are real experiences, real gains, and Menedemus (and Rosalind) do wrong to disparage them. The challenge remains to recognize the seductions of nostalgia for what they are; and to affirm, with Castela, Ogygius, and Jaques, the risk involved in leaving the comfort of home and losing our own lands in the course of the critical pilgrimage.

On taking up, for instance, Rabelais' very particular invitation to have a closer look at the texture of conjunctions figured by the 'marchandises peregrines' bought on Medamothy, we do what Barthes reminds us only children, old people, and university teachers have the economic ability to do: reread.[6] We do so in the knowledge that the figure *occupatio*, beyond occulting the role of the author, also throws into relief the occupation of the reader. Rabelais' particular use of *occupatio*—the central feature of which is his declining to fill out the details of the picture of Philomela sent home from Nowhere—sharpens our attention. For the absence of description here tells us that we already, in reading this text, are implicated in its representative economy: we probably know the story in its broad outlines, and if we don't, we probably know where we can go to find out more details (Ovid, *Metamorphoses*, VI). It is the details of the picture which Rabelais declines to subject to the procedures of fictional representation, even as he addresses the desire to do so. So too

---

[6] Barthes, *S/Z*, p. 11. Rabelais, *QL*, pp. 38–41.

with contemporary reference: the narrator makes no explicit connection between Philomela's story and that of unnamed native inhabitants of the New World, even as the structure of the *Quart Livre* invites such alignment.

If we ask how the picture of Philomela got to be on the wall in Thélème (given that the travellers never arrive at their destination, let alone go home), then the fact that it is a picture of Philomela's rape and not Philomela's own tapestry must matter. So too must Rabelais' gesture in declining to tell us what the picture shows. Rabelais offers two pairs of terms with which to read the painting. It is 'gualante et mirifique' on the one hand; 'bien plus intelligible et autre' on the other. These are pairs which have informed my readings of pilgrimage narratives in their relation to the more canonical forms of Renaissance writing. Each pair speaks both of intelligibility and of that which escapes explication; each pair places the fictional and the nonfictional in close relation, without making one finally subservient to the other. So if Rabelais' fiction does represent historical events, places, or coordinates (home, away, ancient, modern, Renaissance, colonization . . .), then it is important to see that it does so in a manner analogous to that of a copy of Philomela's tapestry: a picture of a tapestry woven by one whose ability to speak directly had been taken from her in the course of a journey.

To fill in those details, to reread the story—as being about medieval/early Renaissance romance, about Philomela, or the Renaissance appropriation of Arabic and classical learning, or European contact with native Americans—is to decide *how* to describe the picture. The figure in the text is not truly an *adynaton* (like the other objects bought on Medamothy), since its transmission to the present day is more unrecounted than impossible. Nor yet is it a relic, a part of Philomela's body; still less a surviving example of her own work, her own voice. The problem, as both Calvin and the Duchess point out, is one of (quasi-legal) representation by subsequent readers of, and in, history. It comes down to how, and by whom, the story which is overheard, or passed over, but mentioned in passing, comes to be told. It is an issue exemplified, intensified, by the details of transmission and translation, as I have suggested throughout this study.

Rereading, then, a final detail, in brackets, in translation, and in euphemism: 'Tereus by force hand-selled [Philomela's] copyhold, and then cut out her tongue, that she might not (as women will) tell tales.' This is Motteux's English version of what the Medamothy picture shows.[7] It compounds Philomela's rape by a defamation which is not in Rabelais' text, where the narrator states quite bluntly that Philomela was raped ('depucellée'—unvirgined) and had her tongue cut out so that she could not 'reveal the crime' ('que tel crime elle ne decelast'). Rabelais' central terms—'depuceller/deceler'—thus echo each other, the echo revealing the connection between the rape and the silencing. It is this connection which Tereus sought to hide, and which Motteux's terms, borrowed from the laws governing the exchange of property, and his addition of the '(as women will)' further seek to elide. This is not so much euphemism, as clarification in a certain direction. It makes clear that this text cannot reasonably be said to present 'heroes who are no tradesmen; [whose] search is for disinterested knowledge'.[8] For Rabelais' texts, like those of Columbus, Georgiewitz, and Calvin, demonstrate the fallacy of such a notion.

Each of the travellers and writers whose pilgrim traces we have followed here is on a specific, and differently motivated, journey. The experience of each is differently formed and policed, and even as they variously demonstrate the price of knowledge, so they lead to different kinds of epiphany. The anthropologist—the traveller who hates journeys, who leaves home with the fantasy of being invisible, of observing, and returning home at no cost to the other—appears as a relative newcomer in the Renaissance. He proves nonetheless to be a relative, a cousin to both pilgrim and merchant, and his concerns reveal the structure of relations between pilgrim, merchant, and fiction-writer all the more clearly. Distant cousin or American uncle, the unwilling Renaissance anthropologist, constantly caught between an assertion and a denial of the worth of his occupation, also raises questions about how we, now, determine the worth of the work of literature and history in which we are engaged.

The writings discussed in this study apply extraordinary pressure to one of the organizing metaphors of Western representation and self-understanding: that of life's pilgrimage. The pressure is applied by mixing this metaphor with a host of others, including, in particular, those of dismemberment, incorporation, and resurrection, all of

---

[7] See Urquhart and Motteux's translation of *Gargantua and Pantagruel* (1653–1694; reissued London, 1994), p. 532.

[8] Screech, *Rabelais*, p. 334 n. 5, echoing Pantagruel's self-description in *QL*, p. 128.

which figure forth both the mysteries and the risks of representation. If we try to attend closely to the still, small voices which are woven into the text of History, or if we seek to remember those bodies whose stories are metamorphosed into Literature, then we need to ask—with each generation, if need be—what forms of subjectivity, pleasure, and understanding our work makes available, and whose interests it can best serve.

For the terms of pilgrimage are not so much consistently recognizable signposts, as the pales which pilgrims and other writers are constantly going beyond; they are the barbed wire fences strung out between the lines in a battle over luggage, food, books, and bodies. The imagery is extreme, but as the texts we have read here repeatedly demonstrate, pilgrimage is a journey which is both 'sans terme' and an attempt to 'come to terms'—both to find words, and to negotiate the value of those words—with the subjective experience of territory, of inexplicable loss, of distance, of separation, and of death. Reading pilgrimage must be, finally—and this is the challenge which Pascal and Sontag inherit from Hamlet and rephrase as a trip projected both towards China and Moses—about how to translate such terms into the kinds of understanding which structure the experience of the living.

Bibliography

THIS is not an exhaustive bibliography of works relating to pilgrimage in the sixteenth century. It is a check-list of works cited in the text and footnotes (except for some primary works mentioned in passing, and a few secondary works of indirect relevance to the argument, where publication details are given in footnotes). Also listed are a few works which, although not cited in the text, have been useful in the preparation of the book. In the case of single early modern works, unless otherwise stated, the edition listed is the earliest of which I am aware. I give place, date and—where known—publishers, of primary works, along with shelfmarks of the copies I have used. For secondary works, I give date and place of publication only. The following abbreviations have been used:

AJFS	Australian Journal of French Studies
BLVS	Bibliothek des literarischen Vereins in Stuttgart
Doubs	*Mémoires de la Société d'Émulation du Doubs*
EC	*Esprit Créateur*
ER	Études Rabelaisiennes
JIRS	Journal of the Institute of Romance Studies
LPPTS	Library of the Palestine Pilgrims' Text Society
PQ	Petrarchan Quarterly
RSH	Revue des sciences humaines
SC	Sources Chrétiennes (Editions du Cerf, Paris)
THR	*Travaux d'humanisme et renaissance*

PRIMARY WORKS

Manuscripts

Besançon:
SAUGET, SIMON, *Album Amicorum*, A.D. Doubs. MSS. 34. 1589.

VALIMBERT, JACQUES DE, *Voyages de jacques de valimbert, à jérusalem, écrit en 1584,* Bibliothèque Municipale, MS 1453 fols. 46–67.

Archives Communales: BB. 45, 1597–9.
  HH. 41–3.
  MSS. Chifflet, 4.

Printed Books

ADAMNAN, *De Situ Terrae Sanctae,* ed. J. Gretser (Ingolstadt, 1619); BL: 10161 11.
—— (trans. J. R. Macpherson), LPPTS, 10 (London, 1889).
ADRICHOMIUS, CHRISTIAN, *Jerusalem, sicut Christi tempore floruit, et suburbanorum insigniorumque historiarum eius brevis descriptio* (Cologne: Kempensis, 1584); Bodleian: Opp Adds 8° II 257.
—— *Theatrum Terrae Sanctae et biblicarum historiarum cum tabulis geographicis aere expressis* (Cologne: Birckmann, 1590); Bodleian: Douce A subt 58.
—— *A Briefe Description of Hierusalem and the Suburbs therof, as it florished in the time of Christ,* trans. Thomas Tymme (London: printed by Peter Short for Thomas Wright, 1595); Bodleian: 4° T 13 Jur.
AFFAGART, GREFFIN, *Relation de Terre Sainte (1533–34),* ed. J. Chavanon (Paris, 1902); BL: 10075 h 19.
AUGUSTINE, ST., *Opera,* ed. Erasmus (Basel, 1526); Bodleian: A 1. 1–10 Th.
—— *Confessiones,* ed. J. O'Donnell (3 vols.; Oxford, 1992).
—— *The Confessions,* trans. E. B. Pusey (Oxford, 1838).
—— *Sensuyt le Manuel de sainct Augustin tresdevot et contemplatif* [Paris? 1505?]; Maz: 31969 a.
—— *De doctrina christiana,* ed. and trans. R. Green (Oxford, 1995).
BALOURDET, LOYS, *La Guide des chemins pour le voyage de Hierusalem, et autres villes et lieux de la Terre Saincte* (Chaalons: C. Guyot, 1601); BN: 02 f. 783.
[BARBARINO, ANDREA DA,] *La tresjoyeuse plaisante et recreative hystoire . . . du chevalier Guerin par advent nomme Mesquin,* trans. Jean de Cuchermoys (Lyon: Romain Morin pour Olivier Arnoullet, 1530); Bodleian: Arch Bd 1.
—— see Cuchermoys, *Le Voyage de Hierusalem.*
BEAUVEAU, HENRI DE, *Relation Journaliere du Voyage de Levant* (Toul: François du Bois, 1608); Bodleian: 8° L 3 Linc.
—— 1615 edition, with engravings and considerably expanded; Bodleian: Douce B 474.
BELLARMINE, ROBERT, ST., *Opera omnia,* ed. J. Fèvre (Paris, 1870).
BELLEFOREST, FRANÇOIS DE, see Granada, *Le Vray chemin.*
—— see also Guevara, *Livre du Mont de Calvaire.*

—— see also Münster, *Cosmographie Universelle*.

BELLORINI, T. and HOADE, E. (ed.), *Visit to the Holy Places of Egypt, Sinai, Palestine and Syria, in 1384, by Frescobaldi, Gucci, and Sigoli*. Publications of the Studium Biblicum Franciscanum, 6 (Jerusalem, 1948).

BELON, PIERRE, *Les Observations de plusieurs singularitez et choses memorables trouvées en Grece, Asie, Judée, Egypte, Arabie et autres pays estranges* (Antwerp: Plantin, 1555 [1554]); Bodleian: Mason DD 386.

BERTRANDON DE LA BROQUIÈRE, *Voyage d'outremer*, ed. C. Schefer (Paris, 1892).

BOURGEOIS, JACQUES, *Institution et fondation de l'Ordre de la tressaincte Trinté et rédemption des captifs . . . Ensemble les miseres et tribulations qu'endurent les chrestiens captifs [by Georgiewitz]* (Douay, 1606); Bodleian: 8° D 422 Linc.

BREYDENBACH, BERNARD VON, *Sanctarum peregrinationum in Montem Syon ad venerandum Christi Sepulchrum in Jerusalem, et in Montem Synai* (Mainz: Erhard Reuwich, 1486); BN: Cartes et Plans Rés. GeFF. 8304.

—— *Le saint voyage et pelerinage*, trans. Jean Hersin (Lyon, 1489); BL: C 20 e 10.

BROCARDUS OF MOUNT SION, *Descriptio Terrae Sanctae* (Antwerp: Joannes Steels, 1536); Bodleian: Mason N 21.

CALVIN, JEAN, *Advertissement tresutile du grand proffit qui reviendroit à la Chrestienté, s'il se faisoit inventoire de tous les corps sainctz, et reliques, qui sont tant en Italie, qu'en France, Allemagne, Hespagne, et autres Royaumes et Pays* [1543] ed. Higman, in *Three French Treatises* (London, 1970).

—— *A very profitable treatise on . . . reliques.* trans. S. Wythers (London: R. Hall, 1561); Bodleian: Douce C 381.

CARLIER DE PINON, *Relation du voyage en Orient* (Paris, 1920).

CARTIER, JACQUES, *Brief recit & succinte narration de la navigation faicte es ysles de Canada . . .* (Paris: Ponce Rosset dict Faucheur, 1545); BL: G 7082.

CASOLA, PIETRO, *Canon Pietro Casola's pilgrimage to Jerusalem in the year 1494*, trans. M. Newett (Manchester, 1907).

CASTELA, HENRI DE, *Le Sainct Voyage de Hierusalem et Mont Sinay* (Bordeaux: P. Arnaud du Brel, 1603); BL: 1570/2716.

—— Second edition (Paris: Sonnius, 1612); BL: 1051 c 4.

—— *La Guide et adresse pour ceux qui veulent faire le S. Voyage de Hierusalem* (Paris: Sonnius, 1604); BN: o2 f. 62.

CHASSIGNET, JEAN-BAPTISTE, *Le Mespris de la vie & consolation contre la mort* (Besançon, 1594); Besançon, Bibliothèque Municipale.

—— *Le Mespris de la vie et consolation contre la mort*, ed. H.-J. Lope (Geneva, 1967).

CHESNEAU, JEAN, *Le Voyage de Monsieur d'Aramon, ambassadeur pour le Roy en Levant, escript par noble homme Jean Chesneau*, ed. C. Schefer (Paris, 1887).

CHESNEAU, JEAN, *see also* Thevet, André (ed. Lestringant).

COLUMBUS, CHRISTOPHER, *Raccolta di Documenti e Studi*, ed. C. De Lollis (14 vols.; Rome, 1892–94).

—— *Journals and Other Documents on the Life and Voyages of Christopher Columbus*, trans. and ed. S. E. Morison (New York, 1963).

CORYATE, THOMAS, *Coryates Crudities . . . [with] Kirchnerus in praise of trauell* (London: W.S., 1611); Bodleian: Douce C 660.

CUCHERMOYS, JEHAN DE, *Le voyage de Hierusalem* [appended to *La tresjoyeuse . . . histoire . . . du chevalier Guerin—see* Barbarino, Andrea da] (Lyon: Romain Morin pour Olivier Arnoullet, 1530); Bodleian: Arch Bd 1. This is the edition to which I refer.

—— *Sensuyt aucun brief traicté du voyage de Hierusalem* (Paris: Alain Lotrain & Denis Janot, 1531); Maz: Rés. 11105 J.

—— Le sainct Voyage de Hierusalem . . . Reproduit par le procédé PLINSKI . . . pour la Société de l'Orient Latin et précédé d'une introduction par le Comte de Marsy (Geneva: Imprimerie Jules-Guillaume Finck, 1889); BN: Rés. Velins, 818.

DEGUILLEVILLE, GUILLAUME DE, *Le Pèlerinage de lhomme* [verse] (Paris, 1511); Bodleian: Douce G 285.

—— *Le Pèlerinage de la vie humaine tresutile et puffitable pour cognoistre soymesmes* [prose; trans. Jean Gallopes] (Lyon: Claude Nourry, 1504); Bodleian: Douce P 339.

DESCARTES, RENÉ, *Philosophical Writings of Descartes*, ed. J. Cottingham, R. Stoothoff, and D. Murdoch (2 vols.; Cambridge, 1985).

DU BELLAY, JOACHIM, *Les Regrets et autres oeuvres poëtiques* [1558], ed. J. Joliffe and M. Screech (Geneva, 1974).

DUBLIOUL, JEAN, *Le Voyage de Hierusalem et pelerinage des Saincts Lieux de la Palestine* (Besançon: Nicolas de Moingesse, 1602); Besançon, Bibliothèque municipale: 249,228.

—— *Hierosolymitanae peregrinationes hodoepicorum. septem dialogorum Libris explicatum* (Cologne: Gevenbruch, 1599); Bodleian: 8° D   15 Th.

DUFRESNE-CANAYE, PHILIPPE, *Le voyage de Levant* [1573], ed. H. Hauser (Paris, 1897); Bodleian: 203 h 304 (1).

EGERIA, *Journal de Voyage (Itinéraire)* ed. P. Maraval, SC 296 (Paris, 1982).

ERASMUS, DESIDERIUS, *Opera omnia* (Amsterdam, 1969–   ).

—— *The Collected Works of Erasmus* (Toronto, 1974–   ).

—— *The Colloquies of Erasmus*, trans. C. Thompson (Chicago and London, 1965).

—— *A dialoge intitled y pylgremage of pure deuotyn* (London: John Bydell?, 1540?); BL: C 53a 25.

—— *Von Walfart Erasmi Roterodami vermanung, wo Christus und sein reich zu suche[n] ist* [n.p., 1522]; BL: 3905 d 113.

—— *Adagiorum chiliades* (Basel: Froben, 1541); New: R C.

—— *Enchiridion militis Christi* (Louvain: T. Martini, 1515); Bodleian: Vet B1 e 18 (3).

ESTIENNE, CHARLES, *La Guide des chemins de France* (Paris: Charles Estienne, 1553); Bodleian: 8° Rawl 791.

—— ed. C. Bonnerot, *Bibliothèque de l'École des Hautes Études*, 265, 267 (2 vols.; Paris, 1936); Bodleian: C Acad 100.

—— *La Grande Guide des chemins pour aller et venir par tout le Royaume de France . . . Augmenté du voyage de S. Jacques, de Rome, de Venise et Hierusalem* (Troyes: Nicolas Oudot, 1623); Bodleian: 8° A 137 Linc.

FABRI, FELIX, *Evagatorium in Terrae Sanctae, Arabiae, et Egyptae peregrinationem*, ed. K. Hassler, BLVS ii–iv (Stuttgart, 1843–9).

—— *The Wanderings of Felix Fabri*, trans. A. Stewart, LPPTS 7–10 (2 vols.; London, 1892).

—— *Eigentliche Beschreibung der hin und wider Farth zu dem heylichen Landt gen Jerusalem* [facsimile of the original German edition, Ulm, 1556] ed. H. Roob (Heidelberg, 1967).

—— *Le Voyage en Egypte*, trans. J. Masson, SJ (Cairo, 1975).

FABRI, PIERRE, *Le Grand et vrai art de pleine réthorique* (Lyon: Pierre Sergent, 1534); Bodleian: Mason FF 55.

FEYRABEND, SIGMUND (ed.), *Reyssbuch des heyligen Landes das ist ein grundtliche beschreibung aller und jeder Meer un Bilgerfahrten zum heilgen Lande* (Frankfurt: Feyrabend, 1584); Bodleian: Caps 18.17.

FLACIUS ILLYRICUS [Matthias Francowicz], *Catalogus testium veritatis, qui ante nostram aetatem reclamarunt Papae* (Basel: per Ioanem Oporinum, 1560 [1556]) Bodleian: Douce P 843.

—— *Quarta Centuriae Ecclesiasticae historiae* (Basel: per Ioanem Oporinum, 1560); Bodleian: C II 4 Th.

GEILER, JOHANN, *Christliche Bilgerschaften zum ewigen Vatterland* (Strasbourg, 1512); BL: 3835 d 13.

GEORGIEWITZ, BARTHOLOMEUS [Dordevic] *Exhortatio contra Turcas* (Anvers, 1545) Bodleian: 8° G 78 (1) Art.

—— *La maniere & ceremonies des Turcs* (Antwerp: pour Gregoire Bonte par Gilles Copyns, [1544]); Bodleian: Mason FF 61.

—— *Les miseres et tribulations que les Chrestines tributaire et esclaves tenuz par le* [sic] *Turcz seuffrent* (Anvers, 1544) Bodleian: 8° G 78 (1) Art.

—— *Discours de la maniere de vivre des Turcs* [appended to *Le Voyage de la saincte Terre et cité de Hierusalem, et combien de lieux il y a, tant par mer que par terre*] (Liège: Leonard Streel pour Lambert de la Coste, 1600); Arsenal: 4° H 486.

—— *The Offspring of the house of Ottoman . . . whereunto is added Bartholomeus Georgieviz, of the customes, Rytes, Ceremonies, and Religion of the Turkes*, trans. H. Goughe (London: T. Marshe, 1570); Bodleian: Tanner 60 (6).

GEORGIEWITZ, *The Rarities of Turkey gathered by one that was sold a slave in the Turkish Empire* (London, 1661); Bodleian: Wood 156 (2).

—— *Opera nova che comprende quattro libretti* (Rome, 1555); Bodleian: 8° B 567 Linc.

GIRAUDET, GABRIEL, *Discours du voyage d'outremer au saint sepulcre de Hierusalem, et autres lieux de la terre Saincte . . . Par Gabriel Giraudet, marchant de la ville de nostre Dame du puy en Velay. Imprimé au despens de l'autheur* (Lyon: Michel Joue, et Jean Pillehote, [1575]); Maz: 35423 (2). This is the edition to which I refer.

—— *Discours du voyage d'outremer* (Toulouse: Arnauld & Jacques Colonnies, 1583) Maz: 33429.

—— *Discours du voyage . . . par Gabriel Giraudet prestre hierosolymitain où nous avons de nouveau adjousté a chacune station une histoire et une oraison propre* (Paris: chez Thomas Brumen, 1585); BN: O2 f 50. Note the change of occupation here, and the adaptation of the merchant's account, printed at his own expense, into a devotional text, for others' use.

GRANADA, LUIS DE, *Istruttione de' Peregrini, che vanno alla Madonna di Loreto . . . Ove si tratta anco della confessione e communione* (Macerata: apresso Sebastiano Martellini, 1575); Bodleian: 110 K 114 (5).

—— *The Sinner's Guyde. A worke contayning the whole regiment of a Christian life . . . perused and digested into English, by Francis Meres* (London: James Roberts for Paule Linley and John Flasket, 1598); Bodleian: Antiq e E 1598 1.

—— *Traité de la confession et communion*, trans. Jean Chabanet (Paris: Guillaume de la Noüe, 1580); Bodleian: 8° H 30 Th BS.

—— *Le Vray chemin et adresse pour acquerir et parvenir à la grace de Dieu . . . mis en Francois, selon l'ordre de l'Autheur, par F. de Belleforest* (second edn. Paris: chez Guillaume de la Noue, 1579); BL: 846 l 7.

GREGORY OF NYSSA, ST., *Opera omnia* (Paris: Sonnius, 1615); Bodleian: Caps. 15.14,15 [The second letter, with notes, is vol. 2, pp. 1084–7].

—— *Lettres*, ed. P. Maraval, SC 363 (Paris, 1990).

—— *de iis qui adeunt Hierosolyma opusculum* [Gr. & Lat.] (Paris: Morel, 1551); California State Library, Sacramento.

—— *de iis qui adeunt Hierosolyma* [Gr. & Lat.] (Paris, 1560) BL: 793 c 10 (2).

—— *de iis qui adeunt Jerosolyma. Juxta editionem Morellianam* [Gr. & Lat.] (Paris: Robert Estienne III, 1606); Bodleian: Byw N 77 (2).

—— *de euntibus Jerosolyma. Epistola, Latinè versa, et Notis illustrata à Petro Molineo* (n.p., 1605); Bodleian: Byw N 77 (3).

—— *de euntibus Jerosolyma epistola, latinè versa et notis illustrata a Petro Molineo, cum ejusdem tractatu de peregrinationibus et altero de alteribus et sacrificii christianorum. Accedunt indices* (Hanau: C Marnium et heredes J. Aubin, 1607); BN: C 2645 (1).

—— *Select Writings and Letters of Gregory of Nyssa* (Select Library of

Nicene and Post-Nicene Fathers, vol. 5), ed. H. Wace and P. Schaff (Oxford, 1893).

GRETSER, JACOB, *Opera omnia* (5 vols.; Ratisbonae, 1734); Bodleian: Caps. 20. 1–17.

—— *de sacris et religiosis peregrinationibus libri quatuor* (Ingolstadt, 1606); Bodleian: 4° G 14 Th.

—— *Notae in notis Petri Molinei Calvinistae super epistolam Nysseno adscriptam, de euntibus Hierosolymam* (Ingolstadt: Adam Sartorius, 1608); BN: D 5907.

—— *Examen Tractatus de peregrinationibus ab eodem Molineo editi* (Ingolstadt: Adam Sartorius, 1608); BL: 476a. 15.

GUERRERO, ANTONIO, *El viage de Hierusalem* (Exeter, 1984 [Seville: Juan de Leon, 1592]); Taylor: ASY 1391 A 1.

GUEVARA, ANTONIO, *Livre du Mont de Calvaire*, trans. F. de Belleforest (Paris: Le Fizelier, 1589 [1571]); BN: Rés. D. 37000.

HALIN, JEAN, *Brief dialogue d'un homme passant son chemin, et d'un honeste et scavant Prestre qui conduit des pelerins à Maestrecht, auquel est monstré le proffit des Pelerinages, et la maniere de bien les faire*: Appended to *La Vie de M. S. Servais* (Liège: C. Ouverx, 1623); BN: Rés. H. 1022.

HARFF, ARNOLD VON, *The Pilgrimage of Arnold von Harff, Knight*, ed. M. Letts (London, 1967).

HAULT, NICOLAS DE, *Le Voyage de Hierusalem* (Chaumont en Bassigny, et se vendent a Paris: Abraham Saugrin, 1601); Bodleian: Mason C 14.

HEIDEGGER, JOHANN, *Dissertatio de Peregrinationibus Religiosis . . . nec non Gregorii Nysseni Epistola Greco-Latina de iis qui adeunt Hierosolymam una cum ejusdem Apologia* (Trier: Schauffelberger, 1670); Bodleian: 8° E 75 Th. Part IV is the letter, followed by the apology, pp. 414–30.

HUEN, NICOLE, *Des sainctes peregrinations de Jherusalem* (Lyon: Michelet Topie & Jacques Herembeck, 1488); BL: G 7203.

—— *Le grant voyage de Jherusalem* (Paris: François Regnault, [1517]); BL: C 32. m. 13.

Itinéraires de la Terre Sainte, ed. E. Carmoly (Paris, 1847); Bodleian: 47.66. This volume collects and translates Hebrew pilgrimages from the thirteenth to the seventeenth century.

LA BORDERIE, BERTRAND DE, *Le Discours du voyage de Constantinoble, envoyé dudict lieu à une demoyselle Françoyse* (Lyon: Nicolas Bacquennois, 1547); BL: C.39.c.58.

LAMBECK, P., *Commentariorum de augustissima bibliotheca Caesarea Vindobonensi* (Vienna: Typis Matthei Cosmerovij, 1672), Bodleian: Douce L 502. Book V, pp. 81–8 deals with Gregory of Nyssa's letter.

LENGHERAND, GEORGES, *Voyage à Venise, Rome, Jérusalem, Mont Sinai, et le Kayre, 1485–6*, ed. Mqs. de Godefroy Menilglaise (Mons, 1861).

304   BIBLIOGRAPHY

LÉRY, JEAN DE, *Histoire d'un Voyage Fait en la Terre du Brésil, autrement dite Amerique* (La Rochelle: Antoine Chuppin, 1578); Bodleian: 576.c.29.

—— *Histoire d'un voyage*, ed. F. Lestringant (Paris, 1992).

—— *History of a Voyage to the Land of Brazil, otherwise called America*, trans. J. Whatley (Berkeley, Los Angeles, and Oxford, 1990).

LESAIGE, JACQUES, *Chy sensuyvent les gistes repaistres et despens: que moy Jacques le Saige marchant de drapz de soye demeurant a Douay ay faict . . . avec mon retour* (Cambray: Bonaventure Brassart au despens dudict Jacques, [1518?]); BL: G 6727. This is the edition I refer to; the modern edition is imperfect in several places.

—— *Voyage de Jacques le Saige de Douai à Rome, Notre-Dame de Lorette, Venise, Jerusalem, et autres lieux saints*, ed. H.-R. Duthilloeul (Douai, 1851); Bodleian: Mason KK 24.

LIPSIUS, JUSTUS, *Le choix des Epistres de Lipse traduites de Latin au Francois—* see Secondary Sources, Doiron, N.

LOARTE, GASPAR, *Opusculum de sacris peregrinationibus* (Cologne: Gualter, 1619); BN: D. 88285.

—— *Trattato delle Sante Peregrinationi* (Venice: Guerra, 1585); BN: D. 42296.

LOYOLA, IGNATIUS, ST, *Exercices Spirituels* (Lille: Pierre de Rache, 1614); BN: D. 42402.

KEMPE, MARGERY, *The Book of Margery Kempe*, trans. B. Windeatt (Harmondsworth, 1985).

MAIGNAN, ELOI, *Petit Discours de l'utilité des voyages ou pelerinages* (Paris: Charles Roger, 1578); Maz: 56464.

MANDEVILLE, JEAN, *Les Voyages* (Lyons: [Barth. Buyer], 1480); BL: G 6775.

—— *Les Voyages* (Paris: Jehan Bonfons, 1550?); BL: C 97 b 30 (1).

—— *Mandeville's Travels*, ed. M. Letts, Hakluyt Soc. series ii, vols. 101–2 (London, 1953).

[MARCOURT, ANTOINE,] *Le livre des marchans, fort utile à toutes gens, pour cognoistre de quelles marchandises on se doit garder destre trompé. Lequel a esté nouvellement reveu & fort augmente par sont [sic] premier autheur bien expert en tel affaire. Lisez et profittez* (n.p. [1541]); Bodleian: Douce C 356 (1) [under 'Livre'].

—— *The boke of marchauntes right necessarye unto all folkes. Newly made by the lorde Pantapole right expert in such busynesse nere neyhbour unto the lorde Pantagrule* [T. Godefray, 1534] (n.p.n.d.); Bodleian: Facs f 51 [under 'Livre'].

MONTAIGNE, MICHEL DE, *Oeuvres complètes*, ed. A. Thibaudet and M. Rat (Paris, 1962).

—— *Journal de Voyage*, ed. F. Rigolot (Paris, 1992).

MORE, THOMAS, *A dyalogue of the veneration and worshyp of ymages and relyques, praying to saints and goyng on pylgrymage* (London: M. Rastell, 1529); Bodleian: Douce M 739.

MÜNSTER, SEBASTIAN, *La Cosmographie Universelle*, trans. F. de Belleforest (Paris: Sonnius ou Chesneau, 1575) Bodleian: Douce B subt. 147–9.

—— *Cosmographia oder Beschreibung aller Länder des gantzen Erdbodens* (Basel, 1578); Bodleian: G 3 8 Art.

NAVARRE, MARGUERITE DE, *L'Heptaméron*, ed. S. Reyff (Paris, 1982).

NICOLAY, NICOLAS DE, *Les quatres premiers livres des Navigations et Peregrinations Orientales* (Lyon: G. Roville, 1568); BL: 455 e 5.

—— *Dans l'Empire de Soliman le Magnifique*, ed. M.-C. Gomez-Géraud (Paris, 1989).

ORTELIUS, ABRAHAM, *Theatre de l'Univers, contenant les cartes de Tout le monde* (Antwerp: Plantin, 1598); Bodleian: Vet B1 b 2.

PAESSCHEN, JAN VAN, *La Peregrination spirituelle vers la terre saincte* (Louvain: Nicolas de Leuze, 1566); Bodleian: Douce PP 245.

PALERNE, JEAN, *Peregrinations* (Lyon: Jean Pillehotte, 1606); Bodleian: Mason C 18.

PARÉ, AMBROISE, *Des Monstres, des prodiges, des voyages*, ed. P. Boussel (Paris, 1964).

PASCAL, *Oeuvres complètes*, ed. L. Lafuma (Paris, 1963).

PASQUIER, ESTIENNE, *Lettres* (Avignon: Jacques Bramereau, 1590); Taylor: Skipworth A 29.

Le pelerin veritable de la Terre Saincte auquel soubs le discours figuré de la Jerusalem antique et moderne est enseigné le chemin de la celeste (Paris: P. Louis Feburier, 1615); Bodleian: Douce T 258.

PETRARCH, FRANCESO, *Opera* (Basel: Henricus Petri, 1554); Bodleian: Douce P 23.

—— 'The Ascent of Mont Ventoux', trans. Nachod in, *The Renaissance Philosophy of Man*—see Secondary Sources ed. Cassirer and others, pp. 36–48.

—— *Epistolae Selectae*, ed. A. Johnson (Oxford, 1923).

PHILIP, *Liber de Terra Sancta* (1377), ed. J. Haupt, *Oesterreichische Vierteljahresschrift für katholische Theologie*, x (1871), pp. 511–40.

POSSOT, DENIS, *Tresample et habondante description du voyage de la Terre Saincte* (Paris: rue sainct Jacques a lenseigne de lhomme Saulvaige, 1536); BN: Rés. 02 f 41.

—— *Le Voyage de la Terre Sainte composé par Maitre Denis Possot et achevé par Messire Charles Philippe 1532*, ed. C. Schefer (Paris, 1890); Bodleian: 203 h 304 k (11).

POSTEL, GUILLAUME, *Description et charte de la Terre Saincte, qui est la propriété de Jesus Christ . . .* (Paris: Guillaume Guillard et Amaury Warencore, 1562) appended to a *Concordance des quatre evangelistes*); BL: 1016 a 8.

—— *De la République des Turcs* (Poitiers: Enguilbert de Marnef, 1560); Bodleian: 4° P 17 Art Seld.

PYRCKMAIR, HILARIUS, *Commentariolus de arte apodemica seu vera peregrinandi ratione* (Ingolstadt, 1577); BL: 10004 a 44.

RABELAIS, F., *Pantagruel*, ed. V.-L. Saulnier (Geneva, 1965).

—— *Gargantua*, ed. R. Calder and M. Screech (Geneva, 1970).

—— *Le Quart Livre*, ed. R. Marichal (Geneva, 1947).

REGNAUT, ANTOINE, *Discours du Voyage d'outremer au sainct sepulchre* (Paris: on les vend auz fauxbourgs Sainct Jacques a lenseigne de la croix de Hierusalem, 1573); Bodleian: 4° V 77 Th.

RICHEOME, LOUIS, *Deffence des Pelerinages contre le traducteur d'une lettre pretendue de St. Gregoire de Nisse sur les Pelerinages de Hierusalem. Avec ung discours des sainctes Reliques, et ung aultre des Richesses* (Paris: Sonnius, 1604); BL: 850 c 7 (1).

—— *Oeuvres* (Paris: Sonnius, 1628); Bodleian; P 11,12,13 Th.

—— *Tableaux sacrez* (Paris: Sonnius, 1601); BL: 4323 bb 48 (1).

—— *La Peinture spirituelle* (Lyon: Pierre Rigaud, 1611); Sorb: TTa 15, in–8°.

RICHER, CHRISTOPHE, *Des Coustumes et manières de vivre des Turcs* (Paris: Robert Estienne, 1540); BL: 1053 i 2.

ROGER, EUGENE, *La Terre saincte ou Terre de Promission* (Paris: Antoine Bertier, 1646); Bodleian: 4° L 82 Th.

SALIGNAC, BARTHELMY DE, *Itinerarium* (Magdeburg: Donatus impensis Kirchneri, 1587); Bodleian: 4° S 9 Art Seld. This includes Brocardus' *Descriptio* as a preface.

Sensuyt le chemin de Paris a Lyon, de lyon a Venise, et de Paris a Romme par lyon . . . Avec le chemin depuis Lyon jusques en hierusalem et combien il ya de lieues de ville en ville. Et avec ce sont toutes les eglises de Romme. Et mesmement les sept eglises principalles que doibvent visiter les pellerins qui y vont. Avec les grands indulgences et remissions quilz acquerent. Et aussi les stations qui se font durant la saincte quarantaine (Lyons, [1510]?); BL: C 107 a 14. [under 'Paris, Appendix-Topography, 1510?'. This edition has the book plate of Henri Cordier, editor of a number of these accounts, with its motto: 'Je flane, donc je suis.']

A Short History of the Order of the Holy Sepulchre of our Lord Jesus Christ, with an account of the English Community of that Order established at New Hall in Essex (London, 1848); BL: 1067/2626.

SURIANO, FRANCESCO, *Il Trattato di Terra Santa e dell'oriente*, ed. G. Golubovich (Milan, 1900).

Tableau de l'archiconfrérie royale du sainct-sépulchre de Jérusalem (Paris: Imprimerie de la veuve Valade, 1789); BL: F 832 (1).

TAFUR, PERO, *Travels and Adventures, 1435–1439*, trans. and ed. M. Letts (London, 1926); Bodleian: 2034 d 60.

TASSO, TORQUATO, *Discourses on the Heroic Poem*, trans. M. Cavalchini and I. Samuel (Oxford, 1973).

TERRAUBE, GUILLAUME DE, *Brief Discours des choses plus necessaires & dignes d'estre entendues en la Cosmographie, reveu & corrigé de nouveau* (Paris: Frederic Morel, 1569); BL: 700 c 2 (2).

THENAUD, JEAN, *Le voyage et itinaire* [sic] *de outre mer* (Paris: a lenseigne sainct Nicolas, s.d.); BN: Rés O2 f 988.

—— *Le Voyage d'Outremer . . . suivi de La Relation de l'Ambassade de Domenico Trevisan auprès du Soudan d'Egypte* [1512], ed. C. Schefer (Paris, 1884); Bodleian: 203 h 304 e.

THEVET, ANDRÉ, *Cosmographie de Levant* (Lyon: Jean de Tournes et Guillaume Gazeau, 1554); Bodleian: Douce T 226.

—— *Cosmographie de Levant* [CL], ed. F. Lestringant, THR 203 (Geneva, 1985); Bodleian: 20606 d 148. This is the edition I refer to.

—— *Singularitez de la France Antartique* [SFA] (Paris: chez les héritiers de Maurice de la Porte, 1557); BL: 797 L 1.

—— *La Cosmographie Universelle d'André Thevet, Cosmographe du Roy. Illustrée de divers figures des choses remarquables veües par l'Autheur, et incogneuës de noz Anciens & Modernes* [CU] (2 vols.; Paris: Pierre L'Huilier, 1575); Bodleian: Douce T subt 40,41.

—— *Les Vrais Pourtraicts et Vies des Hommes Illustres Grecz, Latins, et Payens* (2 vols.; Paris: la Veusve J. Kermert & Guillaume Chaullir, 1584); BL: 134 f 13.

—— and Chesneau, Jean, *Voyages en Egypte, 1549–1552*, ed. F. Lestringant (Cairo: IFAO, 1984).

TURLER, JEROME, *De peregrinatione, et agro neapolitano* (Strasbourg, per Bernhardum Iobinum, 1574); Bodleian: 8° M 37 (2) Art.

—— *The Traueiler of Jerome Turler* [trans. 1575] ed. D. Baughan (Gainesville, Fla., 1951); Bodleian: 2004 e 159.

VILLAMONT, JACQUES DE, *Les Voyages du seigneur de Villamont, Chevalier de l'Ordre de Hierusalem, Gentilhomme ordinaire de la chambre du Roy . . . derniere edition* (Lyon: Claude Larjot, 1611 [1588]); Bodleian: 8° Rawl 918.

VILLETTE, CLAUDE, *La description des lieux de la Terre Saincte, où nostre Sauveur Jesus Christ a cheminé: et les jours des annees de ses oeuvres en ladite terre Saincte* (Paris: Fleury Bourriquant, 1608); BN: O2 f 63.

VOISINS, PHILIPPE DE, *Voyage à Jérusalem de Philippe de Voisins, Seigneur de Montaut*, ed. P. Tamizey de Larroque (Paris and Auch, 1883); Maz: 43043 (3).

Le Voyage de la saincte cite de hierusalem. Avec la description des lieux portz villes citez et autres passages, faict lan mil quatre cens quatre vingtz estant le siege du grand Turc a Rhodes et regnant en France Louis unzieme de ce nom (Paris: Nicholas Chrestien, n.d.); Arsenal: Rés. H 1201.

Le Voyage de la saincte cite de Hierusalem (Paris; Pierre Sergent, n.d.); BL: Jerusalem 6895.

Le Voyage de la Saincte Cyté de Hierusalem, fait l'an 1480, ed. C. Schefer (Paris, 1882); Bodleian: 203 h 304 2.

Voyages en Egypte des années 1589, 1590, et 1591: Le Vénitien anonyme; Le Seigneur de Villamont; Le Hollandais Jan Sommer, trans. and ed. C. Burri, S. Sauneron, P. Bleser (Cairo. IFAO, 1971).

WALTHER, PAUL, *Itinerarium in terram sanctam*, ed. M. Sollweck, BLVS, 192 (Tübingen, 1892).

WAZZAN EZ-ZAYYATI [Leo Africanus], *Historiale Description de l'Afrique* (Lyon: Jean Temporal, 1556); Bodleian: Mason V 157.

WEY, WILLIAM, *The Itineraries*, ed. B. Bandinel (London, 1857).

Woodcuts of Palestine [*c.*1500]; Bodleian: Douce Prints F. L. [under Palestine].

ZUALLART, GIOVANNI, *Il devotissimo viaggio di Gerusalemme* (Rome, 1587); Bodleian: Antiq. E 1 1587 4.

—— *Le Tresdevot voyage de Jerusalem* (Antwerp, 1608) Bodleian: D 20 8 (1) Linc.

ZWINGER, THEODORE, *Methodus apodemika in eorum gratiam, qui cum fructu in quocumque tandem vitae genere peregrinari cupiunt* (Basel: Eusebius Episopius, 1577); Bodleian: BB 103 (1) Art.

SECONDARY WORKS

Works of Reference

ALTENBURGER, M., and MANN, F., *Bibliographie zu Gregor von Nyssa* (Leiden, 1988).

ATKINSON, G., *La littérature géographique de la Renaissance: Répertoire bibliographique* (Paris, 1927).

—— *Supplément* (Paris, 1936).

BRUNET, J.-C., *Manuel du libraire et de l'amateur de livres* (6 vols. plus supplement; Paris, 1860–78).

COTGRAVE, R., *A Dictionarie of the French and English Tongues*, facsimile of the first edition (1611) (Columbia, 1968).

COX, E. G., *Reference Guide to the Literature of Travel*, University of Washington Publications in Language and Literature, vols. 9, 10, 12 (Seattle, 1935–49) This lists primarily texts printed in England.

DAGENS, J., *Bibliographie chronologique de la littérature de spiritualité et de ses sources (1501–1610)* (Paris, 1952).

DRAUD, G., *Bibliotheca exotica* . . . (Frankfurt, 1610).

—— second edition of the above (Frankfurt, 1625).

—— *Bibliotheca classica* . . . (Frankfurt, 1625).

GAZIER, G. (ed.), *Inventaire sommaire des archives communales antérieures à 1790. Série BB* (Administration communale) vol. 2, 1576–1676 (Besançon, 1931).

GOLUBOVICH, G., OFM., *Bibliotheca Bio-bibliografica della Terra Santa* (11 vols.; Florence, 1906–27).

HUGUET, É., *Dictionnaire de la langue française du seizième siècle* (7 vols.; Paris, 1925–67).

LA CROIX DU MAINE, F. G., and DU VERDIER, A., *Les Bibliothèques françoises*, new edition, ed. R. de Juvigny (6 vols.; 1772–3 [1584 and 1585]).

NICOT, J., *Thresor de la langue françoise, tant ancienne que moderne*, facsimile of the 1621 edn. (Paris, 1960) 1st edn. 1606.

Oxford Latin Dictionary (2 vols.; Oxford, 1968).

PRINET, E., BERLAND, P., and GAZIER, G. (ed.), *Inventaire sommaire des archives communales antérieures à 1790, Série BB* (Administration communale) vol. 1, 1290–1576 (Besançon, 1912).

RENOUARD, P., *Répertoire des imprimeurs parisiens* (Paris, 1965).

ROBERT, U., *Inventaire des testaments de l'Officialité de Besançon* (Besançon, 1891).

RÖHRICHT, R., *Bibliotheca Geographica Palestinae: Chronologisches Verzeichnis der von 333 bis 1878 verfassten Literatur über das Heilige Land* ... [Berlin, 1890] rev. D. H. K. Amiran (Jerusalem, 1963).

—— and MEISNER, H., *Deutsche Pilgerreisen nach dem heiligen Lande* (Berlin, 1880).

SCHUR, N., *Jerusalem in Pilgrims' and Travellers' Account: A Thematic Bibliography of Western Christian Itineraries, 1300–1917* (Jerusalem, 1980).

SOMMERVOGEL, C. (ed.), *Bibliothèque de la Compagnie de Jésus* (9 vols.; Brussels and Paris, 1890–1909).

General

ALLEN, D. C., *The Legend of Noah: Renaissance Rationalism in Science, Arts and Letters* (Illinois, 1963).

ALPHANDÉRY, P., *La Chrétienté et l'idée de croisade* (2 vols.; Paris, 1954).

ANDERSON, B., *Imagined Communities* (London and New York, 1991).

ARIES, P., *L'Homme devant la mort* (Paris, 1977).

ATKINSON, G., *Les Nouveaux horizons de la Renaissance française* (Paris, 1935).

AUERBACH, E., *Mimesis: The Representation of Reality in Western Literature*, trans. W. Trask (Princeton, 1974 [1946]).

BAKHTIN, M., *Rabelais and his World*, trans. H. Iswolsky (Cambridge, Mass., and London, 1968).

BALAGNA COUSTOU, J., *Arabe et humanisme dans la France des derniers Valois* (Paris, 1989).

BALMAS, E. (ed.), *Montaigne e l'Italia, Atti del Congresso internazionale di Studi, Milano-Lecco, 26–30 ottobre 1988* (Geneva, 1991).

BARTHES, R., *S/Z* (Paris, 1970).

—— *Sade, Fourier, Loyola* (Paris, 1971).

—— *Fragments d'un discours amoureux* (Paris, 1977).

—— *La Chambre claire* (Paris, 1980)

BATES, E., *Touring in 1600: A Study in the Development of Travel as a Means of Education* (London, 1987 [1911]).

BAUDELAIRE, C., *Les Fleurs du Mal*, ed. A. Adam (Paris, 1961).

BAXANDALL, M., *Painting and Experience in Fifteenth Century Italy* (Oxford, 1972).

—— *Giotto and the Orators: Humanist Observers of Painting in Italy and the Discovery of Pictorial Composition, 1350–1450* (Oxford, 1971).

BELLENGER, Y., *Jacques Lesaige: Voyage en Terre Sainte d'un marchand de Douai en 1519* (Paris, 1989).

—— 'Quelques relations de voyage vers l'Italie et vers l'Orient au XVIe siècle', in *Voyager à la Renaissance*, ed. Céard and Margolin, q.v., pp. 453–65.

BÉNÉ, C., *Erasme et Saint Augustin* (Geneva, 1969).

—— 'Humanistes, et pèlerinages au XVIe siècle: Montaigne à Lorette', in *Montaigne e l'Italia*, ed. Balmas q.v., pp. 597–607.

BENJAMIN, W., *Illuminationen* (Frankfurt am Main, 1977).

BENNASSAR, B. and L., *Les Chrétiens d'Allah: l'histoire extraordinaire des renégats, XVIe et XVIIe siècles* (Paris, 1989).

BENVENISTE, E., *Problèmes de linguistique générale* (2 vols.; Paris, 1968 (I), 1974 (II)).

BERNARD, Y., *L'Orient du XVIe siècle à travers les récits des voyageurs français: Regards portés sur la société musulmane* (Paris, 1988).

BERTHOUD, G., *Antoine Marcourt, réformateur et pamphlétaire du Livre des Marchans aux placards de 1534* (Geneva, 1973).

BEUGNOT, B. (ed.), *Voyages, récits et imaginaires* (Paris, Seattle, Tübingen, 1984).

BIDEAUX, M., 'L'honnesté des autres: Voyageurs du XVIème siècle', in *La Catégorie de l'honneste dans la culture du XVIe siècle, Actes du Colloque International de Sommières II (Sept. 1983)* (Sainte-Etienne, 1985), pp. 79–100.

BIERLAIRE, F., *Erasme et ses colloques: Le livre d'une vie* (Geneva, 1977).

BILLANOVICH, G., 'Petrarca e il Ventoso', *Italia Mediovale e Umanistica*, 9 (1966), pp. 369–401.

BLUMENBERG, H., *The Legitimacy of the Modern Age* (Cambridge, Mass., and London, 1983).

—— 'Augustins Anteil an der Geschichte des Begriffs der theoretischen Neugierde', *Revue des Etudes Augustiniennes*, 7 (1961).

BÖHME, M., *Die Grossen Reisesammlungen des 16 Jahrhunderts und Ihre Bedeutung* (Dresden, 1962).

BOWEN, B. (ed.), *The French Renaissance Mind: Studies Presented to W. G. Moore, EC*, xvi (1976).

BOUWSMA, W., *Concordia mundi. The Career and Thought of Guillaume Postel, 1510–1581* (Cambridge, Mass., 1957).

BRAUDEL, F., *La Méditerranée et le monde méditerranéen à l'époque de Philippe II* (Paris, 1949).

BREEN, Q., 'The Terms "loci communes" and "loci" in Melanchthon', *Church History*, xvi (1947), pp. 197–209.

BREMOND, H., *Histoire littéraire du sentiment religieux en France depuis la fin des guerres de religion jusqu'à nos jours*, I, L'Humanisme dévot (1580–1660) (Paris, 1916).

BROC, N., *La Géographie de la Renaissance* (1490–1620) (Paris, 1980).

BROWN, P., *Augustine of Hippo* (Berkeley and Los Angeles, 1976).

—— *The Cult of the Saints: Its Rise and Function in Latin Christianity* (London, 1983 [Chicago, 1981]).

—— *The Body and Society: Men, Women and Sexual Renunciation in Early Christianity* (London, 1989).

BUISSERET, D. (ed.), *Monarchs, Ministers and Maps: The Emergence of Cartography as a Tool of Government in Early Modern Europe* (Chicago and London, 1992).

BURCKHARDT, J., *The Civilisation of the Renaissance in Italy* (London, 1944 [1860], trans. Middlemore [1878]).

BURKE, P., *The Renaissance Sense of the Past* (London, 1969).

CANART, P., 'Recentissimus non deterrimus. Le texte de la lettre II de Grégoire de Nysse dans la copie d'Alvise Lollino (cod Vaticanus gr 1759)', in *Zetesis: Album Amicorum door Vrienden en collega's angeboden aan Prof. Dr. E. Stryker* (Antwerp, 1973), pp. 717–31.

CAMERON, A., *Christianity and the Rhetoric of Empire: The Development of Christian Discourse* (Berkeley and London, 1991).

CAMERON, E., *The European Reformation* (Oxford, 1991).

CAMPBELL, M. B., *The Witness and the Other World: Exotic European Travel Writing, 400–1600* (Ithaca, NY, 1988).

CARILE, P., *Lo Sguardo impedito. Studi dulle relazione di viaggio in 'Nouvelle France' e sulle letteratura popolare* (Bari, 1987).

CASSIRER, E., KRISTELLER, P. O., and RANDALL, J. H. (ed.), *The Renaissance Philosophy of Man* (Chicago, 1948).

CASTAN, A., 'La Rivalité des familles de Rye et de Granvelle', in *Doubs*, 6e série, 6e volume (Besançon, 1892), pp. 1–130.

CAVE, T. C., *Devotional Poetry in France c.1570–1613* (Cambridge, 1969).

—— *The Cornucopian Text: Problems of Writing in the French Renaissance* (Oxford, 1979).

—— *Recognitions: A Study in Poetics* (Oxford, 1990 [1988]).

—— '*Enargeia*: Erasmus and the Rhetoric of Presence in the Sixteenth Century', in *The French Renaissance Mind*, ed. Bowen, q.v. pp. 5–19.

—— 'Travelers and Others: Cultural Connections in the Works of Rabelais', in *François Rabelais: Critical Assessments*, ed. J.-C. Carron (Baltimore and London, 1995), pp. 39–56.

—— 'Le récit montaignien: un voyage sans repentir', in *Montaigne: Espace, Voyage, Écriture*, ed. Z. Samaras (Paris, 1995), pp. 125–35

CÉARD, J. (ed.), *La Curiosité à la Renaissance* (Paris, 1986).

—— with MARGOLIN, J.-C. (ed.), *Voyager à la Renaissance, Actes du Colloque de Tours* (Paris, 1987).

CERTEAU, M., *L'Invention du quotidien: 1. Arts de faire* (Paris, 1990 [1980]).

—— *L'Écriture de l'histoire* (Paris, 1975).

CHARRIÈRE, E., *Négociations de la France dans le Levant* (Paris, 1848).

CHELINI, J., and BRANTHOMME, H. (ed.), *Les Chemins de Dieu: Histoire des pèlerinages chrétiens des origines à nos jours* (Paris, 1982).

—— *Histoires des pèlerinages non chrétiens: Entre magique et sacré: le chemin des dieux* (Paris, 1987).

CHINARD, G., *L'Exotisme américain dans la littérature française au XVIe siècle d'après Rabelais, Ronsard, Montaigne* (Paris, 1911).

CHRISTENSEN, S., 'The Image of Europe in Anglo-German Trave Literature', in *Voyager à la Renaissance*, ed. Céard and Margolin, q.v., pp. 257–80.

CHUPEAU, J., 'Les récits de voyages aux lisières du roman', *Revue d'histoire littéraire de la France*, 77, Mai-Août (1977), pp. 536–53.

COHEN, W. B., *The French Encounter with Africans: White Responses to Blacks, 1530–1880* (Bloomington and London, 1980).

COLIE, R., *The Resources of Kind: Genre-theory in the Renaissance*, ed. B. Lewalski (Berkeley and London, 1964).

COMPAGNON, A., *Nous, Michel de Montaigne* (Paris, 1980).

—— *Chat en poche: Montaigne et l'allégorie* (Paris, 1993).

CONSTABLE, G., 'Opposition to Pilgrimage in the Middle Ages', *Studia Gratiana*, 19 (1976), pp. 123–46.

—— 'Monachisme et pèlerinage au Moyen Age', *Revue Historique* 258 (1977), pp. 3–27.

COURCELLE, P., 'Petrarque entre Saint Augustin et les Augustins du XVIe siècle', *Studi Petrarcheschi*, 7 (1954), pp. 45–62.

—— *Les 'Confessions' de Saint Augustin dans la tradition littéraire, antécédents et postérité* (Paris, 1963).

CURTIUS, E. R., *European Literature and the Latin Middle Ages*, trans. W. Trask (London, 1979).

DAHLBERG, C., *The Literature of Unlikeness* (London, 1988).

DAINVILLE, F. DE, *La Géographie des Humanistes* (Paris, 1940).

DAVIES, H. W., *Bernhard von Breydenbach and his Journey to the Holy Land, 1483–4: A Bibliography* (London, 1911).

DAVIES, J. G., 'Pilgrimage and Crusade Literature', in *Journeys Toward God*, ed. Sargent-Baur, q.v., pp. 1–30.

DAVIS, N. Z., *Society and Culture in Early Modern France* (Cambridge, 1987).

—— 'Some Tasks and Themes in the Study of Popular Religion', in *The Pursuit of Holiness in Late Medieval and Renaissance Religion*, ed. C. Trinkaus and H. Oberman (Leiden, 1974), pp. 307–36.

—— 'Boundaries and the Sense of Self in Sixteenth Century France', in *Reconstructing Individualism*, ed. Heller, Sosna, Wellerby q.v., pp. 53–63.

DEFAUX, G., *Le Curieux, le glorieux et la sagesse du monde dans la première moitié du XVIe siècle* (Lexington, Kentucky, 1982).

DELANO-SMITH, C., and MORLEY INGRAM, E., *Maps in Bibles, 1500–1600, an Illustrated Catalogue* (Geneva, 1991).

DELÈGUE, Y., *Le Royaume d'exil: le sujet de la littérature en quête d'auteur* (Paris, 1991).

DELUMEAU, J., *La Civilisation de la Renaissance* (Paris, 1967).

—— *La Peur en Occident* (Paris, 1978).

DERRIDA, J., *De la Grammatologie* (Paris, 1967).

—— *La Carte postale de Socrate à Freud et au-delà* (Paris, 1980).

DESAN, P. (ed.), *Humanism in Crisis: The Decline of the French Renaissance* (Ann Arbor, 1991).

DIÉGUEZ, M. DE, 'Un aspect de la thélogie de Rabelais: le chapitre 38 du *Gargantua*', *ER* 21, ed. J. Céard and J.-C. Margolin (Geneva, 1988), pp. 347–53.

'The Discourse of Travel', *EC*, 25, 3 (1985).

DOIRON, N., *L'Art de voyager: le déplacement à l'époque classique* (Paris, 1995).

—— 'L'Art de voyager', *Poétique*, 73 (1988), pp. 83–108.

DUPRONT, A., 'Éspace et Humanisme' in *BHR*, 8 (1946), pp. 7–104.

—— 'Pèlerinages et lieux sacrés' in *Mélanges F. Braudel* (Toulouse, 1973) II, pp. 63–82.

—— *Du Sacré: croisades et pèlerinages, images et langages* (Paris, 1977).

DURLING, R., 'The Ascent of Mt. Ventoux and the Crisis of Allegory', *Italian Quarterly*, 18 (1974), pp. 7–28.

EADE J. and SALLNOW, M. (ed.), *Contesting the Sacred: The Anthropology of Christian Pilgrimage* (London, 1991).

ELIADE, M., *Patterns in Comparative Religion* (New York, 1958).

—— *The Sacred and the Prophane* (New York, 1959).

FEBVRE, L., *Le Problème de l'incroyance au XVIe siècle: La religion de Rabelais* (Paris, 1942).

—— *Philippe II et la Franche-comté* (Paris, 1911).

—— and MARTIN, H.-J., *L'Apparition du livre* (Paris, 1970 [1958]).

FEILKE, H., *Felix Fabris Evagatorium über seine Reise in das heilige Land: Eine Untersuchung über die Pilgerliteratur des ausgehenden Mittelalters (Europäische Hochschulschriften, 155)* (Frankfurt am Main, 1976).

FELMAN, S., *Jacques Lacan and the Adventure of Insight: Psychoanalysis in Contemporary Culture* (Cambridge, Mass., 1987).

FINEMAN, J., 'Fiction and Fiction: The History of the Anecdote', in *The New Historicism*, ed. Veeser, q.v., pp. 49–76.

FINUCANE, R. C., *Miracles and Pilgrims: Popular Beliefs in Medieval England* (London, 1977).

FORDHAM, H. G., *The Earliest French Itineraries 1552 and 1591 Charles Estienne and Théodore de Mayerne-Turquet* (London, 1921).

FOUCAULT, M., *Les Mots et les choses* (Paris, 1966).

—— *L'Ordre du discours* (Paris, 1971).

—— *L'Histoire de la sexualité* (3 vols.; Paris, 1976–84).

—— 'What is an Author', in *Modern Criticism and Theory: A Reader*, ed. Lodge, q.v., pp. 197–210.

FOWLER, A., *Kinds of Literature: An Introduction to the Theory of Genres and Modes* (Oxford, 1982).

FRANKLIN, W., *Discoverers, Explorers, Settlers: The Diligent Writers of Early America* (Chicago and London, 1979).

FRECCERO, J., 'Autobiography and Narrative', in *Reconstructing Individualism*, ed. Heller, Sosna, and Wellerby, q.v., pp. 67 ff.

FRENCH, D. R., 'Journeys to the Center of the Earth: Medieval and Renaissance Pilgrimages to Mount Calvary', in *Journeys Toward God*, ed. Sargent-Baur, q.v., pp. 45–82.

FREUD, S., *Art and Literature*, The Pelican Freud Library, 14 (Harmondsworth, 1985).

FRYE, N., *The Anatomy of Criticism* (Princeton, 1957).

—— *The Secular Scripture* (Cambridge, 1976).

FUMAROLI, M., *L'Age de l'éloquence* (Geneva, 1980).

GARAVINI, F., 'Montaigne rencontre Theodor Zwinger à Bâle: Deux esprits parents', *Montaigne Studies* v (1993), 1–2, pp. 191–205.

GAZIER, G., 'Le pèlerinage d'un bisontin en Egypte et en Terre Sainte en 1584', *Doubs*, Xe série, 2e volume (Besançon, 1932), pp. 35–64.

GODIN, A., "Érasme: 'pia/impia curiositas"', in *La Curiosité à la Renaissance*, ed. Céard, q.v., pp. 25–36.

GOMEZ-GÉRAUD, M.-C., 'Le procès d'une relation coupable. De quelques interprétations des récits de Jacques Cartier', *Études Françaises*, 22, 2 (1986), pp. 63–72.

—— 'Contempler Jerusalem: L'espace optique du récit de pèlerinage', *Littérales*, 3 (1987), pp. 55–67.

—— 'Un colloque chez les Toupinambouts ou du bon usage du modèle', *Littrérales*, 5 (1989), pp. 97–111.

—— 'La belle infidèle aux Amériques: La vocation de Dona Marina interprète de Cortés', *EC* 30, 3 (1990), pp. 5–14.

—— 'Récit de pèlerinage et modèle: le cas de Frère Pantaliao d'Aveyro', *Littérales*, 7 (1990), pp. 71–83.

—— 'La mer: un espace hors-la-loi? La représentation de l'espace marin dans quelques récits de voyage français et espagnols au XVIe siècle', *Révue de Littérature comparée*, 2 (1990), pp. 385–407.

—— 'L'empire turc au XVIe siècle ou l'empire des apparences: regards des voyageurs français et flamands', in *Miroirs de l'altérité et Voyages au Proche Orient* (Geneva, 1991), pp. 73–82.

—— 'Écrire l'histoire des Lieux saints à l'heure de la Contre-Réforme', in *Regards sur le passé dans l'Europe des XVIe-XVIIe siècles. Actes du Colloque tenu à Nancy (décembre 1995), organisé par le groupe de Recherche 'XVIe et XVIIe siècles en Europe' de l'Université de Nancy II* (Berne, 1997), pp. 197–206.

GREENBLATT, S., *Renaissance Self-Fashioning: From More to Shakespeare* (Chicago and London, 1984 [1980]).

—— *Marvelous Possessions: The Wonder of the New World* (Oxford, 1991).

GREENE, T., *The Light in Troy: Imitation and Discovery in Renaissance Poetry* (New Haven and London, 1982).

HALKIN, L. E., 'Érasme Pèlerin', in *Scrinium Erasmianum II* (Leiden, 1969), pp. 245 ff.

—— 'Le thème du pèlerinage dans les Colloques d'Érasme', in *Actes du Congrès Érasme* (Amsterdam, 1971), pp. 88–98.

HAMPTON, T., *Writing from History: The Rhetoric of Exemplarity in Renaissance Literature* (Ithaca, NY, 1990).

—— ' "Turkish dogs": Rabelais, Erasmus and the Rhetoric of Alterity', *Representations* 41 (Winter 1993), pp. 58–82.

HARBSMEIER, M., 'Elementary Structures of Otherness: An Analysis of Sixteenth-Century German Travel Accounts', in *Voyager à la Renaissance*, ed. Céard and Margolin, q.v., pp. 337–56.

HAWICKHORST, H., 'Über die Geographie bei Andrea de' Magnabotti', *Romanische Forschungen*, 13 (1901), pp. 689–784.

HEATH, M., *Crusading Commonplaces: La Noue, Lucinge and Rhetoric against the Turks* (Geneva, 1986).

HEFFENING, W., *Die Türkischen Transkriptionstexte des Bartolomeus Giorgiewitz aus den Jahren, 1544–1548. Ein Beitrag zur historischen Grammatik des Osmanischen-Turkischen* (Leipzig, 1942).

HELLER, T. C., SOSNA, M., and WELLERBY, D. (ed.), *Reconstructing Individualism: Autonomy, Individuality, and the Self in Western Thought* (Stanford, Calif. 1986).

HEYD, U., *Ottoman Documents on Palestine, 1552–1615* (Oxford, 1960).

HOGDEN, M. T., *Early Anthropology in the Sixteenth and Seventeenth Century* (Philadelphia, 1964).

HOWARD, D. R., *Writers and Pilgrims: Medieval Pilgrimage Narratives and their Posterity* (Berkeley, Los Angeles and London, 1980).

HUNT, E. D., *Holy Land Pilgrimage in the Later Roman Empire AD 312–460* (Oxford, 1984).

HUON, A., 'Alexandrie et l'alexandrisme dans le *Quart Livre*: l'escale à Medamothi', *ER*, 1 (Geneva, 1956) pp. 98–111.

HUSCHENBETT, D., 'Die Literatur der deutschen Pilgerreisen nach Jerusalem im späten Mittelalter', in *Deutsche Vierteljahrsschrift für Literaturwissenschaft und Geistesgeschichte*, 59 (1985), pp. 29–46.

HUTSON, L., *The Usurer's Daughter: Male Friendship and Fictions of Women in Sixteenth-Century England* (London, 1994).

HUXLEY, F., 'Psychoanalysis and anthropology', in *Freud and the Humanities* ed. P. Hordern (London, 1985), pp. 130–51.

JACOB, C. and LESTRINGANT, F. (ed.), *Arts et Légendes d'Espaces: Figures du voyage et rhétoriques du monde* (Paris, 1981).

JAMESON, F., *The Political Unconscious: Narrative as a Socially Symbolic Act* (London, 1986 [1981]).

—— 'Cognitive Mapping', in *Marxism and the Interpretation of Culture*, ed. C. Nelson and L. Grossberg (Urbana and Chicago, 1988).

JARDINE, L., *Erasmus, Man of Letters: The Construction of Charisma in Print* (Princeton, 1993).

JEANNERET, M., *Des Mets et des mots* (Paris, 1987).

JEFFERSON, A., 'Realism reconsidered: Bakhtin's dialogism and the "will to reference" ', *AJFS*, 2 (1986), pp. 169–84.

—— 'Roland Barthes: Photography and the Other of Writing', *JIRS*, i (1992), pp. 293–309.

KAHN, V., *Rhetoric, Prudence and Scepticism in the Renaissance* (Ithaca, NY, 1985).

KENNY, N., ' "Curiosité" and philosophical poetry in the French Renaissance', *Renaissance Studies*, 5, 3 (1991), pp. 263–76.

—— *The Palace of Secrets: Béroalde de Verville and Renaissance Conceptions of Knowledge* (Oxford, 1991).

KÖHLER, W., *Das Marburger Religionsgespräch 1529: Versuch einer Rekonstruktion* (Leipzig, 1929).

KOLODNY, A., *The Lay of the Land: Metaphor as Experience and History in American Life and Letters* (Chapel Hill, 1975).

KÖTTING, B., *Peregrinatio Religiosa: Wallfahrten in der Antike und das Pilgerreisen in der alten Kirche* (Münster, 1950).

—— 'Gregor von Nyssas Wallfahrtskritik', *Studia Patristica*, 5 (1959), pp. 360–7.

KORINMANN, M., 'Simon Grynaeus et le "Novus Orbis": Les pouvoirs d'une collection', in *Voyager à la Renaissance*, ed., Céard, q.v., pp. 419–32.

KRISTELLER, P., 'Augustine and the Early Renaissance', in *Review of Religion*, (1944), pp. 57–78.

KRISTEVA, J., *Folle Vérité: vérité et vraisemblance du texte psychotique* (Paris, 1979).

—— *The Kristeva Reader*, ed. T. Moi (Oxford, 1986).

LA CHARITÉ, R. (ed.), *Rabelais's Incomparable Book: Essays on His Art* (Lexington, 1986).

LADNER, G. B., '*Homo Viator*: Medieval Ideas of Alienation and Order', *Speculum*, 42 (1967), pp. 233–59.

LANE FOX, R., *Pagans and Christians* (London, 1988 [1986]).

LEAKE, R., 'Jean-Baptiste Chassignet and Montaigne', *BHR*, 23 (1961), pp. 282–95.

LECLERQ, H., 'Mönchtum and peregrinatio im Frühmittelalter,' *Römische Quartelschrift für christliche Altertumskunde and Kirchengeschichte*, 55 (1960) pp. 212–25.

—— 'Monachisme et pérégrination du IXe au XIIe siècle', *Studia Monastica*, 3 (1961), pp. 33–52.

LEFRANC, A., *Les Navigations de Pantagruel* (Paris, 1905).

LE MOINE, R., *L'Amérique et les poètes français de la Renaissance* (Ottawa, 1972).

LEPSZY, H. J., *Die Reiseberichte des Mittelalters und der Reformationszeit* (Hamburg, 1952).

LESTRINGANT, F., *André Thevet: Cosmographe des derniers Valois* (Geneva, 1991).

—— *L'Atelier du Cosmographe* (Paris, 1991).

—— *Le Huguenot et le Sauvage* (Paris, 1990).

—— 'The Crisis of Cosmography at the End of the Renaissance', in *Humanism in Crisis*, ed. Desan, q.v., pp. 153–80.

—— 'Catholiques et Cannibales: le theme du cannibalisme dans le discours protestant au temps des guerres de religion', in *Pratiques et discours alimentaires à la Renaissance* (Paris, 1982), pp. 233–45.

—— 'Le declin d'un savoir: La crise de la cosmographie à la fin de la Renaissance', *Annales*, 2, mars–avril (1991), pp. 25–41.

—— 'Récit de quête/ récit d'éxil: Le retour de la terre promise (XVIe siècle), *RSH* 54, 214, avril–juin (1989), pp. 25–41'.

—— 'La flèche du patagon ou la preuve des lointains: sur un chapitre d'André Thevet', in *Voyager à la Renaissance*, q.v., pp. 467–96.

—— 'Calvinistes et Cannibales. Les écrits protestants sur le Brésil français (1555–1560)', *BSHPF*, 126, mars–juin (1980), pp. 9–26.

—— 'Le Nom des "Cannibales", de Christophe Colomb à Michel de Montaigne', *BSAM*, 6e série. 17–18, janvier–juin (1984), pp. 51–74.

—— 'Tristes Tropistes: du Brésil à la France, une controverse à l'aube des guerres de religion', *Revue de l'histoire des religions*, fasc. 3, juillet–septembre (1985), pp. 267–94.

—— 'Dans la bouche des géants (*Pantagruel*, 32; *Gargantua*, 38), *Cahiers Textuels* 34/35 (1989), 4–5, pp. 43–52.

LÉVI-STRAUSS, C., *Tristes Tropiques* (Paris, 1955).

—— *La Pensée sauvage* (Paris, 1962).

—— *Le Regard éloigné* (Paris, 1983).

LEYSER, C., 'Lectio divina, oratio pura: Rhetoric and the techniques of asceticism in the "Conferences" of John Cassian', in G. Barone (ed.), *Modelli di santità e modelli di comportamento* (Turin, 1994), pp. 29–40.

—— 'Long haired kings and short haired nuns: writing on the body in Caesarius of Arles', *Studia Patristica*, 24 (1993), pp. 143–50.

LIECHTENHAN, F.-D., 'Theodor Zwinger, théoricien du voyage', *Littérales*, 7 (1990), pp. 151–64.

LODGE, D. (ed.), *Modern Criticism and Theory: A Reader* (London and New York, 1988).

LOVIOT, L., 'Voyages de Villamont', in *Revue des livres anciens* (Paris, 1914), pp. 101–34.

LUBAC, H. DE, *Exégèse médiévale: les quatre sens de l'Écriture* (4 vols.; Paris, 1959–64).

LUSSAGNET, S., *Les Français en Amérique pendant la deuxième moitié du XVIe siècle* (Paris, 1953).

MACLEAN, I. W. F., ' "Le païs au delà": Montaigne and philosophical speculation', in *Montaigne: Essays in Memory of Richard Sayce*, ed. I. D. Macfarlane and I. Maclean (Oxford, 1982), pp. 101–32.

—— 'Montaigne, Cardano: the reading of subtlety/ the subtlety of reading', *FS* 37 (1983), pp. 143–56.

MAJOR, A., 'Vision externe sur l'empire vénétien: Les voyageurs méridionaux au XVe siècle', *Le Moyen Age: Revue d'histoire et de Philologie* 2, 5e série (1992), pp. 213–26.

MARAVAL, P., 'Une controverse sur les pèlerinages autour d'un texte patristique (Gregoire de Nysse, Letter 2)', *Revue d'histoire et de philosophie religieuses* 66, 2 (1986), pp. 131–46.

MARGRY, P., *Les Navigations françaises et la révolution maritime du XIVe au XVIe siècle* (Paris, 1867).

MARKUS, R., *The End of Ancient Christianity* (Cambridge, 1990).

—— *Saeculum: History and Society in the Theology of St. Augustine* (London, 1970).

MARROU, H., *Saint Augustin et la fin de la culture antique* (Paris, 1938).

MARSY, A. DE, *Le voyage à Jérusalem de Loys Balourdet curé de mareuil (1588)* (Paris, 1878).

—— *Les Pèlerins normands en Palestine* (Paris, 1896).

—— *Les Pèlerins picards à Jerusalem* (Paris, 1881).

MARTZ, L., *The Poetry of Meditation* (Yale, 1962).

MEYER, F. B., *Abraham or, The Obedience of Faith* (London, 1885).

MONTROSE, L., 'Professing the Renaissance: The Poetics and Politics of Culture', in *The New Historicism*, ed., Veeser, q.v., pp. 15–36.

MOORE, W., *De la Dévotion moderne à la spiritualité française* (Paris, 1958).

NIETZSCHE, F., 'Vom Nutzen und Nachteil der Historie für das Leben', in *Werke*, i, ed. K. Schlechta (Frankfurt-am-Main, 1984), pp. 209–85.

NORTON, G., 'Rabelais and the epic of palpability: Enargeia and History', *Symposia* 33 (1979), pp. 171–85.

O'CONNELL, M., 'Authority and the Truth of Experience in Petrarch's "Ascent of Mt. Ventoux" ', *PQ*, 62 (1983), pp. 507–20.

O'DONOVAN, P., 'The Place of Rhetoric', *Paragraph* 11 (1986), pp. 227–48.

O'GORMAN, E., *The Invention of America* (Bloomington, 1961).

ONG, W., *Orality and Literacy: The Technologising of the Word* (London and New York, 1982).

ORTALI, R., *Jean-Baptiste Chassignet: Un Poète de la mort* (Geneva, 1968).

PAGDEN, A., *The Fall of Natural Man: The American Indian and the Origins of Comparative Ethnology* (Cambridge, 1982).

PARKER, P., *Inescapable Romance: Studies in the Poetics of a Mode* (Princeton, 1979).

—— with D. QUINT (ed.), *Literary Theory/ Renaissance Texts* (Baltimore, 1986).

—— *Literary Fat Ladies, Rhetoric, Gender, Property* (London and New York, 1987).

PASTOUREAU, M., *Les Atlas français: XVIe–XVIIe siècles* (Paris, 1984).

PENROSE, B., *Travel and Discovery in the Renaissance, 1420–1620* (Harvard, 1960).

PETERS, R., 'Über die Geographie im Guerino Meschino des Andrea de' Magnabotti', *Romansiche Forschungen* 22 (1908), pp. 426–505.

PRESCOTT, H., *Jerusalem Journey: Pilgrimage to the Holy Land in the Fifteenth Century* (London, 1954).

—— *Felix Friar at Large: A Fifteenth Century Pilgrimage to the Holy Land* (Yale, 1950).

RAHNER, H., *Ignatius the Theologian* (London, 1990 [1964]).

RIES, J., 'Pèlerinage et pensée mythique', in *Histoire des pèlerinages non chrétiens*, eds. Chelini and Branthomme, q.v., pp. 24 ff.

RIMBAULT, L., *Pierre de Moulin 1568–1658: Un Pasteur classique à l'age classique* (Paris, 1966).

ROBBINS, J., 'Petrarch Reading Augustine: "The ascent of Mont Ventoux" ', *PQ*, 64 (1985), pp. 533–52.

—— 'Prodigal Son and Elder Brother: The Example of Augustine's Confessions', *Genre* 16 (1983), pp. 65–79.

RÖHRICHT, R., and MEISNER, H., *Deutsche Pilgerreisen nach dem heiligen Lande* (Berlin, 1880, 1889).

—— *Die Deutschen im heiligen Lande* (Innsbruck, 1894).

RONCIÈRE, C. DE LA, *Histoire de la nation égyptienne*, vol. 3. (Paris, 1937) [in Bodleian: 24672 d 11 under Hanotaux, G, who edited all seven volumes, Paris, 1931–40].

ROPER, L., *The Holy Household: Women and Morals in Reformation Augsburg* (Oxford, 1989).

ROUILLARD, C., *The Turk in French History, Thought and Literature, 1520–1660* (Paris, 1941).

ROUSSELLE, A., *Porneia: On Desire and the Body in Antiquity* (Oxford, 1988).

RUBIÉS, J.-P., 'Instructions for Travellers: Teaching the Eye to See', *History and Anthropology* (1996), vol. 9, nos. 2–3, pp. 139–90.

SAID, E., *Orientalism* (New York, 1985 [1978]).

SARGENT-BAUR, B. (ed.), *Journeys Toward God: Pilgrimage and Crusade*, SMC XXX, Medieval Institute Publications (Kalamazoo, 1992).

SCREECH, M., *Rabelais* (London, 1979).

—— *Ecstasy and the Praise of Folly* (London, 1980).

SCRIBNER, R., *Simple Folk: Popular Propaganda for the German Reformation* (Cambridge, 1981).

SHARRATT, P. (ed.), *French Renaissance Studies, 1540–70: Humanism and the Encyclopedia* (Edinburgh, 1976).

SHKLOVSKY, V., 'Art as Technique', in *Modern Criticism and Theory*, ed., Lodge, q.v., pp. 15–30.

—— 'The Resurrection of the Word', trans. Shukman, in *Russian Formalism* ed. Bann, S. and Bowlt, J. (Edinburgh, 1973), pp. 94–127.

SIMONIN, M., *Vivre de sa plume au XVIe siècle, ou la carrière de François de Belleforest* (Geneva, 1992).

SMITH, J. Z., *Map is not Territory: Studies in the History of Religion* (Leiden, 1978).

—— *To Take Place: Toward Theory in Ritual* (Chicago and London, 1987).

SMITH, P., *Voyage et écriture. Etude sur le 'Quart Livre' de Rabelais* (Geneva, 1987).

SONTAG, S., *Styles of Radical Will* (London, 1994 [1969]).

—— *I, etcetera* (New York and Toronto, 1979).

SPENCE, J., *The Memory Palace of Matteo Ricci* (New York, 1984).

SPITZER, L., 'The Epic Style of the Pilgrim Aetheria', *Comparative Literature*, 1, 3 (1949), pp. 225–58.

STAGL, J., 'Apodemiken', in ed. Stagl J., and Rassem, M., *Quellen und Abhandlungen zur Geschichte der Staatsbeschreibung und Statistik* (2 vols.; Paderborn, 1983).

STALLYBRASS, P., and WHITE, A., *The Politics and Poetics of Transgression* (London, 1986).

STRAUSS, G., *Sixteenth Century Germany: Its Topography and Topographers* (Madison, 1959).

—— 'A Sixteenth Century Encyclopedia: Sebastian Münster's Cosmography and its editions', in *From the Renaissance to the Counter-Reformation: Essays in Honour of Garrett Mattingly*, ed. Carter C. H. (London, 1966), pp. 145–63.

STRUEVER, N., *The Language of History in the Renaissance* (Princeton, 1970).

SUMPTION, J., *Pilgrimage: An Image of Medieval Religion* (London, 1975).

TAYLOR, C., 'The Moral Topography of the Self', in Messner, S., Sass, L., and Woolfolk, R. (ed.), *Hermeneutics and Psychological Theory* (New Brunswick, 1988).

—— *Sources of the Self: The Making of Modern Identity* (Cambridge, 1989).

TAYLOR, E. G., *Tudor Geography* (London, 1930).

—— *Late Tudor and Early Stuart Geography* (London, 1934).

THURSTON, H., *The Stations of the Cross: An Account of their History and Devotional Purpose* (London, 1906).

TODOROV, T., *La Conquête de l'Amérique: La Question de l'Autre* (Paris, 1982).

TOURNIER, M., *Gaspard, Melchior & Balthazar* (Paris, 1980).

TRANGMAR, S., and WILLIAMS, W., 'Contemplation', in *Reading the Glass: Management of the Eyes, Moderation of the Gaze*, ed. C. Barber, S. Kivland, C. Leyser (London, 1991).

TRIPET, A., *Petrarque, ou la connaissance de soi* (Geneva, 1967).

TUCKER, G. H., *The Poet's Odyssey: Joachim du Bellay and the 'Antiquitez de Rome'* (Oxford, 1990).

TURBET-DELOF, G., *L'Afrique barbaresque dans la littérature française au XVIe et XVIIe siècles (Afrique du Nord 1532–1715)* (Paris, 1971).

TURK, E. B., *Baroque Fiction Making: A Study of Gomberville's 'Polexandre'* (Chapel Hill, 1978).

TURNER, E. and V., *Image and Pilgrimage in Christian Culture: Anthropological Perspectives* (New York, 1978).

—— TURNER, V., 'Pilgrimages as Social Processes', in *Dramas, Fields and Metaphors* (Cornell, 1978), pp. 166–230.

VAN DEN ABEELE, G., *Travel as Metaphor: from Montaigne to Rousseau* (Minneapolis and Oxford, 1992).

VAN MARTELS, Z. (ed.), *Travel Fact and Travel Fiction* (Leiden, 1994).

VEESER, H. (ed.), *The New Historicism* (London and New York, 1989).

WALKER-BYNUM, C., *Fragmentation and Redemption: Essays on Gender and the Human Body in Medieval Religion* (New York, 1991).

WEINBERG, B., *A History of Literary Criticism in the Italian Renaissance* (2 vols.; Chicago, 1961).

WILLIAMS, W., ' "Marchandises peregrines": Renaissance pilgrimage and the Occupation of Literature', *Paragraph*, 18 (1995), pp. 132–47.

—— 'Salad Days: Revisiting Pilgrimage in the Sixteenth Century', *Michigan Romance Studies* (1995), pp. 151–76.

—— ' "Rubbing up against others": Montaigne on pilgrimage', in *Voyages and Visions*, ed. J. Elsner and J.-P. Rubiés (London, forthcoming).

—— *see also* Trangmar, S.

YATES, F. A., *The Art of Memory* (Harmondsworth, 1969).

ZACHER, C. K., *Curiosity and Pilgrimage: The Literature of Discovery in Fourteenth Century England* (Baltimore and London, 1976).

ZIEGLER, H., 'Die "peregrinatio" Aetheriae und die heilige Schrift', *Biblica* 12 (1931), pp. 162–7.

ZRENNER, C., *Die Berichte der europäischen Jerusalempilger (1475–1500): Ein literarischer Vergleich im historischen Kontext* (*Europäische Hochschulschriften*, 382) (Frankfurt am Main, 1981).

Index

Authors of secondary works are not listed here; nor are certain topics and names occurring *passim* (metaphor, devotion, literalisation, experience, narrative, God, Bible, Christ, pilgrimage, Reformation, Counter Reformation, Palestine, Holy Land). For further orientation, readers should consult the detailed table of contents.